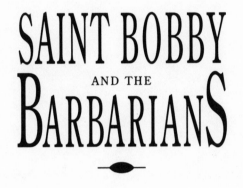

SAINT BOBBY
AND THE
BARBARIANS

SAINT BOBBY
AND THE
BARBARIANS

Ben Brown

DOUBLEDAY

New York   London   Toronto   Sydney   Auckland

For my mother, Nell Rawls Brown, and my grandmother, Ethel McGlathery Rawls.

PUBLISHED BY DOUBLEDAY
a division of Bantam Doubleday Dell Publishing Group, Inc.
666 Fifth Avenue, New York, NY 10103

DOUBLEDAY and the portrayal of an anchor with a dolphin are trademarks of Doubleday, a division of Bantam Doubleday Dell Publishing Group, Inc.

DESIGN BY GLEN M. EDELSTEIN

Library of Congress Cataloging-in-Publication Data

Brown, Ben, 1946–
    Saint Bobby and the Barbarians : the inside story of a tumultuous
  season with the Florida State Seminoles / Ben Brown.—1st ed.
      p. cm.
    1. Florida State Seminoles (Football team) 2. Bowden, Bobby.
  I. Title.
  GV958.F56B76   1992
  796.332'0975988—dc20   92-16299
                                         CIP

ISBN 0-385-42407-8

10 9 8 7 6 5 4 3 2 1

FIRST EDITION

CONTENTS

PREFACE

Exactly halfway through the Game of the Century, Coach Bobby Bowden paced the only patch of open territory left in the Florida State locker room. The players maneuvered for space in front of him, clacking pads as they found places to sit.

"Three minutes, Coach," someone said.

Outside, the stadium was stuffed with football hysterics, momentarily distracted by a halftime tribute to veterans of the Gulf War. Band music filtered through the metal door that led to the ramp and the stadium. But inside, it was quiet, save for the deep breaths of 100 restless young men.

It was Saturday afternoon, November 16, 1991, in Tallahassee's Doak Campbell Stadium. Bowden's undefeated No. 1-rated Florida State University Seminoles were playing the undefeated No. 2-ranked University of Miami Hurricanes, perhaps for the national championship of college football. The Seminoles led 10–7 at the half. And everybody was watching.

Besides the record crowd of 63,442—many of whom had bribed or begged to get the year's toughest sports ticket—there were over 500 reporters and technicians divided between the press box, the field and a windowless room in the athletic center where a large-screen TV provided the ABC feed. The network had its No. 1 announcers in the booth, broadcasting the game to over 11 million homes, the largest college football audience of the regular season.

In the Doak Campbell luxury boxes were boosters and business leaders, many of whom would be asked—or had already consented—to back up their Seminole fever with checks in support of the athletic program. The day before, some had joined with university officials to break ground on the $100 million renovation of Doak Campbell.

Also up high in a private box was the new university president, who had arrived in Tallahassee in late summer in time to preside over painful budget cuts elsewhere on campus. Now he was using the attraction of the No. 1 football team in the country to pitch a select group of corporate

VIPs on the idea of investing in a school that could inspire such a Saturday-afternoon spectacle.

Mingling with the school officials in the president's box were representatives from major bowl committees, who had already made not so secret deals to divvy up today's contestants for separate January 1 matchups. A victory today was worth an extra $1 million to the winning school.

Bowden looked toward the door. "Have the captains gone out yet?"

"Yes, sir," someone answered.

Bowden and his players were crowded into a large anteroom between their lockers and the door to the stadium. Over the exit was a sign proclaiming NO EXCUSES, the slogan the team had chosen as their motto before the season began. Every player, coach, trainer, manager and team doctor would touch the sign on his way out in affirmation.

On an opposite wall were framed enlargements of championship rings from the Sugar, Blockbuster and Fiesta bowls. They represented the postseason past, where the Seminoles had played and won over the past three years. Above them hung an empty frame, waiting for the future, championship ring that had been on their minds since spring practice, through the stifling August two-a-days and through each of the ten contests that so far had required no excuses.

Outside, through the closed door, they could hear the Seminole "War Chant." A roar would again shake the old stadium when they ran onto the field to start the second half. The band would play. Hope and anxiety would be thick enough to breathe.

"You realize we're just thirty minutes away?" said the coach. "Just thirty minutes away from all we've worked for. It's down to guts. Do you want the ring?

"We need somebody to make a great play. We need somebody who'll suck it up and go get that passer, somebody to make that great catch, that great run.

"We need a hero, men. We need a hero."

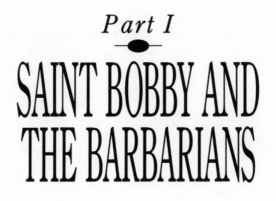

Part I

SAINT BOBBY AND THE BARBARIANS

1

I<small>N</small> the spring of 1991, Bobby Bowden was six months away from his 62nd birthday. He would begin his 16th football season as Florida State's head coach, his 26th as the top guy somewhere, his 38th in coaching. He was a giant in the history of the game, eighth in all-time victories behind such legends as Bear Bryant, Amos Alonzo Stagg and Pop Warner. Already just a step or two away from football immortality, he still lacked one significant career achievement—a national championship.

"Does it eat me alive that I haven't won it?"

Bowden was forced to ask himself that almost daily, because everybody else was asking. The Seminoles had finished second, third, third and fourth in the end-of-year Associated Press rankings from 1987 to 1990. A national championship naturally seemed like the next step.

"Am I obsessed with it? No, I'm not."

The truth was, all the space in Bobby Bowden's life that might have supported that obsession was taken up by the one that got there first: the obsession with winning.

Florida State had been playing football 29 years before Bowden arrived in 1976. There were good, even great teams, with players such as NFL Hall of Fame receiver Fred Biletnikoff. But there's little doubt Bobby Bowden reinvented Seminole football for modern times. When he took over the football program, the school had won a total of four games in the previous three seasons and was thinking about dropping the sport. He won five in his first year and hadn't posted a losing season since. In his first fifteen years at the school, he won 132 games—only 18 fewer than FSU had managed in its entire pre-Bowden football history.

Now, among active coaches, he was second only to Penn State's Joe Paterno in career victories. And like Paterno, he had built a program that became a national model. No major scandals, no NCAA probations, no censures. No serious accusations, in fact, that Bobby Bowden football was anything other than the wildly entertaining, straight-arrow program it appeared to be. What's more, in a sports world rife with inflated egos

3

and stone-faced seriousness, Bowden built a beloved public persona with self-deprecation and down-home humor.

Everybody loved him.

When the coach was hired, Coyle E. Moore, then an FSU dean, said that the coach "fits our needs like a glove. . . . He is a Southern Cracker, to the manner born—perfectly adaptable to us Southern Crackers and rednecks of northern Florida. He speaks our language, adheres to our religious faith."

That was in 1976, when Tallahassee was edging into the transition from sleepy Southern town to Sun Belt capital city and when Florida State University was yearning to boost itself to national academic prominence. In the decade and a half since, Bowden and the university had made the big time. And there were few people in town who thought it was a coincidence that FSU's national reputation had risen along with the school's football fortunes.

Where Dean Moore talked about Bowden's ability to fit in with North Florida traditions, Dale Lick, FSU's new president, was beginning to speak of the whole country adopting Bowden and his Seminoles as their own.

Lick left the University of Maine to take over at Florida State in August 1991. "When I was coming down here, people told me, 'I don't know Bobby Bowden, but he's my coach.' I had people say it to me all over the country. People perceive that he does a quality job, and they perceive that he does it correctly, fairly, properly, and they really admire that. And that's almost bigger than the man.

"In some sense, he's almost become the Nation's Coach, like the Dallas Cowboys tried to become America's Team in pro football and the Atlanta Braves were trying to be America's Team in baseball. I think we have moved up into that area where we've become the Nation's Team in college football."

Bowden managed to do so without losing the qualities that put Dean Moore and North Florida fans at ease, winning at increasingly higher levels and without once embarrassing the university with scandal. "St. Bobby," they started calling him.

The label never set well with his family and friends, who heard it said sneeringly by rival fans. Bowden would joke about it in banquet speeches. "You've got to be careful about that saint stuff. They put that halo over your head, and pretty soon it slips down a few inches and becomes a noose."

But there was no escaping the role. The more successful you are, the steeper the ascent of expectations and the greater the risk in being measured against them. Yet he also knew the bargain offered the opportunity that thrilled him and defined his working life: the chance to test himself in an arena many compared to war. To compete with the best, winner take all.

In that contest, bumped to its most hyperbolic level, the commander is cast as defender of the castle, mounting the barricades to resist with every fiber the barbarian hordes bent on destroying all that is sacred.

At other times, he must lead his own barbarians to seize by force what has been denied them all these years by some elitist, distant empire.

Such a commander must be the protector saint, and he must be the demon invader. It is a brand of spectacular schizophrenia entirely in keeping with the contradictions embodied in both the American mythic story and big-time college football. Everybody needs a hero.

2

BOBBY Bowden was born in 1929 in Birmingham, Alabama, the only son and one of two children in the family. In his early years they shared his grandmother's house in the Woodlawn section of town. His father was a bank teller, one of the few men with a regular job during the Depression. But it was not a bad time to be a boy, especially when your grandmother's backyard was almost under the goalposts of Woodlawn High, where some of Alabama's best schoolboy stars practiced football.

Among Bowden's earliest memories is climbing atop the family garage with his dad to watch the Woodlawn workouts. And every day during the season, he could hear the band playing and the ball being kicked.

When Bowden was five, the family moved a few miles away to the East Lake section of Birmingham and only half a block away from the football field at Howard College, the Baptist school that would become his alma mater. Howard's football field was up on a hill. "And I could look up and see them practicing. I guess I always lived next to football."

Bowden's father taught Sunday school to some of Woodlawn's players, and the two of them would go watch the high school boys play at Legion Field, which was also the Birmingham home of the University of Alabama Crimson Tide. Some of those high schoolers became Bowden's first heroes, and he followed them throughout their careers at Alabama, Howard and Auburn.

At age 13, Bowden was diagnosed as having rheumatic fever and was confined to bed. The doctor, afraid of injury to the young boy's heart, forbade him to exert himself. And for three months "I had to stay in that stinkin' bed. I had to use a bedpan. I had to have every meal brought in. I never got up."

He practically had to learn to walk again when the doctor finally allowed him out of bed. And for another six months, he was permitted only slightly more mobility. Long hours were spent listening to the radio. And over the airwaves and into his bedroom came a procession of heroes and real-life adventures. World War II was on, and Bowden became engrossed in the daily reports. The forces of good and evil were clashing on remote islands in the Pacific and on the deserts of North Africa. Generals were leading audacious campaigns, armies of young heroes were battling to take and retain vital territory.

On weekends came the reports of other kinds of wars, the ones played on football fields by Alabama, Auburn, Notre Dame, Michigan and the other great powers of the college game. He especially loved Alabama's teams. And he would lie in bed charting their drives as they moved down the field.

"I would pray for them not to lose and would cry when they did."

Much of his contact with other people during that time came when neighborhood buddies stopped by on their way home from the Saturday-afternoon movies. They would catch Bowden up on the serials and adventure flicks, and he would bring out the electric football game his mother had given him, a push-button affair that allowed opposing players to match one another in offensive and defensive play selection. The children would play it for hours.

That year, said Bowden, "was probably the influential year of my life." It inspired his lifelong fascination with the strategies of war and football. And it nurtured the private, secret life of a boy who would become one of the most famous men in sports.

3

"WELL, they're pickin' us No. 1 to start the season," Bowden told his booster banquet audiences in the spring of '91. "That's the good news. The bad news is that the same people picked us No. 1 in 1988. That was the year we stayed in contention all the way until the kickoff of the first game.

"I think y'all probably remember that. Miami whipped us pretty good, 31–0. Which is why I can't let myself get too excited about the prospects of being No. 1 before we start playing football. If we didn't have to go out and play the dad-gum games, I guess we'd have won more national championships in August than just about anybody else. In fact, I'd probably be the August coach of the decade."

The coach had been at home in Tallahassee, watching television over the holidays at the end of the '90 season, when he first heard that his team would probably start the season ranked first. After losing to Miami and Auburn in midseason, the Seminoles had gone on a five-game win streak, then wrapped up the season with an impressive victory over Penn State in the Blockbuster Bowl in Miami on December 28. They had looked more invincible with every game.

After the bowl game, Bowden was watching TV for scores and highlights of other contests when he heard Danny Sheridan, the CNN/ *USA Today* sports analyst, telling his viewers, "I know one thing: next year, I'm picking Florida State to be the national champion."

Oh no, Bowden thought. Not that again. The memory of '88 still lingered, and like most coaches, Bowden would rather not be billed as the guy to beat week in and week out. But then he began thinking about the possibilities.

There were no end-of-season playoffs in college football. Rankings were determined by media polls, principally the two run by the Associated Press and CNN/*USA Today*. So if Florida State was voted the top ranking, everybody in the country would consider the Seminoles the No. 1 team whether they liked it or not.

Also, lots had changed since '88. Bowden had two more outstanding recruiting classes work their way onto the depth chart, and he and his assistants had two more years' experience massaging the program into a perennial contender. Maybe this would be the breakthrough year.

"The reason they're pickin' us so high is that we have a team of experienced players returning," he told the boosters. "We have a quarterback, Casey Weldon, who might be a great one. We are so deep at running back that I'm going to have trouble getting them all the ball and keeping them happy. But that's a nice problem to have, ain't it? Our offensive line returns virtually intact from last season. On defense, we'll probably be all right up front. And we have a fine group of linebackers.

"You want to know the weaknesses? Well, if we have any, they might be in the defensive secondary, where we have lost starters. And we don't yet seem to have receivers who will leap and contest for the ball the way we're used to. The Fab Four probably spoiled us.

"And, of course, there's the kicking game. Nobody has stepped up to take the job of punter or placekicker.

"But yes, if we stay healthy and get some breaks, we should have as good a chance as six or seven other teams of winning it all."

Of course, you couldn't plan your way to a national championship any more than you could duck the No. 1 ranking. So much was beyond your control. But if you were lucky enough with injuries and you had the right schedule—one that was tough enough to impress the poll voters, but forgiving enough to allow for players' natural emotional cycles—then your chances were pretty good. And they improved for the Seminoles, the coach figured, when they agreed to add an extra game at the beginning of the year.

Bowden was in Hawaii coaching in the Hula Bowl when the call came from FSU athletic director Bob Goin that the Seminoles had been invited to play in the Disneyland Pigskin Classic on August 29. The opponent would be Brigham Young University, the school that upset Miami in the first game of the 1990 season and spoiled the Hurricanes' No. 1 ranking.

At first, Bowden said no. Why erect another barrier? But he had argued himself into the game by the time he got back to Tallahassee. Despite the return of quarterback Ty Detmer, the 1990 Heisman Trophy winner, BYU figured to be a young, inexperienced team. An early win would solidify the Seminoles' ranking and give them a one-game edge against rivals in case of a tie later on.

We might as well find out how good we are in the first game, Bowden reasoned. If we're going to get beat, might as well be early. And the whole idea of starting off with a name team on national television fit right in with the plan the head coach began developing in his head almost from the moment he heard Danny Sheridan's prediction.

"We're on a mission," Bowden decided.

4

FSU wasn't the only team getting preseason attention in the Sunshine State. All of Florida seemed alive with football promise. Florida had three universities playing football in the NCAA's Division I-A category for big-time programs, and all three were sure bets to be in the preseason top ten.

The University of Miami, which had already won three championships in the past eight years, was going to be ranked among the top three in most polls. And the University of Florida, with second-year head coach Steve Spurrier, would break into the top five in some experts' picks.

"We're going to cut each other to pieces," Bobby Bowden told reporters in Daytona Beach for a preseason media roundup. "The national championship? Heck, we gotta worry about the state championship. We figure Miami knocked us out of three national championships over the last decade. And now Florida is getting into the act."

The prominence of the three schools in college football launched an annual flurry of preseason stories. How did they do it? Primarily by sticking with homegrown talent.

A 1991 Tallahassee *Democrat* survey of university football rosters found that 89 of 106 University of Florida players were from the state; 86 of Florida State's 112 were Floridians; and 58 of Miami's 95 were in-staters. What's more, according to regional recruiting experts, some 120 Florida high school grads signed with Division I-A programs out of state in '91—either because they wanted a change of scenery or because they couldn't attract the attention of Florida's big three. At least another 100 accepted lower-division scholarships all over the country.

Bill Buchalter, one of the best known of the Florida recruiting experts, argues that the annual harvest of talent amounts to an industry. "Well over a hundred major colleges come down here to recruit. I did a study one year and estimated that there's an economic impact of about $2.5 million from all these guys coming down and staying in hotels, renting cars and buying meals."

The football bonanza is created by a combination of forces. The most powerful is simply numbers. Between census counts in 1980 and 1990 Florida jumped from seventh to fourth among the fifty states in population. Of the four most populous states—California, Texas, New York and Florida—the Sunshine State had the fewest colleges with big-time athletic programs. Only the three. Which means that a Florida player who intended to stay in-state had to compete with the best at each position for a freshman slot at Florida, Florida State or Miami.

Most young athletes want to play close to home, where parents and friends can see them regularly and where a visit by a girlfriend or a quick trip back to the neighborhood is not a major production. Schools within a day's drive of prime recruiting territory are the schools most likely to build big-time athletic programs. The big-city playgrounds of New York, Philadelphia and Washington, D.C., fuel Big East basketball. And the coal mines and steel mills of Pennsylvania and West Virginia played a big part in the football prominence of teams such as Pitt and Penn State.

Football was always strong in the South. But for two decades after official integration in the region, old segregationist traditions made it difficult for black athletes to crack the color barrier on teams at predominantly white institutions. It wasn't until the football powers of the Midwest and North made use of the South's great black players that Southern schools decided they could no longer afford to exclude such a large percentage of the football talent pool. Since the mid-'70s, when the region's traditional football powers became more determined to keep talented black athletes at home, the South has made an increasingly convincing case for its dominance in college football. In Associated Press polls at the close of the four seasons before '91, Southern-based teams owned five of the top ten spots in every year but one. In the exception, 1988, four Southern schools made that group.

People who know only the Florida of Disney World and Miami Beach have a difficult time understanding how closely parts of Florida resemble other states in the Deep South in culture and tradition. Tallahassee is 500 miles from the tourist hotels on Miami Beach and 20 miles from Georgia. It is one of the largest cities in a rural region where football is a way of life.

In many rural areas of North Florida and South Georgia, football is literally the only game in town. Those are the places that tend to produce the high school state championship teams, honed by the discipline of a county full of mommas and poppas hauling kids to practice from the time they can strap on a helmet. These are also the places that produce lifelong fans, people who are avid followers of favorite teams in newspapers and on radio and television. Until Atlanta and Miami got pro football franchises, the colleges were the only places in the South for fans to invest all that football devotion after high school.

The game is not just a rural phenomenon, of course. Even in urbanized South Florida, football retains a hold on fan and media attention that's unrivaled by any other sport. One-quarter of the state's largest high schools are in the Miami area, where tough, street-hardened kids play in conferences that produce third-team defensive backs who could beat out other leagues' all-stars. The University of Miami assembled teams that won national championships primarily by making sure they controlled the recruiting territory they named the State of Miami. And the Hurricanes' success fed on itself, creating avid young fans who later became all-star recruits.

School systems in the South may fare badly in academic comparisons with systems in other regions. But the school boards know what their constituents want when it comes to football. In a time when schools across the nation were cutting back on extracurricular activities, high schools in the South found a way to keep football alive nearly year-round. Of the thirteen states with spring football practice in 1991, all but five were Southern states. With 20 extra days of practice each May, a three-year high school player has the equivalent of another entire season in pads by the time he graduates.

Weather, too, is an obvious factor in Florida's football prominence. Because of mild Florida winters, a young athlete has year-round opportunities for playing outside with neighborhood buddies and with organized teams. That means more running, more jumping, more repetition of activities that build athleticism. Those extra reps probably give Florida kids an automatic advantage in speed and skill over children their age in colder climates.

The South has another advantage when it comes to building great football teams, although it's not as widely touted as the weather. In the '80s, elite-level football and basketball became games dominated by black athletes, many of them from desperate situations. And the South, including Florida, is loaded with those kinds of demographics.

According to an NCAA-financed study in 1989, 37 percent of Division I football players, 56 percent of men's basketball players and 33 percent of women's basketball players are black. And those numbers underrepresent black participation at the highest levels of competition. Of the 22 starters on offense and defense when No. 1 Florida State lined up for its first game of the '91 season, only seven were white.

Almost half of black football and basketball players, said the 1989 report, came from families in the bottom 25 percent of the socioeconomic strata, which is territory not unfamiliar to many black families in Florida. For instance, according to a 1990 analysis by the Center for Population Study at the University of Michigan, two-thirds of blacks in the Miami and Fort Lauderdale area live at or below the poverty line.

Football didn't create these conditions. As a matter of fact, for the select few athletes who are good enough to play in college, football provides a way out—a chance for a college education and, maybe, a shot at the NFL. Still, Florida's three Division I-A programs clearly profit by the numbers of kids fighting for the chance to break into the big time.

Coaches have always gone recruiting for "the hungry ones." That used to mean the offspring of coal miners, farmers and steel mill workers, kids anxious to do something with their strength and energy besides backbreaking labor. Now it often means kids looking for a way off the mean streets and out of the day-labor pools.

Part II

—●—

"IT SCARES ME TO DEATH"

1

TALLAHASSEE in late summer is a swamp under a heat lamp. No ocean breezes stir the inland humidity. It either rains or it bakes. In 1991, July brought nearly nonstop rain. August was drier, at least during the hours set aside for two-a-days. Which meant that, instead of mosquitoes, the dominant insects on the practice fields were dragonflies. They swam in the thick air around the punters and beat against the calves of linemen grunting against the blocking sleds. But nobody paid much attention. The heat trivialized everything else.

By 9 A.M. a visitor in a polo shirt could work up a good sweat standing beneath the single big oak that bounded two of the three practice fields. For the players, however, there was no shade. Their jerseys were soaked fifteen minutes into a two-hour practice. The fabric stretched across the ridges of their shoulder pads and hung in wet flaps over their bellies. Some rolled the tails up and tucked them under pad straps to ventilate their midsections. But dirt and grass adhered to the exposed skin, glued there by sweat and ground in by collisions with the earth.

Collision, of course, is the whole point of football. The noise of it, the crackling of pads on helmets, is the most authentic soundtrack of the game. The farther you get from the action, the more it's diluted. So on game day, with a stadium full of fans and marching bands, the violent smacks are distant, harmless pops. On the practice field, however, the sound is clear, rhythmical. It is wince-provoking music. And it is joined with that other familiar melody, the one the assistant coaches sing:

"DRIVE! DRIVE THROUGH THAT MAN! . . . LOCK THOSE ARMS! . . . YOU ARE ONE SORRY EXCUSE FOR A BALLPLAYER! DO I HAVE TO GET A FRESHMAN OUT HERE TO SHOW YOU HOW TO DO THIS?"

This is the way football begins. Every year, in every place the game is played, young men put on pads and run into the hot sun to collide with one another while coaches yell. There are no bands or cheerleaders. And no fans. No one asks any questions about moral character or SAT scores. No matter how sophisticated the academic curriculum, no matter

15

how genteel the faculty and student body, no matter how devoutly religious the coaching staff, it's always the same at football practice.

Do it again. Do it right. And do it harder.

In 1991, Bobby Bowden was in his fifth decade of the preseason ritual. Plenty had changed over those years, mainly because the society that produced players and coaches had changed so radically. But the demands of football had remained remarkably consistent. August practice was still a kind of boot camp, a time to turn individualistic civilians into an army, a team. And the transition was always an agonizing one, especially for players only a year or two out of high school.

For the gifted athlete in a sports-crazy region, high school is a joyous playground. Talent alone can overcome so many little failings and bring so many rewards that athletes can be forgiven for believing that the joy will continue forever. Then they move to the next level, where, suddenly, their talent edge diminishes. They are in competition with other similarly gifted players, and they must submit to the arbitrary authority of coaches who don't seem to appreciate their special gifts.

Like everyone else with big-time ambitions, Bowden went through that trauma too. After doctors finally cleared him to play sports, he leaped at the chance. He played football, baseball and basketball and ran track. And by the time he graduated from Woodlawn, he had achieved something of the same stardom as the boys he admired so much in his father's Sunday-school class. The University of Alabama offered him a scholarship.

Bowden graduated from high school in January and went directly to Tuscaloosa for the spring term. He remembers running out on the field with the rest of the players and looking around. Over 100 athletes, most of them much bigger than the 5-8, 155-pound tailback. "How am I ever gonna get a chance with all these guys?"

Birmingham was only fifty miles away, within easy hitchhiking distance on weekends. But young Bowden had a terrible case of homesickness. "I was just a big baby. Never been away from home and the family." And he was thinking particularly of his girlfriend, Ann Estock, whom he was anxious to marry.

Alabama had a rule against scholarship players marrying. And combined with what he imagined were his dim playing prospects and his homesickness, that was enough to cinch the deal. He would move back home, go to Howard College and marry Ann.

As he grew older and began coaching homesick boys himself, he couldn't help wondering what would have happened if someone had encouraged him more in the other direction: stay at Alabama, accept the reality and face the challenge. And, as a coach, he tried to build a system that could provide the right mix of reality therapy and encouragement.

He wrote freshmen players' parents every summer, telling them how leaving Alabama was the only time he ever quit in his life and how it had haunted him for years. Their sons were likely to come home complaining too. And maybe the best thing they could do for their kids would be to insist they stick it out.

Bowden watched his ballplayers grunt and pant their way through the drills. When you're 19, he thought, it is so hard to connect this tedious labor with the joy of playing on Saturday afternoon. Everything seems a conspiracy against your talent and individuality. It's so hard to trust coaches who demand so much.

As they had done each year, the players had gotten together and chosen a slogan for the '91 season: NO EXCUSES. It was written across the chest of their T-shirts and on a plaque above the exit doors in the locker room. The coach liked the sound of it. It was true. The program had reached a level now where there were no excuses for not being the best.

But did these young men know what that would require of them?

2

Bowden ran his August camp and in-season practices in the time-honored tradition. It was preparation for war, and the head coach was the supreme commander. When he walked onto the practice field or the game sideline, he left behind the good ol' boy of the banquet circuit and the booster meetings. No one called him Bobby. He was the Coach. The Man.

Except for a few words to the players at the beginning and end, Bowden seldom took an active role during practice. He observed in silence, standing apart, occasionally scribbling notes on a card he kept in a hip pocket. The eight segment coaches were the captains and lieutenants. They were the animated ones, striding forward at full voice, teaching and rearranging the bodies in formations. Then they would stand cross-armed to see if anything had sunk in. Sometimes they would lift their eyes at the end of the play to see if the Man downfield had noticed.

After years of working with him, the assistants knew Bowden's confidence in plays and players would rise and fall according to what he saw in practice. No matter how intriguing a play seemed or how potentially superhuman a player might be, come game time, Bowden would rely on what he believed in. And he reached that level of faith only by witnessing successful repetitions in practice.

"Don't depend on the undependables," the Man preached.

Of course, dependability was largely determined by one set of eyes. Shaky plays that worked brilliantly when Bowden was watching had a shot at finding a home in the game plan. Same for receivers who made diving first-down catches the very moment the coach turned his gaze in their direction. The assistant coaches hated to see that card come out of his back pocket, because they always assumed he was noting the screwup—the receiver who blew a pattern, the back who missed an assignment or botched a fake. The notes would reappear as questions in the next day's staff meeting.

"What happened when that linebacker stumbled into the screen pass? Is the quarterback taking too many steps or not enough steps or what on that dropback?"

When the team went into its fall game-preparation routines, those sessions with the boss would become like séances. Most of these men had been together at least seven seasons. They could sense the head coach moving toward or away from plays and players. If they felt him cooling his enthusiasm, they had to make up their minds to mount an all-out effort to turn him or to stop wasting practice time.

"Don't depend on the undependables."

In football, the surest route to dependability is repetition. Which is why football practices demand such elaborate choreography. In 1991, the premium on efficiency rose, with new NCAA regulations limiting the time coaches had with players. The coaches owned the athletes during the preschool two-a-days, but when classes began they would be limited to 20 hours a week of official practice time, including required video review sessions and meetings. That meant maximizing the time when they had it.

On-field practices were divided into a series of five-minute periods. In spring training, practices could go 28 periods or more; Monday-night sessions following Saturday games in the fall might be only 15. Most practices lasted for 22 to 24 periods, not including specialty-teams workouts. An air-horn blast from the tower divided the periods, even though players stayed in some drills for two or three periods, depending on the workout script for that day.

The players' bodies were tuned to the five-minute cycles. So they knew when the horn should sound. They suspected coaches sometimes ordered the managers to string out the periods to squeeze a little more out of them. They were right. But there was no point in protesting. There was no debate. In fact, there were seldom any words that weren't commands. Action was everything. Do it again. Do it right.

Each practice was videotaped from above so that assistant coaches could get nightly overviews of the progress of players and game plans. And each day, coaches would script blocks of periods to hone specific skills or to iron out problems with selected plays.

On most days, there were at least 120 players in practices. And to deal with so many at once, football coaches evolved a system that breaks down the team into constituent parts. Each player is a member of successive subgroups. First he is one individual among others playing his particular position; then he is a member of a position segment, such as inside linebackers or receivers or running backs; then a member of the offense or defense; then a member of the Florida State team. Most practices were a process of assembly into larger parts, then a process of breaking them down again.

During the regular season, Florida State practice blocks usually began with segment classroom meetings, then moved to the field, where players worked first in their own groups, then against their defensive counterparts. Full-contact practices usually ended with 11-on-11 drills, offense against defense in goal-line situations or hurry-up offenses. Then, before heading to the showers, they would break down into segments again for conditioning and agility drills.

A coach, said Bowden, is "like an automobile mechanic who has all the parts of a car laid out. You think you have every part you need; because if you don't, you ain't gonna get it back together. You ain't gonna make it.

"But the only way you're going to know for sure is to put it together piece by piece. There's a piece lying over there, another over there. You get to a point where you realize you may have a piece missing. But if the thing's gonna work, you've got to find that piece. And in the meantime you've got to keep all the other parts greased and fitting together.

"It ain't easy."

3

Iɴ August, the most vocal mechanics were Mickey Andrews and Brad Scott, the two assistant coaches with the double duties of coaching team segments and planning offensive and defensive strategy.

Andrews had been the defensive coordinator and coach of defensive backs since the 1984 season. Before that, the 49-year-old veteran had coached at five colleges and with the Arizona Wranglers of the USFL. But the credential that probably said more than anything else about Mickey Andrews was this one: He played at Alabama for Bear Bryant on two national championship teams in the early '60s. It was like having a doctorate in Southern football.

Football had given Andrews at least two things: permanent back pain from his injuries and a solid appreciation for the hard-nosed tradition he had thrived in. The coach walked like many others with chronic back trouble, as if he'd just as soon not disturb his upper body or lift his feet. When he felt the urge to get the attention of his players, which was often, he would stretch his neck and lean into the yell.

The barely intelligible bellow that Andrews had perfected probably had its roots in Tuscaloosa. The sound came out from somewhere deep in his chest and filtered through a healthy chaw of tobacco:

"YOU CALL THAT TACKLIN'! MY MOTHER HITS HARDER THAN THAT. GET OFF THE FOOTBALL FIELD. GET ME A PLAYER OUT HERE."

The targets of Andrews' '50s-style abuse were the prima donnas of a '90s defense—the defensive backs. And it looked like the worst possible matchup of coaches and players. Andrews wanted hard-nosed football; the cornerbacks and safeties were prejudiced toward speed and finesse. He yelled. They sulked and muttered under their breath. But, generally, they played football Andrews' way.

The Sky Patrol, they called themselves. Errol McCorvey, the senior cornerback, was the off-the-field leader of the pack. But it was Terrell Buckley whom they called the General. And he personified Andrews' problems and his good fortune.

Buck was an All-American as a sophomore and was already being touted as a high draft choice if he chose to leave for the NFL after his junior year. As a punt returner, he was one touchdown away from a school career record, and as a cornerback on defense, he needed six more interceptions to tie another record.

He was small, even for a DB—5-10 and 175 pounds. But his speed—

4.3 seconds in the 40-yard dash—and leaping ability gave him an edge over many receivers. And he definitely had the DB attitude:

"I feel like cornerback is the hardest position on the field, and only the best athletes play there. I could move over to wide receiver and be All-American. But not so many could move to cornerback and become an All-American. If you don't have an attitude you'll get beat to death."

To his coach's way of thinking, however, Buck didn't always practice with the kind of aggressive intensity that would best prepare him for Saturday afternoons. And the two would fight a season-long battle of wills, with Buckley walking the careful line between pride and rebellion and Andrews threatening to demote him every other game.

Most of the noise from the offensive practice field came from the drills run by Brad Scott, the offensive coordinator and offensive line coach. Scott, 35, got those two jobs in 1990, after coaching tight ends and coordinating recruiting for five years. He was raised in central Florida's cowboy country and spent enough time with branding and cutting chores to realize he didn't want to make a career of them. But he preserved the language and tone of the cattle drive for his beefy charges on the football field.

"PUNCH THOSE BIG ARMS . . . LOCK ON 'EM LIKE YOU MEAN IT!"

Unlike the DBs, Scott's linemen didn't play the positions that allowed them to develop much of an attitude. Unless it was grim resignation. Most of the offensive linemen were veterans who had endured the ritual abuse for years, and they knew that the intensity would taper off as the year wore on—especially if they won. Later in the season, Scott's tactics would be to coax the first-teamers and save most of the yelling for the younger linemen he was trying to bring along.

The line lost only one key starter from 1990, which made the '91 first team a group of tested veterans. Mike Morris and Kevin Mancini, both seniors and both All-American candidates, were the guard and tackle on the tight-end side of the line, where most of the power runs were directed. Mancini was a year younger, but had begun playing immediately. Morris, on the other hand, like most of his teammates, was held out his freshman year—redshirted. Under scholarship rules, each player could have his way paid for five years, but was eligible to play only four of them. Because Morris had redshirted that first year, he and Mancini had played side by side for most of their careers.

Mancini, called Cheesy by many of the players and coaches, was a cherub-faced kid who didn't look like a big-time lineman until he began to play. At 6-3, 270 pounds, he was about three inches too short and 20 pounds too light to satisfy the stereotype of the NFL-bound tackle. But he was very athletic for his size, strong and quick off the ball. And in the Florida State offense, which put a premium on quickness, Mancini had found a home.

After a strong summer conditioning program, Morris looked ready to have his best year. The 274-pound Miamian had missed all but four games his sophomore year because of a broken foot. But he had been a consistent first-teamer after his '87 redshirt year.

The returning center was junior Robbie Baker—Boots to most of his teammates, because of his fondness for cowboy footwear. The FSU media guide called him "the Iron Man," which was a nice way of saying he had been beaten to a pulp and still continued to play football. He had had four shoulder operations and one ankle operation already in his career. And because his 6-3, 250-pound body wasn't made to take the pounding in the center of a major-college line, he would probably be back on the operating table. But there was no question about his heart.

On the split-end side of the line were senior guard Reggie (Tricky) Dixon and junior tackle Robert Stevenson. The 280-pound Dixon had played every position on the line but center and had moved in from the split tackle position in the spring. He was one of the best students on the squad, with a better than B average in the School of Business.

Stevenson, at 272 pounds, was another jack-of-all-trades. He had even played center during the spring, when Baker was recovering from one of his operations. And he would probably get the call if anything happened to Boots.

All five began their careers at Florida State in 1987 or 1988. Only Mancini had played in his first year. The others had been redshirted to preserve an extra year of eligibility. The fact that the whole group had sweated through these drills together for three years allowed Scott a measure of confidence. Nothing beats experience. Great athletic ability might make up for lack of it at other positions, but not in the line, where dependability in the heat of battle makes everything else on offense possible.

Fortunately, once they're built, offensive lines stay together better than other team segments. Offensive linemen seem more resistant—or more oblivious—to the kinds of injuries that sideline others. The big guys are toe-to-toe fighters who don't collide with the speed of linebackers and backs, but almost all of them suffer an annual ration of bruises, strains and finger and wrist jams. Their pain is cumulative, building to a permanently distracting, everywhere ache by November. In the off-season, and probably for the rest of their lives, they will be patients of chiropractors and orthopedists. But during the season, they just tape everything up and run back on the field.

Florida State had gotten through the whole 1990 season with its starting line pretty much intact, even though Stevenson had to sub at four different positions to keep experienced people in the lineup. If we can do that again, thought Scott, we'll be hard to beat.

But if he lost one or two starters, Scott knew he would have problems. Which is another truism in the offensive line business. When five guys were getting all the experience, that meant nobody else was. If he had to turn to backups, the drop-off in performance might be disastrous.

He hoped to redshirt his freshmen, including Juan Laureano and Clay Shiver, who were athletic enough to contribute immediately but would lack the experience to be dependable. Forrest Conoly, the 340-pound giant freshman, had arrived overweight and needing knee surgery. He was out for a year.

The others were all question marks. Soft-spoken Patrick McNeil looked as if he could play guard, but he was just a redshirt freshman. And you could never tell what was going on in his mind. Big Steve Allen, 6-5 and 300 pounds, would become the long-snapper for punts and field goals, but his blocking skills were not yet up to first-team standards. And John Flath and Eric McGill, both juniors, seemed to be in the same boat.

If there was a backup who could turn the corner, Scott thought, maybe it was Eric Gibbs. Gibbs was an annual project. He was another overweight 300-pounder, but beneath the fat there appeared to be an athlete. Nicknamed House for obvious reasons, Gibbs had the quick feet demanded of a good offensive lineman. And he surely had the size. It was just that, so far, he had not shown the heart for football.

Gibbs reported out of shape in '91 and was unable to stay up with the others in conditioning drills. Scott stormed at him, drove him to rebellion. But Gibbs couldn't—or wouldn't—perform. He was too burned out from hitting the blocking sled to be of much use in head-to-head blocking. And he never finished his gassers, the end-of-practice wind sprints. That created problems with his teammates, who hated pushing themselves through drills while others sandbagged.

A couple of days into two-a-days, Scott exiled Gibbs to run on his own until he lost weight and was able to keep up with his teammates. He left it to the other linemen: "It's your team. Do you want Gibbs back working beside you? And if he comes back, under what conditions?"

The linemen met with Scott in his office to tell him their decision.

Gibbs could return. But he had to do everything they all were required to do. He had to push the sled. He had to make his gassers.

That afternoon he made every gasser for the first time. But a few days later, a blowup with Scott landed Gibbs in the doghouse again. Bowden, watching from downfield, made a note to caution Scott about not letting Gibbs push him too far. From a distance, it looked as if the two were close to blows.

Of more pressing concern, however, was Mike Morris. On August 13, someone stepped on his sore right foot, breaking it and sending him out of the lineup for three to six weeks. Scott moved McNeil into Morris' guard spot and branded him Rookie. Barring a miracle or a disaster that would require some other plan, Rookie would start in the season opener against Brigham Young on August 29.

"I have to change my approach with Patrick now," said the offensive line coach. "I've been pushing him hard. It's been on the abuse end a lot. Now I've got to start building him up, telling him he can do it."

4

"Aaron Dely, if you flunked out of school, what would you do?"

The freshman wide receiver looked back at John Eason and thought about an answer. Of the players in the room, Dely was one of the least likely to have academic problems. A local Tallahassee kid from a private school, Dely already had a reputation for good work habits on the field and in the classroom. But this was one of the first meetings with his teammates and position coach, and Dely didn't want to seem like either a know-it-all or a dope. He paused. Eason moved on.

"Eric Turral, what would you do?"

Turral had been slumped over in the front row, drifting between daydreams and real sleep. He looked up at the coach and rearranged his body nervously in the seat. Then he looked back down at the floor.

"Probably sell drugs, right, E.T.? That's what you told me last time I asked that question."

The other players laughed. Flunking out of school, losing out on the chance to play football, then ending up on the street selling drugs—it sounded like a soap opera. That kind of stuff didn't really happen, did it?

This was typical of John Eason's regular sessions with his young receivers. For most coaches, the segment meetings were a time for reviewing plays, correcting assignments and watching video of past performances and coming opponents. Eason did that too. But the wide receivers also spent a lot of time in the coach's combination Sunday-school class/consciousness-raising group. If you wanted to play football for John Eason, you had to play this first.

Eason wore two hats. He was receivers coach. And he was an assistant athletic director in charge of academics. A star at Florida A&M in the late '60s, he went on to play two years with the Oakland Raiders in the NFL and, later, with the Canadian Football League. Of Bowden's entire staff, Eason had the most pro playing experience. He was also the only one on the football staff with a doctorate, in education administration from Florida State.

At practice, Eason always stood off to the side near the line of scrimmage and watched his receivers run their patterns. He might raise an arm to correct a player's positioning or offer a quiet reminder about the number of steps a route required before a cut. Yet he almost never raised his voice above a conversational level. Players had to draw close to hear him. But they could always tell what he wanted.

It's not unusual for receivers to be the head cases on a football team. Even the best ones—perhaps especially the best ones—fail to fit the basic football mold. Like the others, they have to learn how to inflict and survive the violence of the game. But they are more zig and zag than straight-ahead thud. They tend to be sensitive types, prone to whining and to constructing elaborate alibis when they miss assignments and to showboating when they make big plays. They are performance artists, unreconstructed individualists in a game that requires undeviating conformity. And they drive everyone crazy when they can't catch passes. Some coaches have great success pounding deviates into line; Eason preferred a different approach.

"I tell them I'm going to treat them like men. I'm not going to yell at them or embarrass them in front of their teammates. Instead, I'll call them over and talk to them individually. I'll remind them what I expect. I want them to take responsibility themselves for doing things the right way. If they can't or won't, they just won't play."

In '91, ghosts haunted receiver segment meetings and the afternoon practices. Florida State, for years, had been known as Receiver U because Bobby Bowden's offensive strategy made heroes of throwers and catchers. And the legacy was renewed with each new group. Two years before, it was the Fab Four—Terry Anthony, Ron Lewis, Bruce LaShane and Lawrence Dawsey. They seemed capable of outrunning and outleaping every defensive back in America. Any ball, anywhere, anytime seemed to belong to them.

Then, in 1990, it was Dawsey alone. He amassed nearly 1,000 yards in receptions, often with short passes broken for big gains.

"The Fab Four would have caught that . . . Dawsey would have turned that one into a touchdown."

Since spring, Eason's young group had heard the coaches and their teammates say those kinds of things over and over. And they knew it wasn't likely to let up until they established names for themselves.

The core receiver group was made up of five underclassmen. Shannon Baker and Eric Turral were juniors. Kevin Knox and Matt Frier were sophomores. And Kez McCorvey, cousin of the defensive back Errol McCorvey, was a redshirt freshman. 'OMar Ellison, another redshirt freshman, had been switched from running back to receiver and was still adjusting to the new position. And Dely, the lone true freshman, would be redshirted this year.

When they came out of high school as all-stars in 1989, Baker, from Lakeland in central Florida, and Turral, from Tallahassee, were among the most heavily recruited wideouts in the country. They were small for major-college football, 5-10 and 5-11, but both had blinding speed and great athletic ability. Baker had been a high school quarterback as well as a receiver, and Turral seemed to do something spectacular every time he caught the ball.

Some schools tried to play them against one another: You guys don't want to end up on the same team; you'll be competing for playing time and end up canceling one another out. But they became friends and decided to come to Florida State together, hoping to play on opposite sides of the formation as the flanker and split end.

Turral, however, had been a partial qualifier under the NCAA's Proposition 48. The rule allowed an athlete who didn't have the necessary high school grade point average or test score to be admitted on scholarship as long as he didn't play or practice with the team while he worked on his academics his first year. The player lost a year of eligibility.

Since Baker played immediately as a freshman instead of taking a redshirt year, the two friends remained in the same football class. Now, they were both juniors and hoping their time had finally come. Nearly opposite in temperament—Baker, the warm and outgoing talker, and Turral, the quiet sulker—they nevertheless were inseparable. Shannon, who played the big brother in the friendship, dreamed for both of them: It would be Shake 'n' Bake and E.T. all the way to the Next League.

Kevin Knox came to Florida State from nearby Niceville, where he was a star on a state championship high school team. At 6-4, 193 pounds, he looked the part of the big-time receiver, and he had lowered his 40-yard dash time to below 4.5 in order to add speed to his size and talent. Bright and outgoing, he was also the group's unofficial lawyer, pleading the receivers' various excuses to Eason and serving as interpreter of the coach's thinking to his teammates. On game days, it would be Knox who ran along the sideline, keeping the other wideouts updated on who was hurt and who was playing well and who was in trouble.

Frier was another little guy—5-10, 189 pounds. But he played tough and hard, the way he was taught on county teams that won back-to-back state championships in the smaller-school division. He cultivated the image of the proud country boy—a truck-driving, deer-hunting, bass-fishing, tobacco-chewing product of Live Oak, Florida. But the sensitive side of him was too apparent to conceal with the swagger.

McCorvey was the youngest and quietest of the five. He came from Gautier (pronounced Goshay), Mississippi, near Pascagoula. At 6-1, 182 pounds, he wasn't big, and he wasn't particularly fast, at least not by Baker-Turral standards. But he had a remarkable ability to get in the clear on pass patterns and seldom dropped the ball.

He was a bright student, with a 3.6 grade point average in high school. But because of his natural shyness and his habit of running his words together in a nervous clip, people tended to underestimate him.

Like most skill-position players at the big-time schools, Eason's group assumed Florida State was an interim stop on the way to the Next League. And like other coaches, he used his players' pro expectations to keep them focused on performing at ever-higher levels and to discipline them. If they didn't do what he required, they wouldn't play; if they didn't play, nobody would know if they were as good as advertised; and if nobody knew them, what shot did they have of being drafted?

Ultimately, that was one of the two threats available to college coaches at the elite level. The other was competition from below, from great young players eager to move up on the depth chart when the starters stumbled.

Those were the sticks. But Eason wanted to work the carrot too.

"Matt Frier, what are you going to do if you flunk out of school?"

"Go work for my father, I guess, installing mobile homes."

"Shannon Baker?"

"I'm not gonna flunk out, Coach. You know I'm not going to flunk out."

Eason turned to the tall blond junior in the second row. "John Wimberly, why don't you tell them."

Since Eason also oversaw the punting game, he sometimes had kickers in his sessions too. Wimberly was a junior from Tampa, a punter who could boom 60-yarders and shank 25-yarders with the same regularity. He had been on scholarship until the previous spring, when he skipped classes and let his grades slip so badly he had to go to Tallahassee Community College for an Associate of Arts degree, then reapply for FSU. Now he was paying his own way at Florida State and competing for the punting job. Bowden told him he would reevaluate him for a scholarship at the end of the season.

"After three years, I had to learn the hard way," Wimberly told the group. "They will take your scholarship away."

"Not for what you do on the football field," said Eason. "But for what you fail to do in living up to your responsibilities in the classroom. The responsibility is yours. Do you understand?

"You have all these dreams of playing in the pros, of what kind of car you're going to drive, of the house you're gonna buy your momma. But if you flunk out, Aaron Dely?"

"I guess the point is," said the freshman, "if we don't get that degree, we could also be flipping burgers at Wendy's for four bucks an hour."

5

On the night before Florida State's final preseason scrimmage, the head coach was sitting in his game room at home, a pile of game-plan notes on his lap and the TV remote control in his hand. He was flipping restlessly through the channels, looking for his second-favorite sport, boxing. He needed something to leave on the tube while he worked his way through his notes.

This was an in-season routine of years. After practice, Bowden would shower in his private-office bathroom, drive home to meet Ann for dinner, then park himself in front of the old Zenith console to look at game film.

The Bowdens bought this four-bedroom colonial-style house on a golf course over fifteen years ago, when they moved to Tallahassee from West Virginia. "I think Bobby walked around the house once then," said Ann. "And I don't think he's done it since."

The coach lived primarily in the four rooms downstairs—the bedroom, the small sitting room that opened onto the patio and pool, the kitchen and the game room/den. A pool table sat in the center of the game room. "He doesn't play pool and he doesn't go into the pool," Ann would say. Both were used primarily by the grandkids. When they weren't around or when recruits and their families weren't visiting, Bowden used the game room as a home office.

Its walls were covered with plaques and photos, celebrating both his life in football and the Bowdens' family of six children and fourteen grandchildren. A collection of Time-Life books on World War II lined one set of shelves. An autographed print of Bear Bryant on the Alabama sidelines dominated an adjacent wall. There was an old leather sofa across from the TV set.

As he zapped through the channels, almost without noticing, Bowden stopped on a local station showing a replay of the Seminoles' 1990 opener against East Carolina. He watched.

Although Florida State beat East Carolina 45–24 in that game, the Pirates jumped out to a 7–0 lead early in the first quarter and stayed within a touchdown until the third period. That was in Tallahassee, with the heavily favored Seminoles ranked No. 3 in the nation. Bowden let himself feel a familiar nervousness. He and his team had not looked ready for that game. They were tentative, sloppy. They could easily have been upset by an inferior team on their own turf.

What about this year, when they were traveling all the way across the country to play Brigham Young, a big-time team with the 1990 Heisman Trophy winner for a quarterback, on national television? A team that upset Miami in the first game last year when the Hurricanes had been No. 1. Back in January, taking on BYU seemed like such a logical idea. But what if they weren't ready? Oh, Lordy!

Bowden was a connoisseur of fear. He cultivated it, especially in the early stages of game preparation. He used it to focus, to bring a sense of urgency to familiar routines. When he first looked at opponents' game tapes, he let it wash over him. The panic: "These guys are so good, so disciplined. How will we ever get to them?"

The only answer was work, all-consuming and exhaustive. No loose ends. Nothing left to chance. He couldn't get enough video, couldn't find enough time to watch opponents' defensive alignments over and over and over. "Are they doing anything we can predict in a certain situation?"

And how about their personnel? "How well do the linebackers cover? When No. 33 is in there, does that always mean blitz? Can their corner stay with our wideouts?"

No matter that Bowden's assistants were studying even more detailed breakdowns of the film. No matter that there would be computer analyses of down and distance tendencies, that scouting reports would diagram every defensive formation the other guys used, that there would be position-by-position talent evaluations for Bowden to peruse later or that all of this would be repeated on demand every time the coach needed to be rebriefed. No matter. Bowden knew he had to prepare as he had prepared for three decades in coaching. He had to touch everything himself, at least on offense. He had to study and work until he reached that point where the confidence began to rise and the fear began to recede.

"Coaches talk about this all the time. Do you do your best because you want to win so bad? Or do you do your best because you're afraid to get beat? Well, I know my motivation. It's built on 'fraid-to-get-beat.

"Some coaches say, 'Oh no, don't even think about that. That's too negative.' But my approach is, I don't want to ever lose, 'cause I can't stand it."

On the night after wins, he let himself relax completely. He slept through the night, even though he might have to rise early to tape his weekly TV show. He would savor the victory, at least for a few hours. Then, sometime on Sunday afternoon, he would grab the first videocassette of the next week's opponent, slide it into the machine in his den and wait for the fear to begin again.

After defeats—and there had been only six of them in the last four years—Bowden slept fitfully. He would awake, painfully relive a key series, then drop off again. "What could I have called instead? Should we have known they were going to be in that coverage? What broke down on our side?"

To out-of-town reporters, Bowden seemed most saintly after losses. "He keeps things in perspective," they would say. His faith, his family, his ability to understand that the world kept on turning despite a football setback—all of that apparently rescued him from the violent depressions common to his profession.

But people who knew him understood that Bowden had no peer in suffering, in feeling utter disappointment at losing. The truth was, it nearly killed him. The color drained from his face. He disappeared inside himself, while the exterior, public Bobby Bowden went through the motions with reporters and well-wishers. It was about the only thing he ever had to fake.

A loss might haunt him for days. What saved him was the ritual of preparation for the next game, for the recruiting season, for the next year. The old cycle of fear and recovery was therapy. It would distract him from moping and point the energy of self-examination toward some useful end. He would learn. He would move on.

What in the world did people do who had no next game, no next season?

Once the routine of the season got underway, it would pull him in. The familiar anxiety would start building on Sunday afternoon when he first looked at film. In the Monday-morning staff meeting, he would be awed at the speed and discipline of an opponent's defense. He would whistle in admiration over their kick-return specialists. And he would express mystification over their alignments.

"Whooee, men, that No. 34 looks like he'll make a million tackles all over the field. And for the life of me, I don't see a way to predict their blitz."

Between media interviews, glad-handing boosters, signing hats and footballs and speaking engagements, the coach would lock himself in his office or pull the chair up close to the TV in his den at home and watch film. Gradually, holes appeared in defenses. Opportunities beckoned. He began filling in a rough game-plan sheet—possible plays for third down and short yardage, third and long, goal line, last chance to win the game. By Wednesday, he had a hundred ideas. And after the morning's general session with the whole staff, he would stay to compare notes with the offensive coaches.

"Do you like this on third and long? Or are they going to jump on our tight ends and backs?"

The assistants would diagram plays, explaining modifications in blocking schemes and pass patterns to account for opposing defensive tendencies. Bowden would ask his what-if questions over and over until he felt confident he knew where everyone should be on a particular play. If he was bothered by the way something looked in practice, he would press segment coaches for assurance that the quarterbacks understood how important a fake was or that the backs knew how to pick up a blitzing linebacker. For the assistants, this was a time for lobbying for favorite plays and for talking the coach out of calling something they didn't like.

When they had gone over everything, Bowden would push himself away from the conference table and say, "Well, men, I feel much better now I know we have a plan."

As the team moved through the regular season, there would be more and more game film of each opponent's previous games, which required more and more time for analysis. But it also meant increasingly more reliable evidence of what an opponent was likely to do in a given situation. Coaches were too afraid of missed assignments to call for plays and alignments they hadn't practiced adequately. And regular-season practice cycles left only a couple of days for working on new ideas. There just wasn't time. Only emergencies could force wholesale changes. Early-season contests—especially the first game of the season—were another story, however.

"It scares me to death," said Bowden, "that they could have changed everything in the off-season and all we've got is film from last year. You don't know what they've been practicing. You don't know who their best players are. That's why most upsets occur on the first day of the season."

Fresh in Bowden's memory was the 31–0 humiliation in Miami in 1988, the last time the Seminoles were ranked No. 1 to start the season. Fans blamed overconfidence for the loss, citing a boastful rap video the players had made in the off-season. But Bowden remembered the more basic things. The Hurricane coach, Jimmy Johnson, had revamped the Miami defense. The Seminoles had prepared a menu of surprises they never got to try. And by the time Florida State adapted, the game was out of hand.

Already, the coach was taking heat for apparently slow-starting Seminole teams. The fact was, Florida State was 12–2 in season openers under Bowden, but both losses had come in the past three years. And last season's opening win against East Carolina wasn't exactly a confidence builder. Now here they were taking on a perennial Western power in Brigham Young and the 1990 Heisman Trophy winner in quarterback Ty Detmer. And they would fly three thousand miles away from home to do it.

"It scares me to death."

6

THE football team squirmed into places on the floor in the locker room and quieted down. Coach Bowden moved to the front, his note card in his hand.

"The big thing tonight, men, is to show me how you're going to hustle. Show me how you're going to play next Thursday. If you're gonna loaf, I'm gonna see it tonight. If you're gonna fight till that whistle blows, I'll see that. That's the main thing you can do, fight till the whistle blows."

The Seminoles were eight days away from their August 29 date with Brigham Young in California. This would be their final full scrimmage, the top defensive and offensive units against scout teams imitating Brigham Young.

"You guys on the scout squad," Bowden continued, "you can make the ball club tonight. If you're on the scout squad, you've got a better chance to show what you can do than the guys on the first unit. You're going against the odds."

The graduate assistant coaches would run the scout teams. Bowden's full-time assistants would be getting their last game-simulated look at the players they had been coaxing and bullying into shape for three weeks. They would play at twilight in the stadium, calculated to be about the same time of day as the kickoff in California. There would be a full complement of officials. The stadium was closed to onlookers except for the sportswriters, who would be getting their first real clue to Bowden's '91 Seminoles.

What the coach most wanted from this scrimmage was no ugly surprises. No injuries, of course. And no major foul-ups that suggested players didn't understand where they were supposed to be. "A live checklist" was the way he put it, "to see if we know how to line up and play a ball game."

Tonight also would be the time to name the captains who would serve until the whole team elected permanent captains at the end of the year. Bowden had taken recommendations from his assistants on who among the seniors would provide strong leadership.

"What I have done," he told the team, "is pick two on offense, two on defense and one specialty player. I wish I could have picked a bunch of you, 'cause we got a great senior class. How long will these seniors serve? Until I think they're not doing the job.

"These are the ones I've picked. On the offense, it will be Edgar Bennett and Kevin Mancini. On the defense, it will be Kirk Carruthers and James Chaney. Errol McCorvey will be the one from the specialty teams.

"I'm proud of what all of you have done, men. You've done good through two-a-days. Now just hope and pray the good Lord will take care of you. Now let's have a little word before we go out and hit the field."

The players knelt or reached out from where they sat to grasp the hand of a teammate. Bowden put his hand on the nearest shoulder pad. And they all bowed their heads.

It is hard to say exactly how and when fundamental Christianity became so entangled in the culture of football. But the connection has been a strong one from the beginning. Especially in the South, where the two most dominant structures in many rural towns are the First Baptist Church and the high school football stadium.

The region's preoccupation with fundamental Protestantism is ripe for parody. And it probably doesn't help that the image of Southerners' religious faith has been contorted by preachers in shiny suits with their own satellite broadcast systems, by the snake handlers and by the speakers in tongues. But those are the fringe characters. The people who have made Protestant fundamentalism the most dominant faith in the Southern states are pretty much the same folks who do everything else. They are the teachers and car dealers and mayors and grocery store owners. They are the establishment. And they sit in the pews on Sunday for the same reasons their counterparts sit in churches in New England and the Midwest: because they were raised in the faith; because their neighbors and business associates are there; because the regular ritual fulfills a spiritual need.

Bobby Bowden was born into the majority Southern faith in Birmingham. His parents took him to Baptist church. The vocabulary of born-again Christianity was as familiar to him as the voices of sports announcers on Saturday afternoons and probably more familiar than the lessons teachers imposed to distract him from sports.

It wasn't until later that Bowden, as a recently married small-college quarterback at Birmingham's Howard College, took the fundamental message of his faith to heart and rededicated his life to its teachings. The beliefs are simple, straightforward:

Christ, the Son of God, came to Earth in the form of a man, Jesus. He was crucified on the cross and rose from the dead. Those who believe in the Story as rendered in the Bible, who accept Christ as Saviour, are born again, regardless of their past sins. And a place will be preserved for them in Heaven.

It's a theology that appeals to two contradictory strains in the intellectual tradition of the South. On the one hand, it rewards individualism; God seeks a personal relationship with each potential Christian. On the other, it demands respect for authority. The Bible is the Word of God; if you don't believe the Word, you can't accept Christ and are condemned for eternity.

Whether they are believers or skeptics, most Southerners have experienced the power of religious faith in the region's culture. They know the hymns and have heard the prayers. A hundred years ago, the shared Southern experience was a war. Now, in this last decade before the turn of the century, perhaps it had become the memory of this fundamental religious faith and all its implications in the culture. It may, in fact, have become the single connection between Southern whites and blacks in an era of racial isolation and distrust. And to all, it offered the comfort of tradition and security when the whole world seemed upside down.

Bobby Bowden's personal faith, though, went beyond merely embracing a tradition. He was a believer in every sense of the word, trusting in the Bible's teachings as a way to make sense of the world beyond football.

He recognized in himself and in others the potential for sin. There was an inner barbarian in all of us, he believed, that could be constrained from horrible things only through self-discipline and obedience to God's will. Football, boxing and other violent sports allowed that barbarian a socially acceptable outlet, a mode of expression. Between the whistles in football, he liked to say, "is about the only time you can try to kill somebody and get away with it." Everybody needed to release the inner barbarian every once in a while. "Why do you think all those people are in the stands watching us?"

Bowden also felt obligated to share his personal faith with any willing audience. And just about every church within 1,000 miles was more than willing. Denomination didn't matter. The Bowdens joined the First Baptist Church in Tallahassee when they came to town. The coach wasn't a stickler about the finer points of Protestant doctrine and always figured he could fit in with the Methodists or the Presbyterians. The churches that asked him to speak ran the gamut.

His habit of appearing in pulpits across the region made Bowden one of the most famous lay Christians in public life. And because so many fans of Southern football were raised in the same tradition, it added to his stature in their eyes and reinforced the St. Bobby legend. To mothers and fathers of recruits, in fact, Bowden's Christian credentials were as important as his coaching strategy. His well-publicized faith reinforced theirs. He is one of us, they thought. And he was.

Before every game there was a Bowden prayer. A devotion began every staff meeting. The lessons of football and Sunday school were entwined. Unselfishness, industry and obedience to authority were to be rewarded; selfishness, laziness and rebellion were sins. The preacher in Bowden clearly influenced the coach. But the coach was never far away. In most prayers and devotions, in fact, were football messages. The lesson was never over.

"Dear Father," Bowden prayed before the last scrimmage, "we thank you again for letting us play. We thank you for letting us survive. These are the survivors. We pray that you'll take care of them and protect them from injury. We pray that you'll help them do their best so that the coaches can evaluate them and be fair to them.

"These things we pray in thy name. Amen."

"Amen," said the men in the locker room.

7

THE first preseason scrimmage on August 14 had produced exactly the kind of flash likely to keep fans pumped for 1991. Third-string tailback Tiger McMillon had run for 113 yards and a touchdown. Charlie Ward, the No. 3 quarterback, had been the usual dazzling innovator, dancing through defenders when the pass protection broke down and completing passes on the run. Wide receiver Shannon Baker had burned the defense for a couple of touchdowns. Even freshman Marquette Smith, *USA Today*'s high school offensive player of the year in 1990, had made his presence known, taking a screen pass from Ward for 55 yards. And he was the No. 4 tailback on a team loaded with offensive threats.

What a team this was going to be.

By the second intrasquad game on August 17, however, the defense was starting to catch up. And then this final scrimmage on August 21 provided a line of demarcation. The torturous two-a-days were over and one week of practice remained before the opening game against Brigham Young. At this stage, the coaches were anxious for proof of the team's readiness and maybe a few hints of championship desire. Many of the players, on the other hand, were tired of hitting one another and eager to get down to the excitement of the regular season.

Maybe that's why a sluggish first-team offense found it impossible to score against the third-team defense for a quarter and a half. The defensive reserves even got the first points, intercepting a Casey Weldon pass and running it back 78 yards for a touchdown. The first-teamers finally won 38–20, but the damage was done. The defense had overshadowed an offense with national ambitions. And Bowden was all narrow-eyed consternation when he addressed the team at midfield after the scrimmage.

"What I saw scared me. There was no offense for one and a half quarters. I hope it's not because we think we can just walk out on the field and win. I hope it's not that."

The head coach left the players to their segment meetings and strolled over to smile and shake hands with the new university president, Dale Lick. Lick had come out for his first look at Doak Campbell Stadium at night. "You oughta see it when it's filled up, Dr. Lick," Ronnie Cottrell, the recruiting coordinator, was telling him. "Every seat filled with fans doing the 'War Chant.' "

While Lick and Cottrell chatted with Bowden, Brad Scott's cowboy baritone was in full bellow twenty yards away, where he had assembled the offense: "This was pitiful, pitiful. You better get it together. You better meet with one another and decide what kind of team you want to be. You've been lollygagging around for a couple of days now. Tomorrow, we go back to work."

The writers waited for Bowden in the end zone. The next day's papers would carry the fullest treatment yet of Seminole potential in '91. The reporters needed a theme. And the coach obliged them with his best "scared to death" concerns.

"Eight days before his highly touted football team travels west to face Brigham Young and its Heisman Trophy-winning quarterback," wrote the Orlando *Sentinel*'s Alan Schmadtke in the next day's editions, "Florida State University coach Bobby Bowden saw another offense to worry about—his own."

The headline over Jim Henry's story in the Tampa *Tribune* said: "Lackluster scrimmage enough to 'scare' Bowden."

In truth, the sloppy offensive show gave the coaches the ammunition they needed to pump more intensity into the next week's practices, to demand a sharper edge for the opening game. "It may have been the best thing that could have happened," said Bowden. "As long as we can use it to get better."

Alarms went off for Mark Richt, the quarterbacks coach. "I was actually nervous before that scrimmage, because I was treating it like a game. But you can't make the players believe it's a real game. There was a total lack of intensity out there, a total lack of seriousness. But at this point, it could be a blessing in disguise."

Under Richt's tutelage were the team's four active quarterbacks— Weldon, Brad Johnson, Charlie Ward and Kenny Felder—and the freshman who would be redshirted in 1991, Jeff McCrone. Weldon and Johnson were seniors in their fifth year and still best friends, even though they had competed with each other their whole careers. Johnson first won the starting job in the spring of 1990 and kept it through the first five games of 1990. Then Weldon took over in the second quarter of the Auburn game and had held it ever since. Each had taken his turn at being an anonymous backup and a nationally known starting quarterback, and neither was blind to the irony.

"Last year," said Weldon, "it was me sitting in the background and Brad signing all the autographs. This year, it's the other way around. We're both very competitive. And we both believe we deserve to start. I didn't think any different when I was No. 2, and I'm sure Brad doesn't think any different now. But we both know it could just as easily be the other guy."

Ward and Felder were developing along the same path. Both were two-sport athletes, Ward in basketball and Felder in baseball. They were both redshirt sophomores, both prime candidates to take over when Johnson and Weldon graduated. And they were good friends. They had even joked, said Ward, that when their time came, "we might be the first co-winners of a Heisman Trophy."

As far as Richt was concerned, this was the ideal way to bring along quarterbacks. Redshirt them their first year so they could get a feel for the offense without pressure, work them in slowly their second and third years and have them confident and competent for starting roles when they had two years of eligibility remaining. By the time they get to their fifth year, "I don't have to teach them so much anymore as remind them of what they already know and help them prepare for the defensive looks they'll get in a game."

Weldon was primed for a great season, Richt thought. He had all the tools, the knowledge, to be one of the best Florida State quarterbacks ever. But potential wouldn't be enough. Not this year. This season, they wanted it all. And Weldon had to bump his intensity and concentration to the next level in order to inspire everyone else to do the same.

For the last scrimmage, Weldon's stats were only fair. He completed 13 passes out of 21 attempts for 127 yards, one touchdown and one interception. Not nearly a match for their ambitions. "If you had really been sharp," Richt told his quarterback, "you would have been 17 for 21—an 81 percent completion record. You would have had 182 yards, two touchdowns and no interceptions."

In a season of no excuses, there could be no complacency either. "We need to get a clean slate now. Let's not let something slip away."

8

THE aw-shucks country boy in Casey Weldon could fool outsiders. He was raised in Tallahassee, went to a small Christian high school and had little need to toot his own horn. Once he started playing sports, everybody else did it for him. By the time he graduated from high school, he was rated fourth in the South among quarterbacks.

He cultivated, consciously or otherwise, an image popular with Southern sports fans. He played the yes-sir, no-sir kid, the kind of guy who would lower his eyes when the master of ceremonies ticked off his accomplishments. In interviews, he let his sentences slur off into nowhere as if he were uncomfortable with all the attention. But he wasn't.

Casey Weldon always had big plans. And this could be a big season, a huge season. He didn't dare talk about the prospect until someone else brought it up, but he knew the Heisman Trophy was waiting for someone who could seize the right opportunities. And quarterbacks always had a leg up, especially on a team slated for maximum TV exposure and a run at the national championship. If they won it all, *he* could win it all—the Heisman, a slot in the first round of the NFL draft, a zillion-dollar pro contract.

At 6-1, Weldon didn't have the height NFL scouts prefer in quarterbacks. But then, neither did Joe Montana, the NFL's most respected quarterback and the athlete Weldon most resembled in style and physical appearance. The FSU quarterback did nothing to discourage the comparison. Besides, he seemed to have every other characteristic of a big-timer. He was intensely competitive, agile—a 4.6 40-yard dash—and maybe a little more mature than the average 22-year-old because of the battles he had fought over the past couple of years.

First came the rush into family life, when he and his girlfriend, Lori, married and had Kendall, a daughter now two years old. Then there was losing out to Brad Johnson in the 1990 spring practice, after waiting three years to become the starting quarterback.

"Boom. It was gone. I had always thought I would play pro ball, that college was just the steppingstone. And suddenly I lost my job."

The shock rippled through his life, threatened his marriage and momentarily made him think of transferring. "I went through a little bit of self-doubt. I didn't understand how it happened." But he stayed, refocusing his life with Lori and Kendall and biding his time, waiting for another chance to assume the role he was convinced he was meant to play.

"I thought I handled it real well. It's tough on Brad now, because he had it and lost it. I never had it."

Coming out of their sophomore years, neither Weldon nor Johnson seemed to be exactly right for the job. Weldon got the reputation of being bomb-crazy, always looking to make the big play. Johnson seemed overly careful, dumping off the pass to the short man before a play could really develop.

Since Weldon hadn't started the 1991 Auburn game, that loss didn't figure in his personal stats. But he had started every game since, and the Seminoles had won them all. It was no coincidence, he figured.

"I feel like we would have been repeating for the national championship if I had been the starting quarterback last year. We would not have lost to Miami and Auburn. It might be cocky, but it's a belief."

9

Bobby Bowden was hard at work on his gum when the door closed and they began the meeting. No sense suppressing the energy now. Direct it. Use it. It was Monday morning of game week. The first staff meeting of the first game week of the '91 season. And the Florida State Seminoles were No. 1 in the country.

"God, you've given us the greatest opportunity of any school in the nation," he prayed after the morning devotion. "It's up to us to do something with it."

Around the conference table in the offensive meeting room sat the nine assistant coaches, dressed for a day of meetings and practice. Despite the Tallahassee summer, they wore long-sleeve warm-ups over shorts and polo shirts. The meeting-room thermostat was wired in with the TV studio air conditioning across the hall, and the temperature never got above a meat-locker chill. Six others, the five graduate assistants and one volunteer assistant, sat in chairs along the back wall. Everyone had a regular seat. Everyone knew the routine.

They rotated duty for the devotion. Someone different each morning read a short inspirational story or thought for the day, then led the group in prayer. The devotion didn't have to be a religious message. It could be taken from any sort of inspirational or motivational lesson, even a coach's biography or something from a speech. And if delivering a prayer in front of the group made someone uncomfortable, Bowden did the honors.

After devotion came the injury report, with head trainer Randy Oravetz going down the list of players who had to be treated after practice the previous day or in the morning. Chuck Amato, the defensive line coach and assistant head coach, would bring up any administrative issues the group should be concerned about. And then Bowden would go over his notes from practice and lead a discussion in what was working, what wasn't and what had to be done next.

The principal injury update on August 26 was Mike Morris. Brad Scott got a glimpse of his worst nightmare when his star guard went down with that broken foot two weeks before. But, lo and behold, redshirt freshman Patrick McNeil appeared to be rising to the occasion. And to bolster that good news, Scott just heard from Oravetz that Morris had taken to rehabilitation with a vengeance. Always prone to gaining weight earlier in his college career, the senior guard was pedaling the stationary bike and lifting weights to keep himself in the 270-pound range. He could be back for Michigan.

In the best of all possible worlds, that's what is supposed to happen. Somebody goes down, somebody else steps into the gap. Nevertheless, if it had been Scott's turn with the devotion, his prayer would be one of gratitude: Thank you, Lord, for this tender mercy in our hour of need.

After the Wednesday-night scrimmage, the team had settled into businesslike practices that satisfied the coaches. And Bowden was turning his concerns to fine-tuning. "Hey, men, we can lose the game with penalties. And penalties are nothing but coaching. No penalties, no penalties."

He was especially concerned about the new no-taunting rule. Already, people were calling it the Miami Rule, because the pressure to enforce it had come after Miami's take-no-prisoners pounding of Texas in the Cotton Bowl the previous year. In the course of beating the Longhorns 46–3, Miami players trash-mouthed and finger-pointed their way into the Cotton Bowl record books with 16 penalties for 202 yards. The Hurricanes had won three national championships with a bad-boy image. And the NCAA worried that the Miami style could be contagious; so teasing and taunting were going to be targeted in '91.

This was likely to be a permanent battle for Bowden. Deion Sanders, the All-World defensive back who left Florida State for the pros in 1989, had already displayed too loose a lip and too high-stepping a style for the North Florida conservatives. And the coach knew he had a half dozen others on his '91 team who would out-Miami the Hurricanes if given half a chance. Despite fans' revulsion at the antics, Bowden wasn't so sure players' natural enthusiasm should be constrained. Playing the games should be fun. They should be excited about scoring, he thought.

He was worried, however, that the NCAA was intent on sending a message. And he didn't want it to be his team that lost a close game because of a stupid penalty. Not this year. In the first scrimmage a couple of weeks back, officials had flagged Shannon Baker twice for hot-dogging in the end zone after touchdowns. That got Bowden's attention.

"No taunting, no baiting other players, no inciting spectators," he said, holding up an official information card on the subject. "You men get that across to your kids.

"Now I want to meet with the offense."

10

Except for the eight-thirty general staff meetings, the assistant coaches spent almost all of their time divided into offensive and defensive groups. Andrews and his coaches studied the opposing offense and plotted alignments to disrupt them. Scott and the offensive coaches mapped out strategy to take advantage of weaknesses they perceived in opposing defenses.

At this level of competition, pregame planning was as computer- and video-driven as time and money would allow. Graduate assistants, former players interested in coaching careers, scouted upcoming teams in person. But most of the analysis came from videotapes of previous games. By Sunday night before a Saturday game, the coaches would have a complete breakdown of an opposing team's games. The in-house video service could isolate whatever situations they were interested in—goal line, third and long, punting, first downs inside the 20, etc. And they could group special situations from several games back to back on one videocassette for study.

In that week before the game, they would know the other team's tendencies for every down and distance and out of every formation from every place on the field. The goal was predictability. They wanted to know: When we get here, in this situation, what are they likely to do? Predictability eliminates surprise. Without surprise, the best athletes have the advantage on every play. And the Seminoles weren't likely to face many teams with better athletes.

Of course, opposing teams were performing this same ritual, with the same kinds of computers and video gear. So part of strategy always had to be deception: You saw us do this out of this formation in the last three games, but now we'll do the other. Clint Ledbetter, a volunteer coaching assistant who worked with the offensive line, would supply Bowden with weekly self-scouting reports, so the coach could monitor his own tendencies. With that information, the head coach could avoid some patterns and plant others in opposing coaches' minds.

For the week prior to a game, the graduate assistants filled the walls in the two meeting rooms with the offensive and defensive formations they could expect to face; and on each back wall was a three-deep roster of opposing players. The best players, the studs, were underlined.

This, of course, was the first game of the year, against a team that lost four of its five starters on the offensive line, the tight end and the starting halfback. That wouldn't seem to bode well for the Heisman-winning passing attack. On defense, the pass rush seemed jeopardized by the departure of just about the entire line. But the linebacking group and the secondary had returning starters.

Florida State coaches knew that BYU staffers had visited Auburn in the off-season. Auburn always played the Seminoles tough and had been the only team besides Miami to beat them in 1990. So Bowden could expect that LaVell Edwards, the longtime Brigham Young coach, had done his homework. But what could anyone do with so many inexperienced players against a veteran No. 1-ranked team?

Maybe change his whole approach. Introduce a new defensive scheme. Florida State could probably adapt with some frantic sketching on the sideline, but it could be a first-quarter nightmare on national television.

And then there were those missionary monsters to worry about.

Brigham Young usually had some of the oldest players in the country on its team, because many were Mormons who left school for a couple of years for missionary work. They always seemed to return bigger and stronger than when they left. For big guys between 19 and 21 years old, a couple of years can mean another 20 to 30 pounds of muscle and maturity. So all week, Florida State strength coach Dave Van Halanger had been worrying aloud about the prospect of the Seminoles colliding with the mystery missionaries.

"These are not boys. These are men," he said to anybody who would listen.

Bowden and his coaches could worry about all that, but they couldn't prepare for it. They could only get ready for what seemed the most reasonable BYU approach to the game. And hope.

When the defensive coaches left, Bowden got his gum back up to speed as he thumbed through his notes and game-plan work sheet. He had a hundred ideas.

"The fake field goal looks good. And man, they look so vulnerable to the reverse, I just hate not to do it."

The coaches smiled at one another. What a surprise, Bobby Bowden, one of the college game's most famous tricksters, was interested in calling a reverse.

"We need a speedster in there, probably Shannon Baker, and we need to be sure of the quarterback fake." The coach pushed back in his chair, rose and assumed a quarterback's stance. He took the imaginary snap and turned, showing how he wanted the quarterback to conceal the ball from defenders and narrating the fake and handoff to the wide receiver.

Everybody in the room, including Bowden, knew the point of the exercise wasn't to teach the coaches something they didn't already know from years of teaching it themselves. It was a way for Bowden to burn off a little of that nervous energy. And it was also his way of sending a signal that, from where he watched practices deep in the defensive secondary, Weldon and the other quarterbacks looked to be getting sloppy with the fakes. For an offense like Florida State's, which thrived on passing when the defense figured run and running when it thought pass, each fake had to be masterful.

Mark Richt made a note to spend a little extra time stressing ball handling with his quarterbacks. Message received.

"That might be the first play, men. 45X Reverse."

Back to his seat and his notes. "Now the whole key to the game . . ." Bowden always had a few "whole keys" to every game. Each time he said it, the assistants had to run through their mental checklists to make sure those plays had been repped well enough to justify Bowden's expectations. If they saw a problem, now was the time to bring it up.

"The whole key is, can we run the 80 game?" Three-step drops for the quarterback. Quick turnarounds for the wide receivers. These were the plays to secure first downs, to stop the clock with out-of-bounds plays and to frustrate the pass rush. When Lawrence Dawsey had been on the receiving end, the 80 game had produced big gains and touchdowns, because Dawsey was so good at picking up yardage after he caught the ball.

Every team had a version of these passes. But while they seem obvious and routine, they require timing and confidence between wideouts and quarterbacks. Patterns had to be run exactly the same way every time. And in '91 there was not yet that routine rapport between Casey Weldon and the wide receivers.

"The whole key," Bowden had said. John Eason knew what he would be reminding his receivers about in today's meeting. He made a note.

Then the coach turned to the plays on his game plan: How does this play look on third and short? What about goal line? Is there a plan to take care of the middle linebacker on that play?

Officially, this was Monday, but it was Wednesday in the coach's routine. The team was playing on Thursday night, two days earlier than usual. Which meant the practice cycle was moved two days ahead. They would have their regular Wednesday practice in shoulder pads today to iron out last-minute wrinkles. Then a walk-through in sweats tomorrow before they got on the chartered plane to Southern California.

He went down his list of plays, comparing it with the coaches' priorities. It took ninety minutes. When Bowden felt sufficiently satisfied that the plan for Brigham Young was on schedule, he gathered his notes and pushed away from the table. "Well, throw out what ain't reppable at this stage. I feel better, knowing we got a plan."

Mark Richt looked up from his notes. "Now if they'll just cooperate and do what they did last year."

Bowden laughed his nervous laugh and left for his office down the hall. Brad Scott leaned forward across the conference table toward his colleagues.

"Is the Man ready to play or what?"

11

IN nearly four decades of selling football to fans, to mommas and poppas, to church congregations and booster luncheons, Bobby Bowden had learned a thing or two about marketing and promotion. So he could sit there in the little fake village square, as the oompah music wafted from the loudspeakers hidden in the landscaping, and listen amiably to the Disneyland producers go over the script for the press conference:

The band would play. Bowden would take Minnie Mouse's hand and stroll out of the castle and up to the lectern for a few words. Then Casey Weldon and Mickey Mouse would toss the football for the cameras.

Music up. And all would exit stage left—the coach, Casey, Minnie and Goofy. They could watch Minnie for their cues. Any questions?

Well, maybe one. "Now, ol' LaVell, he's going to be doing this same thing, right?"

Oh yes, Bowden was assured. The BYU coach and his quarterback would get the same Disneyland welcome. All part of the deal. Welcome to Southern California and the Disneyland Pigskin Classic. Watch Minnie for your cues.

Four teams each year get a taste of an early-season bowl atmosphere when they accept August invitations to the Kickoff Classic in East Rutherford, New Jersey, and the Disneyland Pigskin Classic in Anaheim, California. They are made-for-TV events that can either jump-start national enthusiasm for a team or put it in the hole before the season even gets going.

Once the Seminoles got to California, though, the whole idea of an August bowl game looked a little less appealing. To avoid missing too many days of class, Florida State had cut the trip to the minimum. They arrived Tuesday night, too late for anything other than recovering from jet lag. Wednesday was full of required activities, such as the Disneyland appearance. And they would fly back Thursday night after the game.

For the players, it was a typical bowl routine: stuck in a nice hotel without money, transportation or very much free time. For the coaches, it was a fight for attention for last-minute meetings. And for Bowden, it was a walk down a ramp at Disneyland holding Minnie Mouse's hand.

So far, the principal benefit had been the weather.

When the players piled out of their buses at the Cal. State Irvine practice fields, they looked instinctively to the sky. How curious. There it was, the same sun that baked the energy out of them in Tallahassee. Yet the temperature here hovered around 70 degrees. And there was a cool breeze, blowing from the west, where the Pacific bounded a side of the continent almost none of these young men had ever seen. Wasn't it August here too? You mean this is normal? No wonder everybody wanted to live in Southern California.

The Wednesday-afternoon workout wasn't intended to do more than allow the players to stretch and run a bit. To get them out of the hotel and get their minds back on football. Even then, it was only about half successful.

Rumor had it that Burt Reynolds, Florida State's most famous product, was going to show up at practice. The film and TV star was a Florida native who had played running back for the Seminoles in the mid-1950s. He had stayed true to his school, donating money for uniforms and for the football dorm that was named after him. Florida State's film and theater departments profited from Reynolds' generosity as well. And he made it back to the campus, especially on big football weekends, whenever he could.

Visits were more rare now that his TV series, *Evening Shade*, locked him into Los Angeles for most of the season. But everyone knew that he would do everything he could to see Bowden and the team. So when a long, chauffeur-driven recreation vehicle pulled into the practice-field parking lot, all eyes were on the occupants as they stepped out into the afternoon breeze.

Burt wasn't there. But a group of his Hollywood buddies were, led by actress Loni Anderson, Reynolds' wife. She held a cellular phone that allowed Burt to express his apologies directly. Ann-Margret and her husband, Roger Smith, had taken the ride down from Los Angeles. So had NFL Hall of Famer Jim Brown and a few other friends. Once they hit the field, the workout turned into a photo opportunity, with the stars posing with the players, the coaches and even the university president.

They were all a little hypnotized. Such a beautiful afternoon, so far from where they had come from. Bowden and his team walked leisurely back to their buses. It hadn't been much of a practice.

12

For every coach, there is a point where the festivities surrounding a big game go from being relaxation opportunities to distractions. Bowden probably crossed that line somewhere between Minnie Mouse and the thirty-eighth group photo with Loni Anderson. Reynolds came by to see him privately in his room Wednesday night, and he was appreciative of the compliment. But he was ready to think about football. In his mind's calendar, it was Friday night.

On Friday night before Saturday games, Bowden had a regular ritual. He spoke to the team as a group, often reading them a story of some famous athlete who had conquered adversity and gone on to accomplish great things. Then, after he allowed the offense and defense their last meetings, he had his last skull session with Brad Scott and Mark Richt. Mickey Andrews would have to worry about the defense on his own.

Bowden wanted to cram everything he possibly could into his head for the offensive assault.

The text for the pre-BYU team meeting came from a story about Archie Griffin, the Ohio State running back who was the last player to win two Heisman Trophies. Griffin fumbled on his first carry as a freshman, was put on the fifth team and earned a chance to play only after the tailbacks in front of him were injured. With that opportunity, he gained over 200 yards and launched a legendary college football career.

Griffin attributed his success to his Christian faith, a common theme in Bowden's stories.

"I want you to get an idea where these men get their power," the coach told his audience.

" 'Cause you can get it the same darn way, and I want you to have it.

"Okay, now the ball game tomorrow."

There was no sense ignoring the evidence of bowl-like pressure. Might as well use it.

"National television. National television. A great opportunity, because you'll have the whole nation focused on you. Every play you're in there the camera might run that play back. Every play. But don't worry about mistakes. You're not human if you don't make mistakes. The important thing is to turn it loose, so if they catch you on that camera you'll be going full speed."

Then came the reminders off his note card:

"No profanity. No taunting. You can't get over another player and taunt him while he's on the ground. You can't point. You can't fire your guns off after a touchdown. You can't raise your hands to the crowd. They're going to be watching all that this year, and I don't want to see any of it. If I do, I'm just going to go over to your coach and tell him to get you out of there. I don't want any taunting.

"We need the same attitude we had last year in the bowl game against Penn State, where you have two class programs going at one another. It's a brutal fight, but one of the cleanest games anybody has ever seen. Mean, but clean. If you knock a guy down, help him up after the play is over. Then knock his tail off the next time he picks the ball up.

"When you score, give the ball to the official. Don't throw it down, so that he has to go find it. If you were that guy, wouldn't you look for a time to catch a kid that made him chase a ball? I would. I'd be watching for him to mess up so I could throw that flag on him. So don't infuriate those officials.

"Now just remember this in the game. Whenever you've got a new ball club, you wonder this: How are they going to respond when they get behind? This team will never prove itself this year until you get into a ball game and get down by seven, eight, ten or even fourteen points and have to show what you're made of. Everybody's good when they're ahead.

"I don't know when that day will come, but there will be a game this year when we'll be fourteen points behind and we'll find out what we're made out of. The one thing we must not do is panic. We've got to go ahead and do our thing. We've got to do our thing."

He went down his list of notes, encouraging the offense to open holes, the defense to prevent the long touchdown, the kicking teams to dominate when they were on the field. It would be a weekly checklist.

"Every week, it's going to be like a bowl game, men. They're all after us. Every time we win we take that No. 1 target into the next game and the next game and the next game.

"Now this final thing, men. When it comes down to it, you know why we can't lose tomorrow night? It's because the seniors won't let us lose. It's their last year. And they won't let us lose.

"You won't let us lose, will you?" Bowden looked at each senior one by one: "Kevin? Kirk? You won't let us lose, will you, Casey? James Chaney?"

All but the freshmen in the room had heard Bowden go through the challenge with every previous senior class. But it still worked. It turned the team into individuals who were responsible for the team. It got the requisite "no, sirs." And it quieted the room.

After their group session, the players would go to their offensive and defensive meetings. Bowden headed to his room to watch tape and wait for the last cram session. When the game the next day was a night game, the skull session with Scott and Richt could start late and go through the night. Bowden's enthusiasm for preparation was boundless. And he could stay up later and talk longer than the two younger men he was milking for details. So when they came to his room for the Friday-night skull, they came prepared to settle in.

For these sessions, Bowden was a creature of old habits. Here was a man who was a success by any standard, making upward of $700,000 a year at one of the most competitive professions in the world. He regularly spoke at black-tie banquets and preached from Sunday pulpits. When he didn't have on that garnet game sweater, he seemed to be perpetually in a coat and tie, ready for TV. But for these Friday-night skulls, it was back to Alabama. Off came the coat, the tie, the shirt, the shoes and socks. Even the pants, when he felt less likely to be interrupted.

He would sit on the edge of his chair in a pair of ratty old athletic shorts, barechested and barefooted. A bag of Red Man came out of the briefcase. He chewed tobacco only at practice and on Friday nights. A nervous indulgence from the old days. And a little messy in $500-a-night hotel suites. He lined one of the decorative wastebaskets with newspaper so as not to alarm maids who might be queasy about emptying spittoons.

Usually, the three coaches sat at a table, so that they could have their notes in front of them. And there was always an easel-mounted blackboard so they could draw up defensive alignments. Part of Bowden's pre-skull routine on Friday nights was to arrange the chairs around the table so that the three could see the blackboard. "Now," he would say, smiling at the opportunity to resubmerge into the game, "let's see their personnel again."

Every week, Richt or Scott went to the blackboard to draw up the opposing team's basic defensive alignments, writing in the uniform numbers of the starters and backups in each position: This guy comes in on certain passing downs, this guy goes out. This guy cheats to the middle of the field; this guy will give us the short stuff all day. These are the athletes; these are the stiffs.

None of this was news. They had all seen cassette after cassette of past game situations, and each had personal impressions of the opposing talent. Game-plan decisions had been made days before in order to grease up the plays calculated to take advantage of perceived weaknesses and predictable tendencies. Bowden just wanted to hear it all again, to file it for game day.

"Is there something they do every time? Something we can predict?"

Richt would draw up pass coverages and blitzes. Scott would go through blocking schemes to counteract them. And once he filed it all, Bowden would read through the game plan of possible plays for key downs and field positions.

When Bowden was especially impressed with a play's potential, he would look up from his sheet. "That is a pretty good football play."

For BYU, little had changed since the Monday-morning meeting. Both assistants nodded their agreement as Bowden went through the passes and runs he liked. The reverse was on. So was a fullback vertical pass, straight through the middle, to take advantage of Edgar Bennett's pass-catching ability.

It was early, 11:30 P.M. Pacific time, 2:30 A.M. in Tallahassee, when Bowden, Scott and Richt finished their session. The coach was still restless after the assistants left for their own rooms. Opening games were such question marks. There was just no telling what LaVell Edwards was going to do with his young team. They looked so vulnerable on paper, so filled with holes for the Seminole offense to exploit. It wouldn't be that easy, certainly. And what about Ty Detmer against the Florida State defense? Had they ever faced a quarterback like that?

An old *Star Trek* episode played out soundlessly on the television as Bowden made a halfhearted effort to clear away the coaches' meeting litter. Ann would be coming back soon from a play in Los Angeles. He sat back on the couch and sucked his teeth.

"Boy, if our kids don't contain and Detmer sprints out to throw . . . With some quarterbacks, it doesn't matter so much, but Detmer can kill you."

The door latch rattled, and Ann Bowden entered. "Are y'all through already?"

The coach nodded and walked into the bedroom to retrieve something. "Did you see this?" he asked as he padded barefoot back to where his wife stood in her theater clothes. It was a framed picture of Burt Reynolds with Quint, the young boy he and Loni had adopted. Reynolds, in black tie, held his son in his arms and looked into the camera with one of his classic expressions of bemused resignation. He held Quint's pacifier between his own teeth.

"To Ann and Bobby," it said. "Love, Burt."

13

As the kickers trotted onto the field for their pregame warm-up, John Eason climbed out of the baseball dugout and moved toward the box seats behind the on-deck circle. In an hour or so, the second annual Pigskin Classic would kick off in a baseball park, the California Angels' home stadium in Anaheim. And since baseball still had a month of games left before the playoffs, the field was in better shape for the summer game than for early-season football.

From the 30-yard line to one end zone was the packed clay of the base paths, which would make footing uneasy and landing unpleasant. Some of the receivers and backs had already ventured out to kick the clay with their cleats and make faces.

The game was syndicated nationally on TV and available in most markets. As long as the cameras didn't pan the crowd, maybe it would look like the spectacle Disney planned. But for the second year in a row, even the Disney touch hadn't been enough to drag Californians away from a thousand other recreational alternatives on a Thursday evening. Attendance was expected to be in the 35,000 range, almost 30,000 fewer than the Seminoles attracted at home and considerably below the number of people who packed stadiums anywhere in the South to see Florida State.

Technically, this was BYU territory. The school was only one time zone away in Utah, and the Cougars recruited heavily in California. Because of the Heisman, Ty Detmer was the best known of the players on both teams; this was the first trip to California for a Bowden squad in fourteen years. Still, the locals were intrigued by the coach and the Seminoles, partly because of their national prominence and partly because it gave the contrarians a chance to dump on BYU and Detmer.

Southern California college football enthusiasts didn't have much to cheer about of late, what with Washington stealing the thunder from UCLA and USC in the Pac-10 Conference. Many were tired of hearing about Brigham Young's power in a league, the Western Athletic Conference, where the second-best team was the Air Force Academy. And some had joined the jeers when the 1990 Heisman went to Detmer in his junior year, just before he and BYU lost the final two games of the season to Hawaii and Texas A&M by a total of 82 points.

This was a Heisman-driven offense? The veteran Seminoles would destroy them.

John Eason arranged his 6-3 frame in one of the box seats and thought about the prospects of a Seminole rout. Whoever it was making those kinds of predictions hadn't seen his young receivers struggle with routes and drop passes. Besides, "we've got a punter and a placekicker who have never kicked in a college game, a new long-snapper and two new backs on the kickoff-receiving team. And we're the experienced team?"

He didn't even mention an offensive line with a freshman, Patrick McNeil, starting in place of a potential All-American, and with Robert Stevenson, the tackle on the other side, feeling faint from the flu.

Eason had picked Matt Frier to start at split end. Shannon Baker and Eric Turral would rotate at the flanker position. In playbooks and in game-plan talk, the three potential receivers on the line of scrimmage were designated X, Y and Z: X for the split end, Y for the tight end and Z for the flanker. Although Eason encouraged his X and Z players to know one another's routes, he usually recruited a player with one position in mind. And in the best of all possible worlds, they would rarely have to switch.

The classic X receiver was a guy with passable speed and soft hands. Someone who could get open in the clutch and preserve drives with first-down catches. The Z was supposed to be a game breaker, the guy with burning speed for the long bombs. Against BYU, Eason would start Matt Frier at X and rotate Shannon Baker and Eric Turral at Z.

Matt, he knew, would give it everything he had. E.T. might be the best big-play athlete in Eason's group and therefore the natural lone starter at Z, but no one yet had confidence in Turral to do what he was told on each play. And Eason was as much of a believer in "Don't depend on the undependables" as Bowden.

If the reverse came early, Shannon would temporarily move to the X slot to guarantee speed. Chances are, the Z's were going to get open, because the BYU corners wouldn't be able to stay with Baker and Turral the whole night. But what would happen after Casey threw the ball?

In the Monday offensive meeting, Mark Richt had teased Eason. "Well, John, we've got the schemes. Will they catch the ball?"

A very good question, Eason thought. But he had given the stock coach's answer: "I guess that's why we play the game."

The kicking game was in the hands of walk-on punter Scott Player, who won the job in the final scrimmage, and redshirt freshman place-kicker Dan Mowrey, a cocky Tallahassee kid who had boomed field goals 45 yards in practice but was untested in games. True freshman Marquette Smith and redshirt freshman Tiger McMillon, both tough little water bugs, would be back to receive kickoffs.

Steve Allen, a redshirt sophomore, was the new long-snapper for kicks. At 6-5 and 300 pounds, he looked every bit the part of a world-class jock. But so far he had not shown the agility and athletic instincts that could make him a valuable backup and eventual starter on the offensive line. So, for the time being, his main job was to get the ball back to the punter and placekick holder. A screwup there, of course, could turn into quick points for the other guys.

The experience might be where you wanted it most: on the lines, in the offensive backfield and at linebacker and cornerback. But there were still all those question marks. These, after all, were just kids. Big kids, maybe; some of them with wondrous talent, to be sure. But they were barely more than children who had been alternately flattered and flogged into being gladiators. And now they had been hauled across the continent to debut before a smattering of Californians and a national TV audience.

14

W<small>HEN</small> they came off the field after pregame warm-ups, there were 100 large bodies in shoulder pads crammed into the space designed for 40 baseball players. There was no place to move without stepping on someone. So they sat. They coughed and cleared their throats. It was hard to breathe. The faint noise of rap and rock escaped from their Walkmen and blended into a distant buzz, a barely audible soundtrack of energy suppressed.

The waiting is always the worst. In some pregame locker rooms, players can't hold the energy in. They pound the walls and lockers. Some coaches cultivate the fury, imagining it sharpens the edge of aggression. But that hadn't been the style of Florida State and Bobby Bowden. From time to time, some of the younger guys would explode. A padded forearm would bang a locker; a helmet would fly. Inevitably, Bowden would caution them: "Save it for the game." Mostly, the players would sit silently in whatever space they had, intent on their own mental preparation or lost in the welcome distraction of stereo headsets.

Bowden wrote the schedule on the blackboard:

5:56 Skull.

6:01 Prayer.

6:02 Captains go out.

6:04 Walk out.

6:05 Hit the field.

6:08 Kickoff.

At 5:56 he looked at his watch and began:

"The first play of the game when we get the football is 45X Reverse. I want something good out of it. Backs, I want great fakes. Make it look just like 45." Then Bowden looked toward Baker and Turral side by side at their lockers. "Who's starting?"

Shannon lifted his eyes. "Now look," said Bowden, "I need you to run a 100-yard dash down that field for a touchdown. I'm pitting your speed against theirs. A 100-yard dash."

The receiver nodded. Beside him, E.T. looked down at the floor. Both shifted nervously on their stools until Bowden turned away.

"Second play of the game: 344 Zebra Z Corner. Third play: 644 Z Comeback. By then we should be sending in our kicking team for the extra point or setting up our goal-line offense."

A reverse and two pass plays to start the game. "I feel like they think we're going to run on them, because they lost so many linemen. So they'll be blitzing and everything else, and we might be able to hit 'em with this reverse and get something out of it.

"Okay, captains, if we win the toss, we'll take second-half option." Bowden always preferred letting the other offense go first, saving his option to receive the ball until the second half. The first couple of series are usually times for shaking the jitters and feeling out the other guys, he reasoned. So better to force them to execute their plays first. The defense seemed to make better use of nervous energy anyway.

"Defense, turn it loose. We have always started slow defensively and ended up with one of the best defenses in the nation. Why do we have to do that? Why do we have to do that? Why can't we come out of the blocks? We've got as good material defensively as anybody in the country. As good depth as anybody in the country. Let's turn it loose.

"Are the officials here for the captains? All right, men, no fighting, no penalties. And don't worry about that dirt infield. That was just like what you was raised on. Just like the yard in back of my house. Anyway, the NFL plays on it."

"Okay, men, let's have our prayer.

"Dear Father, thank you for this great opportunity of being on national television. The only two teams in the nation playing tonight. We pray that you help these boys to play their best. Help them do their best; that's all they can do. Protect us from injury on both sides. And give our coaches great wisdom for making decisions. And maybe we can glorify you. We pray in thy name. Amen."

The door opened to the ramp to the dugout and field, and the players crowded toward it, pulling on helmets. The managers had brought a NO EXCUSES sign from Tallahassee to tape over the locker-room door. It was the last thing each of the Seminoles touched as they moved onto the ramp and out on the field to accept the welcome of 38,000 California fans.

15

BRIGHAM Young won the coin toss and chose to go on offense first, which gave Bowden his second-half option by default. Detmer, however, didn't appear to have opening-night jitters. On his first series, he passed the Cougars to a first down six yards short of midfield. And there it was, the "oh God, here we go" feeling.

"Remember," Bowden had said, "if they go ahead, don't panic. We've got to do our thing."

But the defense was conceding nothing. On first down, Detmer dropped back three steps to hit his wide receiver on a short pattern. Terrell Buckley, reading the pass, hovered just behind and beside the receiver, so Detmer had to force the pass high and out of reach.

On second down, the BYU fullback, Peter Tuipulotu, carried on the draw play and gained only two yards. Then an all-out blitz on the obvious passing down hurried the Heisman Trophy winner into a bad pass. Incomplete. Fourth down, and BYU was forced to punt.

When the offense trotted onto the field, both Z's, Baker and Turral, entered the huddle, and Brad Scott signaled Bowden's first play to Weldon: 45X Reverse. The quarterback took the snap, faked to the fullback through the middle, then turned toward the tailback, who appeared headed toward the right side of the line. The young BYU defense, having seen film of Amp Lee gaining hundreds of yards off this play, fought toward the anticipated handoff. Lee closed his arms over his belly where the ball should have been and ran into the line to meet them.

But it was Shannon Baker who had the ball. Turning from his left split end position, the flanker had sprinted back through the backfield, taking the handoff and running left as Lee ran right. He eluded a linebacker at the line of scrimmage, turned the corner and tried to get into full stride down the left sideline. A defender interfered just enough to take him off his feet 19 yards downfield. But it was a first down.

On the next play, the Z corner, Weldon hit E.T. 26 yards downfield, and the Tallahassee high school all-star fought his way for four more yards with two defensive backs holding on. First down, this time in BYU territory on the 37-yard line.

When the third pass play broke down, Weldon scrambled for 10 yards and another first down. Then it was time for the backs to take over. The next five plays featured Lee and Edgar Bennett on the ground and in the air, with the drive culminating in a four-yard touchdown pass to the fullback. Bennett immediately ran over and handed the ball to the official. Mowrey ricocheted the extra point through the goal posts off a defender's helmet. And the No. 1 team in the nation was off to its '91 start. Florida State 7, BYU 0.

In the next two Brigham Young series, Detmer was hounded into turnovers—a fumble after a sack, then a Terrell Buckley interception. Weldon and the FSU offense converted the first turnover into a Bennett rushing touchdown, but Mowrey surprised the crowd and the coaches by missing the extra point wide right.

After Buckley's interception, the Seminoles stalled and had to kick the ball back. Then Detmer took charge, exploiting blitzes with two big third-down passes and handing the ball to Tuipulotu on a draw play for a 21-yard score. That made it FSU 13, BYU 7.

Weldon, however, was not going to be upstaged. He led two more Florida State touchdown drives in the half, finding receivers for big gains on crucial downs. Turral caught a six-yarder for the third Seminole score, and Lee ran it in from five yards out for the fourth. A two-point pass to Frier after Turral's touchdown got the lost extra point back, and Mowrey made the point-after kick following Lee's touchdown. Both drives were solid, time-consuming efforts. Only two things bothered the coaches: a few dropped passes by the receivers that had John Eason cringing on the sidelines, and Turral's little end-zone celebration after his TD catch. When he threw his arms into the air and played to the crowd, the coaches looked for the taunting flags. None appeared. But Eason was waiting for E.T. when he came off the field.

Detmer put together another skin-of-his-teeth effort, escaping a fourth-and-seven situation on the Seminole 34 to keep a drive alive. On the next play, it was again the fullback, Tuipulotu, who ran it in. The extra point put the Cougars within 14 points.

Just before halftime, it looked as if Florida State had widened the gap when Buckley returned a punt 56 yards to the BYU end zone. But the play was called back for clipping, and the score remained 28–14.

As the players ran to the dugout for halftime, Brad Scott caught up to tackle Kevin Mancini. "We had a great half," said Scott. "Now we've got to dig deep."

Inside the locker room, Bowden and his coaches crowded into the tiny office used for visiting managers and coaches during the baseball season. Richt, Ledbetter, Wally Burnham, Greg Guy and Dave Van Halanger had been in the press box, and the head coach wanted to know everything they could tell him about BYU formations. "I can't help thinking the 84 is there every time," he said to Mark.

"It is, Coach," said Richt. "Casey is just not doing a good job of getting it there." But both he and Eason suspected the problem with the 80 game was probably shared by both the quarterback and the receivers.

As fast as he could, Scott moved out among his linemen. "You have had a good half," he told them, "but the war has just begun. We are not going to let them get back into the game. I've got to have fighters out there. If you are tired, let me know, and I'll get you out."

He turned to the freshman, Pat McNeil. "Number 69, I've got to have a running lane. You've got to drive your man."

Richt pulled up a stool in front of Casey's locker to go through the coverages he'd seen. And Andrews gathered his defensive backs at the rear of the locker room. The angry intensity of practice was entirely gone from Andrews' voice now. In its place was encouragement and coaxing.

"Hey, guys, how many intercepts have we got? Just one. We ought to have a bunch by now. We put them in long-yardage situations, and we let them spit it out.

"Hey now, that was a good learning session for us. Now we'll find out how good we are."

When there were just a few minutes left in the intermission, Bowden called them all together. If there was a hint of confidence creeping into the other coaches' voices, the head coach wouldn't let it crowd out the fear and intensity in his. He was scared to death. And angry. This was a great quarterback they were facing, capable of devouring a 14-point lead with two or three plays. This was no time to let up. So he lashed out at the mistakes:

"How long are you going to keep getting penalties? We should have 35 or 40 points by now, but no, the offense is going to get penalties. Defense, you've got penalties that have hurt you. You had a punt return for a touchdown, and you got a penalty. I told you never to drill a danged guy unless you can see the front of his numbers.

"Men, if we don't eliminate these penalties, we're going to be in trouble.

"I haven't seen any killer instinct at all. We've had two chances to completely put them away. And no, we've let 'em right back off the hook. Now, men, are we going to be one of those dad-gum football teams without a killer instinct? Is this going to be just a bunch of good guys? A bunch of nice folks?

"You gotta stop that draw, defense. Every time they get down on the 10 they're gonna run that draw. We knew that. And they just run it for touchdowns."

The volume increased as he built the case of errors. "Receivers, I haven't had any great catches. I've had some good catches, but we've got a chance for you guys to go up and get the ball and I'm seeing those crocodile arms. You reach out only this far, like you're afraid you're going to miss. GET YOUR BODY UP AND MAKE THE CATCH!

"If we've got talent, let's use it. If we don't have talent, I want to find out in this ball game.

"We need to take the kickoff back for a touchdown. BLOCK YOUR MAN! BLOCK YOUR MAN!

"This team can come back and beat us. I need a persistent pass rush. That guy has all day to throw the ball. All day. KEEP FIGHTING TO GET TO THAT PASSER. This kid is a great quarterback. Do you want to come back here in thirty minutes and be beat? That's worth fighting for.

"We've had one big hit out there. What a bunch of nice guys.

"Last year in one game, Brigham Young was down 29–3, and Detmer came back and scored 48 points in the second half and won the dang game. Men, they're probably over there licking their chops right now."

The officials were at the door. "Time to go out? Okay, men, listen now, let's go out there and really fight. Offense, you need to take the ball and score. Backs, I need some great running now. Quarterbacks and receivers, I need some great receptions."

16

As usual, coaching paranoia colored Bowden's version of the game. The seven penalties for 64 yards were troublesome, but Florida State had dominated Brigham Young in the first half, outgaining this traditional super-offense 311 to 205 yards. Casey Weldon had completed 12 of 17 passes for 171 yards, two touchdowns and no interceptions.

Against the Seminole defense, Detmer, the Heisman Trophy winner and holder of 42 separate NCAA passing records, was 11 for 21 for 162 yards, an interception and no touchdowns. He had been sacked once and pressured often. Florida State had held the ball for over 18 of the first 30 minutes. And there weren't likely to be very many folks on the other side, least of all the quarterback, who mistook the Seminoles for merely a bunch of nice guys.

For the first three minutes of the third quarter, the Cougars and Seminoles exchanged possessions without scoring. But not without drama. When the first FSU series went nowhere, Player punted a 13-yarder straight up in the air, giving the Cougars a first down on the Seminole 39. But their version of the reverse lost 12 yards on first down, and they ended up punting it back.

On Florida State's second chance of the half, Weldon led the team on a five-minute, 86-yard drive, capped by Bennett's third touchdown of the evening. To make it even sweeter, he scored on a fourth-and-one smash up the middle. McNeil had cleared a running lane. Florida State 35, Brigham Young 14.

During that long push to the goal line, though, Amp Lee was unable to get up after a 20-yard run. In obvious pain, he was carried from the field by the trainers, and doctors carefully examined the area below his knee for a possible break. A few minutes later, though, he was standing with an ice pack on his shin. Out for the rest of the game, but not seriously injured.

That meant Sean Jackson, a redshirt sophomore and one of the most highly touted high school backs in Louisiana, got regular playing time in Lee's place. And it gave the TV commentators the chance to talk about Florida State's depth at tailback. Behind Jackson was McMillon. Behind McMillon was Smith, the talented true freshman.

Buckley intercepted Detmer but was nailed for pass interference. When FSU got the ball back, penalties for holding and passing beyond the line of scrimmage stopped the next drive. So the third quarter ended with the score 35–14.

Florida State made it 42–14 with a 77-yard drive that took full advantage of Jackson as runner and receiver. And the tailback got his first '91 score with a two-yard run up the middle. The FSU defense added two more points on the next play from scrimmage when Detmer was sacked in the end zone by Dan Footman.

It was a special triumph for big Dan, a 6-7, 265-pound junior-college transfer who suffered what could have been a career-ending injury in the 1990 preseason and was playing in his first game for Florida State. "I'll be back," he had told Detmer when he flattened him on a first-half sack.

With a little less than 10 minutes left in the game and a 30-point lead, the tension on the Florida State sideline finally dissolved. Bowden allowed himself to think about sending in the subs on the next offensive possession, but a ragged 10 minutes resulted, with two turnovers, some blown assignments and 14 unanswered points. Yet it was also a decisive win by two touchdowns. Definitely the most authoritative start in four years and a nationally televised announcement that the No. 1 team in the nation was off and running.

"I'm sorry some of you didn't get to play," Bowden said to his team in the locker room. "I told you that game would be tight, that that guy could come back just like that. And I lose my guts on substituting.

"You just keep in mind the ring. We want the ring.

"I'm proud of you, all of you. One down, right, men?"

The players, already half out of their grungy uniforms, erupted in laughter and shouts.

"One down, baby. One down!"

17

THE front page of the Tallahassee *Democrat* "victory edition" on Friday, August 30, carried the banner: "What a start! 44–28."

Below the four-column color photo of Eric Turral leaping into the arms of Warren Hart after his touchdown reception, just above the story about rising unemployment and beside the latest update on the dissolving Soviet Union, was a piece by general columnist Mary Ann Lindley that began:

> In the afterglow of last night's win against Brigham Young, Florida State football fans will be easy enough to spot today: sleepy eyes, but cockeyed grins, and shoulders thrown back a centimeter or two.
>
> It covers Tallahassee like the kudzu and could last for several days—this unremitting sense of satisfaction that a winning team inspires. Particularly this team already judged best in the nation.
>
> Football remains the most cathartic spectator sport. Talk with fans around North Florida this week and you'll understand: Football is late summer's elixir.
>
> "A winning team stimulates a lot of interest from the backwoods," said retiree Jack Richey, drinking coffee at Governor's Square. "They may have never gone to college—not FSU or anywhere else—but when the home team starts winning, it's Our Team."
>
> There's a certain amount of forward motion in just knowing that, overall, the home team's on a run—again.
>
> Tykes for years to come will be enchanted, looking upon FSU as their alma-mater-in-waiting.
>
> Success is a patina that can permanently change the character of a place, and its luster reflects well. FSU is nationally known because of football, not because of the magnet lab, said John Calvin, a faithful 1948 graduate. And yet FSU did get that magnet lab.
>
> Business owners notice the way a winning football team translates into cash. In gas stations, T-shirt shops, newsstands, restaurants, it's a fact—

people spend more when they're in the feel-good mood a winning team provokes.

The headline on the front page column said: "When FSU wins, we are all winners."

18

THEY were laughing and groaning in the dark in the offensive meeting room. "John, you were taking it real easy there on the sideline last night," drawled Brad Scott.

"Well, it was killing me inside," said Eason as he watched for the fifth time as a sure touchdown pass fell beyond the outstretched hands of Shannon Baker. To add to the torment, Scott backed up the play and let it roll again. Again Baker outran the defender and left his feet too early to catch the pass, and it fell incomplete in the end zone. There was no escape from the obvious. Not when the video was projected five feet by three feet on the meeting-room wall.

The team had flown directly back to Tallahassee after the game. And even though they had gotten little sleep, the assistant coaches were still wired Friday afternoon as they broke down video of the BYU win. This was the usual day-after routine. Game film. Those clackity film projectors were long gone from athletic departments. Even high schools had switched to video from film, as TV technology advanced the art of game preparation and technique isolation. But the old vocabulary remained: coaches watched film.

The day-after review started with segment coaches, often alone in their offices, grading each of their players' game performances. Then they would meet together in offensive and defensive groups to go over problems that needed attention in the next week's practices.

When things had gone well in a game, the joint sessions were fast and loose. Nothing looked so bad that it couldn't be corrected. And everything looked possible. A catch here, a block there, and they could have scored another four touchdowns; a slipped block here, an interception there, and they would have shut them out on defense. Even the screwups that drove them nuts in practice provided comic relief when the end product was victory.

The receivers were entertaining in that way. So were Jimmy Heggins' tight ends. Both regulars from 1990 were gone, and now Heggins was trying to break in three sophomores, who, so far, never seemed to be in the right place to make a block or get open for a catch. One of the three, Marvin Ferrell, had gone down with a hurt knee in the BYU game and would be out indefinitely. That left Lonnie Johnson and Warren Hart. Johnson couldn't always remember his assignments, and Hart's ballooning weight was earning him Crisco Kid barbs from fellow players.

Heggins, the only smoker on the coaching staff, would pull out his cigarettes after practice these days. And the coaches were sure he'd gone up a pack a day out of frustration. Apparently for the same reason, he had begun mumbling at the screen in group film sessions: "No, Lonnie, how many times do I have to tell you? . . . Dang it, Warren."

Ironically, BYU had given Florida State tight ends the benefit of the doubt on pass routes. And Scott delightedly ran the tape back for Heggins to show him how Johnson and Hart had drawn defenders, leaving Bennett open down the middle.

"Dang, Jimmy, haven't they read your clippings? Don't they know you're about to commit suicide because of the tight ends?"

Then there was the kicking game. Billy Sexton, who handled place-kicking and kickoffs as well as the running backs, moaned at the extra-point drama and the short kickoffs of young Dan Mowrey. "What! Let me play that back again," said Scott as he wound back Mowrey's first extra point. "I'll be. I think he bounced that sucker off of one of their guys. He did, he did."

The coaches laughed, and Sexton slid down in his chair. "This guy is testing everything I got. I'm gonna run his tail off in practice this week."

What kept the edge off the criticisms were the numbers: 543 yards of total offense and 44 points against BYU. They averaged over six yards a play and balanced the attack almost equally between rushing and passing. Just what they had intended.

Casey Weldon was still undefeated as a starter. He completed 21 of 28 passes for 268 yards, two touchdowns and no interceptions. And he took home the game's Most Valuable Player trophy.

Ten penalties for 100 yards cost them. So did 15 missed assignments on defense and too many missed tackles. The kicking game needed lots of work. But they had time now. They would be heavy favorites in the next two games, against Tulane and Western Michigan. Both were at home. Then they would have an open date before the big one against Michigan in Ann Arbor on September 28.

Plenty of time. Already, they had faced an unknown opponent a long

way from home. They had played on national television. And the un-
knowns were a little more knowable now. This was a good team, maybe
a great team.

A week ago they had sat in this room, wondering, as they would at the
beginning of every season, if they were kidding themselves about the
quality of their players and the level of their preparation. Maybe BYU
would embarrass them the way Miami was embarrassed a year before.
Now the game was less than twenty-four hours old and already ancient
history. It flickered away on the wall, showing Brad Johnson running out
the clock on a game that had been long decided in their favor.

One down. Twelve to go.

Part III

"YOU GET WHAT YOU DEMAND"

1

WHEN the players returned from California it was to a campus suddenly in full gear. Classes had begun shortly before they left, but practice and trip preparation had consumed their attention. Now, after an August on a nearly deserted campus, they were students again.

In 1991, Florida State University had 29,000 students attending classes on a 347-acre campus in the middle of Florida's capital city. The male-female ratio was almost 50-50, but it had taken four decades to reach near parity. From 1905 until 1947, the state had designated the University of Florida in Gainesville as the men's school and Florida State College for Women in Tallahassee as the women's. And it wasn't until the applications from returning World War II veterans overloaded the University of Florida that the state legislature made both schools coed and changed the Tallahassee school's name to Florida State University.

Through the '50s and early '60s, FSU was still "the girls' school," especially to the boys who went to Gainesville. Male Florida State graduates always resented the prejudice, and it added to the rivalry between the two schools. For years, the scarcity of older male alums put Florida State at a disadvantage in fund raising and in getting the attention of the state legislature. Most FSU alums were convinced that Florida Gators conspired against them in corporate boardrooms and legislative chambers to make sure the University of Florida remained the favored son.

About the time Bowden came to FSU in 1976, male graduates from the first decade of FSU's coed history were reaching the stages in their careers when they could help the university financially and politically. Bowden's success with football helped the school galvanize that support, and it provided him with an expanding alumni and booster network that treated him with enormous respect. There was no 100-year tradition of Florida State football for those folks, so Bowden became the tradition. And that gave him more clout than coaches in other big-time programs.

Provided, that is, he regularly pounded the Gators.

Dale Lick, the new university president, thought there was an advantage in the women's college heritage: "There's a very positive feeling on the campus of this university. I've been trying to put that together since I got here. It may be that the fundamental factor is our history. We came out of a history of being a women's college. And I think there's a nurturing feeling, a caring tradition."

Football players needed a little of that caring tradition if they were going to survive at a school like Florida State. Especially in a program that made a big deal about not cheating to keep them around.

In an ideal student-athlete world, you wouldn't be able to distinguish the students from the athletes. Indeed the NCAA and various reform commissions have advocated rules that attempt to close the gap and integrate jocks more fully into student populations. Special athletic cafeterias and dorms were to be phased out by 1995. Entrance requirements were being toughened. And there were new policies to ensure athletes' progress toward degrees. But the separate realities of university life and big-time intercollegiate competition would always conspire against the ideal.

Football, like war, puts a premium on physical sacrifice of the individual for the good of the group. It requires a willingness to endure pain and abuse for long periods with only the faintest prospect of glory. Lots of kids start out playing the game, but as the demands increase, those who have an array of other alternatives—athletic, social and intellectual—are more likely to drop out of the talent pool. So by the time college recruiters visit high schools, the best football prospects are often those whose talent has been shaped by desperation: the hungry ones. It is no coincidence that there are stark differences between that group and the privileged majority on college campuses.

In 1991, the FSU student body was overwhelming white, with only about 8 percent black students. Yet the football team was about 65 percent black. To avoid the sense of social isolation, most of the black players cultivated a tight circle of black friends on the team and from the nearby campus of historically black Florida A&M University.

Academically, football players were different as well. Most FSU students came to Tallahassee with strong college preparation credentials. The 1990 freshman class, for instance, had an average SAT score of 1097 and a mean high school grade point average of 3.5. Many of the football players, on the other hand, would not have been accepted to the school had they not had athletic talent.

According to a self-study of intercollegiate athletics at FSU, football players admitted for the fall 1989 and spring 1990 terms had an average SAT score of 859 and an average high school grade point of 2.81. And those numbers were most certainly inflated by the inclusion of nonscholarship players. Even so, almost half the group were considered official exceptions to the normal admissions process.

Once they were students, their size, their backgrounds, their notoriety and the demands on their time and energy often set them apart. If they followed all the rules, the players lived a relatively monastic life, moving between the dorm, the athletic center and the classes that could be arranged around football. During the season, they had to sign in for breakfast every morning, be available every afternoon for meetings and practice, report to nightly study halls when their grades slipped, be in their rooms for nightly bed check and reserve every weekend for travel and games. If they skipped or were late, they had to do extra running or report to 6 A.M. study halls.

Their books, tuition, room and board were part of their scholarships, but NCAA rules forbade them to accept jobs during the school year or gifts of any kind. So those without help from home rarely had any extra cash in their pockets.

The faculty and the athletic department tried to provide counselors and tutors who could help the players bridge the distance between the demands on their lives and the opportunities the university offered. But those who came to Florida State ill equipped to take advantage of traditional college activities would have to make a heroic effort to do much more than merely survive. And for most of them, that only made football seem more important. It might be all they had.

2

CASEY Weldon won the Most Valuable Player award in Anaheim. Edgar Bennett had a career day running and catching. But it was Dan Footman who had the coming-out party.

The junior defensive lineman was the defensive player of the BYU game, with four unassisted tackles, two sacks and a safety. Almost exactly a year ago, he had dropped off the depth charts with a knee injury that could have ended his football days and left him with a limp for life. No one had written his name in the August stories of probable Seminole stars. But now everyone wanted to know who the heck this guy was.

Given the evidence of the BYU game and even a casual glance at Dan Footman in a football uniform, one thing was apparent: "This is the prototypical defensive lineman in the National Football League," said defensive line coach Chuck Amato.

At 6-5 and over 270 pounds, Dan quickly got the Big Foot nickname and a hefty measure of respect from his teammates. He was very big, very strong and, for his size, very fast. In high school in Tampa, he had anchored the state championship 4X100 relay in track and had been a running back in football. He ran a 4.5 40-yard dash, a good time for a 220-pound fullback, let alone someone 40 to 50 pounds heavier.

In junior college in Mississippi, he switched to linebacker to increase his chances of playing in Division I and, eventually, the pros; he expected to play the same position when he transferred to Florida State in 1990. But the coaches needed him more as a down lineman. "After they told me that, I was ready to transfer, but a couple of practices later, I hurt my knee in a scrimmage. Then, I *knew* I was ready to go."

He was operated on in the first week of September and began a long, painful rehab process. It was the worst ligament damage the Florida State doctors had seen in a football player, and it required a complete rebuilding.

Footman felt betrayed by the coaches who recruited him as a linebacker and forced him to play tackle. He blamed Bowden and the assistants for his pain. He hated life. And his anger forced everyone to give him a wide berth when they saw him laboring in the training and weight rooms.

"I couldn't have gotten any more down than that. School hadn't even started, and I was going through a crisis.

"When I first got into the training room, and they told me my leg was all torn up, I started crying. I hadn't cried in so long, and I cried for a long time. I said, 'Go out there and ask Coach Bowden if he's happy now.'

"I don't know why I didn't quit. I guess if I had quit there wouldn't have been anywhere I could go to rehab."

Assistant trainer Jack Marucci made him a special project. And the two became good friends. For eight months, often in sessions of four hours a day, Marucci coaxed and harassed Footman into rehab work. And the big man's own determination slowly brought him back.

At first, the goal was to walk again, then to walk without a limp, then to run. After six months he became encouraged that he could play football. In August, he led all the big men in running both the 40-yard dash and the 1.5-mile run. He pounded the offensive linemen in pass-protection practice. Then, in his first game as a defensive tackle, he chased the 1990 Heisman Trophy winner all over Southern California. And his teammates had seen the angriest man in Florida State football start to smile.

But it was too soon to write the happy ending, cautioned Amato. "In two years, Dan has practiced as a lineman only twenty-seven or twenty-eight times," he said. Letting him loose in an undisciplined pass rush was one thing; relying on him in run and pass situations on the base defense was another.

"He's still kind of a virgin. And he's coming off one of the worst knee injuries you can have. After the game, his knee swelled up. And it swelled again in practice. We pulled him out, because I don't want to rush him. I don't want him to become discouraged. We've got to bring him along."

There was not much in Footman's background to encourage him to believe other people had his best interest at heart. His father and mother had split up when Dan was in elementary school. He had worked through high school while playing football and running track. Sometimes that meant walking home from the fast-food restaurant or the produce market at midnight and not getting to sleep until three or three-thirty in the morning.

"There wasn't too much studying. That's probably why I didn't get the math I needed."

He lacked the core courses to qualify for a Division I scholarship out of high school, so he ended up at Northwest Mississippi Junior College. And when he transferred to Florida State before the 1990 season, he was suddenly confronted by everything at once—the demands of the new position, the pressures of student life and the debilitating injury. "It was probably my worst semester ever. But I couldn't just sit here and flunk out. I guess I didn't have no choice but to go to class."

That was typical Footman. Dr. Doom. He had made a miracle recovery by virtue of his—and Marucci's—effort. He hung in there academically when it meant going to class on crutches. And he had earned a place on the No. 1 college football team in the nation. But he was reluctant to give himself credit. And even more reluctant to trust that others would appreciate his achievements.

"It ain't nothin' but a business. If you ain't doin' what the coaches want you to do, they won't listen to you anyway. You can just see it. It's like you have to be a favorite. If you're not a favorite, you ain't gonna get nothin'.

"All the favorites are on offense. You go down to the grocery store and buy every magazine you see with their face on it and you come back with a stack of magazines with pictures of Casey, Edgar and Amp. But you try to find a magazine with a defensive face, there ain't no way.

"I don't think I'm gonna be one of the people they're highlighting. Maybe because of my attitude last year when I was hurt. I ain't never gonna be a favorite."

3

WHEN Bowden watched his players attack practice drills on the Monday of Tulane week, he got nervous. Where was the energy, the evidence of commitment?

After the long buildup to the opening game, maybe the win robbed them of their intensity. Maybe it instilled too much confidence. "I want them to smell the perfume, not throw their heads back and gargle," he told reporters.

Oddsmakers were making the nation's No. 1 team a 41-point favorite in the home opener. And if Bowden needed a little extra shot of paranoia to launch him on his fear cycle, that was it. He appreciated the value of being the underdog. In fact, he had made a mini-career of it. He had stood in many a visiting locker room and preached to young men: "They say you can't do it." And then he had sent them out, onto somebody else's home field, to punish the favorites for their arrogance.

He became the "King of the Road" in the early '80s, building a reputation for his Seminoles by taking them to play in the big guys' backyards and beating them. So he was a master at turning opponents' overconfidence and complacency against them.

Now his team was a 41-point favorite.

"It's like fighting a guy and starting off by slapping his jaws. That just makes him furious."

The assistants knew the routine for avoiding the upset, for focusing players on a threat they could easily underestimate. "Tulane up front will be better than BYU," Jimmy Heggins had told the offense in their Monday scout meeting. "Hey, this is a bowl game for them when they come in here."

When you're No. 1, Brad Scott preached, you're going to be everybody's bowl game. "It has to be our job every time we go out now to be physically intimidating, to beat the will out of them."

Tulane always seemed overflowing with will against Florida State, even though the Green Wave had beaten the Seminoles only once in nine consecutive games. And that '83 win in New Orleans was turned into a forfeit in the record books because Tulane used an ineligible player. They would come to Doak Campbell primed for an upset, Scott argued, "because they've got a roster of twenty or so guys who are from Florida. They wanted to come to FSU, and we turned them down because we wanted you men.

"We told them they couldn't come, and now they want to show us we were wrong."

With so many Florida athletes ending up on rosters of out-of-state schools, this argument was always a safe one. But it probably lost a little impact with every retelling.

In any event, the scout-meeting challenge seemed to have no real effect on the practice that followed. And the listlessness set Bowden to fretting about discipline and mental preparedness. On the plane trip back, some of the players had gotten rowdy, and Sterling Palmer, the 6-7 sophomore linebacker, had lobbed a soft-drink can over his shoulder. It would have been terrible to lose someone for a game because he was smacked in the eye by a flying Coke can. The coach was going to have to sit Palmer down and talk about that.

When he reviewed the game highlights for his Sunday TV show, Bowden didn't like what he saw of Eric Turral's personal celebrations either. And E.T. had further complicated things for himself by getting kicked out of the game protesting an official's call in the closing minutes. Bowden hadn't heard the official say anything about the ejection at the time, but he saw it on the TV tape. Bowden wrote a note to himself to talk to Eason.

The game film had also exposed some of the defensive breakdowns, notably the second-half touchdown pass that apparently victimized Buckley. And that was right after he fumbled the kickoff. If Buck was going to play the star, he had better make sure he consistently performed like a star.

Corey Sawyer, the redshirt freshman cornerback, had been suspended for the first game as part of his continuing punishment for a run-in with the police in the off-season. But Sawyer had dutifully taken his punishment, and now Bowden noted to himself, "Sawyer is ready."

With a little more experience, Sawyer might be able to push Buckley a little. In fact, in two-a-days, Andrews had moved Sawyer to the top of the depth chart ahead of his All-American in an attempt to get Buck's attention. But no one on the team believed the coaches had the nerve to hold Buckley out. Down deep, Bowden suspected the same thing. But it would be nice, thought the head coach, if the younger kid progressed so well he could press the star defensive back. The competition would make both players better.

The coach's offensive notes were unsurprising. Dropped passes and bad routes. "Hand the ball back to officials! . . . If we could have executed the 84s, we would never have punted."

All this was still in Bowden's mind as he left the Monday practice field and approached the writers waiting for items for the next day's papers.

"It was just a so-so practice," he told them. "Nothing excited me today. I sure hope they pick up the pace tomorrow."

4

"MATT Frier, what is class?"

John Eason went around the room to each of his receivers, asking them to define what they thought it meant when somebody said the word. Frier looked up, but was in no mood for conversation. Eason had demoted him to second team because of the dropped passes in the BYU game and in practice.

The sophomore had lost confidence. It might help him to remain in the starting split end job and work his way out of the slump. But competition at this level of football didn't allow for self-esteem therapy at the expense of winning. Redshirt freshman Kez McCorvey would get his first start against Tulane.

"I expect you to come back," Eason told Frier.

The day's lesson on demonstrating class was aimed at Eric Turral, who had been punished for his showboating during the BYU game with extra running after practice. Lawrence Dawsey had even called the receiver over the weekend to recommend laying off the grandstanding.

"I want you to show enthusiasm," said Eason, "but I want you also to exhibit class."

And E.T. had apparently taken the cautions to heart. Coming off his six-catch performance in last week's game, he was having a solid week of practice. Maybe, thought Eason, his problem child was finally coming around.

When E.T. joined the squad in 1990 after his Prop 48 year, it took the full season for him to get back up to athletic speed. He sulked and pouted. And he continued to struggle academically. He refused to take part in off-season workouts along with the others, digging a discipline hole for himself with the coaches.

Academically, he lived on the edge. Dismissed once and readmitted on probation, Turral was forced to make better than B average grades in summer school just to get another chance in 1991. And to survive into '92 he would have to continue the bailout with a B-minus average in the fall semester.

The odds had been against Eric Turral from the beginning. But Eason always thought he could perform the rescue mission. The kid had come so far. He had learned to study. He faithfully attended study halls and never missed class or tutor appointments. And there was always that promise of his potential on the football field. He could put on a display when he wanted, outrunning just about everyone on the team, leaping for balls and snagging them one-handed. If there was one player who could single-handedly salvage the season for the receivers, thought Eason, it could be this troubled kid.

And wouldn't that be a kick for them all—for his teammates, for the school and, most of all, for Eric who desperately needed football and school. Because below him, back in the neighborhood, an abyss awaited.

Matt Frier wasn't going to disappear into any hole. He was the son of a proud and prosperous family in Live Oak. He was a solid student in advertising who would graduate and move easily into a world of regional commerce where it didn't hurt to mix a little country with business-school savvy. Matt Frier had only one problem: the pressure of expectations. All of Live Oak was watching its favorite son. All he had to do, he was always told and always believed, was outwork the other guys, and success would be his.

Eason noted sarcastically that Frier may have been the victim of a racist stereotype. Because he was white in a position dominated by black athletes, he was assumed to be slow and awkward. But Frier's straight-ahead speed probably put him in the middle of the pack among the receivers and running backs. And his desire and toughness were unrivaled. Ironically, it was that fierce desire that was probably inhibiting his improvement as an athlete. He was so determined to push himself to succeed, the effort stiffened his body and, on occasion, turned his hands to stone.

It was an interesting collection, thought Eason. Turral was unpredictable. Frier was falling over himself. Shannon Baker would get dropsy attacks. Kevin Knox, the largest and potentially the most physical of the group, was still tentative on his routes. And quiet Kez was just a freshman.

Until someone stepped up to become the hero, Eason was going to have to piece together one receiver from spare parts.

"Maybe what we need is a trip to Oz," Mark Richt teased him. "We've got guys who need heart, some who need brains, some who need courage. Let's go see the wizard."

5

BEFORE the Wednesday staff meeting got underway, Mark Richt asked the other assistants, "Okay, did anybody promise number 45 to anybody? That's what big Crock says he wants."

The Seminole with 45 on his jersey in 1991 was senior linebacker Kirk Carruthers, who probably would have been surprised to know that a discussion was already underway about who would be wearing his uniform next year. But this was serious business. It was about recruiting. Henri Crockett was a top linebacker from Pompano Beach, Richt's recruiting territory. And he was asking for something the coaches might be able to deliver.

Recruiting was the third tier in the coaches' three-dimensional planning routine. Their first job was to get their starters and top backups ready for the next game. Then they had to make sure the younger players were developing properly so they could compete for first-string jobs a year or two down the road. And, finally, they had to cultivate prospects for the future.

Each assistant was responsible for a geographical recruiting region, and, of course, each kept a special eye on prospects who played the position he coached. But Ronnie Cottrell's only responsibility was coordinating football recruiting.

Next to Bobby Bowden's, Cottrell's was the biggest of the football offices. But there was seldom any place to sit. Files and letters littered the couch and chairs and the filing cabinets. He was always plugged into his computer or talking on the phone. Coach Telephone, the players called him.

It was Cottrell's job to stay in touch with a network of high school coaches, to keep on top of the stream of correspondence that went out to young high school players, coaches and parents, and to field the endless calls that came back. Yes, he told them, Florida State was indeed interested in this great quarterback or that superb lineman. They should keep up the good work. Take algebra. And by the way, had they signed up to take the Scholastic Aptitude Test yet?

On Coach Telephone's wall was a grease board with a sliding panel. Most of the time, the panel remained hidden behind the wall, invisible to players and athletic department visitors who frequented the football offices during working hours. Cottrell closed his door when he slid the panel out to work on the names posted on it. But there really wasn't much need for secrecy. The names were those of top high school prospects. And since they were among the best-known young players in the nation, lots of other coaches had the same names on their recruiting bulletin boards too.

Many are spotted as sophomores and, certainly, as juniors. So the rumors about who will go where often begin before a high school senior even begins his last season. Before the NCAA passed regulations to prohibit contact with high school underclassmen, college coaches would routinely write and phone promising underclassmen to get a head start. Beginning in '91, though, they had to wait until July of a prospect's junior year before contacting him.

Cottrell's list started out as a big one, with maybe 500 names at the beginning of the summer. Then it was gradually whittled down to 100 or so. Throughout the season, prospects would be invited to come up and watch the Seminoles' home games. But it had to be at their own expense. Florida State could provide only the tickets.

Every night during the season, assistant coaches made calls to prospects on their list. Even though a big Florida State game was coming up, they would say, they wanted the youngsters to know they were thinking of them and wishing them well in their own games. This was a time for building relationships, not only with the prospects themselves but also with the network of family and friends that might matter to the kids.

Later in the season, the assistants would fan out to high schools on Friday afternoon to evaluate film and talk with coaches. Then in December, after the last regular-season game, the intense recruiting would begin. Coaches would be out visiting prospects in their schools and in their homes. The ones at the top of the list would get a visit from Bobby Bowden himself, flying in especially to meet with them and their parents.

After the bowl, prospects would make their official, paid visits to the school to be seriously romanced. All of January would be taken up with the courtship, a time of emotional ups and downs, with coaches convinced they had snared their best prospects, then just as convinced they had lost them to competitors. No one would really know until the first week of February, when recruits officially signed letters of intent with schools of their choice.

Henri Crockett was one of the names at the top of the list on Ronnie Cottrell's grease board.

If he wanted number 45, said the other coaches, no problem.

6

THE Holiday Inn in Thomasville, Georgia, is forty miles north of Florida State University's athletic center. Every Friday night before Saturday home games, the Seminole football team boarded a bus for the hour-long ride. In Thomasville, they met briefly with the head coach for his usual Friday-night inspiration session. Then they would spend the night and return to Tallahassee the next day in time to say hello to friends and family at the football dorm and walk over to the stadium.

A Friday-night hideaway is a tradition at most schools, even though now it may have more ritual value than real function. Bowden was of two minds about the Friday trips. He would just as soon sleep in his own bed, and he frequently drove back home after his Friday skull meeting with Scott and Richt. But there was something to be said for getting the boys out of town, especially for big games. And the coach dearly loved the escape it gave him on Friday afternoons. He had a video machine set up in his Thomasville hotel room so he could start watching tapes in midafternoon without the interruptions of phone calls and drop-by visits in his office.

On the Friday afternoon before the Tulane game, Bowden was already settling into the pregame stage of his fear cycle. He was confident but anxious to get on with it, to get past it, really, and move a step closer to the challenges that lay further down the line.

His early-week concern about the players' lack of intensity had been communicated to the coaches—maybe overcommunicated, he now thought. The Tuesday practice had gone 22 periods in full pads. "Some of the older guys were asking what day of spring practice this was," Scott had joked in a morning meeting. And the assistants had gone at them hard on Wednesday, when Bowden figured they'd be tapering down.

Edgar Bennett, the fullback, had been losing weight. "Oh Lord, Bowden," he said to himself, "I hope you haven't blown it."

Coaches lose football games by overtraining as often as they do by undertraining, he thought. Probably more often. Maybe they got away with it this week. But it was one of those things you have to worry about throughout the season: How much is too much? How much is enough?

"We're supposed to win this one. We should win this one. In fact," the coach admitted, "if we play as good as we can play, it will be very bad for them. But if we go out there and make mistakes, lay the ball on the ground, then that's the way we can get beat."

Bowden said all the right things about anticipating every week's contest. But he really wasn't excited about games like this. All the worry was about the upset or about winning so ugly he'd have to spend the whole next week defending his calls and his team's talent.

Before the season began, he had drawn a blackboard depiction of peaks and valleys for his team. This is the season, he told them. There would be mountains of different heights to climb. The Brigham Young mountain was a big one, because that was the opener on national TV. Michigan loomed huge, as big a challenge as any of them had ever faced. The mountains would be even bigger in November for Miami and Florida.

In between those summits, however, were lesser peaks. They couldn't be dismissed, but they wouldn't require every ounce of talent and energy for victory either. "There is no sense lying to them," Bowden said. "They know Western Michigan is not Michigan. They can't peak every week for every game. It's not humanly possible. You just better hope you're ready for the big ones and that you can survive the others with a professional attitude. Just go out and do your job."

Tulane was one of the little peaks, but it was a perennially scrappy team. And Scott was right about all the Florida kids who considered this an opportunity to shine before home folks and to show up the nation's No. 1 team.

Bowden decided to remind his players of the struggle they had last year against this same team. Chance Miller, Tulane's tough little running back, had gotten 96 yards on the ground—more than Amp Lee and Sean Jackson combined.

The Green Wave was proud that it had not been shut out in 150 consecutive games. Maybe that was a good goal for the defense. It would have to stop Miller. And it would have to avoid getting burned with the long pass. Remember last week?

The offense would have to mash 'em at the goal line. Mississippi had beaten Tulane last week, but had to settle for field goals five times when the Rebels drove inside the Green Wave 20. Ole Miss could not push into the end zone against the Tulane goal-line defense. Can we?

Those would be his challenges tonight, along with this:

"Are we the No. 1 team? Well, they voted us the No. 1 team. Tomorrow, men, we don't need to go out there and play down to their level—whatever that level is. You go out there tomorrow and play like you're the best at your position in the United States. And when that first team goes out there and the second-teamers come in, play like you're the best. Let's keep pressure on them for sixty minutes.

"We're not going to lose tomorrow. We're going to win, because we've got a bunch of seniors who are not going to let us lose."

7

"WELL, you get so much publicity, your boys start believing it."

The coach of the nation's No. 1 football team was seated in an empty TV studio off Thomasville Road. Just he and a lone cameraman. He was playing his role via satellite for NBC, which was taping the interview Saturday morning to replay in the afternoon during the halftime of the Notre Dame–Indiana game.

"They get to listening to all the bragging, and it can be very distracting. You have to learn how to live with it and how to act."

Bowden paused, listening to the question from New York in his earpiece. "Well, I don't know if there is such a thing as a 'best shot' at a national championship. This is another shot. And I hope we get a shot every year."

Pause again.

"Do you mean, am I obsessed with getting a national championship? No, I'm not obsessed. There's more to life than that."

The coach answered a few more questions about the astounding performance of college football in the state of Florida. "You talk about a national championship. Man, I'd just love to win the state championship." Then, he thanked the voice in his ear and unplugged himself.

Kickoff wasn't until 7 P.M. Which meant he could steal a little time at home with the family for his wife's birthday party, then slip away in midafternoon to his office to impatiently endure the three hours before the game.

In the Friday-night skull session with Scott and Richt, they had pretty much settled on a plan of attack, at least for the early part of the game. Bowden had bought Scott's argument that the passing game should set up the runs and not the other way around.

"Here's what I think they'll do early on," said Scott. "They'll be locked in there for the running game, and those linebackers are going to be in there tight. If we come out throwing and move the chains, I'll bet they'll start getting back. Our deal has always been to mash 'em and take control of the line of scrimmage. So I believe they're going to be anchored down, especially the way we ran the ball last week and most of last year."

Bowden thought he had a first play: 7 Waggle Special, which could go to the fullback in the flat or the tight end right down the middle. He had watched tape after tape of the Tulane defense double-covering the wide receivers and trusting the backs and tight ends to linebackers. Bennett was certainly no secret out of the backfield after last week. But either he or the tight end was likely to be open if they expected a run or a pass to the wideouts.

"Now, y'all be sure and tell Jimmy Heggins that that tight end ain't got no choice but to get out there on that play," the coach had said to Richt and Scott.

"Coach," laughed Scott, "you owe it to Jimmy to say, 'Now I'm gonna call that play.' He'll smoke two packs of cigarettes before the game. We razz him about that more than we should. But we can't help it. He all but plays the game for those boys. He's so conscientious.

"And, Coach, don't forget you can't call that three-tight-end formation on the goal line. Ol' Jimmy has only got two of them suited up this week."

Heggins had indeed reached a frustration peak over the last couple of weeks. Warren Hart had been told to come in at 250 pounds. He showed up in August at 275. Marvin Ferrell had gone down in the BYU game. Lonnie Johnson was still having trouble remembering whom he was supposed to block and where he was supposed to be as a receiver. But Heggins had plateaued.

"The BYU game was the first time Lonnie and Warren had ever been to war," said the tight-end coach. "Now they've had a taste. It's not like you have guys without the talent to do the job. They are just so young, you have to repeat everything over and over. And there's just so much to teach them. At some point, the light will go on, and then they'll just be able to turn their athletic ability loose.

"Saturday, I'll know I've done the best I can do with them at this point. And I'm just not going to worry."

Richt had grabbed a few minutes with his quarterbacks after the morning meeting to remind them: "Think the vertical on 7 Waggle Special. If we throw and catch on first down and have success, the boss will probably keep doing it. Make it work, make him more comfortable.

"If that tight end gets open and you miss him, you better keep running right on out the gate."

8

DOAK Campbell Stadium, named after FSU's first president, was probably the most famous Erector Set in the South. The steel latticework rose from a patch of lowland property on the southwest corner of the campus like an abandoned project of student engineers. It was on an island bounded by heavily traveled roads, isolated in every sense from the look and feel of the buildings and of the tree-shaded grounds of the old campus. It was of too recent a vintage to be nostalgic and too ugly to be anything else.

Built to hold 15,000 in 1950, it had been expanded to a capacity of over 40,000 by the time Bowden arrived in 1976. Since then, another 20,000 seats had been added, bringing the official 1991 capacity to 60,519. But it remained one of the smaller and least attractive facilities in big-time college football and seemed a fitting monument to the university's inferiority complex in the pre-Bowden era. For down the road in Gainesville, the Gators had a campus shrine in Florida Field. It already had room for 40,000 when Doak Campbell was built and sat 72,000 in 1982.

Plans for a $100 million renovation of Doak Campbell had been working their way through the university, Tallahassee and state bureaucracies for a couple of years. And in 1991, work was finally scheduled to get underway. If all went according to plan, in five years, Doak Campbell would be enclosed on three sides, pushing capacity to 70,000; huge Gothic classroom and office buildings would be erected on the east and west sides, tastefully obscuring the look of the undergirding; and the five-year-old Moore Athletic Center would be expanded to house all FSU sports administration. In that plan, the football offices would overlook the field from the north end zone, with a patio off Bowden's office offering recruits and visitors a view of the revitalized stadium.

While FSU was working to get those plans approved, the University of Florida, between the 1990 and 1991 seasons, enclosed its north end zone, which raised capacity to 83,000.

Most people's more lasting impression of Doak Campbell was probably the atmosphere inside when games were about to begin. Here was a school that prides itself on the number of Ph.D.s it grants annually, on the advanced physics and computer labs it has attracted, on the rising scholastic standing of its undergraduates, and it had for its most prominent symbol a white kid in war paint and an Indian suit, mounted on a horse and waving a flaming spear.

National surveys have suggested that Florida State's Chief Osceola astride Renegade is one of the most recognized images in college football. After the coin toss, with players from each team facing one another, Chief Osceola rides between them and waves the flaming spear above his head at midfield, milking the crowd. Then he flings it into the circle at the 50-yard line. And 60,000 people go nuts.

So powerful is the theater that some visiting teams have refused to come onto the field until the spear is planted. Some turn their backs during the ritual. The bad boys, notably Miami's Hurricanes, have, on occasion, tried to counter the aggression with threats of their own, moving toward the Chief as if to yank him from his mount, but there are always those hooves to contend with. Renegade, they have been warned, gets wide-eyed and cranky about close approaches.

In 1991, Native American protesters reminded baseball's Atlanta Braves and the NFL's Washington Redskins that they were offended by the stereotypical depiction of their culture. But leaders of Florida's tribe of real Seminoles shrugged their shoulders. They even lent their official sanction to the mascot and the pregame ritual. And they helped design the regalia.

Not surprisingly, the Chief Osceola and Renegade tradition owe as much to Bobby Bowden's intuitive marketing sense as to anything else. In the mid-'70s, Florida State's mascot was a cartoon Indian, Sammy Seminole, who looked more like an ethnic Dennis the Menace than a real warrior. Then, in Bowden's second season in 1977, the Seminoles made a trip out West to play the San Diego State Aztecs.

"When San Diego State came out on the field," Bowden remembered, "they had this Indian mascot. He was a Samoan, a big, heavy guy with this black head of hair and his face all painted. And he was holding this burning spear.

"He comes out there on the field and throws that spear down, and the team comes out behind him. And boy, are they fired up. All during the game, this guy is walking around in the stands gettin' the fans going."

Maybe it was because Bowden's team, which went on to win a school record 10 games that year, was pounded 41–16 by the Aztecs. For whatever reason, the coach and his wife, Ann, were unable to shake the memory of the Samoan with the spear. And when they got back to Tallahassee, Ann began hatching a plan with local FSU grad Bill Durham, who had always wanted to get an Indian on horseback involved in the Doak Campbell football spectacle. Bowden, the consummate showman, was an easy sell. And together, Durham and Ann Bowden convinced the athletic director, John Bridgers, it could work.

There were two obvious possibilities: The idea could expose the program to jokes and ridicule just as Bowden was breathing new pride and life into it. Or it could be the beginning of something unique and spectacular.

The Chief and Renegade premiered September 17, 1978, with the first rider wearing a woman's bathrobe because the Seminole Indians hadn't yet finished the official coat. And it took only a couple of seasons for the image to become so associated with the school and its athletic success that it seemed as if Chief Osceola must have founded the university.

9

"You have never come out of that tunnel before as No. 1 in the nation," Bowden told his players before the game. "No. 1 in the nation. You don't deserve to be No. 1 unless you go out there and hit. Unless you go out there on that first play and take your man and let him have it, don't tell me you're No. 1."

The intensity was back in Bowden's voice.

"If we kick, go down there and play like you have got to make the tackle. Captains, if we win the toss, we want second-half option.

"First play: Linemen, we want to make it look like a run. Twins. 7 Waggle Special. Quarterback make a great fake. Tailback make a great fake. Fullback is gonna take it to the flat and turn it up.

"Second play. 344 Z Bench. And I'm thinking tight end down the middle.

"Third play will be Fort Worth. Fullback, don't be in a hurry."

Pass, pass, pass. Count on the double coverage to the receivers and look for the fullback and tight end. The third play was a screen pass, hoping to catch an anxious defense overrunning the play.

"Defense. Chance Miller. No. 27. He's their biggest threat. I'm sure they're going to try to take that ball and run it down our throats.

"Men, let's punish him. Get him on the line. Wear him down.

"Secondary, don't give up anything deep. If you don't give 'em anything deep, I don't think they'll score.

"Now, men, I don't want you getting out there acting like children. No shoving. And don't use profanity. Don't start jawing with one of their guys.

"No penalties.

"I'd like you to go out now and just play the best you can play. Now, let's have a word.

"Dear Father, thank you for letting us play. Thank you for this great opportunity to be No. 1. Are we really No. 1? God, give us the energy to go out and play like No. 1. Help us play the best we can. That's all we ask. We ain't asking you to help us win. Just help us be the best we can.

"Protect us from injuries, both sides. Heal our injuries. Give our coaches wisdom. Help us to be good examples to you and glorify you.

"We ask these things in thy name. Amen."

Three minutes later, they were crowded into the ramp beneath the end zone. Then the Chief and Renegade led the first charge of the season. They were No. 1 at home and the roar was deafening.

Florida State got the second-half option, and Tulane's first offensive series stalled short of the Green Wave 30. But the punt and then a clipping penalty on Buckley's runback forced the Seminoles to start at their own 22.

The new faces in the lineup were Lonnie Johnson at tight end and Kez McCorvey at the X receiver spot. Both were starting for the first time in their college careers. Brad Scott signaled in the first play, the 7 Waggle Special out of a twins formation, which put both wide receivers on the left side of the line. The tight end was on the right side.

On the snap, Casey faked to the tailback, holding the linebackers in for the expected run. Edgar Bennett, the fullback, drifted right and headed toward the sideline. When Casey turned after the fake and looked downfield, he saw exactly what the coaches had drawn on the blackboard.

The Tulane defense had chosen to take away three of the four receiving threats. From seasons past, everybody feared Florida State wide receivers. And the BYU game had left no questions about Bennett's pass-catching ability. So between them, the X and Z receivers attracted three defenders to the left sidelines and the fullback pulled a fourth to the right. There, in the middle of the field, all alone and on the run, was Jimmy Heggins' star pupil.

The pass was a little high, and it pulled Lonnie Johnson almost off his feet as he leaned and reached for it. When he gathered it in and recovered stride, there was still no one within 10 yards. Lonnie was off to the races.

Brad Scott would tease Heggins the next day as they watched film of the reception and run: "You can just see ol' Lonnie here thinkin': Now, what did Coach Heggins tell me? Look the ball in, tuck it away, cover it in traffic and score, score, score."

Indeed, at about the Tulane 30-yard line, Johnson eyed the pursuit and wrapped both arms around the ball like a fullback, expecting the hit. But he was chugging toward the goal line at a fast enough clip to have momentum. And when the last-ditch tackle came, he fell into the end zone for the score. One play, 78 yards, touchdown.

Weldon ran down the field and butted helmets with Johnson. Scott laughed on the sideline. And Heggins tried to hold off his own excitement while he counted heads to make sure he had his guys in the game for the extra-point attempt.

Mowrey nailed the point, then put the ball into the end zone on the kickoff. It was Billy Sexton's turn to relax a notch. Maybe the kicking game was coming around.

Bowden paced the sideline, talking into his headset with Richt in the coaches' booth. Might as well stick with the plan on next possession.

The Tulane quarterback, Billy Duncan, got the Green Wave out of a third-and-14 hole on the next series by connecting with flanker Steve Ballard for a 37-yard gain. Another annoying defensive breakdown when they had the other guys penned. But Tulane got no closer than the FSU 35-yard line and had to punt.

Bowden ordered up play No. 2, the 344 Z Bench. Now Tulane jumped the tight end with double coverage, and Turral was open on the sideline for a 12-yard gain. The next play, the screen pass, however, fooled no one. And then a broken play and an incomplete pass forced the punt. Scott Player boomed one 52 yards.

Tulane took advantage of its own running game and an FSU pass-interference penalty to move down the field on the next series. Backs Shawn Fagan and Chance Miller helped push the ball from their own 17 to the Seminole 18, where Andrews' defense drew the line. Tulane settled for the field goal. Florida State 7, Tulane 3.

Back on offense, Florida State mixed pass and run for over five minutes and 11 plays until it was first and goal on the Tulane 8-yard line. Bennett lost a yard. Then Heggins' No. 2 guy, Warren Hart, let a pass slip through his fingers in the end zone. But Bowden called a similar play on third down, and this time Hart held on for the touchdown.

On its next two offensive possessions, the Tulane offense held the ball for three downs and punted. Florida State scored twice—once off Mowrey's first college field goal and then with a 10-play, 67-yard drive that again starred the tight ends. Lonnie Johnson snared a 37-yarder to give the Seminoles a first-and-goal on the Tulane 6. And on third down, Hart caught a four-yarder, slipped a defender on the 1-yard line and plopped his 265 pounds into the end zone.

"He outfatted the guy on that one," Bowden quipped the following week when he narrated the highlight film for boosters.

At the half, the score was 24–3. The young tight ends had accounted for 143 yards of offense and three touchdowns. And Amp Lee already had 76 yards on the ground. Weldon was 12 for 18 for 184 yards and three TD passes. And Bobby Bowden was beside himself.

10

"THEY are sticking it down your throats, defense. That No. 27 has 58 danged yards.

"They are sticking it down your throats and up your ass."

The players looked at the coach, then glanced out of the corners of their eyes at one another. The Man was definitely steamed.

It wasn't that Bobby Bowden didn't know the words. You don't grow up in football locker rooms and remain innocent about the language. Vulgarity and fierce obscenities are so common as to be utterly unremarkable. Unless the speaker is Bobby Bowden.

Over the years, the coach had adapted to the times in some ways. He was tolerant of different approaches to faith, of different modes of dress, of earrings in men's ears, of hair that grew up or out or down. But Bowden's memory held the voices of too many old Sunday-school teachers to permit him to curse without shame. And he rarely gave in to the temptation.

The assistant coaches tried to respect Bowden's example. Giving up cursing was a perennial resolution for them. They fined one another a dollar at a time for obscene talk. But only Bowden could have afforded a really strict accounting. Even with random enforcement, the coaches' cuss box grew fat with contributions.

But when Saint Bobby slipped, it stopped everything. Sometimes the shock worked to his advantage, focusing the emotion and energy of players and coaches. Other times it was a distraction. Did we hear what we thought we heard?

The players stared. Minutes later, as they strapped on helmets and moved toward the tunnel beneath the end zone before the second half, some were still grinning.

What had set Bowden off were the second and third Tulane series in the first quarter, when three running backs picked up 57 of their 58 total yards in the half. That the Green Wave ended up with only three points on those drives, and that No. 27, Chance Miller, actually accounted for just 36 yards by himself, didn't sway Bowden's perception that the defense was taking the night off.

"It's only natural," he had told the players Friday night in Thomasville, "that a defense tends to relax when they're ahead and they know their offense can score a lot of points." But he wanted them to fight the tendency. He needed them to practice domination. They must learn to immediately shut down the teams like Tulane so they would be ready to stay on the same field with teams like Michigan and Miami for sixty minutes.

Bowden had a picture in his mind of what he needed to see. And those two series had scared him out of the fantasy. "Hey, men," he pleaded, "let's get out there and kick some tail, so I can play some substitutes."

Brad Johnson took over at quarterback with just under ten minutes left in the game. A deflected pass ended up in the arms of a Tulane defender, halting an FSU drive into Green Wave territory. But Johnson picked up where he left off in the next series, finding Warren Hart in the end zone for the tight end's third TD catch of the night. The No. 3 quarterback, Charlie Ward, under orders to keep the ball on the ground, took over in the last two minutes to kill the clock. He couldn't resist hitting Shannon Baker for a nine-yard gain, though, and he had the team on the Tulane 1-yard line when time ran out.

Final score: Florida State 38, Tulane 11.

"I'm not disappointed," Bowden told the players in the locker room after the game, although his voice betrayed him. "I just wish I could have gotten more of you in there.

"Now, I think, when the writers come in here to talk to you, you have to say nice things about Tulane. I didn't think they could hold us like that. Men, we've still got a lot of work to do. But you won.

"Defense, if you can just cut out the penalties, you'll be about the best in the country. Mistakes. Penalties. We had them shut down and we gave them momentum with penalties. We can't do that and beat top-ten teams. You know that.

"Let's correct those mistakes. That's the only way to get better."

11

"A soft answer turneth away wrath, but grievous words stir up anger."

Jim Gladden, coach of the outside linebackers, had the Monday-morning devotion. And he chose that opening verse from Proverbs 15 as a text. Which immediately struck a chord with the head coach.

"I cut one loose at the half the other night I wish I could take back now," said Bowden. "We ask the kids to discipline themselves. And when we don't, we wonder why they can't."

He would guard his language. He had let his frustration get the best of him. Call it an attack of coach's paranoia. His review of the game film dissolved some of the panic. Saturday night, he had the sense that Tulane refused to give up the ball, that his offense got too few chances. But maybe he had just looked up at the wrong time. The Florida State offense had run 81 plays, only six fewer than against BYU; Tulane got just 55.

But there was still that nagging anxiety. Were the breakdowns correctable aberrations or fatal flaws? Were they taking advantage of every opportunity during this three-week buildup to the Michigan game to get themselves ready?

At this stage of the season every year, the coaches usually had made up their minds about the freshmen they were going to redshirt in order to preserve four more years of eligibility. Some of the redshirts would remain with the first and second teams in practice; some would go to the scout teams that imitated upcoming teams' offenses and defenses for the varsity to practice against. Ideally, almost all the freshmen should sit out their first year, learn the system and acclimate to college; then they would have four full years to work themselves into first-team spots.

But this season was different. To redshirt a player who might play a crucial backup role in even one game might cost them everything. "We've got eleven games more to play, men. Do we want to save a guy for next year? Or do we want to start working him in now so that he has at least stood out there in uniform and heard 'The Star-Spangled Banner' if we need to stick him in later?

"We're trying to win a national championship right now, men. Don't play yourself too thin. You might be coaching at Michigan next year. I'm the one planning to stay here until I retire, and I'm the one asking why we are holding these boys out."

The two big worries were in the offensive line and at tight end. Besides Mike Morris's injury on the line, Eric Gibbs had damaged a knee at the very moment he seemed ready to start pulling his weight as a second-team tackle. He had been operated on the Friday before, and it would be weeks before they knew whether he could return. The situation needed backup security. When Brad Scott had sent in reserves to give them experience during the Tulane game, they had been pushed around by the exhausted Green Wave defense.

That, of course, frightened Bowden. So did hearing from the trainers that Warren Hart was limping around after the Saturday game, trimming the tight end depth to exactly one—Lonnie Johnson.

The '91 freshman class included six high school All-Americans who should one day contribute. But if they were rushed, they could end up wasting a year of eligibility for only a few plays; or worse, they could become so intimidated it would take a couple of years to get them back on track. Once a freshman got into one ball game for one play, he couldn't be redshirted unless he was injured badly enough to sit out the rest of the year. So far, the only true freshmen to get playing time were Marquette Smith and Derrick Brooks. Both were probably going to help right away. But of the rest, the only ones who seemed capable of playing even a backup role were offensive linemen Juan Laureano and Clay Shiver and tight end Matt Platto. None of the others were close.

Bowden's assistants didn't share his worry. The need wasn't any greater than in past years, except in tight ends. And there maybe they could switch over a backup lineman like Johnny Clower to help out with blocking while Hart and Ferrell nursed their wounds.

Brad Scott loved the way Laureano and Shiver were coming along. They were definitely future studs. But he wanted to get them a full redshirt year of experience before he asked them to go to war. Look how the rookie Patrick McNeil stepped in as the perfect sixth man. If they could get a little luck, if maybe Gibbs or one of the other guys would just come alive, they could make it without wasting the freshmen. Heggins felt the same about Platto. Let him sit one out. His time would come soon enough.

For most of the other coaches, the opposite problem was more pressing: how to find playing time for all the qualified candidates.

The defense was rotating 25 or so players in every game and still couldn't get enough snaps for some of its future stars. Billy Sexton had an anxious crew of running backs lined up behind Amp Lee and Edgar Bennett. And Mark Richt was trying to figure out a way to get Weldon some big numbers every week while preserving some meaningful snaps for the three backup quarterbacks.

"It's bad right now," said assistant coach Wally Burnham, who had sophomore stud Ken Alexander behind one of the best inside linebackers in the nation, Marvin Jones. Alexander was showing his frustration. In fact, most of the second-teamers were sulking when they didn't get in. And the grumbles and tantrums were building.

"It's absolutely normal," said Bowden. "I saw the same thing in Edgar Bennett and Lawrence Dawsey. I remember Dawsey standing on the sidelines, and he wouldn't even talk to me 'cause he wasn't getting enough passes thrown to him."

Good for them, thought Bowden. You don't really want them to take it happily. You want them to have pride, to be chomping at the bit. But you had to manage it so that their disgruntlement didn't affect the team.

"Oh yeah, we got a problem, men. We got too many good players. I tell you what the answer is. It's communication. You've got to talk to them. If you can't talk to 'em, bring 'em to me."

For Mickey Andrews, these issues always boiled down to his fundamental football belief:

"They need to take pride in the team. They've got to trust us to make the right decisions."

They all nodded, aware that the days in which that trust came easily were long gone.

In any event, said the head coach, "this is stuff we better tend to right now. We sure don't want to worry about it when we play Michigan.

"Now, I need to talk to the offense."

The coach had a list of problems he spotted in the film. But his first approach was always to let the assistants give their version first.

The least happy assistant in the room was John Eason, who was fighting what he sensed was a rising tide of suspicion about the wide receiver talent. He had run Eric Turral the previous week for overcele-brating his receptions, and when the receiver seemed to respond well and take practice seriously, Eason had bragged about him in the morning meetings.

"Coach, E.T. had his best week of practice ever."

Then, when the offensive coaches had gone over Tulane game film Sunday, Eason had watched depressed as the video revealed again and again how Turral had dogged it on every play he wasn't getting the ball. Terrible blocking. Awful fakes.

Bowden had noticed it, too. But one look at the receivers coach and he knew he didn't have to say a thing. "Coach," said Eason, "I may fire the Z."

A demotion might be the only thing Turral would understand. Maybe it would bring him around. But this guy was still the best hope to become the big-play man among the receivers. They had to make him want it—and soon. Michigan was three weeks away.

Would firing Turral for the time being get his attention? "Well, if you're going to do it," said Bowden, "now is the time."

12

THE Tulane game was pretty much out of Bowden's system by the time he boarded the state airplane and buckled his seat belt Monday afternoon. He had met with reporters Sunday morning for their usual morning-after breakfast. He had reviewed the film, discussed it with his coaches on Monday morning, then faced the local critics in the season's first weekly booster luncheon.

Now he was headed to Alabama to kick off the Tuscaloosa Quarterback Club's season of dinners while Mickey Andrews put the players through a light Monday-night workout. On the coach's lap were the Western Michigan offensive and defensive scouting reports. He would read a little, nap a little and think about Alabama.

Originally, Bowden had turned down the Tuscaloosa invitation. He spoke in Birmingham regularly, because it was his hometown. And he made it to Montgomery now and then. But during the season, he rarely interrupted his weekly practice routines for out-of-town speeches unless it was to shore up recruiting connections. And he wasn't likely to gain much recruiting ground talking to folks at Crimson Tide headquarters.

Hootie Ingram, the University of Alabama athletic director, had made the personal call to get Bowden to change his mind and make the trip. Bowden and Ingram had been friends for years. When Florida State had been looking for an athletic director in 1980, Bowden lobbied for Ingram and got him the job. Then, after a decade at Florida State, Ingram accepted the 1990 offer to return to his home state and alma mater.

Only a half dozen years ago, Bowden had figured Tuscaloosa was his ultimate destination as well. He had grown up sixty miles away under the spell of the Crimson Tide and even had that one semester on the team in 1949. He had transferred to Howard (which later became Samford University), had gone on to become a Little All-American quarterback, a husband, a father and a young football coach. But he never severed his Crimson Tide connections.

After he graduated, he got his master's and worked as an assistant coach at Howard, and then, from 1955 until 1958, was head coach at South Georgia, a two-year school in Douglas. In 1959, Howard called him back to be head coach. A year earlier, Paul (Bear) Bryant had left Texas A&M after taking the Aggies to national prominence (and NCAA probation) to become head coach at Alabama. And the aura of possibility in Tuscaloosa drew Bowden into a circle of young coaches whose mentor was the Bear.

In those early years, Bowden would make the drive from Birmingham to Tuscaloosa to draw formations and argue strategy with Bryant assistants—other future head coaches such as Gene Stallings and Jerry Claiborne. Bryant respected Bowden's ambition and intensity, and he regularly funneled to him Alabama-bred players who would get more college playing time in a lower-division program. The Bear remained a Bowden mentor as the younger man worked his way up to Division I prominence. And as his national reputation grew and Alabama's faltered in the post-Bryant era, Bowden did nothing to discourage growing speculation that, eventually, it would be he who would revitalize the legacy and return Alabama to national football domination.

But Bowden had to leave his home state to build his Division I reputation. He led West Virginia to two postseason bowls and a 42–26 record over six years. When he came to Florida State in 1976, he figured he was another step closer to home. What he accomplished in the next ten years—an 83–32–2 overall record, a 5–2–1 record in bowls—made him a giant in Southern football and a worthy candidate for anybody's list of legends. So when he received a call in 1986 from a prominent Alabama booster asking him to meet with the president of the university, Bowden figured the time had come. He left Tallahassee for a secret meeting fully expecting to be officially offered the Alabama coaching job and fully expecting to accept it.

"I felt a sense of loyalty. It was where I was born and raised. It was almost like I had been called."

But when he arrived for the secret meeting, it turned out to be before some fifteen university board members and trustees as well as the president. "I thought they had already decided they wanted me. And all of a sudden this began looking like a job interview. I didn't like that. I wasn't doing no tryouts."

He left without being offered the job and without agreeing to take it.

By the time Bowden arrived back in Tallahassee, the rumors were hot that he was leaving. Cameras were set up on his front lawn. Ann was talking to writers in his living room. What was he going to do?

"My place is here," he told them.

And looking back, as he flew from Tallahassee to Tuscaloosa that day in 1991, he thought: *I'm very lucky I didn't take the job. It might take to the year 2000 before people up there forget about the Bear. Until then, any coach will have that ghost lookin' over his shoulder. And I ain't so sure I could have done it.*

There's no doubt he would have tried, though. "There was only two or three jobs worth leaving what I had at Florida State. And that was one of them. And I guess I felt nearly obligated to take it. It was as if I would have betrayed my state. My emotions wouldn't have let me refuse."

The sense of obligation was diminished by the '86 experience, however. And when Alabama began looking for a coach again in 1989 and the boosters and politicians placed those long-distance calls to Tallahassee, Bowden told them to take his name out of the hat.

"My sentimental home will always be Birmingham. But my real home is here. Florida is my state now."

Ingram met the coach at the airport to take him on a tour of the latest Alabama facilities: the new indoor practice building and the redesigned outdoor fields. As they stood and talked, sprinklers coated the practice fields, which shone green and lush in the late-afternoon sun. Beyond the fences, the old school rose cozily around the stadium and the football domain. It looked every bit the confident capital of Southern football, so unlike Florida State's Doak Campbell, out of sight of a single building to connect it with a university or with a cultural tradition.

But Bowden was unfazed by the gap in imagery. Facilities are built by committed programs. Committed programs are built by winning teams.

And no state university in the nation could match the winning record of Florida State under Bobby Bowden.

Sometime this season, ground would finally be broken for that Doak Campbell renovation. And sometime in the next decade, maybe while Bowden was still head coach, there would be that massive Gothic complex of offices and athletic facilities. The old Erector Set would be bowled in. The coaches' offices would look out on the manicured grass of the playing field. And mommas and poppas and their football-playing sons would be awed by such a monument to tradition.

The Bear himself couldn't have built a better tribute.

"It is a pleasure to get back to Tuscaloosa," the coach told the Quarterback Club after a warm greeting. "There's no way I could express what the University of Alabama means to me. I was raised on Alabama football in Birmingham. I have always loved the University of Alabama. It was always one of the greatest dreams I had to coach here.

"But I just don't believe God meant for it to happen."

13

THE pines on the outside edge of the upper practice field partially blocked the sun's rays. But the heat was still oppressive late in the day, and the air felt thick and damp. Those poor Michigan kids, Bowden thought, as he left the players' end-of-practice huddle and walked toward the writers.

It was Wednesday, September 11. It had been like this all week, heat in the upper 90s and humidity to match; and the prospects were nil for a letup through the weekend. The Western Michigan Broncos, who hadn't played in the South in over a decade, would get a true Florida welcome come Saturday. They would play the nation's No. 1 team in a steam room.

Western Michigan was a perennial power in the Mid-American Conference against teams such as Kent State and Toledo. But it was way out of its league on this road trip. Bowden had been complimentary in interviews and speeches during the week, telling his team and the media that the Broncos would come into Tallahassee well prepared and upset-minded. But it was impossible not to look beyond this game toward that other Michigan team, the one in Ann Arbor, two weeks later. And he could summon little enthusiasm for attacking the overmatched Broncos. He had already decided to turn the play calling over to Brad Scott and Mark Richt. Let them have the fun this week.

Maybe because he wasn't as absorbed as usual in preparing the offense, his thoughts had turned to the problems on the other side of the ball. Bowden trusted Mickey Andrews so much he knew little of the defense's complex schemes and substitution strategy. He seldom watched their drills on the upper field, and he wasn't always sure who was starting and who was second team. That may have made him even more nervous when he thought he spotted breakdowns. Especially breakdowns that threatened to become habitual. In both previous games, apparent screwups in the secondary had resulted in long gains on obvious passing downs. Terrell Buckley's name kept coming up.

Buckley looked to have been way out of position on the second-half touchdown by BYU, and Tulane had scored its only TD in his territory Saturday night. The fans were already grumbling that Buckley was afflicted with Deion-itis without the talent to back it up. Which meant Bowden had been fielding Terrell Buckley questions all week. He had some of his own too.

Andrews rode the All-American cornerback mercilessly in practice, but he was his fiercest advocate everywhere else. The BYU breakdown was a missed assignment. "Poor coaching," was the apologetic explanation offered by Buckley's coach. But don't blame him for that Tulane touchdown. The videotape showed that the receiver pushed off on Buck to get a better angle in the end zone. He had been in position to make the play and had been neutralized by an illegal move. It should have been offensive pass interference, Andrews insisted.

Bowden accepted the explanation and believed it. But he also knew the questions would continue as long as the big plays did. And Buck wasn't likely to help his case with his prideful attitude. Andrews knew the same thing.

For all of practice on Tuesday and Wednesday, Andrews had been relentless. "Hit him. Hit him. Wrap your arms. I want him on the ground."

He had driven free safety Leon Fowler from the field. "You don't deserve to be out here if you can't do any better than that. You're fired."

And he had lauded the play of Buckley's backup, Corey Sawyer, until Sawyer suffered an ankle injury: "You keep working like that, No. 8, and you'll be the first-teamer out here."

After the team broke for conditioning runs, Andrews had kept his defensive backs behind. He dragged a one-man tackling sled to the bottom of the six-foot grade between practice fields and had his backs, one by one, hit the padded metal dummy and drive it up the hill.

When Bowden got to where the reporters waited, he saw them watching the exercise. He looked too.

"Whooee, ol' Mickey is in a bad mood."

The reporters chuckled with the coach. But they had heard the players grousing all week about the intensity of the workouts. About the heat. About the morale problems this might cause.

Bowden played down the issue. "When it's hot like this," he told them, "nobody wants to work. You can't hardly blame them. But we've got to practice. I don't think anybody in the country can stay with us if we play up to our best. But we can't play our best unless we practice at that level."

The next morning in the eight-thirty staff meeting, the coach was even less conciliatory: "I heard the kids complaining about morale on Tuesday and Wednesday this week. Well, they better not have good morale on Tuesday. They better not have morale on Wednesday. Saturday is when we want them to have morale.

"Don't forget, men. You get what you demand. YOU GET WHAT YOU DEMAND. If you don't demand it now, we ain't gonna get it later."

14

WHEN John Eason called Eric Turral into his office to discuss his sloppy play in the Tulane game, the coach hadn't decided yet whether to demote him or let him run out the punishment in practice. He would just watch his reaction, see if he understood how badly he had blocked and run the decoy patterns.

Sometimes, Eason thought, Turral begged for even negative attention as reassurance that somebody cared. The kid had been raised by a single mother struggling to make ends meet. No money, not much attention, no real discipline. As in the case of so many other young athletes, coaches may have been the only authority figures in Turral's life. And even they had let him slide. Who could blame them after they saw what he could do on the football field? Just make sure he shows up for the game and get him the ball.

In the three years Eason had known Turral, he had tried to establish a consistent standard. If you do this, you get this; if you fail to do this, you lose this. These are the rules. They are fair. And they are immutable.

Turral would agree with the standards, then argue for exceptions when he fell short. In the spring, he had resisted the off-season workout routine. He had threatened to quit school and football and got another chance only after he was dragged back into the fold by his teammates.

This season, he seemed finally on the verge of making it on the field and in the classroom. He had a career game against BYU—six receptions for 96 yards and a touchdown. Then he had to be disciplined for showboating.

Eason worried about that. Maybe they had all overreacted to the taunting threat. All the kid did was raise his arms. "The only time he shows any emotion, any joy at all, is when he's on the field. And we take that away from him."

Yet E.T. had accepted the punishment running. And he had played as if he were on a mission every day of practice before the Tulane game, leading Eason to brag to Bowden that the star wideout may have finally arrived. Then he fell apart in the game.

When Eason called him in to talk, he got the old E.T., full of denial and anger. So he had made the move.

"Shannon, you will start on Saturday against Western Michigan. Not because you have won the job. But because E.T. lost it."

It was a grim time for all the receivers. Matt Frier was still in a funk over his demotion. Shannon Baker had been hit with the realization that his future might not include the NFL and had brought his mother by for an emotional talk with Eason after the Tulane game. 'OMar Ellison was morose, convinced that he would never get the chance to play and was thinking about transferring. And Kevin Knox, always sensitive to the moods of the others, was depressed out of sympathy.

About the only one in the group who could be expected to feel encouraged was Kez McCorvey, the redshirt freshman starter at split end. He was quietly becoming the most dependable receiver. And he was also turning out to be the slipperiest on pass routes. But he was driving the coaches crazy with his habit of stopping after a catch to put a move on defenders. "Can we get him to keep running, John?" Bowden asked. "I tell you, that scares me to death."

So even McCorvey, the lone good news of the '91 receiver corps, was getting his share of grief.

"What is adversity?" Eason probed. "Matt Frier?"

Frier had been sitting silently the whole session, his eyes on the floor.

He looked up for the first time. "All I know," he mumbled, "is it's still hitting me."

It came out in such a sincere Live Oak drawl that, for a moment, it cut through the solemn mood and broke up the room. Eason laughed in spite of himself. Even Frier smiled. And the coach immediately tried to build on the spirit by turning to the main target.

"What is adversity, E.T.?"

Turral had been slouched over in the front row, refusing to look at Eason. He tilted his head up and tried to say something. But tears came immediately, and he had to bury his face in his hands to choke back sobs.

Eason paused a moment, then shifted the attention away from Turral. He had to salvage something from all this.

"You know, sometimes we focus so much on football here, we put so much emphasis on this game. But do we come into this life to play football? I think it would be a pity to do nothing with your life but play football. Football is an ego trip. It's entirely self-satisfying, selfish.

"But at the same time, it's a way of realizing other goals, of learning to aspire to other things. The way you handle adversity on the football field is the way you handle adversity in life. It would be a shame to be here four years and not accomplish anything else, to not move toward other goals in your life."

Then Eason shifted gears again.

"I know it's hard for you to believe this, but I was a great one out there." He rubbed his chest in a low-key show of self-satisfaction, playing to the snickers. "I was beautiful. I had the moves. I had the great hands. Just like you think you do.

"I also went through all those two-a-days, all the aches and pains and the times I hated it all. All that adversity. But you know, I don't remember that now. All I remember are the touchdowns and the great catches. I remember the way the crowd roared when they saw me break into the open and the ball was coming, coming . . . and I was reaching out like this." The professor pantomimed, looking up and back over his shoulder for the pass.

"I remember what it felt like to catch those, to run away from everybody, to score. Those are the memories I have.

"That's what you'll have too. That's what you're doing here, building the memories you'll have. You'll forget the bad times. But you must get through them to make the memories.

"You know, you can't live in the past. But you can make a past you can leave from. That's what you are doing right now, making a past to build on.

"Okay, let's talk for a few minutes about this halfback pass you should expect this week."

Time was running out, Eason knew. The dropped passes, the tentative routes. If it kept up, it would be like a treasure map on the game film for the opposition. Dig here, it would say to Michigan and Miami. Forget the famous Florida State wideouts. Shut down the backs and the tight ends, and this was a mediocre passing team.

McCorvey would not embarrass him. Frier would kill himself trying. But it wouldn't work with just the X. Eason needed a bona fide deep threat, a potential game breaker at Z to keep defenses honest. Somebody had to step forward.

So far, there had been time for Sunday school, for fathering and counseling. But soon the big boys would be lining up against them, and Eason would need the segment meetings for X's and O's. He wanted a dependable lineup. He wanted the bleeding to stop. Because football at this level was a shark tank. And blood on the water attracted a crowd.

15

"Boy, I'll just be glad when we get this game over with and get on with Michigan."

It was 4 P.M. on September 14, three hours before the Seminoles were to meet the Western Michigan Broncos in Doak Campbell. Between shaking hands with high school prospects and their parents and attending to obligatory hi-y'alls with boosters, Bowden was restlessly zapping through the TV games. Already it was starting to look like an interesting week in college football. Thursday night, No. 2-ranked Miami had thrashed Houston 40–10 on national television. And all day Friday, the coaches couldn't stop talking about the game and its impact.

"That Miami," Brad Scott had said the previous night in Thomasville. "Man, they had the whole world watching that."

Houston had gone to the Orange Bowl with a highly touted quarterback in David Klingler and an attention-grabbing run-and-shoot offense that scored 73 points the previous week. But Klingler was sacked five times and didn't pass one into the end zone until the closing seconds of the game. It had been brutal.

"I went to bed and pulled the covers over my head," Scott joked.

The Hurricanes would come to Tallahassee November 16 for the Seminoles' 11th game of the season. Florida would be No. 12 in Gainesville. Let 'em all roll until then, Bowden told his assistants. "It's the best thing that could happen to us. If we falter early in the year, we've still got two great teams back to back. And then we'll catch another top-five team in a bowl. It's there, men."

The coaches generally enjoyed big victories by Miami and Florida, as long as they weren't the ones on the losing end. Their rivals' successes validated the toughness of Florida football and stirred their competitive juices. Already the media drums were beating. Maybe No. 2 Miami might deserve the top ranking for pounding Houston while Florida State picked on little Western Michigan. Things could get even more complicated with the Saturday lineup: No. 3 Michigan playing No. 7 Notre Dame, and No. 6 Florida facing No. 16 Alabama.

It was worth mentioning to the players, Scott argued in the Friday-night skull session, that "if we slop things up tomorrow, we could lose ground in the polls."

Bowden had told Richt and Scott to make sure that didn't happen. "Y'all are calling the plays," he reminded them. "If I see something really good, I will come to you between series. I might want to take a series, but I hope I don't. Y'all just do it as if I weren't there."

The two assistant coaches smiled when the boss paused. "Then, about the second play, I'll remind you that I am."

Neither of them doubted that for a moment.

So here it was game day, and Bowden was pretending, halfheartedly at best, to be taking the day off from plotting wars. He climbed up on his exercise bike for a couple minutes of pedaling, then got bored and began flipping through the channels again.

He found the Michigan–Notre Dame game in time to see the Wolverines' talented wide receiver, Desmond Howard, pick up 29 yards on a reverse. "That's our play, dad-gummit. This is the first time in years I haven't had somebody to run that play. Shannon Baker has the speed but not the knack for cutting upfield. Eric Turral could do it, but he hasn't learned how to turn it loose yet.

"If I had that kid Howard, I'd be running the reverse so much his tongue would be hanging out."

Bowden turned up the sound so he could hear the announcers talking about how relaxed Notre Dame coach Lou Holtz had become since he turned over much of the offensive preparation to his coaches. "Hah! I ain't believing that."

Holtz had been a friend and coaching rival for years, so Bowden hated to root against him. But he wanted the Wolverines to win and keep the high ranking, so Florida State would meet them at their best. "The bigger they are, the more I love to stab 'em."

He watched as Michigan ate up the clock on a long drive. "Boy that scares me the way they control the ball. And look at those linemen's splits. I don't know what to do about that."

When they got down in their three-point stances, the Michigan offensive linemen left barely a foot's width of space between center and guard, guard and tackle, tackle and tight end. They looked like huge doorstops. And when they moved off the ball, they blocked in unison left and right. Zone blocking, it was called. It would take a jackhammer to get through there.

Bowden could feel the anxiety creeping in. Too early, he thought. The Seminoles would have two weeks after today to prepare. Save the panic for next week. There was a game to play tonight.

"The only thing I'm worried about is that my kids might be looking at this right now and don't have their minds on the game. I sure hope that's not the case. But maybe they're just like me.

"This game is like a roadblock."

Friday night, Richt and Scott had reiterated their conviction that this could be a big X and Z week. They saw nothing in the Western Michigan defensive personnel or schemes to suggest the Broncos could hang in there with Florida State receivers. They would set up the play-action passes with the run, then hit 'em with the long ball.

"We need to get those boys the ball," Richt said of Eason's wideouts. "They've got to build a little confidence."

Scott had stressed only about four basic running plays, which should be enough to establish the rushing game. Ideally, everybody would get his chance to get some stats and score some points. They would run in all the subs and stop some of the grumbling about lack of playing time.

The home field, the heat, the talent gap. "Florida State has every conceivable advantage in this game," Bowden had told reporters all week. "But we can lose it if we fail to execute."

Privately, he had little worry about offensive performance. He was pleased that, even without big-play production from the wide receivers, Casey Weldon and company had taken the ball on possession after possession and driven down the field for points in the first two games. They had done that without the help of defensive turnovers or kicking-game heroics. If those kicked in, nobody could stop them.

"The thing is, the defense should dominate tonight. If they don't get some turnovers, I'm gonna worry. 'Cause Michigan is a lot better ball-control team than we've played."

Bowden watched as much of the TV game as he could before heading down to the locker room. Notre Dame appeared poised for one of those classic Irish comebacks in the fourth quarter, when Michigan led by only three points and had a fourth-down decision to make on the Irish 25. Instead of the field goal and instead of the predictable mash play behind the huge offensive line, Wolverine quarterback Elvis Grbac drilled one into the end zone, and Desmond Howard dived and snagged it for the touchdown.

The catch would make everybody's highlight film and would catapult the brilliant receiver to the head of the class of '91 Heisman Trophy hopefuls. But Bowden didn't see the play. He was threading his way through parents and boosters in the athletic center atrium, heading toward the locker room.

"How are y'all today? So glad to see you came."

16

WESTERN Michigan was able to make a show of resistance for about seven minutes of the first quarter. Although they failed to make a first down in their first three offensive series, the Broncos' kicking team created a field-goal opportunity deep in Seminole territory after FSU bobbled a punt. The 32-yard attempt, however, was no good. And the evening went downhill for Western Michigan from there on.

Florida State stalled on its first possession, then punted. But the defense got the ball back immediately, deep in Western Michigan territory, with a sack and a recovered fumble. When the Seminole offense took over, Amp Lee ran it in on the first play.

The Broncos lost seven yards on their next possession, and Buckley ran the punt back 14 yards, setting up another touchdown—this time on a three-yard pass to Eric Turral. The picture in the next day's *Democrat* caught E.T. at the top of his leap, his eyes riveted on the ball as his hands reached and squeezed in the touchdown.

After he scored, Turral immediately dropped the ball and thrust his arms in the air in celebration. Then, just as quickly, he yanked them down, retrieved the ball and tossed it back to the official.

Let it be an omen, thought Eason.

Those first two touchdown series took exactly four plays and 59 seconds. And except for its initial series, the Florida State offense scored each time it got the ball in the first half. Weldon completed seven of eight pass attempts for 111 yards and two touchdowns. And with 11 minutes to go in the second quarter, he was relieved by Brad Johnson, who was three for four. The score at the half was 38–0.

Bowden could think of little to say except to fire up the reserves: "Subs, you've got to do the job. Go in there and play like first-teamers. We've got a shutout going. Don't lose it now.

"Offense, protect your passer. If he has the time, he can cut them to pieces."

After the second-half kickoff, Brad Johnson and a corps of reserve backs began a 12-play, 74-yard push to the Western Michigan end zone that consumed more than five minutes. The only incomplete pass on the drive was a 15-yarder dropped by Baker. But Johnson went right back to him on the next play, and he caught one for 13 yards and a first down. Fourth-team tailback Marquette Smith did most of the running on the series, gaining 16 yards on five carries. And fourth-team fullback Felix Harris got the three-yard touchdown.

Kenny Felder went in at quarterback with six minutes remaining in the third quarter. He got his first touchdown pass of the season, a screen pass to backup fullback Paul Moore, after a 61-yard drive.

When the defense got the ball back on a Bronco fumble in the next series, it was Charlie Ward's turn to call the signals and Marquette Smith's turn to run it in. The freshman scored the Seminoles' 57th point, and Dan Mowrey kicked the 58th when the game was only eight seconds into the final quarter.

The Seminoles passed only once more and disdained field goals. So even though the two remaining FSU drives ended deep in Bronco territory, the game ended with no more scoring.

Florida State ran up 459 yards of total offense, 257 of it in the air, using all four quarterbacks. The Broncos were held to 142 total yards and managed just nine first downs. Brad Tayles, the unfortunate Western Michigan quarterback, was sacked four times and was able to complete only seven of 20 passes for 80 yards. The Bronco rushing game netted 44 yards. The Seminole defense forced four turnovers—three fumbles and an interception—and stopped Western Michigan 10 out of 12 times on third down. It was Florida State's first shutout since 1988, Western Michigan's worst beating ever.

Of the 101 Florida State players dressed for the game, 77 played.

Seven different running backs scored. Nine different receivers caught passes—including the offensive lineman just converted to tight end, Johnny Clower.

The bombs never materialized, partly because Western Michigan gave up the medium passes to prevent getting beat deep and partly because the game got out of hand so quickly it would have been cruel to keep throwing. But Eason's top five—Baker, Turral, McCorvey, Frier and Knox—all caught passes. McCorvey led the group with three catches for 65 yards, including a 49-yarder, the longest of the season so far. Turral accounted for the lone wideout touchdown.

"They totally outclassed us," said Western Michigan coach Al Molde after the game.

"I liked everything I saw," Bowden told reporters later. "But it don't mean a darn thing. We're fixin' to get into another league now."

The players, weary of the brutal workouts the previous week, were going to get a couple of days off before practice began for Michigan. And they felt vindicated. They had dominated. They had fulfilled their obligations on a college football weekend that had seen Miami, Michigan and Florida roll over rivals. They were No. 1 and deserved it.

Not everybody was happy in the Seminole locker room, however. Derrick Brooks had separated his shoulder on a series of tackles in the first half, and trainers had strapped his arm to his chest to keep it immobile. The freshman's eyes were big with the pain and the confusion. "A partial separation," they had called it. Routine.

But there was nothing partial or routine about the pain. Nothing like this had ever happened to him in football. What did it mean? Wait and see how it responds to rehabilitation, they told him. Wait and see.

Casey Weldon had lost interest in the Western Michigan game as soon as he was yanked in the second quarter. He wasn't pleased about coming out so quickly. Nor were Edgar Bennett and Amp Lee. They all could have accumulated eye-popping stats on a night like this. And the numbers might have helped to dilute the impact of Desmond Howard and the other stars vying for sports headlines and award votes.

But at least the waiting was over. No more mind games to keep the team focused for lesser opponents. No one to look past. Nothing mattered more than what was immediately ahead. So the excitement returned to Weldon's eyes as he ran into the locker room with the other players. He clenched his fist.

"Now it begins," he said.

Part IV

---•---

"HAIL TO THE VICTORS"

1

In the late '80s, the University of Michigan represented everything most state universities aspired to. It attracted bright students, big research bucks and talented athletes. And it was steeped in tradition, especially football tradition.

For over 100 years, the Wolverines had played big-time college football. They had won more games than anybody. Their fight song, "Hail to the Victors," was as familiar to most fans as "America the Beautiful." And their ballpark, Michigan Stadium, was the nation's largest. When Florida State came to visit on September 28, it would be filled with 100,000 or more fans for the 99th consecutive game.

So to play Michigan in Ann Arbor on national television was to be at the center of college football culture. But Michigan had not won a national title since 1948; and it had lost each of the last five times it met a No. 1-ranked team. The Wolverines had won more Big Ten championships than any other school in the league, but were 2–4 in Rose Bowl matchups against Pac-10 powers since 1979. Nevertheless, the image of the game, its status in the minds of fans and the media, was still heavily rooted in places such as Ann Arbor. Bobby Bowden wouldn't have it any other way in 1991.

"I don't think I've learned anything," the coach liked to say, "that would overcome the advantage of being the underdog."

Bowden had built Florida State's program by exploiting that advantage. And now he was running out of teams that would consent to being the favorite. Here, maybe, was one last opportunity.

Even though his Seminoles would go into the Michigan game as the top-ranked team in the nation, Bowden knew their edge would dwindle in the minds of the legend worshippers: Michigan was so big, so strong, so disciplined, how could his little speedsters ever survive the crunch? And don't forget that long Wolverine football legacy. Two weeks before the game, the point spread was dropping. The experts on TV would argue the game into an even proposition by kickoff. Perfect. Playing at even money when you were No. 1 was the next-best thing to being an underdog.

In the competition for prestige among institutions, FSU really was out of its league compared to the University of Michigan. Florida State stood to gain much in national stature by just appearing in the same arena. Anticipating that moment, boosters had been clamoring for places on the chartered planes for months, and the president's office was busy organizing a giant alumni reception in the southern Michigan area. In their thinking, Michigan vs. Florida State signaled the arrival of this ambitious state university, a school that was still a Southern women's college when Michigan was in its 70th year of playing football. And if the Seminoles won, what a message that would send.

Bowden would do everything in his power to accommodate them.

There was also the Sod Game business to deal with. Even before Bowden, the underdog attitude at Florida State had inspired a tradition of carrying back to Tallahassee a piece of the turf of opponents favored in key away games. These Sod Games had been celebrated since 1962. And the pressure was on to make the Michigan contest the latest one, even though the Seminoles, officially, were slightly favored.

The players were at first indifferent to the media and local booster pressure. Did people really believe they were underdogs? But as they heard more and more about invincible Michigan Blue, they agreed: If they won in Ann Arbor, a chunk of the Wolverines' new grass field would find a final resting place in their Sod Cemetery just inside the gates to the practice fields.

Bowden would play along with that as well—for the time being at least. But it was nearing time to relegate the Sod Game legacy to the museum.

Back when Bowden's program had to build a name for itself, he and the athletic directors were forced into schedules with big-name schools that required the Seminoles to do all the traveling and to get none of the prestige and money that came with hosting the Michigans, the Notre Dames, the Oklahomas at home. They had no choice; they had to become road warriors. In his first year at Florida State, Bowden's team played five homecomings. For five consecutive games with LSU, the Seminoles had to go to Baton Rouge. The upcoming Michigan game was the last remnant of that era.

Florida State had traveled to Ann Arbor once before, in 1986. But future deals would require a home-and-away swap. If, that is, there was a spot open on the schedule.

In 1992, the Seminoles would begin an Atlantic Coast Conference schedule of eight games. That left only three out of the league, and

Florida and Miami would always take two of the slots. In 1993, Notre Dame and Florida State would meet in South Bend; the Irish would return the favor by coming to Florida, probably to the larger Citrus Bowl stadium in Orlando, for a future game. There would be no more need for road warriors and Sod Games. Bobby Bowden's Seminoles no longer had a right to the underdog role.

Unless, of course, someone insisted.

"I'm hearing the TV analysts say they'd pick us if the game was in Tallahassee," said Bowden. "But since it's in Ann Arbor, they're going with Michigan. Boy, I love to hear that."

Even though it was a Southern coach's specialty, poor-mouthing was no longer an effective weapon in Bowden's arsenal. The time was long past when he could get away with running down his own team's chances in order to manufacture the underdog advantage. Still, he was a master at using other folks' prejudices to accomplish the same thing.

In the two weeks before Michigan, out-of-town reporters probed on conference calls for story angles they'd already determined: Isn't that an imposing setting, that enormous stadium with 105,000 people cheering "Go, Blue"?

"It's gonna kinda excite us just being there," Bowden said.

And how about that Michigan offensive line? The starting five averaged 293 pounds. Tackle Greg Skrepenak was 6-8, 325 pounds, and all-everything in preseason.

"Ooh, I tell you, they scare me to death. We haven't been tested like we're fixin' to get tested. It's a game that'll definitely be won or lost up front. I'm not sure if we can play with them."

Desmond Howard ran a 4.2 40-yard dash and had a knack for the big play. He caught passes, ran reverses and received punts and kickoffs. How do you deal with that? "We don't have any 4.2 guys. We got some 4.3s, though, so maybe we can surround him."

All of that was true, but it didn't represent everything Bowden believed about the game. Even though he wouldn't contradict himself, when he was pressed on those same questions Bowden would expand in ways that clued the local media into what he was really thinking.

Yes, they would be excited to play in Michigan Stadium. They would be excited to play the No. 3 team anywhere. This, in fact, would be the highest-ranked matchup in Florida State history. But the crowd would not be a factor, the coach was convinced.

"That place is real open, so the sound just seems to travel up and out. And they're real polite folks up there. Nothing like we're used to at Auburn or LSU or Florida. Football is life and death down here."

The Michigan offensive line was indeed a major force. But the Wolverines hadn't yet played in the fastball league. They had something to prove too.

Seminole defensive linemen would have to keep from getting blown off the ball in order to shut down the run. But Mickey Andrews' defense was designed to do exactly that, with a front that clogged the line of scrimmage so that the linebackers could make the plays. And so far, the '91 defensive line was turning out to be one of the Seminoles' best ever. True, the FSU defensive linemen were smaller than the Michigan offensive front. But they could be as strong or stronger, and they surely were quicker. There were also more of them available on the bench. Fresh talent could be rotated in to aggravate the 300-pounders and wear them down.

But keep on questioning our defensive line, Bowden thought. It won't hurt us one bit if those boys had a mad on after two weeks of hearing how great Skrepenak and the Blue meanies were.

Desmond Howard? There was no denying his game-breaking potential. When Andrews answered Bowden's first inquiry about No. 21, the defensive coordinator said simply, "Well, I guess he's just about as good as you're gonna see."

In that case, thought Bowden, it might be a good idea to see to it that ol' Desmond never got within a mile of a punt or a kickoff. As for the passing game, it would be up to Andrews to figure out how to make sure Howard attracted lots of company every time he ran a pattern. The truth is, he might burn the Seminoles a couple of times, but they didn't deserve to win if they couldn't outscore Desmond Howard all by himself.

2

Since it was two weeks until they next played, the players had a couple of days off after the Western Michigan game. But the coaches couldn't have stayed away if they had wanted. Stacks of game tapes awaited them: Michigan's '91 games against Boston College and Notre Dame, plus all of last season, plus key selections from years past. The assistants had been sneaking looks since the season began. Now they could bury themselves without guilt.

Bowden always claimed he could completely relax in the first few days of an off week. He could just let go and free his mind of football for a couple of days, then return rejuvenated for battle. That's what he always said. After the Western Michigan game, his mental vacation lasted maybe twelve hours.

"This is a serious week, men. There is absolutely no room for a mistake. We've got to have everything covered."

It was 8:30 A.M., Monday, September 16. Twelve full days before the kickoff in Ann Arbor. And the coach's eyes were already narrowed into game-face tenacity. He had listened restlessly through the devotion and the injury report and through part of a discussion about keeping backup players better organized on the bench during home games. His impatience got the best of him.

"Let's get something done about it, dang it. Let's don't just talk."

Now, on to Michigan. He had watched film Sunday and was already worried about the kicking game: "Let's make every effort to get it perfect. That No. 21 scares me."

Another thing: "I've got to have great imitation from the scout squad. If a Michigan receiver has his foot back a certain way at the line of scrimmage, we want the scout team's guy to have his foot back. We want it so they can't do anything we're not ready for."

Where was his self-scouting report? Make sure, by the way, that it broke down calls by hash mark. Bowden wanted to know his own tendencies on the left and right sides of the field. It could make a difference.

The assistants absorbed Bowden's energy. But they didn't want to get too caught up in it. Not yet. Better to pace themselves. The competitive tension would engulf them next week anyway. So why rush it?

Big games have a kind of gravity all their own, a force that bends people and ideas toward a concentrated mass. Soon the out-of-town reporters would arrive to rev up the myth machine. Their columns and features would identify the heroic themes: old against new, North against South, power and size against speed and finesse.

And they would nominate pregame heroes. For Michigan, that would mean Desmond Howard, fresh off the cover of *Sports Illustrated* for his performance against Notre Dame, and the huge tackle Greg Skrepenak. For Florida State, it would be Casey Weldon, suddenly mentioned with Howard as early-season Heisman hopefuls; Terrell Buckley, the defensive back who would match up against Howard; and, of course, Bowden himself.

"I'm not telling you not to talk to the writers and the TV people," Bowden had told the players. "I trust you. I think you ought to know how to talk to the press. It's part of growing up. But you gotta remember that once you say something, you can never take it back. You can never take it back.

"There will be lots of Michigan press here. And some of them might try to get you to say something controversial about the other team so they can show it back in their area. You should be thinking about that when you talk to them."

Inevitably, media coverage on a game like this broke down along regional lines. The Midwestern press would be polite, but suspicious of Florida State's upstart credentials. The Southerners, respectful of the Michigan football tradition, would either overreact with tributes or mask their fears with an in-your-face attitude. The national TV commentators would stick with on-the-one-hand, on-the-other-hand. Except, of course, for former Michigan head coach Bo Schembechler. He was an expert commentator for ABC in New York on college football on Saturdays and looked as if he wanted to be back on the sideline for this one.

On Monday, the coaches were wading into the shallow end of this vast pool. They were enjoying the happy implications of Saturday's big win before immersing themselves in a game plan for Michigan. Their head coach, however, was already doing the backstroke in deep water.

"Let me meet with the offense."

Bowden was fascinated with the idea of catching Michigan with a cheap offside penalty on third or fourth down and short yardage. It was an old tactic, a freeze play, where the quarterback goes through a long signal count, varying the cadence to pull the other team offside. The offensive team must make no move, so that it's obvious to officials that the defensive team encroached.

"You must be able to freeze against Michigan. They are an attack team. Get that sucker in."

Naked bootlegs were a Bowden favorite as well. An athletic quarterback could fake the handoff and run opposite the apparent direction of the play, then pass or run to the unprotected side. The surprise value of nakeds seemed to be highest in short-yardage and goal-line situations against a defense braced for the mash play over guard or tackle. Against Michigan, accustomed to grind-it-out rushing teams in the Big Ten, the tactic could work even on first down, Bowden thought.

"Nakeds could blow their minds."

3

GOING into the biggest game of their college careers, two-thirds of "the best backfield in college football" were feeling unloved. Fullback Edgar Bennett and tailback Amp Lee were still among the most popular players at Florida State with fans and media. But suddenly the coaches were on their case, questioning their commitment and focus.

Were agents getting to these guys? Were they more worried about their pro careers than the team or their studies?

Bennett, the senior, had been talked into returning to Florida State to play out his eligibility instead of turning pro last season. Lee was a junior who, no doubt, would be tempted to make the leap to the Next League after this year. Both, so far, seemed on track for All-American performances in 1991. And it wouldn't have been unusual for agents to be snooping around the two roommates, turning their heads with offers of cash and clothes.

To coaches, who inhaled paranoia with every breath, the warning signs seemed obvious. Both these guys seemed to have their minds elsewhere.

Bennett had always resisted the mash-'em blocking techniques preferred by his coaches. At 212 pounds, he saw himself as a fullback in a tailback's body. And he preferred cut blocks that took the legs out from under onrushing linemen and linebackers, who usually outweighed him by 30 or more pounds. But cuts didn't always do the job, especially with athletic defenders who could leap over a rolling block and collide with the ballcarrier.

The Western Michigan game video showed that all the fullbacks had had a "Nolan Ryan kind of Saturday—a no-hitter," said running backs coach Billy Sexton. But most of the concern was with the starter.

"It was the worst I have ever seen," said Sexton.

When his offensive linemen saw the tape, said Brad Scott, "it pissed all of them off." What good was it for them to block their men if Bennett was going to play footsie with his guy every time?

"Along with all this celebrity," said Scott, "goes a little responsibility."

And what about Amp? He clearly had been moping after being taken out of the Western Michigan game. And for the first time in his career at FSU, he had skipped a couple of classes, then a tutor's appointment and a study hall. If he didn't raise his grade point over 2.00 this term, he would be out.

Was he blowing off his eligibility?

John Eason called in both Bennett and Lee to talk. No, they weren't talking to agents, they insisted. And no, neither was happy about his playing time in the Western Michigan game. They had done everything asked of them in practice all these years, and then it seemed they were penalized for playing too well in a game.

On occasions such as this, coaches are obliged to pull out the team argument: We do these things together, as a team, to make the team better; individuals have to sacrifice sometimes for team goals. But Eason's heart wasn't in it. He sympathized with the players. Neither was an egomaniac. Both had contributed plenty to team victories.

"Maybe you should talk to them, Coach," Eason said to Bowden.

The head coach was as susceptible to paranoia as his assistants, but he also had great affection for his star backs. He thought he owed Bennett the benefit of the doubt for sticking around another year. And Lee had never given anything less than full effort since he earned a place on the team as a true freshman. Bowden wanted to hear them out.

As with most coaches, Bowden's first reaction was to ask why Lee and Bennett could possibly feel hurt. We were able to save them for the next game, he thought. They were able to rest. And we didn't risk an injury when we had the game won. And all the other guys got to play.

When he called the players into his office at midweek, Bowden said he was concerned about Lee's class attendance and Bennett's blocking. And he told them the coaches' suspicions that agents had been talking to them, distracting them from the season before them.

Even as he asked about that and heard the players deny it, the coach was retreating from the theory in his own mind. "Most of that is really our imagination, our fears. It ain't really happening."

There was no need for the do-it-for-the-team speech either. "The more I got to thinking about it, dad-gummit, I might have pulled those boys out too early. I knew I did what was best for the team. If you had gotten a broken arm or something when you were that far ahead, you never would have forgiven yourself.

"But now you look back at the boy. He's worked his tail off and then doesn't get to play but a quarter or a quarter and a half. I think if I had to do it again, I wouldn't take 'em out that fast."

Amp and Edgar would understand the team argument, accept it. But at the same time, they had a right to think it was unfair.

"At my age, I learned another lesson. I've never had this before. It's one of those good problems: What do you do if you're ahead 28–0 in the first quarter? My thinking now is that I'm gonna let my first team play a little more and do my substituting in the second half."

4

AMP Lee would be 20 years old on October 1, but he carried himself—
on and off the field—like a much older man. Already, as a junior, he was
creeping higher among FSU career leaders in scoring. He had sure hands
as a receiver and was one of the most elusive running backs in the nation.

Amp was a make-'em-miss specialist. Not great straight-ahead speed,
but superb vision and terrific body control. He embarrassed linebackers
and defensive backs, disappearing from in front of them. As a true
freshman in 1989, he gained 110 yards in 25 carries in his first start. And
in 1990, he was third in the nation in scoring.

Yet out of uniform Amp Lee could also disappear in a crowd. He was
quiet and unfailingly polite. He looked smaller than his advertised 6-0,
195-pound height and weight, and he walked with a little stoop in his
shoulders. With that gait and his mature, sad face, he looked like the
oldest 19-year-old in the world.

Amp was from Chipley, a small town an hour west of Tallahassee. He
was raised by his mother and stepfather. And back there in the same
house, his brother, Tony Davis, was now creating the same kind of
sensation Amp had sparked in high school: spectacular running back,
great basketball player, surefire top prospect.

What troubled the coaches about Amp Lee was that it was hard to
know what was going on in his head. He was so dependable, apparently
intelligent about so many things. Yet he seemed unable to focus on
decisions he had to make off the football field.

He just got by academically, was dismissed once and reinstated
provided he raised his overall GPA above 2.00. He would need a B-minus
average this term to do it or he would be gone.

Rumors abounded that he had already decided to skip his senior year
and declare for the NFL draft. Yet whenever Bowden or the other
coaches pressed him on the issue, he assured them he intended to stay.
No matter what happened with the NFL, he said, he wanted his degree.
Eventually, he wanted to coach.

Maybe the reason they found it so hard to believe him was that he
looked so confused and distracted when they talked to him. Things
seemed to be caving in around him.

Sports used to be such a wonderful release, Lee thought. So much
joy, so much fun. Now everything was pulling in a hundred different
directions. Every practice was a test of commitment, a grind. Are you

practicing like the No. 1 tailback on the No. 1 team in the nation? Are you giving 100 percent every day?

Everybody wanted a piece of him. Got a minute for an interview? He gave the TV guys and the writers what they asked for. He paid tribute to FSU and to Chipley and his parents. Now word was getting back to him that his biological father was complaining that he was being shunned. The family was upset. What could he do?

And then there was school. Every time he sat down to take a test, he couldn't help thinking it would determine his whole future. Now all this labor, this pressure, these questions. "I feel like this is all I've been doing all my life." And he was so tired.

5

JIM Gladden, coach of the outside linebackers, put together the weekly scouting reports for the defense. His presentations began each week of practice. They were masterpieces of the military briefing style, perfectly suited to Gladden, who could crank his coach's voice up the necessary decibels and rescue the oldest football clichés with sincere intensity.

"We must stuff the run, men."

Gladden had gone through the big names: tackle Greg Skrepenak, quarterback Elvis Grbac, wideout Desmond Howard and tailback Ricky Powers. "In critical situations, they will go to Howard," said Gladden. But he spent most of his time in the scout session talking about the Michigan running game and Ricky Powers.

After two games, Powers was third in the nation in rushing. He had run the ball 65 times for 340 yards. That was an average of 5.2 yards a carry, enough to remove the pressure of obvious passing downs and free Howard to roam the secondary against tentative coverage. The threat of the run set up the play-action pass. So to make the passing game unpleasant for Grbac and Howard, Florida State would have to neutralize Powers and his blockers.

"Can this guy run 30 times against our defense? We've got to punish him. We've got to stand him up and call roll on him with our hats."

After the defensive scout meeting, the segments broke into their own meetings, and the defensive linemen joined their coach, Chuck Amato. There would be no video today, just talk.

The byword for the Michigan game, Bowden had declared, was "leverage." "The man with the lowest pads wins." And Amato told his guys he wanted them "playing at their kneecaps the whole game. You don't need to see. You're not going to look for the football with this team. The football will come to you."

The plan was to punch holes in Michigan's blocking wall, frustrating the Wolverines' attempts to spring Powers and giving the Seminole linebackers a clear shot at him. Amato turned to nose guard James Chaney, the smallest guy on his DL.

"I want you to GO on the snap. I don't want their center to block this stud right here." And the coach pointed to the number 55 on the grease board. No. 55 was FSU's Marvin Jones, the All-American inside linebacker.

Chaney said nothing. Reporters all week had been bugging him about going up against the most famous offensive line in college football. This little nose guard against those huge guys? And he had tried to say, in a dozen polite ways, that while he had the highest regard for the Wolverines, he nevertheless intended to show up for the game.

The whole DL had been getting it. They were the apparently overmatched little guys against the Michigan monsters. The biggest among FSU's front three starters was defensive tackle Carl Simpson at 275 pounds. Henry Ostaszewski, at the other tackle, was 264. On average, they were outweighed by the Michigan offensive line by 30 pounds each. Only when Dan Footman and Sterling Palmer came in on passing downs did they look like a big-time DL.

But Amato's confidence in these guys was growing with every practice. He had a good mix, he figured. Some great athletes who were still rough around the edges—a category that included Footman and sophomore end Toddrick McIntosh. Plus the group he called the Clydesdales: the Ostaszewski twins—Henry and Joe, who backed up Chaney at nose guard—and Troy Sanders, a 260-pound tackle who alternated with Simpson. They were the steady bulls.

Because they had gotten so little attention, they were anxious to make a statement. And wasn't this just the perfect time for it?

Amato was a Pennsylvanian who wrestled and played football at North Carolina State, one of only two Northerners on Bobby Bowden's staff. And while his personal style was more aggressive than that of the Southerners, his coaching technique was less confrontational. He was seldom in the faces of his players. He goaded them when he thought he had to and inspired them when they seemed receptive.

In his playing days at North Carolina State, Amato had been a little guy who played with a big attitude. As a wrestler, he had been unde-feated in dual meets. The beat reporters called him Coach Chest because of his enormously developed upper torso and because his chest seemed to poke out a little more whenever he was challenged. Which meant he would be a bantam rooster for Michigan.

"You know," said Amato, "I thought I was through dealing with the million-dollar question until I went to lunch today. There were four reporters all asking, 'What are you going to do with that huge offensive line, the best in the country, with your little bitty line?'

"Well, when we leave that stadium next week, there will be no doubt in the minds of America about who the big men are.

"Men, you have got to lift the intensity level this next week to be ready for Michigan. When you get tired out there in practice, just look down at the fourth finger on your right hand. That's what it is all about. That's what it is all about. The ring.

"And if we don't get the job done next week, who do you think is going to get the blame? The defensive line. Do you want that stigma the rest of your life?"

6

BOWDEN looked at his watch as he closed his office door before walking the twenty feet down the hall to the athletic department's broadcast studio. He had about three minutes before his Thursday-night radio show. And, as usual, he would slip into his seat and pull on his headset at least a minute before the host, Gene Deckerhoff.

Deckerhoff was a veteran at timing his entrances. For thirteen years he had been the voice of Seminole sports. He was also radio play-by-play man for the NFL's Tampa Bay Buccaneers. Some fifty stations carried Florida State games in Alabama, Georgia and Florida; and the local outlets usually picked up the weekly call-in show. So the voices of Deckerhoff and Bowden had become two of the most familiar on sports radio in the region.

The Thursday-night callers were a pretty good barometer of fan concerns. Many were regulars. All were consumed by the prospects of their team and their favorite players. And all addressed Bowden as if

The Seminole team slogan for 1991: No Excuses.

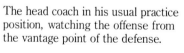

The head coach in his usual practice position, watching the offense from the vantage point of the defense.

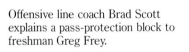

Offensive line coach Brad Scott explains a pass-protection block to freshman Greg Frey.

The daily offense meeting. Bobby Bowden at the head of the table. Clockwise, beginning on Bowden's left: offensive coordinator and line coach Brad Scott, tight end coach Jimmy Heggins, volunteer coach Clint Ledbetter, quarterback coach Mark Richt (hand on cheek), receiver coach John Eason and running back coach Billy Sexton (back to camera).

Quarterback coach Mark Richt
watching game videos.

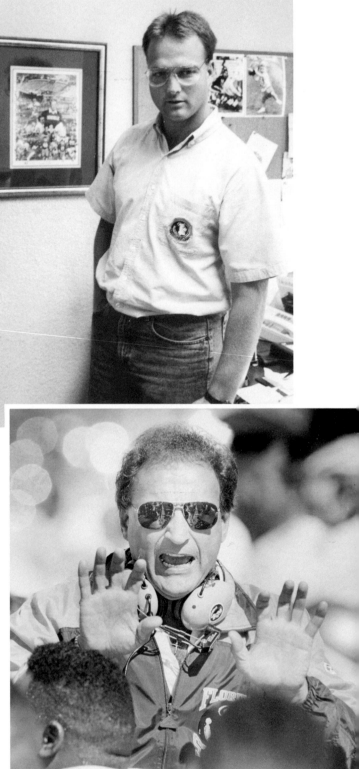

Defensive line coach Chuck Amato.

"Get me a football player out here!" Defensive coordinator Mickey Andrews rides cornerback Errol McCorvey in practice.

Receiver coach John Eason makes a quiet point.

The receivers: Shannon Baker (1), Matt Frier (12), Kevin Knox (81), Eric Turral (7), Kez McCorvey (88), Jeff Beckles (83) and Aaron Dely.

Eric Turral tries to celebrate with Warren Hart and hand the ball back to the official at the same time after a TD in the BYU game.

Casey Weldon and daughter Kendall.

Mr. Make-'em-miss, Amp Lee, against Western Michigan.

they were partners in the Seminole football enterprise: "Are we ready for Michigan, Bobby?"

This Thursday, nine days before the Michigan game, the fans were clearly worried. They were worried about the weather way up North in Ann Arbor, about the Wolverines' no-huddle offense, about those huge linemen and Desmond Howard, about Michigan Stadium, about the Florida State wide receivers and Terrell Buckley.

"Why are we playing them anyway?" one caller wanted to know.

Bowden explained that he didn't think this was "a suicide game." Even if the Seminoles lost, they would have their chance to redeem themselves down the line, no matter what. And besides, it was probably a good idea that teams with No. 1 ambitions took on all comers.

September 28 was a little early for a Midwestern blizzard, the coach said. "If we get freezing weather, it would change our game plan." But snow? "The good Lord wouldn't do that to us."

The Michigan no-huddle wasn't really a hurry-up offense. They just seemed to meander to the line and call the play from there. So it shouldn't frustrate Seminole substitution strategy. "But it's good that we've already seen it. You don't want to be surprised by anything like that."

To the two separate questions about the Wolverine offensive line and Desmond Howard, Bowden gave the same answer: "That's what scares me the most."

Playing before 105,000 screaming Michigan fans would be no problem, though. "I'm gonna tell my kids there are just 60,000 up there. They won't have time to count."

As for the receivers, they were coming along. And Buck? Well, he was a gambler, and with gamblers you won a few and lost a few. If the losses mounted up, that kid Corey Sawyer just might challenge for the job.

Bowden chomped on his gum and answered every question with friendly appreciation. Thanks for callin' now. He could do it in his sleep. And as long as his team won, he knew, the fans would play along. They would fret, but they would be friendly. Of course, if you lose a big one or—God forbid—two, then all bets might be off.

His own anxiety had been alleviated somewhat as he had seen his assistants crank up this week. One of his functions as a manager, Bowden figured, was to balance the energy of his subordinates. He could be the firebrand when things got too mellow; he could defuse the tension, usually with humor, when he sensed everyone was too tight.

They had gotten away with head-butting practices in the last couple of weeks. They may even have profited by them. But now, with the players already antsy for combat, there was no sense taking the risk of injuries. "This is not the time," he cautioned, "to find out who's the toughest guy in camp."

That didn't mean, however, that there was a cease-fire in the war Bowden was plotting in his head. He had been telling the media after practice how this was going to be "a game of basics. They're too smart to trick." But he couldn't help himself.

A fake field goal, the freeze play and a double-quarterback pass using Charlie Ward as a receiver-passer were already getting practice reps. And now he was waking up in the middle of the night to jot down alternative pass routes and to hatch devious ideas for a Seminole version of the no-huddle offense.

"I think that would drive them nuts," he told the coaches Thursday morning. "And we need to drive them nuts. They're giving us fits with their no-huddle offense. We'd get even with them with our own."

Bowden's no-huddle would be more pro-style, a steady one-minute drill right down the field. No pause. No time for defensive substitution. Maybe they would write the plays on Casey's armband or signal in two at a time from the sideline.

The coach laughed as he ran through plays he liked out of a no-huddle. "You want to confuse somebody? That's the way to confuse 'em."

While Bowden talked excitedly, the assistants around the conference table had been respectfully silent. They would do anything he wanted. But they wanted to make sure he settled on his priorities. If they scripted every idea, they would spread their time too thin and go into what might be the biggest game of the year without the confidence that comes only with focused repetitions on the practice field.

Mark Richt doodled in his notebook. He was committed to Bobby Bowden football. Still, his basic indoctrination in the sport came at Miami under Howard Schnellenberger. It boiled down to: Get the talent you need; train them in a simple system that exploits their gifts; then line up and play.

They had recruited right and planned right at Florida State, Richt liked to argue. Why not just play ball? Finally, he spoke up: "We don't want to give our guys the idea that we have to do a lot of fancy things to beat these guys."

Bowden leaned back from his notepad. "I got a million ideas. Y'all decide what you have time for. We don't want to end up confusing ourselves.

"But I definitely like the fake field goal."

7

IF Miami's destruction of Houston in the Orange Bowl reminded the Seminoles of what lay ahead in November, the University of Florida's visit to Syracuse on September 21 was another kind of wake-up call.

The Gators were a cocky No. 5 in the nation when they went to New York. They returned to Gainesville victimized 38–21 by the No. 18 team.

Apparently on a roll after a 35–0 whipping of Alabama the previous week, the Florida offense had been averaging over 460 yards a game. Against the Crimson Tide, the Gators got 216 yards on the ground. But they hit a brick wall in the Carrier Dome. Minus 17 yards—that was Florida's net rushing performance on Saturday. And while Gator quarterback Shane Matthews connected on 27 of 43 passes for 347 yards, he also threw two interceptions and was sacked three times.

Syracuse used two quarterbacks and an option scheme to drive the Florida defense crazy. Even the Orangemen's kicking game produced. They scored on the first kickoff with a reverse handoff. And the Gators never seemed to recover from the shock.

"We got a good tail kicking," Florida coach Steve Spurrier told reporters. "From the opening kickoff to the last play of the game, Syracuse was better than us."

Maybe there was a lesson here for Florida State. "I suppose that's encouraging to Michigan," Bowden told the players before their Monday practice. "A Southern team that's supposed to be good gets beat when it comes up to play a Northern team."

The coach peered at the seated players over his bifocals. "I suppose that's encouraging to them."

Bowden had missed the televised Florida game. He was in a small state plane navigating the West Virginia mountains on Saturday afternoon, en route to a Fellowship of Christian Athletes conference. "Why I agreed to talk way up there in the week before Michigan, I'll never know. But they asked me a long time ago. And I can't hardly turn these kinds of speeches down, especially when they ask me so far in advance."

But he had seen some of the game highlights and listened avidly to the other coaches' discussion in their meetings. "They just quit," said Amato of the Gators.

The Seminoles could at least be grateful for the advance warning Florida provided. Syracuse was coming to Tallahassee the week after the Michigan game. And if anybody on Bowden's staff had been tempted to take the Orangemen less seriously than some of the more familiar

Southern opponents, that inclination was now history. But for the time being the coaches had enough to keep themselves occupied.

Mike Morris had rejoined the offensive line, his broken foot apparently healed enough to test it in combat. Brad Scott let himself grin at the sight of the senior guard taking his place beside his teammates. During his entire rehab period, Morris had kept his weight down and his mind on football.

"It's like he never left," said Scott.

Rookie Patrick McNeil had been heroic as a replacement. And it was great to know he would be around for another three seasons. But there was no substitute for experience. Morris had been to war. And he knew all the tricks. He knew blocking assignments so well he could help those on either side of him.

"I tell you, Coach," Scott said to Bowden, "you hear him in there calling out those blocks and you realize what you've been missing all this time. He makes ol' Robbie a better center, because half the time he's telling him what to do."

Morris' return worked right into Bowden's motivational plans. He addressed Scott's players directly in his prepractice notes on Monday: "All I hear is how good the Michigan offensive line is. It's a pro OL, they keep saying. Well, our OL has got something to prove. Let's see who has the best offensive line."

Billy Sexton's backs did not share the enthusiasm of the rekindled line. They were in a funk. Even though they were both doing everything asked of them in practice, there was still an emotional hangover from last week for Edgar Bennett and Amp Lee. William Floyd, the No. 2 fullback, had been demoted to No. 3, behind Paul Moore, for following Bennett's blocking example on "no-hit Saturday" against Western Michigan. And he wasn't talking to Sexton.

Moore took the promotion cynically. He had been No. 2 before, and it didn't seem to increase his game opportunities. Now, as a senior, he was running out of chances. Marquette Smith was favoring an arm injured in the last game and appeared to be working himself out of contention for playing time.

But at least they were all there, taking their reps and working through the drills. Coaches tend to believe the routine of practice itself is therapeutic. Just shut up and do it; you'll feel better.

On defense, Buckley was getting most of Mickey Andrews' attention. He was fired and rehired several times during the week. Andrews always wanted more physical play from the star corner. Buckley resisted collisions he didn't think were necessary. The other defensive players watched the daily battles, convinced that no matter how many times Buck got fired, he would be rehired come kickoff.

8

TERRELL Buckley entered the 1991 season as a probable All-American, an almost certain contender for the Jim Thorpe Award for the nation's top defensive back and a natural heir to Deion Sanders' swaggering, outspoken style.

Now, three games into his junior year, Buck was tiring of the Sanders comparisons and the nagging criticism of fans. "Fans don't know what they're talking about."

Which was true, but irrelevant.

Like other highly visible players and coaches, Terrell Buckley was both the victim and the beneficiary of fantasies and fears over which he had little control. Reporters and fans didn't have playbooks, didn't know the calls on offense or defense and wouldn't see the frame-by-frame analysis of game film that was standard procedure for players and coaches. They could never really know what was happening on the field. Heck, the players didn't know half the time. What most people saw was a game played out in their imaginations.

But the fact was, the game in fans' minds was the one that ultimately mattered most and lasted longest. It generated the emotion that inspired the business that made the money that built the empire that gave Terrell Buckley and Bobby Bowden a chance for a career in sports. Of course, a certain amount of injustice was built into the deal: You get more credit than you deserve when things go well, more blame when they don't. It was one of Bowden's coaching axioms.

Through long experience, coaches and veteran players learned to live with the irony. Or else they imploded from the pressure. But young athletes had the hardest time adapting to the contradictions. Buck wanted it all, the glory, the chance for the Next League, everything generated by fan fantasies. But, understandably, he resisted being held accountable to others' unrealistic—and often misinformed—expectations.

Buckley never really had a chance to duck them. He arrived at Florida State in 1989, in the fall following the spring that Deion Sanders was selected in the first round of the NFL draft. He was fast and smooth—

like Deion. And he had an attitude—like Deion. Both were of the in-your-face school of defense. One on one. Me and you.

When Buckley was recruited out of Mississippi, he came to see the Seminoles in the fall of his senior high school year. There was Deion, finger-pointing and talking trash, waving his arms to incite the crowd. It horrified many of the white conservative fans and electrified many of the young black players like Buckley.

"They were out there talkin' the fool: 'Man, did you see me cover him? I could do that with my eyes closed.'

"I used to tell guys in high school that I could cover them with an ice cream in one hand and a Coke in another and on one leg. That kind of thing pumps you up. It's funny. It's sarcastic.

"Then I came to Florida State. Deion was gone. And they start comparing me to him, saying, 'We can't have another guy like Deion Sanders playing for the Florida State Seminoles.' "

The Deion Effect had indeed left ripples at FSU. Two years after Sanders had left to become a two-sport star in the pros, Bowden was still answering questions about him: Couldn't you control that guy more?

Sanders' legacy even extended to the Florida Board of Regents, who enacted a special academic regulation in his honor. The all-star corner-back had made no secret of his disinterest in his studies. In 1988, he was already a minor league baseball player under contract to the New York Yankees, who were paying his way at Florida State while he played football. He wasn't on scholarship, wasn't living in the football dorms and wasn't nearly as concerned about his academic future as he was about tapping into the millions waiting for him in the NFL and the major leagues.

Too bad for him—and for those who might emulate him—that he couldn't work a little study time into his career planning. But given Sanders' abilities, there was little chance that he would be unemployed when his days at FSU were through. So when he knew he was in his last season, he skipped some of his classes and final examinations. When it became national news prior to the season-ending bowl game, Deion's disdain damaged the football program's image and embarrassed the school and the Board of Regents. Once again, it seemed, Deion Sanders was thumbing his nose at the system. And the system struck back. The Board of Regents enacted what unofficially became known as the Deion Sanders Rule, requiring athletes to go to class and take tests or be suspended from games.

The coaches weren't nearly as worried about the Deion Effect as the fans. Great players, such as Buckley, came to programs that provided a stage for stars. And great players made great coaches. Besides, if even mediocre players had the work habits of Deion Sanders you could build a heck of a football team. Sanders' practice intensity was legendary at Florida State. He talked on Saturdays, but he practiced all week.

Bowden liked Sanders and defended him in booster speeches and media interviews. He could have done without some of the showboating. And certainly a team of Deions would be a nightmare for media relations. But if the head coach were given a choice between world-class football played with spirited arrogance and run-of-the-mill athleticism from a group of Southern gentlemen, he'd take his chances with the problem children.

Bowden liked Buckley too. He didn't trust athletes without competitive spirit. And Buck, so far, had risen to every challenge. The coach had seen the young Mississippian turn games around with an interception or a punt return. He had watched Buckley in the last full-contact scrimmage before the Michigan game, when the offensive team had gone for a short pass on the sideline, a quick out that should have been a cinch score. Buckley had appeared out of nowhere to knock the ball from the receiver's hands.

Gosh, he closes on the ball fast, thought Bowden. He is this close to breaking something big. You just know it.

Andrews was also a Buckley fan. For all the same reasons. But Buck wouldn't turn up the juice in practice the way Deion did, and Andrews demanded the assurance that his people could do what was required on every down, in every drill, every day. In that same last scrimmage, Andrews yanked Buck when he missed an assignment. The two had shouted at one another, and the defensive coordinator had demoted his star. At least for the moment. Buck sought out Bowden the next day to complain about the treatment.

Bowden listened, but he had no intention of undercutting Andrews. The problem between them was one of pride. Mostly Buck's pride. He hated having his nose rubbed in his mistakes. He reacted to criticism with defensiveness, with defiance if pushed too hard.

"He is a special guy. So much pride," said Bowden. "And when you get on him, it hurts. But he is getting better at handling it. I am not worried in the least about Terrell Buckley."

Still, this did not feel like such a wonderful time to Buckley. In fact, it felt terrible. "I practice harder than anybody. I do all the things they want me to do. I go to class. I lift weights. I expect them to see all I'm doing and realize that they have a special kind of player who's trying to do all the right things out there. And they never reward me."

On top of everything else, reporters were bugging him with Desmond Howard questions: Could Buckley stay with this guy? Was he intimidated?

Intimidated? Man, this is what he signed on for. This was why he put up with all the stupid rules and abusive coaches.

"I know all this stuff is hype. But I also know this is a make-you-or-break-you situation. If I end up on Desmond Howard one on one and I have a good showing, then it could lift me and give me a little more exposure. But if I have a poor showing it could push me down in people's estimates."

Buckley had no intention of letting his stock go down in anybody's book. Especially not on the notepads and charts of NFL scouts. After the bowl game, he wanted the option of skipping his senior year and heading directly into the Next League. After a week like this, January couldn't come fast enough. The pressure and the criticism were diluting the pleasure he got from playing. And without the fun, the dreary routines of practice felt like a straitjacket.

"Football is not fun for me anymore, because they put so much emphasis on work, work, work. You can't be yourself in the four years you're an athlete. You have to be somebody else.

"They try to tell us how to walk, how to sleep, how to eat. Don't curse, don't do this, don't do that. Don't, don't, don't. When you hear 'don't' so much it's human nature to rebel. It will get to the point where you don't even want to play.

"They want you to give the ball back to the ref after you score a touchdown, then go sit back on the bench. They don't want you to say nothing fun when you're getting interviewed. They want to do all that to make it seem like a business. Well, then we ought to treat it like a business."

As for Desmond Howard, bring him on.

On the locker-room bulletin board a wall of Michigan newspaper clippings featured No. 21 prominently. "You're mine, Buck," had been penciled in a cartoon balloon on one Howard photo.

Fine, thought Buckley.

"When I'm hyped, I'm gonna do my best. I just wish it was me and Howard, one on one. I feel like double coverage hinders me. If I'm gonna be the one who gets beat and gets criticized for it, I want it to be me, by myself, with the responsibility. One on one."

9

THE last twenty minutes of the September 23 practice was a progress check. The No. 1 offense against the No. 2 defense, the No. 2 offense against the No. 1 defense. Full teams, full speed. It was a time for evaluating plays, for spotting weak links and testing timing.

When the ball moved to about midfield on the right hash mark, Weldon broke the huddle and moved to the line of scrimmage with the other first-teamers. To his left, in a receiver's slot, was Charlie Ward, the No. 3 quarterback. At the snap, Weldon dropped back and passed to Ward, who was still behind the line of scrimmage. The defense shifted to block Ward's path downfield. But Ward suddenly turned and threw back to Weldon, who was headed down the right sideline, with three offensive linemen clearing the way.

The quarterback-turned-receiver picked up 40 yards before being pushed out of bounds. The offensive coaches roared their approval.

This was Crocodile, named after a similar play by the Florida Gators. Bowden would later tell reporters that he hated calling it Alligator and giving Florida the credit, so they named it Crocodile. But the truth was, there was already a Gator pass in the playbook, and they wanted no confusion.

Crocodile wasn't a made-for-Michigan play. The team had been practicing it since the beginning of the season, waiting for an opportunity to use it against a fired-up, overpursuing defense. "Work on it, work on it, work on it. And don't use it unless you have to," was Bowden's trick-play philosophy. "But sometimes I just don't feel comfortable unless I have one of these babies in my back pocket."

This particular one hinged on Ward's talent and judgment. He was a cool ball handler, a starting point guard in basketball and a sure-handed quarterback in football. He could be relied upon to make the crucial run-pass decision. If Weldon looked to be in too much traffic to risk a pass, Ward could take off down the left side of the field. But it was the kind of thing that would work only once.

"It's kind of a desperation play or a tone setter. It either backfires or you make a big play," said the head coach.

It was also better early in the game, when defenders were fresh and pumped with adrenaline. A sluggish defensive lineman who ignored the leftward flow of the ball could stumble into the middle of the play and knock down the cross-field pass. Or worse. When the offense was practicing Crocodile against the scout team, a tired defender walked into the path of the pass-back and got a surprise interception.

"I might like this on the first play," Bowden warned his offensive coaches. "So make sure it's in there."

The Seminoles' offense also worked on the fake field goal every practice. After studying Michigan game tapes, the coaches thought the Wolverines cheated inside on field goals and point-afters, looking to make the block. And that made them vulnerable to the fake.

William Floyd, the big backup fullback, was usually a left corner blocker on placekicks, lining up just behind and to the left of a tight end. On the fake they were working on for Michigan, Floyd spun with the snap of the ball and ran just behind the line of scrimmage. Brad Johnson, the kick holder, would hold the ball on the ground as the kicker pantomimed his kick. Then, still on his knee in the holding position, Johnson would shovel-pass the ball toward Floyd as he crossed in front, and the fullback would try to slide behind the tight end on the right side. In practice against the Seminole defense in short-yardage situations, it seemed to work every time.

Under Bobby Bowden, Florida State's reputation for trick plays— "rooskies," in Bowden's parlance—had taken on a life of its own by the mid-'80s. Few profiles of the head coach ever appeared without the Riverboat Gambler analogy. Everybody remembered the classic Punt-rooskie play in the '88 Clemson game, in which LeRoy Butler turned a fake punt into a 78-yard run to set up the winning field goal. Bowden dearly loved anything that surprised and confused the enemy. "You know what ruins football players? Confusion. They can't play if they're confused."

But confusion works in both directions. For every football game won with a gimmick, the coach knew, he could lose five by robbing the team of practice time on fundamental football. Proper execution is crucial, whether it's a straight-ahead fullback dive or Crocodile. And smoothness only comes with repetition. So he had to be careful to get enough work on a trick play to assure its chances of success, without sacrificing the meat-and-potatoes game. That usually meant narrowing his repertoire of gadgets to three or four that could be worked into the 40-odd plays in the weekly game plans.

"The key," Bowden said, "is when to call 'em. If you're gonna try something like that, it's better to try it early. If you've got a one-point lead with a minute to go, you're afraid to try anything. So you might as well get it over with. If it doesn't work, and they come back and score on you, then you know what you got to do to win the game. Sometimes that takes the pressure off.

"If you get in a game and start moving the ball, then you don't worry about the special things you worked on. You carry those sweet things on until the next game. Maybe, you carry them with you all season and use 'em in the bowl."

The superior athletic talent at Florida State seemed to make the gadget plays especially effective. How many teams had a Charlie Ward to sneak into the game? Amp Lee could run or catch out of any back or receiver position. Shannon Baker and Sean Jackson were both former quarterbacks who could throw the ball downfield 40 yards. When Florida State was on offense, anybody could end up with the ball.

But, paradoxically, the better the talent, the more powerful the pull toward simplicity. "There's a mistake in thinking that the better your athletes are, the more you can do. The truth is, they don't need to do more. You just let them execute, and you don't make mistakes."

10

"A RE there any announcements?"

It was the team's end-of-practice gathering in the center of the field. And before Bowden would give any last words, he reserved time to tend to administrative matters—details about travel and meal schedules, a reminder to players to shave the stubble, plane etiquette. Mark Meleney stepped up to the circle of kneeling players.

Meleney was academic adviser to the three principal men's teams at Florida State—baseball, basketball and football. For all the players on those teams, he was the day-to-day liaison between them and the academic side of the university. He helped them register, advised them on courses and majors and acted as a go-between with deans and professors.

This was another one of his duties in the fall.

He said he knew how excited they all were about the Michigan game. He was excited too. "But there are twenty-two of you who are in danger of being dismissed at the end of this term if you don't make high enough grades to pull up your grade point averages."

A couple of the players shifted knees nervously, but most kept their blank meeting faces on. Shave, behave on the plane, hit the books. So what else was new?

"Now listen, men," said Bowden. "you can't forget your academic responsibilities. Wouldn't it be a shame to come this far, to go all the way through this season, win 'em all and then for some of you to be ineligible to play in the bowl for the national championship? You don't want that to happen, men."

That was about the only thing Meleney could do at this stage, he thought. He had to come out to practice and call attention to the problem. Let the coaches hear. Let Bowden say something.

It sounded terrible—22 out of the 130 scholarship players and walk-ons were about to flunk out of school. But it was only slightly worse than usual. There would always be a core group who would try to figure the minimum effort it took to get by in class, and they would, from time to time, slip below the line. When they came under the gun, most would find a way to pull up their averages.

Maybe seventeen or eighteen of these guys would get official dismissal notices. Then Meleney would go to their college deans and try to negotiate terms under which the players could return to school under some sort of probationary status. It was an appeal process open to any students at FSU. It was just that few others had full-time advocates like Meleney. Or the kind of support system available to athletes.

If there was a difference this year, Meleney thought, it was in the increased pressure from two directions. One was from the university, which was evolving tighter restrictions on academic appeals. Every year, the quality of the student body—as measured in test scores and high school grade point averages—improved. More people were applying from out of state. There was more grant money. And since the new president and faculty were anxious to keep that trend going, it was getting tougher to last as a marginal student.

The other pressure was from the larger world of football. At this level, thought Meleney, there seemed to be an inverse relationship between achieving in academics and winning in athletics.

"What frustrates me the most is that the freshmen come in with pretty good attitudes. Most of them do everything they need to do in their freshman and sophomore years. Then, all of a sudden, they lose that edge and get away.

"I've had a number of guys who were average college students all through their freshman and sophomore years when football was not the center of their lives. Then football kind of took over, especially when the team was doing well. And when there's a lot of talk about the guys who will be going pro, it just balloons."

Meleney saw an academic "red zone, a place where you lose a lot of student-athletes, between the second semester of their sophomore year and second semester of their junior year." That's when the best athletes are beginning to compete for starting roles, beginning to get their pictures in the paper and their names announced over the stadium public address systems.

In the old days, that kind of notoriety often allowed jocks to slide in the classroom. There were friendly professors, forgiving deans and presidents, ever-supportive boosters and alums who winked at academic indiscretions. But not anymore.

11

"HAIL to the Victors" blasted over the Doak Campbell public-address system. Then came crowd noise. Then the Michigan fight song again. All at deafening volume, played through the speakers to a stadium deserted but for the 100 players and coaches in shorts.

It was the Thursday-afternoon run-through, the final opportunity to grease the game plan. Assignments, assignments, assignments. That's what Bowden preached. Make sure everyone knew where he was supposed to be; hit every block; run every pass pattern.

"This will be a game of execution, men. Low pads win. Explode off the ball. If there's any question left unanswered, let's deal with it now."

The crowd-noise tape was a standard exercise when the team was preparing for an unfriendly stadium. The offense might have to work without hearing the quarterback's signals. They would move on the snap, sacrificing the advantage of knowing the count for the security of avoiding false-start and motion penalties.

"Crocodile, on movement. Ready, break."

Casey Weldon called the plays in the first-team huddle after taking Mark Richt's signal from the sideline. The players—dressed in shorts, jerseys and helmets—trotted to the line of scrimmage with the tape blaring. Across from them, the scout-team defense held body-size pads to cushion the blocks. This was a minimum-contact rehearsal, intended to imprint the game plan in players' minds.

They ran Crocodile and the fake field goal. They went through the passes and the runs. The nakeds, the screens. The defensive line practiced Check Blue, a made-for-Michigan switch into an eight-man line to frustrate run blocking. Behind the front lurked No. 55, linebacker Marvin Jones, a guided missile tuned to Ricky Powers' frequency.

The specialty teams blooped kickoffs. Keep it away from No. 21, whatever you do. If things went according to plan, Desmond Howard would have to buy a ticket to see the ball on kickoffs and punts.

"Hail to the Victors" crackled at distortion levels. How many times would they hear that on Saturday?

The noise attracted the curious to the stadium, but Bowden had security guards shoo them away. Who knew what Wolverine sympathizers lurked in northern Florida? Was it mere coincidence that night on the radio show when a caller asked about the chances of using Charlie Ward in some kind of double pass? Bowden stopped chewing his bubble gum for a moment when the question came through his headset.

Could they know? Nah, he thought.

"I like your concept," he told the caller. "It would sure catch 'em flat-footed the first time they saw it. You could probably do it once."

By now, Bowden was in the confident stretch of his fear cycle. The two weeks of practice had been enough to put in everything he wanted. More than enough, in fact. "It's a good thing we're finally going to play this dang game," joked Brad Scott. "We're already back into 1984 film."

The players, Bowden thought, had responded about as well as could be expected. Coaches were always probing for proof of intensity and commitment. But the truth was, you could never know how players really felt or what their attitudes implied about their readiness to play. Bowden had seen teams self-destruct on game day after a week of perfect concentration, and he had watched teams miraculously coalesce on Saturday afternoon after stinking up the practice field. You never could tell.

Still, the head coach was pleased to see they had called a players-only meeting after one practice. "This is for the ring," Kirk Carruthers had reminded his teammates. And that was a phrase they repeated together when they broke their last huddle of the day: "We want the ring. Together."

Bowden had stopped practice early on Wednesday, fearing the hitting had grown so intense during the 11-on-11 segments that someone would get hurt. "They would've killed each other if I let them."

The worry over Michigan's offensive front, the concern about Desmond Howard—all that had been diluted by Bowden's growing confidence in his own offense. He could outscore them if he had to.

Except for the fake field goal, the offensive attack was pieced together from plays already in the repertoire. Crocodile had been in the plans since two-a-days. The coaches had altered a pass route here, a block there to customize a strategy for Michigan. But there were no massive rewrites of the basic Seminole script: hurt 'em with a run-pass mix; keep 'em off balance; attack, attack, attack.

Scott had talked to Tulane coaches over the last week and had been comforted with a truism of football preparation: No matter how dedicated your scout team, there was no way to simulate the full-speed attack of a team like Florida State's.

Maybe the grind-'em-out tradition of the Big Ten was a tired cliché. Certainly, the Midwestern schools had been recruiting passers and pass catchers for years. Yet their schedules still provided little exposure to the fastball offenses of the great Southern teams. Who had Michigan played with the team speed of a Miami or a Florida State?

This would be a test for his line, Scott knew. But, finally, he had his best five starters together for the first time all season. Mike Morris' foot was healed sufficiently to allow him to reclaim his spot from McNeil. Now the rookie could be the valuable sixth man. If only he had a reliable seventh and eighth at tackle and center.

Eric Gibbs, the second-team tackle behind Kevin Mancini, had made a surprise comeback from his knee operation. He had practiced this week—tentatively and inconsistently, to be sure, but he had practiced. And that alone was encouraging, thought Scott, because the old Gibbs would have dragged out the rehab period for another couple of weeks. Maybe he was ready to contribute.

When Gibbs went down, Scott had warned him about letting his weight creep up over 300 pounds. He had asked to see his weight every day. And so far, it had held around 300. Another good sign.

Ever since he and Gibbs had their shouting match at the end of two-a-days, Scott had been refiguring his approach with the big guy. Challenging him hadn't worked. So he tried encouragement. When Gibbs had returned to practice, Scott coaxed and complimented him.

"I don't want to give him a sense of false security, but if he thinks I'm proud of him and that I think he's coming along, it helps his confidence. And I think he needs to feel that right now." Scott was determined to redshirt the freshman tackle Juan Laureano, and Gibbs was the closest he had to a ready-to-play backup to Mancini. So Gibbs, who had been left behind on the California trip to punish him for lethargy in practice, would be on the plane to Michigan. And if Mancini needed a break, he would get a chance to prove how far he had come.

Of more immediate concern to Scott, though, was the prospect of playing the Michigan game without his starting center, Robbie Baker. Baker was the roommate of defensive back Leon Fowler, who attracted every virus in North Florida. Both of them were now down with the flu. And the head trainer, Randy Oravetz, had held Baker out of the Thursday run-through, hoping the rest would help him recover for the game on Saturday.

That might mean switching the other tackle, Rob Stevenson, to center. Morris would move to the vacated tackle spot and McNeil to guard. That put two out of the five offensive linemen in positions they didn't normally play. Dangerous, but probably better than the alternative. Which was to simply sub the backup center, Jeff Deremer. Deremer, a junior, was feisty, but overmatched. He stood barely six feet tall and was already playing with a soft cast on one hand.

If Scott chose from all the players available to him, the best backup to Baker might have been Clay Shiver, the freshman. But, again, Scott was determined to preserve a redshirt year. Holding the two freshmen out would pay future dividends, Scott knew. Still, it meant he would become increasingly dependent on the durability of his starters and on the development of Gibbs and the other backups. Once the redshirt decision was made, Scott had to deny the freshmen the practice reps and game experience they'd need to bridge the gap in an emergency. Every week, it would become more difficult to reverse the decision. Already, perhaps, they had reached a point of no return.

It was precisely the risk Bowden had cautioned about in the first week: Don't hold anything back that can help win the national championship. But linemen were not like running backs. You couldn't just give them the ball and count on natural skill and instinct to make up for what they didn't yet know. It took years to build a solid front, hundreds of practice snaps and hundreds more in games. Only desperation could force a coach into throwing true freshmen into the heat of battle on the interior line. And they weren't that desperate. Not yet, thought Scott.

On the other side of the ball, the confidence had grown with each game. And even if Bowden was willing to settle for a scoring contest, Mickey Andrews and his coaches weren't. They wanted to stop the Wolverines in their tracks.

"This," said Andrews, "is what it's all about, to get into a position to play the best. I don't think that offensive line of theirs has been beaten in a couple of years. It's a difficult challenge. But this is why you're a coach. This is one of those times that the only thing better than being on the sidelines is being in the game."

Ironically, if Baker shook the flu, it might be Florida State with the most experienced front five on offense, despite Michigan's much-advertised strength. Wolverine center Steve Everitt had broken his jaw in the Notre Dame game. And replacing him required the same kind of shift Scott had considered. The starting Michigan guard would move to center, and a backup would get his first start at the guard spot. See, thought Scott, no offensive line—not even the nation's top-rated line—could survive key injuries without taking risks.

To fans and the media, the Michigan line without Everitt was still a mythical force. The Big Blue tradition had a life all its own. But to Chuck Amato, who had recruited Everitt for Florida State when he was still a South Florida high schooler, the damage to the Michigan front with Everitt out was one more edge for his guys. When he took his linemen aside Thursday after the run-through in Doak Campbell, Amato used the time for one last speech:

"Michigan has every advantage in this game but one. They've got the tradition. They've got the home crowd. They've got the stadium. They've got Desmond Howard and that huge offensive line.

"But our advantage is that we're better.

"I've studied film for two weeks, men. And I'm convinced we are a better football team. Play as hard as you can, and we'll be sitting here next Friday 4–0."

The betting spread was hovering around two points. The commentators were calling it a toss-up. And Bowden was sensing that he'd get his underdog advantage.

12

Traffic on the freeways and surface roads to Ann Arbor began slowing to a rush-hour crawl three hours before the noon kickoff on Saturday. There would be over 105,000 in the stands. Millions more would watch on ABC. But those who chose to fight the crush to be on hand in person got the extra reward of a perfect September day.

By game time, the temperature would be 60 degrees. Bright sun. Nearly cloudless skies. A brilliant, crisp day that relaxed even the

Floridians, who lived in morbid fear of ice and snow. In the sun, the new grass, replacing the artificial turf that had been Michigan's playing surface since the late '60s, looked thick and deep green. And maybe a little high.

The coaches had been joking for weeks that the Wolverines wouldn't bother with much lawn mowing. They'd want it high and unruly to slow the Florida State speedsters. But speed was relative. And everyone knew that whatever slowed the fast guys would turn the slow ones to statues.

Oh man, finally, thought Bowden. Now, finally, the target was in sight.

The entire offensive coaching staff had gathered in Bowden's suite the night before for the skull session. One last rehearsal of their strategy: "We gotta attack the whole football game," Scott stressed. "Say we jump on them 14 points, and we're lookin' pretty good. Well, there's nothing to say they won't get their running game cranked up and start putting those eight-minute drives together and we don't get the ball.

"Then, when we do get it and get conservative, we'll end up going three and out. We have to attack. We gotta try to score every time. Outscore 'em and force them out of their running game. Then we got 'em where we want 'em."

For his Friday-night closer with the players, Bowden had saved something he'd been thinking about since the pre-Michigan hype began:

"Here's what they're proud of up here in the Big Ten—and if you listen to anything I say, men, listen to this: They say they play smash-mouth football up here. We play finesse football in the South. We're a bunch of finessers. They play smash-mouth. And the nation wants to see, can their smash-mouth beat our finesse?

"Are we finesse? I kinda thought we were a little smash-mouth. I kinda thought we got some bad guys. Let's go smash-mouth them. I'd feel a lot better about that. Let's make those running plays go. And let's smash them."

The players had shifted restlessly when Bowden said that. Some nodded. It was what they had been thinking too. That big Michigan line, Go, Blue, the Big Ten, grind-it-out, smash-mouth football. Enough already. They say we can't do it? They really think that? Well, fine. Nothing beats the advantage of being the underdog.

Bowden watched them closely. He monitored himself too. His juices were flowing. The gum was chomping. It was time to play.

"I want you to play with reckless abandon and total disregard for personal safety," he had told them Friday night. It was another of football's perfect contradictions. Success came from absolute discipline and reckless abandon.

The warm-ups helped ease the pressure. It always felt good to go through the familiar routines, to run and hit. But it was never enough, especially in games like this. Too soon, they had to go back into the tunnel and crowd into the visitors' locker room and try to breathe the stale, anxious air for another twenty minutes.

Sean Jackson and William Floyd couldn't hold it in any longer. They threw forearms into lockers. Equipment flew. The whole row of metal shuddered with each bang.

"Save that dang stuff for the field," Bowden scolded. "Sit down and reflect on what you're going to do."

Most of the Florida State coaches had been in this stadium before in 1986, when a far different Seminole team had lost to the Wolverines. The world of college football had shifted in those five years, but one thing remained: this was a glorious place to play. That crowd—so enormous, spreading up and out from the very edge of the playing field. The top rows looked miles away. Front-row fans could almost touch the players. Now, with the carpet replaced by real grass, Michigan Stadium truly was a kind of shrine. And on this breathtaking day in early autumn, who would want to be anywhere else?

"Now look," said Bowden, "this is a fun place to play. I hope you're loose. Some of you are wound up too tight, and that will hurt you. You'll play better when you're loose.

"You've already paid the price. You've worked hard the last couple of weeks. Now comes the fun time. Keep a smile on your face, and go out there and have a good time. Don't worry about a mistake. Just try to do the best you can. Play as hard as you can. If you make a mistake, it just means you're human."

The coach paced as he talked, moving up and down the row of lockers so all the players could hear. He stopped in the middle of the room, near where the linebackers sat. And he stood almost directly in front of Kirk Carruthers.

"Now, captains going out for the coin toss, I want you to listen. Their offense is so good I'm afraid to kick off to them. I want the ball, 'cause I'm scared they'll get it and run it down our throats. I'm scared they'll get the ball and we can't get it back."

The defensive players glared. What was he saying?

"If I win the toss, I usually take second-half option. But today, I'm scared that they might run it down our defense's throats, so I'm gonna take the ball first."

He paused. No one breathed.

"The hell I am."

The players exhaled almost in unison. Then they laughed.

"Oh no, oh no. That's what they think. If we win the toss, we turn it immediately over to our defense. Of course, if they choose second-half option, we have to receive. But that ain't all bad either.

"Hey, men, when we get the ball, we're gonna come out there attacking. We ain't gonna play scared, we ain't gonna play afraid. We're coming after it. We've worked too hard. Everything is not going to go, but we'll keep throwin' it at 'em and throwin' it at 'em and throwin' it at 'em until something does."

Bowden had made up his mind to start the offensive series with 37 Naked, a rollout pass that gave Weldon the option of running or passing. Two more passes would follow. And the first time the ball was on the right hash, leaving the open field to the left, it would be Crocodile.

Before the pregame prayer, Bowden looked toward the door to make sure the captains were making their way there to be the first out. "And let 'ol Heath go out there with 'em," Bowden said suddenly.

Mike Heath was a Michigan native and a scout-team quarterback. There was no chance that he would play, but Heath had offered to fly up to Ann Arbor on his own if Bowden would let him dress before the home crowd. At the last minute, when a player had come down with the flu, Bowden found a seat for Heath on the team plane. Now he was sending him out with the captains for what might be the biggest game in Seminole history.

"I know he wouldn't like that," the head coach said with a smile as Heath pushed his way to the door.

"Dear Father," Bowden prayed, "thank you for this greatest of all opportunities. It's just like you kinda planned it. All we're gonna do is our best. We might not win it, but we'll try our best. If we play hard, we can't complain.

"I pray that you protect my boys from injury. We pray that nobody gets hurt out there today. Help our boys do the best they can do. Give our coaches wisdom, so that we can be an example for you.

"Lord, we just pray that the best team wins.

"In thy name, Amen."

13

THERE was just one tunnel leading from the locker rooms to the playing field in Michigan Stadium. It emptied onto midfield, across from the press box. So both teams—first the visitors, then the Wolverines—spilled onto the field from its mouth.

Florida State's bench was on the tunnel side of the stadium, but Bowden didn't want the Michigan players running through his team when they entered. So he had the Seminoles take a left when they came out and move out of range of the midfield hoopla. If he had his way, the head coach told his players the night before, "I'd outwait 'em." But ABC was probably calling the shots on the order of entry, said Bowden. "And when they give you $400,000, you come out when they say come out."

Still, when Michigan ran onto their home grass, some of the Seminoles had edged to within shouting distance of the men in blue. Just to let them know they were there. And that it was about to begin.

When Michigan won the toss, Bowden got his wish—the second-half option. And Mickey Andrews' defense collected itself on the sidelines, waiting for the kicking team to bloop the first kickoff high and far short of No. 21. Elvis Grbac and the Wolverine offense took over on their own 29.

To no one's surprise, Ricky Powers, the workhorse tailback who was averaging 170 yards a game, took the first handoff. He bounced off shoulder pads, dodged linebackers and made six yards before he was stopped by a Seminole defensive back. Welcome to the Big Ten.

On second down, Desmond Howard initially lined up in the backfield in the fullback's slot. Then Grbac signaled a shift that split him right. On the opposite side of the line, Terrell Buckley shifted with him. At the snap, Grbac dropped back three steps and fired in the direction of Howard. It was to be a short hitch pass, a chance to immediately get the great receiver into the game and make the Florida State defense respect both the run and the pass. Let the Seminoles get an early taste of Desmond Howard's speed and elusiveness.

But Buckley had read Grbac's drop, had anticipated Howard's position. And he leaped in front of the receiver to snag the interception. Howard slipped down behind him. And only a Michigan tight end was within range to pursue Buckley the 40 yards to the end zone. No contest.

Buck taunted the Michigan player the last ten yards, holding the ball out toward him as he cruised to the touchdown. And as soon as he crossed the goal line, he dropped the ball and ran straight to the end-zone section, where most of the FSU fans were. He leaped high on the stadium wall to return their high-fives, then was engulfed by his defensive teammates.

"How do you do!" exclaimed Keith Jackson in the ABC booth.

Less than a minute was gone; the Florida State offense had not yet been on the field; and the Seminoles were up 7–0 after Dan Mowrey's low point-after kick cleared the crossbar.

As planned, Mowrey again blooped the kickoff, this time to the Michigan up man at his own 34, where the Wolverine offense took over. Six times in a row, Powers carried the ball. Then, when the drive stalled at fourth and one on the FSU 40, the fullback, Burnie Legette, got the call and the first down.

Seven smash-mouth plays. Just as advertised.

Now it was Howard's turn. On first down, he faked an inside move ten yards deep, then ran to the sideline. Buckley lost his footing and didn't catch up until the receiver had hauled in his first reception. A 15-yarder for another first down. An offside penalty against the Seminoles moved the ball five yards closer to the end zone, and Powers took it up the middle for five more. It was first down on the Florida State 13.

"This is power football," Jackson told his TV audience, "and the kind of football that will work most of the day for the Michigan Wolverines."

But Coach Gary Moeller went right back to the pass. On first down, Howard fought off Buckley in the end zone as Grbac lofted the ball high over the cornerback's head. It appeared out of reach for the receiver too; but the Michigan superstar made a diving catch for the touchdown.

It was 7–7 on the scoreboard and 1–1 in the Terrell Buckley–Desmond Howard All-American one-on-one sweepstakes.

After Felix Harris' 16-yard return of the kickoff, the Seminoles started their first offensive series on their own 34. The center, Robbie Baker, was well enough to assume his starter role. So Weldon had the veteran offensive line in front of him for the first time all season.

Scott signaled in 37 Naked. Weldon faked the handoff and rolled left. He eluded the outside linebacker and found Shannon Baker on the left sideline for 13 yards.

The second play was another pass. Again to Baker, this time on the right side of the field. And again for 13 yards. First down now on the Michigan 40. Right hash. And Scott signaled for Crocodile.

When the players on the Florida State bench saw Charlie Ward run onto the field, they edged closer to the sideline for a better view. Would the Michigan coaches spot the substitution? In the TV booth, Jackson and color commentator Bob Griese were still reacting to the back-to-back first-down passes and didn't note Ward's presence until the play was underway.

Ward took Weldon's low throw and only glanced downfield momentarily. He had time. Edgar Bennett had shifted left before the snap to handle the defensive back trying to get at Ward before he ran or threw. The Michigan defense reacted quickly, shifting toward the left side of the field to cut off Ward. And he passed back to Weldon, who had his linemen running interference down the right sideline.

Weldon had every intention of running the ball all the way into the end zone. No slides, no running out of bounds. He could score if he could stay behind the linemen and if they cleared a path quickly enough to escape the pursuit building behind him. But Weldon hit heavy traffic near the 15-yard line and was slowed enough to be a target from the blind side. Linebacker Eric Anderson came across the field behind and to the left of Weldon at full speed.

The impact sprawled the quarterback at the 11 and spilled the ball forward another five yards. Seminole offensive lineman Reggie Dixon recovered it, but the officials had blown the play dead back at the 11.

Weldon felt as if he'd been shot. Get up, he told himself. Don't let 'em see you hurt. The adrenaline helped him to his feet, but pain in his side was intense. He tried to shake it off as the officials moved the chains for the first down. It would be okay. Especially if they could score.

But the Seminoles could get only seven yards in the next three plays and were left with fourth down on the Michigan four. The field goal team ran onto the field.

Dan Mowrey, the kicker, looked up at the goalposts, focused, then nodded to Brad Johnson, his holder. Johnson took the snap. And Mowrey was kicking through empty air just as Floyd crossed in front of him and tucked away the shovel pass. The big fullback's forward momentum carried him through a tackle on the 2 and allowed his shoulders—and the football—to fall into the end zone.

Crocodile, Fake Field Goal Right. Six points. And the trick plays were over.

Mowrey's point-after kick was blocked. Too low. That kept Florida State's margin to six points. And as the Wolverines cranked up another drive, picking up three first downs in the first six plays of their next series, Weldon worried on the sideline. His hip was killing him. He had told Johnson to get ready to go in in case he couldn't make it on the field the next time they got the ball. And the No. 2 quarterback was warming up.

We can't stop these guys. We have to score every time we get the ball, Weldon thought. But what if he couldn't play?

On the field, the Wolverines had run out of steam on the Florida State 30-yard line. On fourth and five, J. D. Carlson—a former Tallahassee high school kicker, just like Mowrey—came out to try a 47-yard field goal. His kick hit the upright where the support post joined the crossbar and bounced through. Now it was a three-point game.

Tiger McMillon made 17 yards on the kickoff return, giving the Seminoles the ball at the 33. And Casey Weldon ran back on the field, inoculated against the pain by his own adrenaline. The only thing this series would require, fortunately, was someone to get the ball to Amp Lee.

The tailback ran right for three yards on the first play, then picked up 20 on a screen pass. On first down at the Michigan 44, he danced through the left side of the line, eluded the linebackers and zagged toward the goal line as the Michigan secondary zigged helplessly in his wake. The 44-yard run was classic make-'em-miss, the longest run of the season. And it qualified for every highlight film of the week.

Mowrey's point-after attempt smacked into the crossbar, just like Carlson's field goal. Only his bounced back. It was shaping up to be a terrible day for the freshman kicker. But the Seminoles were out front by nine, with a little under two minutes left in a breathtaking first quarter.

The Michigan fans had been eerily quiet for most of the first quarter. About 100 of FSU's 400-person marching band had made the trip by bus, and were making more noise than 100,000 Wolverine partisans. The "War Chant" carried well in the giant stadium, and the ceaseless tom-tom drumming was going to leave Michiganders with headaches long after the Seminoles pulled out of town. This was not Go, Blue football. In fact, it was something of a track meet.

For the remainder of the first half, the two sides exchanged possessions with no score. Then early in the second period, after Buckley set up the FSU offense with a 30-yard punt return, Weldon hit Warren Hart with a 20-yard touchdown pass. A try for two points failed, but the Seminoles led by 15 points. At least for a few seconds.

On Michigan's next possession, Grbac, throwing from midfield on third down, again found Howard streaking for the end zone. Buck tried a last-second dive to deflect it from Howard's fingertips, but the Michigan receiver caught it falling forward in the back of the end zone. Carlson's kick narrowed the gap to eight points.

Michigan got even closer on the next series after intercepting Weldon on the FSU 20 and powering the ball into the end zone. The Wolverines' attempt to tie the score with a two-point play failed, however. And after the kickoff, the Seminoles killed Michigan's hopes for catch-up momentum by driving the length of the field to reestablish the eight-point margin. Mowrey again missed the extra point. Then he delivered the ball to Desmond Howard on the kickoff, giving the most-feared returner in college football the chance for a 48-yard return. The kicker had to prevent the touchdown himself with a last-ditch tackle.

With five and a half minutes left in the half, Michigan took over on the Florida State 40-yard line and made good use of Powers and wideout Yale VanDyne to move the ball to the 3. But the Florida State defensive line stiffened when Legette and Powers tried to mash it over. On third down, when Grbac attempted to lob a pass to tight end Tony McGee in the end zone, Howard Dinkins snatched the interception, robbing Michigan of a chance to pull within two, or even tie the score, before the half ended.

14

THE crowded visitors' locker room was a high-energy tangle at halftime. Weldon headed immediately to the trainers' area, where the doctors examined his bruised left hip. They injected him with cortisone and painkiller. He would feel like a cripple tomorrow, but he needed thirty more minutes of football.

Mowrey wouldn't let his disappointment show, but he was shell-shocked from the missed kicks. John Wimberly, the backup punter, pleaded for a shot at the point-after attempts. He would return to the field during halftime ceremonies and try a few practice kicks. Richie Andrews, a former Florida State kicker recently cut from the NFL, would coach him.

Go for it, Wimberly was told. What was there to lose? Besides, if the first half was any indication, an extra point or a field goal here or there wouldn't be enough to win. This game was going to be about making and stopping touchdowns.

The pregame anxiety was history. With only a few minutes left before the third period began, the cramped locker room all but vibrated with the sense of looming possibility. It was in their grasp.

"Hey, men, you've got an eight-point lead. If they don't score, you and I could be celebrating right now," Bowden told them.

"Now listen, those guys are not going to quit fighting. And we're not going to quit fighting. Defense, don't let them get the big play. They can't score on you if you don't give up the big play.

"Offensive line, I tell you again, the game is in your hands. Protect the passer."

The offensive coaches had made up their minds to come back out with the mash attack, to establish the running game in the first possession of the second half. So when the Seminoles took over on their own 26 after the kickoff, the first five calls were for Edgar Bennett and Amp Lee. And the Seminoles muscled their way to the Michigan 25.

There would be no score, however, because Bennett, in a determined effort to reach the ball over the goal line on a first-down power play, fumbled. But the Seminoles got the ball right back when the defense forced Michigan to punt from its own end zone, and Weldon was able to hook up with Turral for a 20-yard touchdown.

The catch was classic E.T., or at least the E.T. the coaches and players knew to be hidden under the surface of his unpredictability. He was the primary target on a pattern to the outside, and he had a half step on the defensive back when Weldon drew his arm back to throw. But just as he was releasing the ball, the quarterback was blindsided, and there wasn't enough on the ball to lift it into Turral's path.

When the receiver saw the falling trajectory of the pass, he was running at nearly full speed and his forward motion should have taken him out of reach of the short ball. But he curled quickly to the inside, throwing his right leg out as a braking pivot, sliding to the ground as he reached back toward the ball. The Michigan defender, almost on Turral's back, tried to make the same turn. But by the time he got around and reached out to block the pass, the ball was already below his hand and dropping into Turral's grasp an inch above the turf.

When he got back to his feet, Turral raised his arms with the ball and leaped into his teammates' arms. Then he looked for an official to hand over the ball. It was the best catch by a wideout so far. And maybe, thought Eason, it was a harbinger of what was to come.

Weldon clenched his fist: Yes!

For the remainder of the third period and early into the fourth, the two defenses dueled. Both quarterbacks threw interceptions, but neither offense seemed capable of capitalizing on the turnovers. As time became a factor, however, the two-touchdown spread put all the pressure on Michigan.

The Wolverines had their best chance to reclaim the momentum when Howard returned a punt to the FSU 20. Three consecutive running plays left them with fourth-and-one on the Seminole 11, and just about every one of the 106,145 people in the stands had a pretty good idea of what had to happen next. This was a Michigan team with 100 years of grind-it-out tradition. Position by position, its offensive line averaged over 290 pounds, outweighing Florida State's by 30 pounds a man. The Wolverines had come into this game averaging 4.8 yards a carry when they ran the ball. Now they needed just one for the first down.

Powers was back in the backfield. But it was the fullback, Legette, who took the handoff from Grbac and took one step toward the left side of the line behind guard Doug Skene, who was starting his first game. There he immediately ran into two problems. Carl Simpson, playing across from Skene, had beaten the guard off the ball and pushed him back into the fullback's lap. At the same time, the guided missile, No. 55, was filling all the airspace over the intended hole.

It was a Marvin Jones specialty on goal-line, short-yardage pushes. Anticipating a leap over the top by the fullback, Jones timed his own jump to collide in midair. He was bigger than most backs and had a better running start; so the laws of physics usually were on the linebacker's side. The only thing that saved Legette from decapitation was that he had no time to jump. Jones sailed by.

By this time, though, the line of scrimmage was utterly clogged. Lavon Brown, the Seminoles' strong safety, had run around the pile on the outside and was closing in on Legette from behind. And linebacker Ken Alexander completed the sandwich from the front.

The official spotted the ball on the 11. No gain. The Seminoles took over on downs.

If Chuck Amato had been looking for proof that his defensive line could rise to a big-game challenge, he needed only that play. So far, in fact, the second half belonged to Mickey Andrews' three-deep platoons, which had arrived in Ann Arbor rated second best in the nation statistically but untested against the big boys. There would be no doubters after this.

Still, Weldon was frustrated that he and his offensive teammates couldn't put the game away once and for all. They had to make something happen on this drive. But when they took over on the 11, they again struggled against a determined Michigan defense and soon were backed up to their own 12 with a third down and nine yards to go for the first.

Just as everybody in America figured the Wolverines would be running on fourth and one, it was a safe bet that Florida State, in this situation, would pin its first-down hopes on a pass. So far in the second half,

Michigan's defensive tactic on obvious passing downs was to drop most of its people into coverage, hoping to tie up Weldon's receivers until he was forced to throw it away or until he was chased down by the defensive linemen. The trade-off in that strategy was the lack of a pass rush. With the extra guys committed to coverage, the defensive linemen had no help in putting pressure on the passer. And if they couldn't beat their blocks and chase down the quarterback, Weldon could hold the ball until his receivers got open. It would turn into sandlot football: everybody out for the pass. And no one wanted to play a Bobby Bowden team under sandlot rules.

Weldon dropped back, looking for receivers. The Seminole offensive linemen stayed with their blocks until finally the pocket slowly collapsed. Still, the quarterback waited, looking for an open man. He rolled back into his own end zone, then out to the five. Mancini turned his man inside and pushed him to the ground, giving Weldon outside scrambling room on the right sideline. Seconds passed. Thousands were on their feet in the corner of the end zone screaming for the sack.

When a quarterback scrambles, the receivers' rule is to work back toward the ball. So Shannon Baker, who had run his pattern on the left, had turned back inside and was moving into the open in the middle of the field. Bennett, who had been covered on the right sideline, now reversed himself and moved back toward the center too.

Weldon finally was overtaken at the 10 and was hit as he winged the ball toward Baker. Bennett, however, was already at full speed and got to the spot first. His leaping catch in front of the surprised wideout was good for 28 yards.

Bowden came back with another passing call, a dip pattern with the tight end as the primary receiver. And the way it played out may have illustrated more than anything else how Weldon and his offensive line meshed this day.

When the quarterback pulled away from the center and looked to Warren Hart, he saw Hart was covered. He turned to the No. 2 target in the progression, the Z wideout. But Weldon saw a defender in the passing lane. Too dangerous. How about No. 3? That was the tailback, but someone was on Lee too. So it was back to option one, the tight end, who after all this time was wide open on the right sideline. Hart caught it for 31 yards and another first down.

The Seminoles moved it to the Michigan 15, where they had seven yards to go to turn a fourth down into first-and-goal. Weldon called time-out.

When the quarterback, Bowden and Brad Scott convened on the

sideline, the discussion was a hot one. They were on the 15-yard line. Their kicker had missed three of four extra points. A field goal seemed out of the question. So what do you call?

Bowden wanted to go right to the end zone. Maybe with 7 Waggle Special, the pass they hit for the first-play touchdown against Tulane. Scott counseled caution. How about something safer? Something that put the ball into the hands of Amp Lee in the open field. Let Amp make 'em miss.

Bowden let himself be persuaded. They would go for a screen pass to Lee. It might go all the way. It might go for the first down. But it wouldn't be intercepted and run back. At worst, it would leave them short of the first and force the Wolverines to operate deep in their own territory. The Seminole defense had proved what it could do. And no matter what happened on the next Michigan possession, with over six minutes left, the Seminoles would get another chance to ice the game.

Lee caught Weldon's short screen pass and danced his way close to the 8-yard line. There was confusion over the spot. And there would have to be a measurement. But there was also a flag on the play. A Michigan defender had grabbed Weldon's face mask in the Florida State backfield. When the measurement came up short of the first down, the Seminoles opted for the five-yard penalty and another fourth down on the 10.

Florida State took another time-out. Weldon argued on the sideline for the mash play. The offensive line had been moving the Michigan defense off the ball. Give it to the fullback. Let Bennett get the two yards they needed for the first. Then they would have four downs to play with.

Bowden, however, saw the second chance on fourth down as a message from the gods: Attack. He wanted the pass into the end zone. Weldon looked at him, then shrugged. He would never turn down the chance to throw.

"7 Waggle Special on 2."

The Wolverine defense was coming on the snap. Weldon rolled right and looked into the end zone. There was Lonnie Johnson, wide open. And the quarterback zipped the ball just as he was caught from the side. Touchdown. John Wimberly kicked his first-ever college point-after, and the Seminoles were up 44–23.

Three touchdowns should have been enough to put them out of danger with six minutes left. But the thought never occurred to Bowden. To him, it was still a shoot-out. Especially while No. 21 was on the field. And Michigan did nothing to make him feel more relaxed.

The Wolverines took over near midfield and drove the ball into the end zone in five plays. Four were passes, but none to Howard. Grbac kept the ball on a quarterback draw for the two-point conversion. Then, Carlson kicked the perfect onside kick, and Michigan recovered on the Florida State 46 with just under five minutes left to play.

Suddenly, the fans were alive again, on their feet and stomping to "Hail to the Victors." On the Florida State sideline, whatever sense of relief there had been after the last Seminole touchdown was now replaced by something else. Not panic, maybe, but surely concern.

Enough, thought Andy Urbanic, the assistant athletic director. He didn't even want to watch. He had been the logistics guy for the trip, booking the team planes, worrying about the boosters' reservations and hotel accommodations. The whole thing had been an ulcer since August. And now it wouldn't end.

The game had been going on for hours. It would keep going like this, apparently. Like some nightmarish tape loop of football anxiety. His boss, athletic director Bob Goin, had been right. Asked by reporters before the game how he felt, Goin had told them he just wanted to go into a coma and wake up when it was over.

Well, if it was going to end badly, or even if they were going to win but endure five minutes of anguish until the end, they could do it without him. So Urbanic left the sideline and made his way back to the locker room. It was cool and dark after the brilliant afternoon sun. He stretched out on a training table and closed his eyes.

Back on the field, the Seminole defense now had the luxury of ignoring the run threat. To make up the 13-point deficit, Michigan had to play come-from-behind football. Which meant passing. And which, for Florida State, meant coming after Grbac with a vengeance.

The Michigan quarterback picked up a first down and found receivers for a total of 26 yards. But he was sacked twice for minus 14. So after five plays, the Wolverines faced a fourth and 14 on the Florida State 36. And the Seminoles threw the whole defense into the rush.

Grbac never had a chance.

Outside linebacker Reggie Freeman hit his arm just as it came forward with a desperation pass. The ball blooped straight up, and Toddrick McIntosh gathered it in. For the next couple of weeks, teammates would tease the 270-pound defensive lineman about how long it took him to rumble the 49 yards to the Michigan end zone. But it was the crowning blow for a defense that ended up accounting for two touchdowns on its own as it derailed one of the most lauded offenses in the nation.

Urbanic was still lying on the training table when he heard Goin shout. The athletic director had been unable to stand the tension on the sideline and had retreated to the locker room too. He had been pacing and listening to the game on the radio in an adjacent alcove, out of Urbanic's sight.

When McIntosh made the interception, Goin ran into the main locker room yelling. The two men looked at one another, then ran out into the tunnel to rejoin the team. McIntosh was still heaving on the bench when they got to the sideline.

There were three minutes left. Michigan was driving against Andrews' last batch of substitutes. But everybody in the stadium knew that whatever happened in the remaining time was meaningless.

James Chaney was standing on the bench, facing the crowd and crowing: "I'm the little Florida State nose guard that had to face the big Michigan line, and here I am, still standing." Marvin Jones held an "Elvis is dead" sign for the ABC cameras. And on the field, Elvis Grbac was replaced by backup Todd Collins.

Collins completed four consecutive passes to put Michigan within 17 yards of the Florida State end zone. But Jesse Johnson fumbled a fifth reception at the 13 and lost the ball. The backup defense had refused even Michigan's last-ditch push for pride.

Weldon came on the field to run out the clock for the last minute.

"That is the greatest feeling in the world, to kneel down and watch that clock tick away, to see that scoreboard and know the game is over and that we won."

The scoreboard showed 51–31. Kirk Carruthers stood in the end zone facing the cheering Florida State fans and held aloft a chunk of Michigan turf destined for the Sod Cemetery. Everywhere around him, his teammates danced the frenzied dance of relief and victory. They held their fingers high. They were No. 1. And there was not a dissenting voice in college football.

Part V

"ARE YOU REALLY NO. 1?"

1

THE deep, disabling pain didn't hit Casey Weldon until Monday. Victory adrenaline had kept him and his teammates flying even after they stepped off the plane Saturday night in Tallahassee, where an excited crowd greeted them. Incredible, thought the quarterback. Absolutely incredible.

Fans lined the wide corridor between the arrival gate and the airport lobby. They held signs and cheered when they saw the players, many of whom deplaned wearing new blue Michigan caps. They would be the headgear of choice for the remainder of the season.

Hands reached out to touch players. There were cheers of excited gratitude. Thank you, thank you. "We're No. 1."

No team before them had come to Michigan Stadium and scored 51 points against the Wolverines. "Who's No. 1? Don't even ask," wrote Joe Falls, in the Detroit *News*. "Never in the more than 100 years they've been playing football around here has a team like Florida State ever played in Ann Arbor."

Saturday night, Weldon ended up at Ken's, a college tavern near the campus, with some of the other players. Robbie Baker lifted the quarterback atop a pool table when ESPN showed highlights of the game and featured Weldon in a special case-for-the-Heisman report.

"Casey, Casey, Casey!" the crowd chanted. It was glorious. And there was no point paying attention to the dull throb building in his side.

Monday, however, was another story.

One of the great myths about sports is that the more you play, the healthier you are. That's true only for the noncompetitive, recreational athlete. Those who aspire to elite levels quickly move through training for fitness and health and into another zone. At the top, whether it's in Olympic track and field or professional basketball or football, the stress of training and competing increases the risk of injury and sickness. In football, of course, the collisions greatly add to that risk. So much so that most players in top college programs and in the pros can assume they will sustain crippling injuries.

Three doctors were always on the sidelines for Florida State games. Head trainer Randy Oravetz had a staff of two full-time assistants and numerous student helpers working exclusively on football during the season. All were devoted to tending the torn muscles and tendons, the twisted joints, the broken and dislocated bones, the open lacerations and the concussions that are routine in the sport. A player who practiced and played for Florida State for the full five years faced an 80 percent chance that he would have to undergo major surgery.

It was part of the game.

Because they spent so much time there, getting taped before practices and games and tending to hurts afterward, the training room was the players' lounge. Reporters weren't allowed. Coaches made infrequent visits. A dozen players at a time might stretch out on the big pads atop the training tables. Most needed attention for some wound or assurance they were healing from the last one. Some were just there to hang out while their teammates got treatment.

On Sundays, every player who got into a Saturday game was required to check in to have bruises and sprains evaluated. Many of them hung around to catch Bowden's afternoon TV show. As the coach walked viewers through the game highlights, the players would razz one another for tackles missed and passes dropped. They all made mental notes of whom the coach picked out to compliment and who didn't get noticed. After big games, the push to be near the TV created two tiers of viewers, those perched up high on the pads and those who sat on the floor below them.

On the Sunday after the Michigan game, the training room filled faster than usual. And not just for the Bowden TV show. Oravetz would have a long list of walking wounded for the coaches' meeting Monday morning.

Even without the added effect of bouncing off 290-pounders all afternoon in Ann Arbor, the players were at that stage in the season when they had little chance to be free from pain. They had recovered from two-a-days and cruised through a couple of games with minor hurts. But now they were entering the middle third of the season, when the cumulative effects of football would begin to overcome conditioning and luck.

On every Saturday but one from now until December, the players would be asked to sacrifice their bodies, to play with reckless abandon and with utter disregard for personal safety. All of which meant that from now on the team would be in a state of steady physical disintegration. Their bodies could never fully recover from any hurt. And each week new wounds would come.

As the season wore on, Oravetz would, by necessity, become more and more of a factor in the coaches' sessions. Football coaches made a distinction between being hurt and being injured. They expected players to play hurt. It was a test of will, of pride. It was natural for players to exaggerate a bruise or a muscle pull to get out of practice. But only a certified injury should excuse them.

Oravetz and the doctors were in charge of separating the hurts from the injuries, of catching the practice shirkers and—most important—of identifying those players who would hide real problems for fear of losing ground in the competition for a job. But the doctors had little direct contact with the coaching staff. It was Oravetz who sat in the chair just behind Bowden in the morning meetings, when the coaches were desperate for good news and cranky about medical setbacks.

The coaches were at war. No matter how humanistic their approach, they were training soldiers for battle. Didn't Randy know they needed these guys?

In those sessions, the trainer would have to be sure of his opinions and diplomatic in his answers. The conference room could be a minefield. Although his desire to win was as strong as everybody else's, Oravetz had a slightly different mission. His clients were somebody else's victims.

Complicating everything, of course, was the suck-it-up tradition of the game. The presumption of virility is so built into football that an injury that takes a player out of action is sometimes seen as a character flaw, as a sign of weakness. Players could easily be made to feel defensive and guilty about their hurts. Were they really injured or just afraid?

Coach Bowden knew that much of his motivation to win came from his fear of losing. Similarly, fear of humiliation—of being thought weak or cowardly—is a major motivating force for athletes at all levels. So while many football players might welcome a chance to skip practice drills to heal, almost all resisted a diagnosis that would keep them out of a game. Playing hurt was a point of pride and an antidote to anonymity. Each Saturday they didn't play, they disappeared a little.

Coaches, in their hearts, knew the danger of exploiting players' fragile sense of self-worth, especially if it meant risking further injury by allowing them to play with serious injuries. But the heat of battle altered the context of decision making. Twisted limbs and nasty bruises that might turn lives inside out in normal households and everyday offices were simple annoyances in football. Unless a player was clearly disabled by broken bones or major surgery, the issue was always up in the air. When can we get him back? And how effective is he going to be when we do?

Inevitably, a brutal kind of calculus came into play: Am I better off with my starter at 75 percent than I am with his backup at 100?

Oravetz always found himself playing the coaches' conscience. "You can rush him back if you want," he would say, "but if he reinjures it, you've lost him for the season and maybe for his career. You make the call."

The coaches would grumble that "ol' Randy is trying to do our coaching for us." But they would give in, especially when they saw the trainer's face redden with the attempt to control his anger at being challenged. Sometimes, he simply had to say the words: "He cannot play."

Casey Weldon could play. But it wasn't going to be easy. He lay atop a table in the training room, grimacing, while an assistant trainer wired him into a machine that would electrically stimulate the muscle and tissue to accelerate the healing process. He would do this twice a day for the next couple of weeks. Maybe he would get another cortisone injection. But no matter what he did, the welt on his hip would grow huge and blue-black ugly. And it would be at least three days before he could throw with any authority.

Weldon, however, never considered sitting out a week. The team—and he himself—had too much at stake. And once the Florida State doctors and trainers cleared him, no one questioned the decision.

Playing football is what football players do.

2

IT took less than a day after the team's return from Ann Arbor for the panic to begin. The first hint may have been Bryan Burwell's column in the combined edition of the Detroit *News* and *Free Press* on Sunday, September 29:

All game long, Florida State's No. 1 ranked Seminoles had stomped up and down Michigan Stadium's thick emerald field as if they owned every precious inch of the manicured grass. And now, as the final gun sounded at the end of FSU's 51–31 belting of third-ranked Michigan, college football's newest dark knights of deportment were dead set on proving this land was their land.

An entire phalanx of Seminoles swept across the south end of the field, snatching up huge clumps of thick green turf, waving it in the air like a prized trophy worthy of mounting, then tossing large divots into the end zone seats to an excited entourage of Seminole fans doing their rhythmic tomahawk chop. Along the sidelines, Casey Weldon, the satin-smooth FSU quarterback, gripped a patch of grass in his hands, wiggled his index finger in the air, then mugged for ABC's cameras.

Linebacker Marvin Jones stood on an aluminum bench, stretched his arms out wide and hooted, "Is THAT all the Big 10 is about? Come on, is THAT it?" A few paces away, linebacker Kirk Carruthers, FSU's East Lansing import, gazed wild-eyed into the stands and hollered, "No finesse, baby! Just pure smash-mouth, just pure smash-mouth! . . ."

Ah yes, here we go again. Just when college football thought it had rid itself of Miami's gloating Hurricanes, along comes a team with even more talent and with even less capacity to blush. Say hello to the brashest, most talented team in college football, Florida State.

It was the inevitable reaction to an invasion. As sour grapes go, Burwell's column was practically a tribute. "Like 'em or loathe 'em," he wrote farther down in the piece, "Florida State is the most dynamic, most electric, most entertaining football team in the land. . . .

"This was supposed to be the best game in college football, and for a while it looked like it. But then football's greatest law took over: Talent prevailed.

"There was too much of it on Florida State's side of the ball for Michigan to handle. The Wolverines could have scored 48 points or 68 points. Somehow Florida State would have scored 88."

But deep in the paranoid souls of Florida State fans, something snapped. They were stirred by suggestions that Seminole players might behave indecorously. They had seen Weldon on TV after the game, grinning and waving in triumph. They could imagine the players mounting the benches to taunt the crowd. And they cringed at the thought of the assault on the end-zone turf. One alum wrote:

I hesitate to write this letter because I hate to "swim against the tide" or urge you to do so. However, yesterday I was talking with Chancellor Reed and he confirmed that the reported taunting by our football team in Michigan actually occurred—even though it was denied by Coach Bowden. This incident, alone, would be disappointing enough; but it is merely a continuation of conduct which has been condoned by our University for several years— since Deion Sanders.

As a graduate from FSU's Business School and College of Law, former student leader . . . and loyal alumni [sic], I urge you to initiate immediate action within our athletic department to return our athletic programs to the level of respect that the University and, we alumni, deserve.

The letter to Florida State president Dale Lick came from J. Michael Huey of Tallahassee. Copies went to Bowden, Weldon, faculty representative Chuck Ehrhardt and Board of Regents chancellor Charles B. Reed. Others, far less articulate and far nastier in tone, poured in, echoing similar sentiments. As usual, Sue Hall, Bowden's secretary, trashed the ugliest ones and passed along only those that seemed to require the coach's response.

Letters to the editor in the *Democrat* reflected the same apparent concern. A debate was building. Within forty-eight hours of a victory that seemed the perfect symbolic culmination of their long efforts to be included on the party lists of the nation's elite, Florida State boosters were consumed with worry about their table manners.

Bowden knew he had a responsibility to monitor those manners, but he also was determined to allow for reasonable displays of emotion. In fact, he encouraged them. But the issue worried the sports information director, Wayne Hogan, who came to Bowden's office Monday afternoon. The media attention would only increase, Hogan warned, and if players didn't watch themselves they would be victimized by ambush interviews that embarrassed everybody.

"You or somebody has to say something to the players," he told the coach.

The Michigan game situation may have been unique, with TV crews hanging around the bench in the closing minutes of the game. "I tell you what happened," said Hogan. "They got mugged by cameras on the field as soon as the game ended, before they could get to the locker room. And some of them said some things on camera that didn't come over so good."

"Such as?" Bowden wanted to know.

Hogan explained how Casey had waved the chunk of Michigan turf and told the ESPN camera that this was the same grass that ESPN commentators had predicted they'd never take back to Tallahassee for the Sod Cemetery.

"I think you're worrying about something that's not worth worrying about," said the coach.

But Hogan wanted to make his point. "It's just that the reaction from the public is that this just didn't come across well. Our kids have been so respectful, and this wasn't really their fault. They stuck those cameras right in their faces. Maybe the way to handle that in the future is that when the game is over, they don't need to be standing around out there."

Bowden was less than convinced. "But that's the biggest win they ever had. Let 'em enjoy it. That don't worry me, to tell you the truth. If we said derogatory things, that would be one thing. If we called those guys yellow-bellied something or other or said, 'Michigan stinks,' that would really bother me. But gosh, you can't take the excitement out of winning a game like that. That was a big game for Florida State University.

"I hate to shut 'em out from the press. I ain't worried about it."

Hogan tried a different tack. "I guess I'm more worried than anything about Casey."

Weldon and Michigan's Desmond Howard were everybody's front-runners for the Heisman Trophy. Howard was the epitome of the self-made, say-and-do-no-evil athlete award voters loved. And he played in a program that allowed for little backsliding. Weldon was also a likable straight arrow. But too much smirking on national TV could undercut that impression quickly and doom him with the Heisman voters.

Bowden, however, threw the concern right back in Hogan's lap. "Now, you can help him more than anybody by telling him how people will react to that sort of thing, with him in the running for the Heisman. I don't want to talk to him about that, because I don't want him to get the idea that I'm promoting him. 'Cause I got Amp Lee, who might want it; Edgar Bennett, who might want it; Terrell Buckley, who might want it. But you can say, 'Hey, you can hurt yourself.' "

Was he ignoring a genuine trouble spot in the program? Bowden thought not. He knew he couldn't afford to be inattentive to image concerns. Public perceptions counted for too much in college football. But he had to think of the players too. Emotional rewards were the principal paybacks for the effort he required of them.

When they were heavily favored, coaches tried to appeal to players' "professionalism" to carry them to decisive victories without mental letdowns and sloppy play. But they seldom got away with it. Colleges have structured sports to minimize the rewards of professionalism and to maximize the appearance of the amateur ideal. They have created an arena where the institutions get the money and the athletes get the intangibles—pride in self and in team and the temporary satisfaction of being the best.

Supporters of college sports were proud of that distinction. So why were they so embarrassed when the emotion spills out in every direction?

Bowden was a master at cultivating fan relationships with Florida State football. But there was a time to rein in players for public relations reasons and there was a time to preserve a little space for them to enjoy themselves. As long as they won, Bowden suspected, it would be his voice that carried the most weight.

To Huey, Bowden wrote his own reply:

You sent me a copy of your letter to Dr. Lick about the conduct of our football team, FSU vs. Michigan game.

We go to Ann Arbor and win the biggest game of our career, before the biggest crowd of any event in FSU history, our players play their hearts out and win and you expect us not to be enthusiastic.

When TV cameras are allowed on the football field immediately after an emotional game and stick a camera in the faces of our players, anything might be said that is regrettable the next day.

I would like for you to list for me, categorically, exactly which players did what and said what that gives you a right to write such a letter.

3

"You might as well enjoy whatever you're going to do this morning," Brad Scott told Bowden in Monday's eight-thirty meeting. "Because you're not going to like this."

As soon as they had graded out the Michigan tapes on Sunday, the assistant coaches had jumped into preparation for the following week. And when Bowden had asked first thing Monday, "What can you tell me about Syracuse?" Jim Gladden had been the first to answer.

"They are a bitch, Coach."

That's when Scott told Bowden to be prepared for the worst. After escaping the runback threat of Desmond Howard in Ann Arbor, they were now set to go against Qadry Ismail, brother of former Notre Dame great Rocket Ismail. Qadry's nickname: the Missile.

After four games, the Missile was averaging nearly twice as many yards every time he touched the ball as his brother had at this point in 1990. He was also nearly doubling the output of that other Notre Dame superstar, Tim Brown, after the first four games of his 1987 Heisman-winning year.

Ismail had already scored on reverses, kick returns and pass receptions. He was a frightening weapon and one reason Syracuse would come into Doak Campbell undefeated and ranked 10th in the nation. The Orangemen had plenty of reason to be upset-minded. They had already trashed one fabled Florida team, the Gators. And if they could get past

the Seminoles, they seemed to have a downhill run through the remainder
of their schedule.

"They can quietly and secretly be in the national championship game
on January 1," said Scott. "And don't think their coaches aren't pumping
that."

So this week, Bowden wouldn't be operating alone in the fear zone.
Everything the assistants saw pointed to trouble. The players were too
beat-up to push hard in practice. Which meant mental preparation was
crucial. And coming off the Michigan win, they were likely to be flat.

There couldn't be a worse time for a letdown.

Syracuse was not one of those stereotypical Northern teams with big,
immobile linemen and a cloud-of-dust running game. The Orangemen
had speed demons on both sides of the ball, including six recruited out
of Florida under the noses of Florida State and Florida. They had a
kicker, Pat O'Neill, who had put 23 of his 25 kickoffs into the end zone
so far this year, 19 of them unreturned. They played an option offense
with two quarterbacks. And that could be bad news.

Mickey Andrews' defense didn't see enough option attacks to feel
entirely at ease with assignments and adjustments. The coaches could
scheme a plan against it, but they might not be able to get the scout
team to simulate the pace of the game.

How about bringing Charlie Ward over to the scout team to help? His
speed and elusiveness were the closest thing the Seminoles had to the
Orangemen's offensive game.

The offensive coaches wanted to help the defense, but they were
nervous about donating Ward's services. Weldon was hurting and might
not be able to play. That left Johnson, then Ward, then Felder as backups.
And Ward was considered a kind of secret weapon.

Anyone who had seen Charlie Ward take over a scrimmage was
tempted to believe he could win a game entirely on his own. If a game
plan exploded in their faces, if nothing else seemed to work, sending in
No. 17 and letting him improvise was always a desperation alternative.
They probably wouldn't risk it, but it was fun just to think about it. And
none of the offensive coaches wanted Charlie Ward too far away from
their huddles. What if they needed him to win the game and he had been
running Syracuse plays all week?

Bowden sided with the defense. "Scout teams must have the perfect
look." But they all knew that there would be a tug-of-war in practices,
with the offense gradually subverting the defense's plan to keep Ward on
the upper field. As the week wore on, the offense would find it impossible
to do without him. Fortunately, another scout-team quarterback would

move into the option role, diminishing the demand for the offense's secret weapon.

There was a more pressing issue—the kicking game. Mowrey had missed three of four extra-point attempts against Michigan. And that had scared Bowden out of even thinking about field goals. It hadn't cost them anything in Ann Arbor, but what if a game came down to a kick? Something had to be done.

Bowden thought aloud with his coaches: "You've really got a problem when you're scared to kick an extra point. I think he'll be all right at home. It just gets to him on the road. He'll outgrow it one of these days, but the point is, can we get away with sitting back and waiting?"

Probably not. So they had better find a reliable backup fast. Maybe it was Wimberly. Maybe it was Gerry Thomas, a walk-on who had kicked well in high school. But they had to get on it. By the time Florida State hit the road against Louisiana State and Louisville, Bowden intended to be confident—at the very least in the ability to kick extra points.

"I ain't giving up on Dan, but I can't guarantee he'll be our No. 1 guy either."

The other side of the kicking game was troubling too. They had planned to kick away from Howard in Ann Arbor, and he still got a couple of runbacks. Now they were facing the Missile. Were they giving up too much yardage with bloop kicks away from dangerous return men? "We can't do that all year, can we?"

For part of every meeting before the Syracuse game, the coaches would debate kick coverage. It was hard not to point fingers. Maybe, griped the defense, if the offense would let the specialty teams have some of its more talented players, they could do better. Maybe the defense should be contributing more of its studs, came the rejoinder. The bottom line was unavoidable: Script more time in practice to work on kick coverage and returns.

What was oddly absent in all of this fretting about option attacks and kicking was time to relish the position Florida State had found itself in. Just last week it had achieved one of the greatest victories in school history, a win by 20 points against the No. 3-ranked Wolverines at Michigan. Now the Seminoles owned the nation's longest winning streak, 10 games. They were America's No. 1 team for the fifth consecutive week and were scheduled as ABC's principal TV game for the second Saturday in a row.

This was the top of college football. And, one of the most precarious, most agonizing perches in athletics.

In Bowden's scenario of the chase for the championship ring, the

Seminoles could have afforded one loss at this point. They could have been toppled by either BYU or Michigan. That would have dropped them in the polls, but they would have had three major games left to regain the title—Miami, Florida and the bowl game.

Miami, Bowden believed, could be counted on to remain near the top until the Hurricanes came to Doak Campbell on November 16. Florida was churning its way through the Southeastern Conference and would probably be highly ranked when Florida State arrived in Gainesville two weeks after the Miami game. And a bowl bid against another top-five team would guarantee their opportunity in the final stretch.

Florida State could have lost one early, then come back strong against Miami, Florida and the bowl team. That way the Seminoles would have ducked the pressure of being the No. 1 target in college football through half the season and still controlled their own destiny.

But now, there was only one realistic route to the national championship. They had to win them all.

Each week they remained the top-ranked team they risked everything. Gone for good was the psychological edge of being the underdog. Now they would be *expected* to win. It was their job. Already, they were 18-point favorites against Syracuse. And after Saturday came a five-game series in which they could embarrass themselves if they failed to dominate each opponent.

From now on, the teams they faced risked nothing. A win turned them into heroes. By upsetting the nation's No. 1 team, they could turn their programs around, win security for their coaches and get a leg up in recruiting. The Seminoles could only hope to maintain the status quo—to defend the championship they had not yet won.

"Don't let 'em take our ring."

Whether that was enough to motivate young men 19 to 22 years old, whose principal rewards were in the currency of emotion, remained to be seen. But from Monday on, there was precious little joy in the meeting rooms and around the lockers in the athletic center. Fans were writing letters to the editor. The coaches were getting faxed suggestions for how to improve the kicking game. And while ABC was wiring Doak Campbell for Saturday's national broadcast, everybody settled into the grim routines of self-preservation. Florida State was under siege.

4

"Dɪᴅ everybody go to class today? Shannon? Matt? Knox?"

John Eason went down the list of his receivers. It was part of the routine for his segment meetings. But academics were on the coach's mind even more today. They were nearing midterms, and early reports were not good.

Of primary concern were the twenty-two players Mark Meleney had reported on before they left for Ann Arbor. Some had already exhausted all appeals and probations and would certainly be gone if they didn't make the target GPAs. For most, it would mean appealing to deans for second chances. Although the worries over keeping players eligible was a regular ritual, there were just too many names showing up on lists of those who had missed study halls, tutorial appointments and classes.

Bowden had looked surprised in that morning's meeting when Eason had read off the names of students in apparent trouble. Part of it was just bad timing. Professors tended to turn in absence reports in batches, and their most recent totals, plus pre-midterm grade estimates, probably made things look worse than they were. But so much had been competing for the players' attention lately, what with the two weeks of total intensity prior to the Michigan game and then the trip to Ann Arbor. Who could blame them for letting the books slide?

But somebody would be blamed, they all knew. The players themselves, to a certain extent. Then the coaches, especially if a star had to be suspended or dismissed. So Eason had spent much of the day handing out penalties for missed appointments and reminding players of their other jobs—as students.

"Did you go to all your classes, E.T.?"

"Yes," said the Tallahassee receiver.

Eason stared at Turral for a second to shame him into changing his answer if he had lied. It was an old teacher's tactic that still worked for the coach. The young receiver held his ground.

If life was getting more complicated on the academic side, at least the football part of Eason's world seemed to be looking up. Shannon Baker and Kevin Knox were having a good week of practice. The day before, Baker had pulled in a long touchdown pass in the one-minute drill. And E.T., after making the great touchdown catch against Michigan, had also come down with a circus catch in practice. Bowden and Mark Richt had complimented his guys in the morning meeting.

"Shannon, you and Knox get a banker for being the subject of discussion in the meeting this morning. They were talking about that 4.3 speed."

The coaches assigned extra gassers—wind sprints—for missed assignments and sloppy play. Players got bankers, a credit in the bank against the next penalty gasser, for extraordinary effort.

"E.T., you made a good catch out there. But everybody expects that of you now."

Eason hoped the point sank in. He was trying to draw a floor of expectations under Turral, encouraging him to rise to his maximum performance level and to remain there, without lapsing into his trademark indifference. The coach had no idea if he was getting through.

Now it was on to the theme of the day. "Knox, what is courage?"

The receivers batted the idea around for a few minutes. Courage was an attitude, a style, a kind of fearless aggressiveness. The coach nodded. But didn't it also imply the willingness to take risks?

"It takes a different kind of courage to perform when you know your body is at risk," said Eason. "You have to have courage to sacrifice your body. Sometimes I think that a wide receiver has to have more courage than anybody else on a football team, because they have to go out at full speed and come down with that ball, knowing all the time they're going to get hit."

Kevin Knox was Eason's target for the courage lesson. The tall receiver had the speed and the hands to make big-time catches, but he was clearly uncomfortable coming down with the ball in front of defensive backs who were likely to nail him. In other contexts, that healthy fear was a sign of intelligence, but it was excess baggage in football.

Knox shifted the focus of the discussion. "You know, Coach, I think quarterbacks are right there too. Casey Weldon will stand there and stand there, knowing he's going to get hit. I'd have to say quarterbacks are right behind wide receivers in courage."

Shannon Baker had been thinking about the subject while the others were talking. In these discussions, Baker was the perfect student. He took every word to heart, thinking how the lessons applied to him. Then he would often burst out with a little confession or with an observation that either cracked everybody up or moved them almost to tears.

"You know, sometimes I feel like a knight," offered Baker. "The king hasn't issued me a suit of armor. I may not have it now, but by the time I leave college, I'll have my suit of armor."

Eason smiled. "Yeah, but remember, just because you're a knight, it doesn't mean you can't get your tail whipped."

5

D<small>AN</small> Footman was trying to arrange his 6-5, 270-pound body on his couch in some way that minimized the pain. He hurt all over, which was nothing new during football season. But his back bothered him so much he could think of nothing else.

"I must have pinched a nerve or something."

The trainers had given Footman some Tylenol, and he was wondering whether to take it now or wait until he studied for a couple of hours and take it before he hit the sack. Maybe it could help him sleep all the way through the night. And he wanted the rest.

"Man, I need this ABC game. Got to get my stock up. Pain or no pain, I gotta go on Saturday."

Since the BYU game, when he was defensive player of the week primarily because of his pass-rush power, Footman had been integrated more and more into the defensive game plan. Coach Amato had gradually worked him into the base three-man line as a second-teamer and kept him on the first team in the pass-rush alignment. Because of the rolling substitution system of the Florida State defense, Footman was seeing plenty of action.

On-the-job education was taking its toll on Footman's body and mind. There were all these new hurts to worry about. And the new assignments in the base defenses were hard to assimilate. If he had to think too much about what he was doing, it neutralized his assets—speed and power. But it would work in the long run, Amato was convinced. Even with his occasional lapses, Footman, so far, was leading the defensive line in unassisted tackles.

Success had done two things for the big guy: It made it harder to maintain his reputation as the prophet of doom. And it was making him an increasingly recognizable factor on an increasingly respected defensive squad. Television commentators knew the story of his miraculous rehabilitation from knee surgery, and his picture had flashed on national TV screens during replays. Now everybody knew his name.

When that happens to most players, they suddenly hear from all sorts of new friends. Dan Footman heard from his father.

His mother and father had split when he was still a youngster, and Footman couldn't remember any contact with his dad since he was 13 years old—even though he and his mother lived only about thirty miles from his father in central Florida.

"I guess he figured I was going to be a nobody, 'cause that side of the family was known for trouble. I guess he thought I was just going to be another troublemaker, so it ain't like you go out of your way to make contact with the average troublemaker.

"But when you see somebody on TV, I guess that would be enough reason to try to suck up like you miss 'em or something."

He dismissed the possibility of reconciliation. "You know, that only happens on TV, man. You know, where parents are gone for fifteen or twenty years. Then they all of a sudden come back and all make up in a weekend. To me, that only happens on TV.

"My mother doesn't want anything to do with him, but she says it's up to me what I do. I feel like my momma. He didn't leave us with nothin'. And I can't do nothin' for him."

Footman sighed. He shifted again on the couch, couldn't find a position that was bearable and moved to the floor. He tried to stretch his back, but the pain stiffened him.

"Man, oh man. This is ridiculous."

6

A<small>T</small> the end of the Thursday run-through in Doak Campbell, Mickey Andrews took his defensive team aside. No one ever had a problem hearing the defensive coordinator during practice drills, but when he talked directly to his players, they had to lean in to make out the words.

"I don't care how hard you try," he told them, "you won't be able to get up to the emotional level you did last week. Don't fool yourself. That may mean that you'll have to be better in technique to win."

The truth was, nobody, including the players themselves, knew what kind of emotional state they were in for Syracuse. It had been a weird week in practice.

To start with, Syracuse hadn't played enough snaps against Florida State-style offenses to provide good video previews for the Seminole offensive coaches. The Orangemen appeared to run a defense that was similar to the Seminoles'. Which would make it easier to guess what they would do when they saw certain Florida State alignments. But it was still a guess. And, as a result, it took longer than usual to come up with a game plan.

It wasn't until Wednesday's practice, in fact, that the full complement of plays and adjustments was in. That was also the first day Casey Weldon was able to throw. So the first-team backfield was still working the kinks out of their bodies and the game plan in the next-to-last practice before the game.

Flu and the aftermath of the previous Saturday's war with the 300-pounders had dinged up the offensive line. So it took until the Thursday walk-through before Brad Scott's first-team line looked healthy enough to go through an entire workout. Scott had nearly yelled himself hoarse earlier in the week trying to work his backups into practice repetitions. Kevin Mancini's hips were hurting, and Scott wanted to test the game potential of Eric Gibbs and Steve Allen. They ended up testing him.

"Do I have to get the dad-gum freshmen in here?" Scott demanded on Tuesday. "I've got two older guys who don't want to play. One has no heart and the other is so dang spastic he can't do nothin'."

The only good thing, as far as the players were concerned, was that there were no full-contact scrimmages. Afraid of adding to the long list of injuries, Bowden had kept them in shells—shorts and shoulder pads.

"It's the first time in my life that I've done that. If we go out there and get pushed all over the field, you can bet it will be the last time."

The defense worked against the scout team's version of the Syracuse option offense. But who knew if it was close enough to be of any real value?

When ABC's Bob Griese came by Bowden's office on Friday to get a feel for what to expect in the game, Bowden told him the Syracuse offense "scares me to death. I expect them to get that thing and move the ball on us. Then we'll gradually get used to the speed." So Bowden and his offensive coaches once again wanted to make sure they could win a scoring contest.

"Maybe we can help our defense," said Scott, "if we can put together some of them long drives and keep their option offense off the field."

Syracuse would come into this game ranked fourth in the nation in rushing defense. The Orangemen had held Florida to minus 17 yards on the ground. And no opponent had yet run for more than 105 yards. "But I don't believe they've been tested," Scott argued. "The teams they've been playing are either one-back-set teams or teams that got behind early and had to start throwing the ball to catch up—like Florida.

"They're good on defense, but they seem to play the same defense our guys play. And the only thing that let me go to sleep at night this week was the thought that we play in the spring and in two-a-days in August against a defense that's better than Syracuse.

"So we're gonna test 'em."

7

IT had been raining all morning on Saturday, providing a classic dose of the North Florida humid zone for the visitors from New York. There was a steady downpour, then a pause, then another sheet of rain. Concessionaires did a record business in plastic ponchos. But a record crowd of over 61,000 was still on hand.

Syracuse was spared the heat. It was only 74 degrees at kickoff. But even when the rain stopped, the humidity was 94 percent.

Welcome to Florida.

The Orangemen won the toss and put Qadry Ismail back to receive the first kickoff. When he returned it only 15 yards to his own 20, the Florida State coaches relaxed a little. But only for one play. On the first play from scrimmage, Syracuse quarterback Marvin Graves scooted right. Then, when he was challenged by the outside linebacker, he flipped the ball back to tailback David Walker, who turned the corner and zipped 36 yards down the right sideline. That was the option.

On first and ten at the FSU 45, Walker again got the ball, then pitched back to Graves before he reached the line of scrimmage. The quarterback planted his feet and lifted a bomb toward the end zone. Ismail ran under it for the touchdown. That was the Missile.

Twenty-three seconds had elapsed. The Seminoles were down 7–0. And it was raining.

Florida State started on the 20 after Syracuse kicker Pat O'Neill booted the kickoff to the back of the end zone. It was time to test 'em on the run. Amp Lee carried for three consecutive plays of 21, then seven, then four yards. Edgar Bennett got the first-down call on the Syracuse 48 and got one yard. Lee picked up one more on second down. Which made it third and long near midfield.

Bowden figured Syracuse would think it was about to see the Seminoles' first pass of the day. And hoping for an excited defense and a hard pass rush, he called for the Irish Screen.

Named after the Notre Dame play that gave the Florida State coaches the idea, this was a version of the screen pass that targeted a wide receiver moving laterally across the field at the line of scrimmage. The quarterback pedaled backward, drawing rushing linemen and blitzing linebackers with him. That opened up the territory behind them. And if the play worked, the pass would get into the hands of a speedster already on the move. Shannon Baker was the fastest man on the team, and he was in perfect position for Weldon's pass. But he dropped the ball. And the Seminoles had to punt.

Florida State narrowly escaped another Missile attack when Graves overthrew Ismail on third down. The punt forced the Seminole offense to begin at the FSU 16, but Weldon and his receivers put together a drive that ended with a touchdown catch by Matt Frier with a defender on his back.

The sophomore split end had lost his starting job to the redshirt freshman, Kez McCorvey. And during practice the past couple of weeks, the team's speedsters had seemed to be getting all the attention. Frier took pride in being a clutch receiver, someone who could catch the ball over the middle, take the hit, pick up the first down. He needed balls thrown his way. When he caught the touchdown pass, he immediately dropped to a knee: Thank you, Lord. I needed that one.

Mowrey's point-after kick was good, which brought more sighs of relief. The drive merely tied the score, but the six-minute possession was exactly what the offensive coaches had in mind. Set up the pass with the run. Keep 'em guessing. Eat up the clock.

What they didn't have in mind was giving Qadry Ismail another chance to quiet the home crowd and scare the life out of the specialty-team coaches.

The Missile took Mowrey's kickoff at his own 5 and didn't stop running until he crossed the goal line at the other end of the field. It was a 95-yard return, the first kickoff return for a touchdown against Florida State since the '84 season. And after the extra point, the Orangemen were ahead 14–7.

When they received the ball after the Ismail touchdown, the Seminoles seemed sluggish, and they failed to make a first down. But the lethargy was temporary. The defense allowed Syracuse no maneuvering room. And when Weldon and his teammates came out on the field for their next two series, it was clear that the control of the game had shifted their way.

Bennett concluded a 12-play, 74-yard drive by catching a nine-yard touchdown pass. And the next time the FSU offense got the ball, Mowrey kicked a 27-yard field goal.

Syracuse tried once more to make magic with Ismail. But Buckley intercepted the pass at the FSU 23, and the half ended a little over a minute later with the score 17–14.

8

"THIS team hadn't been behind in ten or eleven games," said Bowden at halftime. "For the first time, we got behind. We came back. We got behind again. We came back again. We got ahead. And now we got a three-point lead.

"They're good, aren't they? I think they're good. But, men, they're tired. They are tired, but they will fight.

"Now they gotta kick off to us. We need to break this kickoff back. Hey, men, doesn't it mean enough to you to get your man?

"They are so tired, they can't rush the passer. So if you receivers can't get open at first, keep scrambling around.

"We need to get the running game going again, men. It went the first two series. Then they just shut us down. Through our own mistakes.

"Offensive line, the best way for us to win this game—I told you y'all were the key—is for us to take this kick off and drive it for a touchdown and not have to throw it every down.

"Defense, all you have to do is stop the long play. Don't let 'em have anything deep.

"Men, it's just down to your heart. You just play as hard as you can play. Don't do anything dumb. Just go out there and execute."

He paused. It was hot in the room despite the air conditioning. With the players all crowded into the large anteroom between their lockers and the door, the air was made thick with their own humidity. Everything was wet and muddied. It felt like a tropical cave.

"Men, they are trying to take our ring. In thirty more minutes, they will take our ring away from us.

"Oh no," said the coach, clenching his fist. "Oh no. We will be the ones who'll take it."

Although this was the closest halftime margin in the Seminoles first five games, there was no panic in Bowden's voice. There was less concern even than in the Tulane game, when the Florida State lead seemed far more secure. As the second quarter wound down, it was impossible not to sense that his team had taken charge of the game. Without a dropped pass here, a missed assignment there, they could just as easily be ahead by 20. And now they had another whole half against a tired New York team in 94 percent humidity.

"Just don't do anything dumb."

After Syracuse put the kickoff out of reach in the end zone, the Seminoles took over at their own 20, determined to run the ball. Lee picked up nine on the first carry. Bennett got the first down on the second. Then came 344 Z Bench, again to Baker, who picked up eight yards.

On second down and two on the Florida State 41, Bowden invited Syracuse to think play-action pass and called for a run. Lee picked up seven yards. Now it was first down near midfield, an apparent running down. And it was back to the pass, this one sending the Z on a post pattern toward the end zone. Baker was way out in front of the defender when Weldon uncorked the bomb, and he was just a yard short of the end zone when he was tackled. The play was good for 51 yards. And Bennett mashed it in for the touchdown on the next play.

Mowrey missed the extra point. But the soggy crowd barely noticed.

The Seminole defense dug in for the rest of the day. On its next four possessions, Syracuse managed to convert only one first down. And that was through a penalty. The Orangemen went three and out on the next series, then were forced to punt from near midfield on their second possession of the half.

When Florida State took over after the punt, Weldon again went for the bomb on a pattern especially designed to take advantage of expected Syracuse coverages. Baker was open, but he couldn't run under Weldon's pass. It fell incomplete. Lee picked up four on the next play, and Bennett preserved the drive with a third-down grab over the middle for 21 yards.

The Seminoles still needed five more yards for the first down when they apparently stalled on the 50-yard line. On third down, Bowden called Smoke and Go, another play that would give Baker a chance to outrun the defensive secondary.

At the snap, the wideout took off parallel to the right sideline. He faked an inside move toward the goalposts to buy a little space between him and the defensive back, then he shifted into high gear as he cut back outside and headed for the goal line. Weldon's pass was perfect, hitting Baker in stride. And he and the defender splashed down and slid deep into the end zone.

Mowrey's kick made the score Florida State 30, Syracuse 14.

The two big catches by Baker would lift some of the pressure he had felt since the 1990 Florida game, when he failed to come down with a similar ball. "That's all they remember," Baker said, "the one I missed." But this was a new year. He was a giant step closer, he figured, to his suit of armor.

Cliff Abraham, the freshman backup cornerback, stopped the next Syracuse series with an interception and ran the ball back to the Florida State 48. When the FSU offense had to punt back, Sterling Palmer downed the ball on the Orangemen's 3-yard line. And three plays later, Todd McIntosh sacked Graves in the end zone for the two-point safety. That was eight points for the defensive lineman in two games.

Now, two minutes into the final quarter, Sean Jackson was in for Lee. And he and Bennett combined on most of the yardage that led to Florida State's fifth touchdown. Jackson ran the last 12 yards of the six-play scoring drive. And after Mowrey's kick made it 39–14, the offensive coaches got their second- and third-teamers ready to go in for the remaining 10 minutes of the game.

When Syracuse ran out of downs on the FSU 31, Brad Johnson took over for Weldon and led the final nine-play drive that ended with a touchdown pass to Lonnie Johnson. Syracuse failed to make another first down. And the clock ran out with the Florida State offense handing the ball off to backup running backs. The final score: 46–14.

What had been feared as a trap, as a gift-wrapped invitation to a mental letdown, had turned out to be a continuation of the Seminole party in Ann Arbor the previous week. This was the fifth quarter of the Michigan game transposed to Doak Campbell for the entertainment of the home fans.

In back-to-back games against top-ten opponents, Florida State had scored almost 100 points. Casey Weldon, who had not been able to lift his arm without pain on Wednesday morning, had a career day on Saturday afternoon—347 passing yards. He had never lost as a starter.

Syracuse, whose proud defense had throttled the Gators and earned national prominence, had given up the most ground in school history— 642 yards of total offense.

"We got our butts kicked in every way," said Syracuse head coach Paul Pasqualoni.

Bowden, talking to reporters after the game, was careful to admire the opposition. "Dad-gummit, that Ismail is so good. After playing Howard last week, we thought we were through with those kinds. This guy might be better."

And he deflected the tributes to his coaching by crediting climatic conditions. "Really, the heat just took it out of them. You can coach a lot of things, but humidity is not one of them."

But in the locker room with his team after the game, Bowden had let himself feel the relief, even if it was to be only a brief respite from the ordeal ahead. For the moment, he was as excited as the players.

"This was a great game, a great game."

Chuck Amato had given Bowden one of the defensive stats as they entered the locker room, and Bowden wanted to share it with the players. "They got 80 yards in the first twenty-three seconds of the game and didn't get but 105 more for the rest of the game. Defense, you were fantastic."

The players applauded one another. "And, offense, you weren't bad either." Everyone laughed. Indeed, 642 yards of offense was not half bad.

"I'm proud of you. You didn't put full pads on a single day this week. I might have to do that again."

The room cheered.

"Now, men, don't say foolish things. Some of you are making great names for yourselves. Don't get some TV commentator mad at you. You need those guys votin' for you for those awards. Watch what you say.

"No bed check tonight. And don't come by my house either. I ain't gonna be there."

"Ooooooh," went the players.

"Well, you know what I'll be doin'. I'll be rocking my grandchildren."

9

THE truth was, Bowden had been going home to grandchildren most nights this season. Ginger Madden, the youngest of the Bowdens' two daughters and four sons, had been staying at the house with her two kids all season while she attended Florida State's Law School. She and her husband, John, went to their Fort Walton Beach home on weekends.

That kept two of the Bowdens' fourteen grandchildren close, which pleased Ann, who was a doting grandmother. During football season, though, Grandpa wasn't doing much rocking or storytelling. He was up before them in the morning and arrived home at night about the time they were headed to bed.

Saturday night, the coach came home alone after taping his TV show. Ann was in Auburn, Alabama, where Tommy Bowden, one of their three coaching sons, was offensive coordinator under Pat Dye. Auburn had played Southern Mississippi on Saturday. And their youngest son, Jeff, was receivers coach for that team.

Ann planned to switch sides at the half, and her balancing act was in keeping with the struggle on the field. Southern Miss won by one point. Which meant Tommy was the only Bowden to lose that Saturday.

Samford, Bobby Bowden's alma mater in Birmingham, had won under head coach Terry Bowden, the No. 3 son. Son-in-law Jack Hines—who was married to the Bowdens' elder daughter, Robyn—was Terry's defensive coordinator.

The only Bowden son not coaching was Steve, who was an ordained minister and an administrator at Flagler University in nearby Jacksonville.

Normally after wins, the elder Bowden slept easily. "I slept okay after this one," he said. "But I started worrying about Tommy, of all things. I talked to him Saturday night after Auburn's loss.

"I don't think Tommy will worry. If he does worry, he'll hide it. But their offense is just not clicking, and that's what he was hired for.

"There's nothing I can do about it. They rebroadcast the game here Sunday, and I saw the whole thing. The problem is, they just ain't throwing and catching well."

All the Bowden coaches shared their father's enthusiasm for the balanced offensive attack. So their gatherings at the family condo on the Gulf of Mexico easily turned into play-drawing clinics in the sand. They traded plays and ideas. They talked all season long by phone. And when something stalled in one of their offenses, they all knew the problem and suspected they knew what had to be done about it.

"To use our kind of offense, you must be able to throw and catch well. And it don't take long to see Tommy and them ain't throwing and catching very well."

The strategy was simple enough, said Bowden. His teams were designed to force defenses into alignments his offense could move on. He wanted to create gaps by increasing the defense's responsibility to cover the whole field. "They can bring everybody up and stop the run, but then they can't stop the passes. But if you're dropping passes and they're stopping the run, boy, then you are in trouble."

Bowden had a pretty good idea Auburn was going to stay in trouble until some of its young players grew into their abilities. Which, he suspected, might not be fast enough for fans in his home state. So between his meetings early in the week, Bowden couldn't stop thinking about Tommy's probable state of mind. "Of all our children, he's the most like me." Which meant that losing hit him hard. The father collected some of the thoughts and Bible scripture he used to console himself in tough times and put them in a letter to Tommy.

He would see most of the other children and grandchildren the following week in Orlando. Local organizers had made Saturday a Bowden doubleheader in the Citrus Bowl, with Samford going against the University of Central Florida in a night game after FSU's afternoon meeting with Virginia Tech. The coach and Ann would stay over to see the game and visit with friends and family. That meant a big weekend for Ann Bowden, who was still not back from her Auburn visit early in the week, when Bowden joked with reporters about his wife's priorities.

"We were only the No. 1 team in the country trying to hold off the No. 10-ranked team in Tallahassee. And, of course, she had to be in Auburn with her boys. Never mind that they are grown with children of their own. They are still her boys.

"She's such a front-runner she's probably in Hattiesburg right now," home of Southern Miss and son Jeff.

And just wait until next week when they were all in Orlando and he couldn't hide on the sidelines, said the coach, rolling his eyes for effect. "Sittin' next to Ann in the stands is just awful. She is one of those very loud fans. I keep lookin' around tryin' to pretend she ain't with me."

10

ERIC Turral was trying to duck his coach's gaze. But John Eason pressed him: "Eric, do you feel like you're hustling?"

Eason wanted his receivers to see some of the Syracuse game video before he moved on to preparation for Virginia Tech. He wanted to let Shannon Baker and Kevin Knox take a few bows. Between them, they had caught 10 passes for 198 yards. But he also wanted to make some points about opportunities missed. And about attitude.

Frozen on the video screen was a play that went away from Eric Turral's side of the field, and he had made a halfhearted effort at decoying his defender. "Do you feel like you're running when you do this?"

"Not always," said Turral.

"Why not? What causes you not to hustle?"

Silence.

"I'm not mad at you. I'm just trying to figure out why. What causes you not to try? You were in there for six straight plays in this series, and on the sixth play, you loafed."

Turral tried to make a joke. "It was probably six straight running plays."

They were back to that.

For most high school stars, the transition to the next level in college required a new kind of commitment. To play regularly they needed to prove the team was better when they were in the game. They had to hit their blocks, run their patterns, hold on to the ball consistently. They had to become one of the dependables.

In high school, lapses in preparation and concentration could be overcome by pure talent. Not many coaches had the courage to bench an all-star for loafing or missing blocks. Not when they could save a game—and a coach's job—with one big play.

At the highest college levels, however, the talent gap narrowed. Advantages were measured in half steps and two extra inches of vertical leap. Disciplined skill almost always won.

After two years, Turral was still adapting to the transition. He might sleepwalk through a week of practice, then panic on game day, hanging on to Eason's every word and asking a hundred questions about assignments. He would have a game like the one in Ann Arbor, stealing that touchdown pass and blocking half of the Michigan secondary to spring Amp Lee. Then he would try to play his way through a game like last Saturday's on cruise control.

Eason left the video frozen on the single frame and looked right at Turral. "You know, I keep thinking about the Michigan game, when you're running your patterns and Shannon is standing there beside me on the sideline. He's all excited, because he wants you to do so well. He's yelling, 'Y'all better put two on 'em. One guy is never gonna handle ol' E.T.'"

"How do you figure that? You're in there playing instead of him, and he's rootin' for you. He's your biggest fan."

Eason moved back to the screen and indicated the line of scrimmage, where the Seminole offensive linemen were fighting off the pass rush. "See these guys? They never get their names in the paper. They gotta run and block on every play so y'all can catch the ball. That's a team thing. You all have to fight. Whatever it takes, you gotta make the adjustment."

Eason let the video run and spoke over the action. "If you're not careful, you're gonna let the fact that you can't control your emotions ruin your career."

The play on the screen now was a running call, with No. 42, Amp Lee, squeezing through a narrow hole at the line of scrimmage and sliding for extra yards into the secondary. Eason backed it up and let it run again.

"Watch this guy. He may be the best running back we ever had here. You know why? Because he does it all."

Fast-forwarding back and forth through the game video, Eason picked a half dozen plays to focus on. He went back to the opening drive and stopped on the third-down screen pass that Baker dropped. "Shannon, what were you thinking about?"

"About being on TV, Coach. About scoring. About making the big play. I thought: Man, if I ever get back in I'll try to make up for it."

Eason backed up the play again. "Let's just see what would have happened if you had caught the ball." The path across the middle was open. One defensive back may have been within range. "Oh, that guy would have got you," said the coach. But everyone knew that with Baker's speed it would have been a footrace for a long gain, maybe a score. Instead, it had cost Baker his job on the next couple of possessions.

"As a coach, I just can't let one guy do that."

Eason moved to the series that brought Knox into the game. "It was like, finally," said the sophomore. The receivers teased him about getting balls thrown his way in the touchdown drive. "Coach Bowden probably thought E.T. was in there," laughed Baker.

"I thought I was coming in to block," said Knox. "But we thought as wide receivers we'd all do it."

Indeed, Knox's and Matt Frier's receptions had kept the drive alive. And Frier's grab in the end zone had tied the game.

Eason fast-forwarded.

"You know, I'm always on your backs. I'm always demanding things from you. But you know, y'all are extensions of me. When you drop one, I drop one. When you catch one, I catch one. I use y'all's hands and feet to get down there and catch it. And when you score, I'm running around with my finger in the air too."

The figures on the screen froze again, then backed up. Turral missed a catch. The room was quiet again as the coach ran the play twice. "I'm listening."

"I dropped the ball," E.T. said quietly.

Eason moved on to the second half, now speaking barely loudly enough for anyone beyond the first row of receivers to hear. "You gotta block if you want to play."

On the screen, Baker splashed into the end zone on his two second-half bombs. Eason froze one frame at the point of the catch. "What were you thinking about?"

"About last year's Florida game."

Okay, but Eason wanted him to feel the achievement too. "I think this was the best game of your career at Florida State."

Baker smiled.

11

MICKEY Andrews had the Monday devotion. And gratitude was his theme. It would do them all some good, he told the coaches, to take a moment to reflect on how fortunate they were. Not only for the performance of their football team but also for all the other things that made their lives so rich. Everyone around the table nodded in agreement.

Then they listened to the injury report.

Mancini's hips and sore knee would keep him out of contact until Saturday. Tiger McMillon was slowed. Buckley couldn't go full speed because of a sore muscle in his thigh. Footman was out with back pain.

A few eyebrows lifted. They hadn't yet let themselves believe that Dan Footman could be counted on. He had come so far. And he could be such a dominating force if he could learn the position and survive the pounding. Yet every small setback seemed to suggest he wasn't ready.

Chuck Amato, though, refused to let the topic of Dan Footman's condition be anything but positive. "Coach," Amato said to Bowden, "Dan was hurting all last week, and he was out there every day doing everything and never complaining."

Bowden chewed his gum and nodded. They would just have to wait and see.

Randy Oravetz continued down the injury list: Casey Weldon was back to tentative, with the bad left hip and the bruised right calf from the Michigan game and now sore ribs from Syracuse. He wouldn't be throwing until midweek. Sean Jackson had a hip pointer too.

Marvin Jones had been thrown into a mirror in the dorm trying to break up a fight between two teammates. He had to have stitches to close lacerations in his right calf.

The flu was making its way through the team now, with three or four more players suffering high fever, vomiting and diarrhea each morning.

The coaches looked at one another, sensing the gratitude for all their good fortune ebb. They had four more days to prepare for a team that, every year, possessed the capability of humiliating them.

Virginia Tech was better known as VPI, for Virginia Polytechnic Institute, back when it was an all-male military school. The official name remained, shortened to Virginia Tech as the student composition changed to nearly 50-50 male-female. In 1991, only about 2 percent of the 23,000 students were in the Corps of Cadets.

What Virginia Tech had retained over the years, however, was a leather-helmet kind of ferocity for the sport of football. The school still attracted hard-nosed bruisers who always threatened to physically snatch victories from higher-profile teams such as Oklahoma and Florida State.

"You know," said Bowden, "sometimes we'll play teams who are intimidated by the idea of facing Florida State University. But not this team. Not ever."

This was an old rivalry. Only Florida and Miami had appeared on Florida State football schedules more often than the Virginia Tech Hokies. This would make the 29th meeting of the two teams. And probably the last, since both schools were entering conference play in 1992 and wouldn't have room on their schedules. Virginia Tech was moving to the Big East, where it could harass Miami in the future.

Bowden was 10–0 against Hokie squads, including two wins when he was coaching West Virginia. But it hadn't been easy. Last year's game in Tallahassee, in fact, was a nightmare. The Seminoles had to come back from a 21–3 deficit and were still trailing 28–25 late in the third quarter.

The Hokies' big left-handed quarterback, Will Furrer, threw for three touchdowns. Fortunately for the Seminoles, he also gave up four interceptions. Terrell Buckley got two of them, returning one 53 yards for a score. And Errol McCorvey picked up a fumble and ran 77 yards for another touchdown. Those two turnover touchdowns provided the margin for the 39–28 victory.

Furrer was back in '91. So were eight other offensive starters and seven on defense. Technically, the Hokies would be the home team in Orlando, because Florida State had guaranteed them $800,000 to move the game from their 51,000-seat stadium in Blacksburg, Virginia, to the 70,000-seat Citrus Bowl. But this was really their fifth road game in a row.

In their last two, they had lost to Oklahoma by 10 points, then beat West Virginia by six. Now they were 2–3 and anxious for a turnaround. There was every reason to believe they would be fired up at being four-touchdown underdogs and playing the nation's No. 1 team before a big crowd in central Florida.

"There couldn't be a better time for an upset," the coaches told the Seminole players in their meetings. They harped on last year's struggle, on Virginia Tech's pride in rough-and-tumble football. They reminded the offense of how the Hokies had frustrated them and how if it hadn't been for the defense, they would have lost in '90. But there was no way to tell whether the players were buying the need for a sense of urgency.

Between the Michigan and Syracuse games, everybody was sore and sluggish. The practices had been ragged. And look what they had done to the Orangemen. Now here they were again, still beat-up and facing a team that was even more of an underdog.

"The only people who can beat us is us," Bowden told them in practice.

"The whole nation is looking to see if you'll stub your toe," said athletic director Bob Goin. "You're in a fishbowl."

If Bowden and the offensive coaches wanted to pick out something to worry about it could be Virginia Tech's old-style defense, one that put eight men on the line to rush. Teams had moved away from that defense as the passing game developed blitz-reaction tactics to take advantage of it. And taking so many people out of pass coverage would seem to be particularly dangerous against Florida State.

"The scouting reports on us," Bowden explained, "have always been: 'Whatever you do, don't blitz 'em. They'll kill you in the blitz.' That's because when you blitz you have to leave all kinds of holes open. And if quarterbacks and receivers adjust quick enough, you'll get burned for the big play. Everybody is usually so afraid to cover our receivers one on one they stay away from the blitz."

Last year, Bowden had spent much of the pre-Virginia Tech week working on anti-blitz packages that he never got to use. The Hokies crossed him up by dropping people in zone coverage. This year, he and Brad Scott and Mark Richt would remind themselves not to get carried away.

But every time Bowden looked at game tapes, the Hokie blitzes jumped out at him. "The more I look at film, the more I'm inclined to say y'all oughta get your passin' shoes on. But you better pick up the blitzes, 'cause these guys can kill you."

They had nearly killed them without the blitzes last year.

"We just all kinda took turns messing up," Richt said. Reviewing the 1990 game tape had sobered them all, because it clearly had not been Florida State's offensive attack that won. Without the big turnovers, the Hokie experience might have been terminal.

"You know, if they hadn't thrown the ball late, they would have won it," said Eason. "If they had just run the ball and played defense, they would have beaten us."

Bowden's gum got a little more workout as he considered that. "Whooeeee, it scares me to death."

12

With Casey Weldon nursing bruises until midweek, Brad Johnson was getting more and more first-team snaps in the Tuesday practices. It felt good to be in charge again, even if he knew he was just filling in until Weldon could take over later in the week.

The 1990 Virginia Tech game had been Johnson's best as a Seminole quarterback. He had led the Seminoles' comeback with a career-high 254 yards and two touchdown passes.

"I think that was pretty good for the team and for me. I had a bad game in the sense that I threw interceptions, but I think I improved as a quarterback, taking charge in the middle of the game and throwing the ball downfield. When you're down like that and people start pointing fingers, it's important to come back the way we did."

The real finger pointing had started the next week, when Florida State lost to Miami. The game after that against Auburn was Johnson's last as a starter. Watching his best friend win every game since had been the toughest experience of Brad Johnson's life. He didn't resent Casey, but he hated life as a runner-up.

He had never been No. 2 in sports. Not in basketball, when he was the high school player of the year in his division in North Carolina. And certainly not in football, where his 6-6 height and solid 217 pounds made him look like a pro scout's dream. Now he was watching the last games of his college career from the sideline, hearing the Heisman hype and all the speculation about how high Casey would go in the NFL draft.

Even Casey said this just as easily could have been Brad. Why wasn't it? Why, out of all the places that could have used a big, strong quarterback, did he have to end up here, behind the guy who might win the Heisman Trophy?

When he came to Tallahassee from Black Mountain, North Carolina, one of the *Parade* magazine All-Americans, he looked like the future. He played basketball for the Seminoles. During the '88 Sugar Bowl week, he flew back and forth between football practice and basketball games. Then he had won the starting quarterback job in the spring of 1990 and looked poised for bigger things. Now he was in danger of becoming the answer to a trivia question.

"People only remember the last time they saw you. Last year in Casey's first couple of games, people were pointing the finger at him too, saying they ought to switch to Charlie Ward. Then the more he played, the better he got.

"I've improved too. But the only place I get to show it is in practice. I hate that. And I hate it that people still remember me primarily for being taken out of the Auburn game. But I can't worry about other people."

A year had changed everything.

Weldon's father was beginning to screen the agents who were calling to get in line for Casey's consideration in the postseason. Weldon would go to the Senior Bowl in Mobile and the Hula Bowl in Hawaii, where pro coaches would watch his every move. Johnson knew that for him it would be a battle just to get the pros' attention.

He wouldn't be in the all-star games. Somehow, he would have to get an invitation to the Combine workouts in February, when pro scouts measured and tested the nation's top senior prospects. If he was drafted at all, it would not be in the top rounds. But all he wanted was a chance.

His teammates called Johnson Bull because of his size and his work habits. A physical education major, he had always taken conditioning seriously. And he threw himself into training when he lost the starting job, partly for the therapy and partly to raise his market value for the NFL.

Between his junior year and midseason '91 he had taken two-tenths of a second off his 40-yard dash time and added bulk in the weight room. "I'm sharper in terms of reading my coverages and in my timing too." And he relished chances to demonstrate his development.

His coach, Mark Richt, teased him about the keen edge he developed in practice when the scouts were around. Of course, said Bull. It was his future.

Johnson was looking forward to this five-game stretch of teams the Seminoles should dominate. He wanted those fourth-quarter snaps. And with Weldon hurting, he was focusing even more intently on the drills and the video sessions. It was impossible not to feel good about taking those first-team reps in practice, impossible not to watch closely in the games as Weldon took the big hits. If the starter stayed down a few seconds longer than usual, the adrenaline started pumping in Brad Johnson. He couldn't help it.

In the third and fourth quarters, when the Seminoles were up by 20 or more, Johnson would edge closer to the sideline territory where Brad Scott and Bowden paced. He wanted to remind them he was there, ready. It was about all he could do for now.

"I think I've handled this pretty well. It was really tough last year. But I've eased up on myself lately. When you come to a program like this, so much of your future is in the hands of other people. There are things you just cannot control.

"But I also understand that if I'm satisfied to sit in the back and wait, I'll never get anywhere.

"I'm cheering for Casey. In the long run, that's what is best for the team and best for me. But sometimes I hate being around here. There are twelve or thirteen seniors on this team. And I'm the only one not playing, the only one not contributing.

"Sure, this is the No. 1 team in the nation. A lot of people would kill to be here. But there can be only twenty-two people at a time who are really happy. Everybody wants theirs. That's why we're here."

13

"You can't prepare a lot with all the junk they throw at you and still feel good. But I just don't believe they've proved they can do all this stuff against a team that can pass."

Brad Scott was making his Friday-night pitch in Bowden's hotel room as the head coach drew up opposing defensive formations on the black-board.

The extended Bowden family was spread all over the Orlando resort hotel. Ann and their elder daughter, Robyn Hines, had headed out to dinner, leaving the coach in charge of a couple of his grandchildren in a nearby room. The kids were under orders to play quietly while he met in his suite with Scott and Mark Richt for their usual Friday-night skull session.

Bowden was down to his Friday-night thinking gear. His shirt was open and his pants were loose at the waist. He had lined the wastebasket with newspaper for a spittoon and was helping himself to Red Man. He needed lots of chew. He had been watching game tapes for the umpteenth time that afternoon, and he was restless. All those danged Hokie blitzes.

He knew the answer to the question about how to beat a blitzing defense: You just throw and catch.

But had the players gotten enough reps to be comfortable with the blocking schemes? Backs and tight ends had to know whom to pick up and when. And this had not been a practice week to inspire confidence, not with the No. 1 quarterback limping around and half the starters taking up residence in the training room.

Scott tried to assure the head coach that the right protections were built into the offensive scheme. Casey would have the time. And if he had the time, hadn't he proved what he could do?

"Receivers, you ought to have a field day tomorrow," Scott had told the offensive players earlier that night.

Richt and Scott went through their evaluation of the Virginia Tech personnel. The Hokies' strengths seemed to be the two tackles, the two inside linebackers and the "robber"—a free-floating safety in the middle of the field.

If they rushed all eight linemen and linebackers, and the Seminoles blocked the extra men with the tight end and backs, that left three men in pass coverage against two Florida State wide receivers. Excellent odds, the coaches thought, for big plays.

"If they want to play a blitz package, they will have a quick death," Scott had told the offense. "But you gotta hat 'em up."

On Bowden's blackboard, Scott wrote some stats he thought would build a case for first-down strategy. Of 90 second-down situations against the Virginia Tech defense so far this year, 65 were second and seven-plus. Which suggested the Hokies were stuffing other teams' running game on first down.

So far in '91, the Seminoles' own first-down tendencies leaned toward the ground game. According to Bowden's self-scouting report, they had run 67 percent of the time on first down. But against these guys, said the coach when he saw Scott's figures, "we're gonna have to pass."

Richt laughed. "Oh, darn it." Here was a team willing to bet their pass rushers against your passer and receivers. Bring 'em on, thought the quarterback coach. Let them even see us in our favorite formation for protecting the passer. We'll dare them to stop us.

Fine, said Bowden. "I need to give Casey a chance to make things happen."

Just as long as they were sure they could pick up the blitzes. Bowden wanted to hear assurances on every play Scott and Richt recommended that protection had been repped sufficiently in practice. They were working their way through Bowden's pages of notes when the phone rang.

The coach crossed the room to answer it, giving Scott and Richt a chance to thumb the remaining pages of his notes. It was getting late, and they were beat. "We gotta get him to turn that dang machine off," moaned Scott, motioning to Bowden's VCR and stack of game tapes.

Bowden was talking into the receiver. "Okay, I'll take care of it." He hung up and giggled, then crossed to the customized spittoon to empty a little tobacco juice.

He went back to the phone and dialed a number. Someone evidently picked up on the other end.

"Beau, this is your granddaddy. I just got a call from the front desk that y'all are jumping on the beds and disturbing people in the next room. Now, I don't have time to come down there. But they said they were going to send a policeman up there if you don't stop."

When he hung up the phone, he turned, grinning at the two assistant coaches. All three men laughed.

14

ON the first play from scrimmage against Virginia Tech, Casey Weldon's pass was complete to Shannon Baker for 19 yards. It wasn't a perfect throw. Baker had to leap for it and was hit hard from behind while he was still in the air. But he had been open, and he had come down with the ball for the big gain.

Just throw and catch. Maybe this was going to be exactly as advertised.

Amp Lee picked up a yard on the first-down pass play. Edgar Bennett was open on the sideline for the third consecutive pass of the opening series, and Weldon hit him in stride, but he couldn't hold on. Now it was third down.

The call was for a play-action pass that would put the fullback in a delay pattern over the middle. But Weldon never got to see Bennett. He was sacked from behind by Virginia Tech's John Granby, the left-side cornerback, who moved up to the line of scrimmage and let the wide receiver run right by him. He was the extra guy on the blitz, and no one touched him.

Mark Richt watched the play develop from the coach's booth and pounded a fist on the narrow table that separated him from the window to the field. "That's crap." Somebody had missed an assignment.

Richt and Clint Ledbetter, the volunteer line assistant, were the offense's eyes in the booth. Wally Burnham, who coached the inside linebackers, and graduate assistant coach Greg Guy were the defensive representatives. Strength coach Dave Van Halanger kept track of plays for both sides.

The five men occupied the first row of the Florida State coaches' booth in the press boxes, both home and away. Their headsets wired them in to the coaches on the sideline, who were too engulfed in the action to have even a fan's overview. They provided two things: a constant reminder of the situation—the position of the ball on the field, the down and the distance for a first down; and a bird's-eye view of opponents' defensive and offensive alignments. Everything the other guys did could be monitored so that coaches on the sideline could adapt blocking assignments and defensive alignments.

The men in the booth had all played football themselves. They had spent the better part of their lives in the heat of the action, then had moved to the sidelines to help direct it. So on game days, their bodies were more attuned to the rhythms of the competition on the field than to objective analysis from the press box.

On the headset, Richt, the former quarterback, disguised his intensity with understatement: "I wouldn't call that one here, Coach." Burnham, a friendly Alabaman in most other ways, had to fight off the linebacker inside. Sometimes he would snatch off the headset and jump to his feet, looking as if he intended to leap through the glass to make the tackle himself. "Draw! Draw! It's the draw play!"

If Burnham forgot to take off his headset when he leaned forward to yell instructions to the players four stories below, the first to know about it was Chuck Amato, who was on the other end of the phones down on the field. Amato would give a little jump and hold the headset away from his ears until the official whistled the play dead.

Ledbetter watched without emotion from the waist up. But his legs, barely scrunched into the space beneath the table, would vibrate so intensely that cold drinks and peanut shells walked across the tabletop.

Guy was more like Richt, suppressing the competitive fires to advise Mickey Andrews on opponents' pass routes and breakdowns in the Seminoles' coverage. Van Halanger was the designated worrier: "Oh my God, if we don't stop them now . . ."

This game, evidently, was going to test the nerves of everyone in the booth.

The Seminole defense gave up almost no ground in the Hokies' first series, forcing them to punt from their own 26-yard line. And after Virginia Tech was penalized for not giving Terrell Buckley enough room for his fair catch, Weldon and the offense took over seven yards short of midfield.

The call was the same as the play that sacked the quarterback in the first series. This time, Weldon found Eric Turral, who had slanted into a crease deep in the Virginia Tech secondary. But the ball popped out of his hands straight up into the air and a Virginia Tech cornerback got the rebound for the interception.

On the first play of the Hokies' possession, Buckley was called for pass interference. And three plays later, Will Furrer launched a 45-yarder into the end zone to Michael Sturdivant. Buckley and Seminole safety John Davis weren't close. Touchdown.

Bob Goin, the athletic director, had been pacing the enormous Citrus Bowl press box during the drive. And he slipped into the coaches' booth just before the touchdown. This was going to be one of those games; he just knew it.

Orlando should have been a home away from home for the Seminoles. But central Florida was still Gator territory, and many of the FSU season-ticket holders hadn't made the four-hour trip. Prominent among the 58,000-plus here today were folks who were prepared to jump on the No. 1 bandwagon and do that Seminole "War Chant" stuff they'd seen on television—provided, of course, Florida State cooperated by running up and down the field on this unranked team from the mountains of southern Virginia.

The Citrus Bowl was full of high expectations. Goin, for the most part, felt nervous dread. After Furrer's touchdown pass, the athletic director murmured to no one in particular, "All this is going to do is give that quarterback confidence."

On the next offensive series, Florida State came back with the run. Amp Lee picked up nine yards, and Bennett got the first down on the first two plays. On second and third downs, Weldon overthrew first Lee, then Kez McCorvey. Both were wide open.

On fourth down from the Florida State 36, the Seminoles called time-out and yanked the punt team. Bowden called a play intended to put the ball in the hands of Lee, but it was Kez McCorvey who made the drive-sustaining catch when Weldon had to throw under pressure.

Back-to-back Lee runs advanced the ball another 25 yards, and Florida State had a first down on the Virginia Tech 30. On the next two plays, the Seminoles lost 18 yards. The Hokie rush batted down a pass, then Weldon was nailed for intentionally grounding the ball when he was about to be sacked.

The third-down pass to Lee got back only four yards, and Player punted again.

Richt listened to Scott's questions from the sideline. This was not going the way they planned. If it hadn't been for the run, they would have had almost no offensive yards after two series. The backs were missing the blitz pickups. Receivers were dropping the ball. They were favored by four touchdowns and already down by one. And the Heisman-nominated quarterback couldn't seem to buy a completion.

"All I can say," the quarterback coach told the offensive coordinator, "is that he is playing like crap."

Richt grabbed another set of headphones that connected him with Brad Johnson. "Put Casey on," he said. And when the quarterback plugged in, the coach asked, "Are you hurt?"

He suspected Weldon was feeling the cumulative aches of the last two weeks. But if Weldon was physically hampered, he wouldn't admit it. He had just blown the throws, he told his coach. It was his fault, and he would get them back.

While they talked, Will Furrer was having his own quarterbacking troubles. On the Hokies' second play, Leon Fowler intercepted him, and Weldon and the rest of the Seminole offense got another chance at the Virginia Tech 48.

Granby, who was already having a dream day on defense for the Hokies, swatted down the first-down pass attempt. And later in the series, Weldon overthrew first Warren Hart for a sure first down, then Eric Turral in the end zone. The only advance of the ball by passing, in fact, was on a pass-interference penalty that gave the Seminoles a first down on the Hokie 22. From there, Lee, Weldon and Bennett ran it the rest of the way into the end zone. Mowrey's kick tied the game at seven apiece.

On the next series, the Virginia Tech fullback, Phil Bryant, pulled Burnham out of his seat in the booth with a 29-yard carry. And Furrer was able to escape a third-and-17 hole with a 19-yard screen pass to back Mark Poindexter as the first quarter ran out. It was the kind of defensive play calculated to drive Andrews and Bowden crazy—push 'em back, push 'em back, then give up the big play.

But once the Hokies crossed into Seminole territory, the defense tightened, and Furrer was left with another third-and-long dilemma at the Florida State 36. It was an obvious passing down, which gave the advantage to Terrell Buckley when Furrer tried to find a receiver in his territory.

Buck intercepted the ball at his own 29 and picked his way through the Virginia Tech offensive squad for the 71-yard touchdown. The air in the press-box booth immediately got easier to breathe. At least for the defensive coaches.

Richt, Scott and Bowden argued among themselves over the game plan. "I still don't think we have to abort anything, Coach," Richt told Bowden. "No. 11 is just not sharp."

While they talked, the Virginia Tech offense was moving down the field. Suddenly it was fourth and three from the Florida State 8. Virginia Tech sent in the field-goal team.

Backup placekicker Scott Freund served as the Hokies' holder on field goals and point-afters. When the snap came to him, instead of putting the ball on the ground for Ryan Williams' kick, Freund stood up, tucked the ball and tried to barrel through an enormous hole in the left side of the line. He was stopped at the 1, but still got the first down. And tailback Tony Kennedy ran it in on the next play. The score was tied again.

Marquette Smith, playing his first game since his biceps problems, ran the kickoff back 33 yards. It was a little show for the home folks, since he had been an Orlando high school all-star. But it also settled the question of whether Smith would take a medical redshirt his freshman year. Since they had passed the five-game deadline for declaring medical redshirts, the option was gone.

No matter what happened from now on, Smith and Derrick Brooks— *USA Today*'s high school offensive and defensive players of the year in 1990—were both using their first years of eligibility at Florida State. They were the only two freshmen from last year's class not redshirted.

Smith's runback gave the Seminoles the ball on their own 43. Less than a minute later, Weldon hit Kevin Knox with a perfect 38-yard pass for the go-ahead touchdown. But because Mowrey bounced the point-after kick off the right goalpost, no one on the Seminole sidelines could allow himself to feel confident things were back on track. And it turned out, the suspicions were justified. Even though the defense shut down Furrer and the determined Hokies for the remainder of the half, the FSU offense seemed derailed. Weldon missed wide-open receivers. And when he made the right throws, somebody dropped the ball.

It could have been worse. They could have been losing as they walked into the locker room at the half. But Bowden felt only frustration.

What the heck happened to throw and catch?

15

Bowden read aloud from unofficial stats: "We gained 153 yards of total offense. We've got 65 yards rushing. We've got 88 passing.

"Now, I ain't worried about stats. All I want are them points. But, offense, that's awful. That is awful.

"Now, quarterback, you gotta make something happen. You didn't make nothin' happen in the first quarter.

"Receivers, we've got to have great catches. Quarterback, you've got to get back and fire. And runners, you've got to make something happen.

"Defense, the only thing they've done to you is take the ball and drill it, just exactly like they did last year. They've drilled two touchdowns on you. Right down your dad-gum throats."

Bowden paced. The anger was apparent in his voice.

"Now, men, we've got to get with it this half now. We've got to kick off to them."

The very mention of the need to kick riled the coach. And as was his habit when upset or distracted, he momentarily forgot the name of his kicker, Dan Mowrey.

"Lowrey, kick the stinkin' ball out of the end zone. Defense, you've got to take that ball away. And, offense, we've got to come back and score. Then I think we'll have momentum our way. If we don't, we're going to have a fight on our hands all day.

"We've already missed an extra point. So if they score, they can go ahead of us. It's precarious. It's precarious, men. It's all inside your heart now.

"Okay, men, we've got thirty more minutes. Can you imagine what it would be like to walk back in here in thirty minutes and not have won this thing? That's what will happen unless you fight your guts out."

Someone at the door signaled five more minutes until the second-half kickoff.

Bowden turned to Amato, who had charge of the captains. Virginia Tech had deferred to the second half their right to receive the kickoff, and Florida State had the choice of end zones to defend. "Chuck, make sure you check that wind now. I want every advantage I can get when we go out there. And, Lowrey, you kick the ball exactly where they say kick it."

Mowrey did blast the opening kickoff into the end zone for the touchback. And the defense kept the Hokies inside their own 20-yard line. The punt and Buckley's 10-yard return gave the Seminoles a head start on Virginia Tech's 44. Then three consecutive runs by Lee and Bennett created another first down on the 31.

Bowden called for passes on the next three downs. Weldon took a sack for an eight-yard loss; the second-down pass was batted down; then he was sacked for six yards more on third down. It was fourth and 24 from the Hokie 45. Player's punt went into the end zone.

Richt had Weldon on the player headphones again. "All I know is that we're killing 'em with the run and stinkin' it up on the passing game. What is going on?"

Furrer and flanker Steve Sanders tested Buckley on three consecutive passes. They completed the first for 13 yards, but Buck had Sanders covered tightly on the next two. On third down and 10, a collision in the Virginia Tech backfield put the ball on the ground, and Dan Footman was there to fall on it.

Once again, the FSU defense had given the ball to the offense deep in Hokie territory, this time on the 32. And once again, the offense was able to take advantage of the opportunity. Bowden, however, was taking no chances on the passing game. The Seminoles mashed it into the end zone in four plays, with Lee carrying on the final six-yard toss sweep.

Mowrey missed the extra point. Boos rose from the bored Citrus Bowl crowd. The freshman's season as anything but a kickoff specialist was clearly in danger, but the coaches were surprised to hear the fan reaction. They couldn't remember ever hearing boos for one of their own players in home territory. This season was shaping up to be so different. And so weird.

When Florida State scored again in the third quarter off a short dump pass to Lonnie Johnson, John Wimberly came in to kick the extra point. That made the score 33–14. But the Hokies fought as if they expected to make up the three-touchdown spread in the remaining 15 minutes. Furrer mixed passes and runs to drive 66 yards to the Seminole 11-yard line, but he had to relinquish the ball when the FSU defense held on fourth-and-two. On its next series, though, Virginia Tech put together an impressive 82-yard scoring drive, missing the attempt to add two points when Howard Dinkins sacked Furrer on the conversion attempt.

Bowden had sent in subs to get game experience, but the first-teamers were back when the Seminoles received the kickoff. Still, they were stopped at the Virginia Tech 42 when Weldon and Bennett couldn't connect on the third-and-two pass. It was left to the Florida State defense to keep the Hokies at bay. On the next series, Furrer threw deep on first down from his own 20. Buckley picked off the pass 40 yards downfield and ran the ball back to near midfield with five minutes left in the game. Florida State didn't score again. But it didn't give Virginia Tech another chance with the ball until less than two minutes remained. Even then, Furrer and his offense fought to put something into the end zone. The effort ended with Buckley breaking up a fourth-and-11 pass attempt from the Seminoles' 31-yard line.

The final score: Florida State 33, Virginia Tech 20.

"Dear Father," prayed Bowden, "thank you for this beautiful day and this great opportunity. We pray that you heal our injured. I don't think we did as good as we could, but we won the ball game, and that's the most important thing."

Amen.

The 343 yards total offense was the lowest output of the season for the Seminoles. Virginia Tech's 420 yards was the most allowed by the defense.

It was Casey Weldon's worst performance as an FSU starter, 13 completions in 31 attempts for 186 yards and an interception. He was sacked five times. So when the doors were opened to them, the reporters headed straight for the quarterback's locker.

Game adrenaline still prevented the quarterback from feeling the damage to his body. But he had a pretty good idea he had added to his misery. The hip, the calf, the ribs all hurt from before. And today he had landed on his throwing shoulder. Now that was throbbing.

He was gingerly peeling off his pants and pads when the crowd encircled him. So he stood up to face the reporters and the TV lights with his pants around his knees.

"I was just awful," he told them.

16

THE Florida Gators beat conference rival Tennessee 35–18. And the Miami Hurricanes edged past the last significant hurdle on their schedule before Florida State, defeating Penn State 26–20 on the same Saturday FSU faced Virginia Tech. So the Seminoles didn't generate much excitement with their win, especially given the struggle it took to get past the Hokies.

The Tallahassee *Democrat* pronounced the Orlando victory a "technical knockout." Bowden, nevertheless, let himself feel a little better about the game after he looked at the videotapes on Sunday. Virginia Tech coaches had done a masterful job preparing themselves for the Seminoles.

In the week after the game, Seminole coaches talked to their Virginia Tech counterparts by phone. Since this was the last time the two teams would be on one another's schedule, they could exchange information that would help with self-scouting. Were they doing anything on offense or defense that tipped their hands? What did the other guys fear the most?

The first thing the Seminole coaches learned was that, from scouting earlier games, Virginia Tech had isolated Florida State's signs for offensive formations. And they were decoding Brad Scott's signals to Casey Weldon at the same time the quarterback was getting them from the Seminole sideline. This didn't mean they knew the play, just the formation. Bowden could run any number of plays out of those formations. But knowing the Florida State offensive set gave the Virginia Tech defense the chance to counter with an alignment most likely to disrupt things.

Virginia Tech used the advantage to try to neutralize Edgar Bennett. Bowden might call for a formation that gave Bennett three options, depending upon the play call and the defense. He could be the runner, a receiver or a pass protector. In an obvious passing situation, such as third and long on the Seminole end of the field, he would be more likely to be a receiver or a pass blocker. Bennett was one of the best receiving backs in college football. So knowing the formation and Bennett's responsibilities as soon as the signal went to Weldon enabled the Hokie coaches to signal their own defense to move into an alignment more likely to force Bennett to stay back and block. The Virginia Tech game was the first game in the season in which the fullback caught no passes.

It was a guessing game, sure. But even a hint of advantage was welcome.

The head Seminole guesser took some of the blame too. "I outsmart myself sometimes," said Bowden. "And I may have done some of that this game.

"I pride myself in staying a jump ahead of the other guy. You don't want to be a play behind, always saying, 'Golly, I should have called 15.' So then you call 15, and they smear it. 'Aw, gee,' you say, 'I should have called 12.' Then they smear that.

"I went out there Saturday with the idea of throwing, and they stopped it. So I went to the run, and it was working just fine. Now I'm thinkin': Oh, they're gonna change any minute. They ain't gonna let us run the ball down their throats all day long.

"So I guess when they're likely to change and pick that time to throw something. And they ain't changed. They just batted it down our throats.

"I finally realized they ain't gonna change, but it took me half the game to figure that out. They just did a great job of scheming."

In the process, Amp Lee quietly picked up another 100-yard game, running for 114 yards on 16 carries. And when Weldon was able to find a receiver, it often was Knox, who had his best performance as a Seminole—132 yards and a touchdown on four receptions.

Despite giving up 420 yards, the defense had rallied to stop Virginia Tech when it had to. And Terrell Buckley's reputation as one of the nation's top big-play defensive backs had been enhanced by his two interceptions and the 71-yard runback for the touchdown.

By those standards, it had not been a terrible game. They had won. They were still No. 1 in the nation and still owned the longest win streak in Division I-A football, 12 games.

But standards for Florida State in 1991 had changed. Victory had diminished some of the frustration, and surely, Virginia Tech's scrappy determination deserved some of the credit for the Seminoles' disappointing performance. But none of that was going to overcome the growing fear that, if they were not very careful, things could quickly spin out of control.

Gone now was any pretense of the low-key campaign they had begun the season with: One game at a time; don't look beyond this week. Every newspaper and TV sports show was beating the drums for the November 16 clash with Miami. They were calling it the Game of the Century. And everything the Seminoles now did was going to be an indicator of their readiness to meet the Hurricanes. "No Excuses" was no longer just a slogan of commitment. If they lost, it would become a sealed indictment.

That realization would drive the coaches' practice planning for the next four games. Against Virginia Tech, the players had botched assignments and lapsed into undisciplined play. "We worked a dad-gum hour on blitz pickups," grumbled Brad Scott, "and they spent most of their time with their fingers up their butts."

They had won because the Hokies couldn't match up with them, position by position, in athletic talent. They would have the same advantage again in this Saturday's homecoming game against Middle Tennessee State. Which meant this was likely to be another week in which it would be hard to instill a sense of urgency.

After Middle Tennessee State, they were on the road against Louisiana State and Louisville. Then it was back to Doak Campbell to play South Carolina before Miami came to town. If the Virginia Tech game was allowed to remain as a kind of model of practice discipline and game-day execution, they could go downhill fast and end up losers before they even got to the Game of the Century.

"You get what you demand, men," Bowden repeated to his coaches in the Monday meeting. If there was a time to pull in the reins of discipline, to experiment with new starters, this might be it.

Jimmy Heggins, the tight end coach, was toying with the idea of sitting Warren Hart down for defying orders to drop some weight. Hart was pushing 280. John Eason was going to promote Kevin Knox to starter; he'd earned the chance with his performance the last two games. And Coach Scott wanted to make an example out of his junior center, Robbie Baker.

Baker had been a reliable starter since last year, but he had missed some key blocks in the Virginia Tech game and now seemed to be slacking off on his academic responsibilities. Maybe it would do him some good to miss a game. So Scott moved Robert Stevenson from tackle to center and promoted backup tackle John Flath to Stevenson's spot. There could be a double profit from Scott's standpoint: He could get Baker's attention and experiment with a backup alignment he might need later on anyway.

"Whether Robbie Baker plays or not, we're not risking our chances, 'cause we're supposed to win this game no matter what. So it's not a very brave thing we're doin'," Bowden admitted. "Yet it's still a punishment to him because he wants to play, whether it's against Miami or Middle Tennessee State."

Ultimately, that was the only power the coaches had over the young men they directed. To be who they wanted to be, the players needed to be on the field on Saturdays.

But the tactics the coaches employed in the weeks before they faced heavy underdogs was not exactly a secret. And the players accepted the maneuvers with cynical resignation. Anybody who moved up a slot when starters were demoted before a game with Middle Tennessee State knew they couldn't count on being there when the guys across the line of scrimmage were Miami Hurricanes and Florida Gators. Those games inspired their own kind of practice discipline.

The pressure to do something about the kicking game pushed Bowden beyond the tinkering stage. "We can't continue like this," he had told reporters after Dan Mowrey missed two more extra points in the Virginia Tech game. That gave him eight misses for the season.

"As soon as we play a close game, we'll lose."

John Wimberly had come in to kick the point-afters at Michigan and in last week's game in Orlando. But Bowden was nervous about his tendency to kick line drives. Gerry Thomas, the walk-on sophomore, was a better bet. He would get his chance in practice this week.

They could spend most of the week on fundamentals and on correcting mistakes, because Saturday's opponents didn't appear to present anything complicated or challenging to scheme against. Mark Richt and Brad Scott would call the plays, as they did against Western Michigan, when the Seminoles shut out the Broncos 58–0. Middle Tennessee State might not offer even that much resistance. The school was a respected competitor in Division I-AA, but was clearly overmatched at this level.

"We can run just about anything we want if we execute," said Scott.

Bowden's practice plan was to concentrate on getting the backups prepared to contribute. They would surely have a major role in Saturday's game, and this might be a last chance to get them some controlled, concentrated work before an emergency thrust them into the action. To make sure the second- and third-team players got the attention in the scrimmage sections of the workouts, Bowden excused the starters on defense and offense from wearing full gear on Tuesday. They would practice in shells—shoulder pads, hip pads and shorts.

"That's dangerous to let one group go out in pads and one group not," admitted Bowden. "But the thing is, if you put 'em all in pads, the coaches won't coach them second- and third-teamers. They will spend all their time with the starters. I nearly had to do that to get the coaches to work with them."

But it was touchy territory. "There's always the chance of introducing the possibility of disturbing something that was going good."

17

THE air was cool on Wednesday afternoon. Some of the players moved out of the shade of the practice-field oak tree and into the sun while they waited for the punting teams to finish their drills in the ABC portion of prepractice.

When those periods were over, they knew, Bowden would whistle them all together for a few words before they split into offensive and defensive segments for the rest of practice. All of them were in shells today, except for Marvin Jones and Kirk Carruthers. The two linebackers were fighting the flu and were permitted to come out in just sweat suits.

That got the grumbles started again. First the starters didn't dress in full pads on Tuesday. Now these guys were out here in sweat suits. The coaches were always talking TEAM this and TEAM that. If Kirk and Marvin were so sick, let 'em stay in their rooms or work out with the rehabbing players way off on the side with Coach Van Halanger. Seeing them out here in no pads, with no chance of giving or receiving hits, just rubbed it in.

Instead of moving to the shade, where he usually talked to the players, Bowden remained in the sun in the middle of the upper offensive field. He whistled for the players to join him there.

This break in the routine got the players chattering as they jogged toward him. The coach was notoriously susceptible to chills. Maybe he just didn't want to stand in the shade. Or maybe, whispered one young player, he was going to do something special, like letting them out of practice altogether today. The Tuesday practice, with the first-teamers on the side, had been a bust. And they were in no better mood to work today. So maybe the Man was gonna cut them some slack.

Bowden motioned them into a circle around him, then backed them off where they would have some space to move. He peered at them, emotionless, from behind his sunglasses. When he spoke it was with an even intensity, enunciating each word.

"Now, when I blow the whistle, I want you running in place, knees up. And when I say, 'On your belly,' I want you to hit the ground on your belly. When I say, 'On your back,' flip over on your back.

"All right." He blew the whistle. "Start running. Get 'em up."

The assistant coaches worked the circle like drill instructors, yelling at players who were too slow to move on Bowden's command.

"On your belly!"

"On your back!"

"On your belly!"

"On your feet!"

It took about two minutes of this to have even the receivers and backs sweating and puffing. The linemen were exhausted and lagging a command behind. Looks of utter confusion were on all their faces.

This was a penalty drill, Bowden explained to the panting players after he ended it. The football locker room was being left in worse and worse shape after practices and games. And earlier in the week, Carruthers and Todd McIntosh, horsing around in the shower area, had dumped a whole barrel of foot powder onto the floor, creating a mud slick.

"What are you trying to do? Isn't the locker room our home? Now, I don't know who threw that powder all over the floor in there. But they are the reason you had to go through this little drill."

In the last row of the concentric circles of players, one of the redshirt freshmen was still panting, and just out of earshot of the coach. "If he asked me," he rasped to a teammate, "I sure woulda told him who done it."

18

ALTHOUGH it was one of football's oldest traditions, Bowden rarely turned to physical punishment as a way of getting his point across. In the old days of college football, when most of Florida State's assistant coaches had been players and Bowden had been a novice coach, "on your belly, on your back" drills wouldn't even have qualified as physical punishment. Back then, it wasn't unusual for coaches to dig pits for players to fight out of. Drills, especially in preseason, were designed to leave one person standing. A previous Florida State coach had been criticized for forcing linemen to do low-attack drills under a cage of chicken wire, a common technique back then.

"It was survival of the fittest," remembered Bowden.

When he took over Howard's program in 1959, he had organized one of those boot-camp-style preseasons to drive out the players who wouldn't play tough enough. But those days, for the most part, were gone.

The Seminole coaches would assign penalty gassers, runs up stadium steps and sit-ups for careless mistakes and minor rule violations. But nobody wanted players burned out from drills and punishment when it was time to play on Saturday. The tough stuff was saved for out-of-season workouts. Spring practices were day-after-day scrimmages. And in February and early March, there were the dreaded mat drills, the early-morning calisthenics designed to drive players to exhaustion, then beyond, to teach perseverance and mental toughness.

But Bowden was convinced the modern athlete wouldn't put up with the old brutality. "These kids would walk right out on you.

"Bear Bryant couldn't come back to Alabama today and coach like he did in 1959. And I couldn't go back to Samford and coach the way I did.

It was a boot camp back then. Nowadays, that won't work anymore. You gotta go another route. You got to motivate better. You got to be more understanding. You gotta show them where they can gain more by doing what you ask.

"I think when I went to West Virginia is when I began to see the change starting, the players demanding more input. It was more 'Why are we doing this?' and 'We've got our rights too.' That movement started in the late '60s, and I learned to adapt with it.

"Coaches who don't learn to adapt are gone. If I can't keep up with the modern times, my day will be gone.

"I think raising six children probably helped me. From 1970 to 1982, I always had one of my own boys on the team, either playing for me or coaching for me. So I could always get a feeling for how they thought about things. And now that we're all coaching, we confer a lot.

"We're getting more talented players now and ones that are stronger academically. You can be a little more lenient. As long as they're gonna abide by the rules, you try to have as few rules as possible.

"When they don't, you gotta throw on the restrictions and dish out the punishment."

19

Boots Donnelly, 12-year head coach of the Middle Tennessee State Blue Raiders, arrived in Florida in spirit far in advance of Saturday's game.

How did he expect to do against the nation's No. 1 team? "I think we got a better chance of survival if the plane goes down."

The Tampa *Tribune*'s Tom McEwen led his Wednesday, October 16, column with that quote, then followed it with the complete Donnelly routine:

"I got five kids on this team I don't like, so I called 'em in and told them they are going to play the whole game. I told them to write their mommas and warn them."

On the Seminoles' ranking:

"Hah! I think they are No. 1 in the human poll and No. 1 in God's personal poll. I think he even has them rated ahead of Notre Dame, with St. Bobby Bowden the coach."

If the Middle Tennessee State coaches did their jobs well, said Donnelly, they should be able "to make one first down and force one punt. I want to make them punt once."

As for his own preparation:

"I don't spend a lot of time watching Florida State films. I don't want to put myself through that misery. . . . We will get us up as good an offensive plan as we can and as good a defensive plan as we can, go down and play the game and have some fun—if experiencing death is fun."

Bowden read all this and grinned. Coach Donnelly was clearly going for the Southern football coaching Oscar. And he had a true admirer in the Florida State coach, who had played this role enough times to recognize another master. Donnelly would have his team ready to run through walls.

In giving Middle Tennessee State the slot left by Auburn's late cancellation, the Seminole athletic department had made Donnelly's season. His school, which played in a 15,000-seat stadium in Murfreesboro, Tennessee, was guaranteed $175,000 for showing up. And since they were expected to lose big, almost anything the Blue Raiders did on the field would boost their prestige.

The program was already a power in the lower division. Middle Tennessee State lost in the I-AA championship quarterfinals last year but was ranked first in the country before the playoffs. Under Donnelly, the Blue Raiders were 86–51 in 12 years and 11–2 in 1990. No other Florida State opponent this year had won that many games the previous season.

Donnelly's players, many of whom had been passed over for Division I-A scholarships, had everything to prove and nothing to lose. And he and his assistant coaches would test their skills against the nation's top-ranked team.

Those guys would be primed to play the best game of their lives against the Seminoles, thought Bowden. And this week he had a team whose greatest show of enthusiasm was a foot-powder fight in the locker room.

"Y'all better not be taking that stuff seriously you're reading in the newspapers," he told them. "Those players can't wait to get at you."

20

THERE was a month left until the November 17 pick-'em day for the postseason bowl games, but the Florida State athletic director, like everybody else in the business of college football, already had bowl season on his mind. It was impossible not to.

In Orlando the previous weekend, Bob Goin had been to a Friday-afternoon reception sponsored by Miami's Blockbuster Bowl, then went to dinner with the Citrus Bowl people. On Saturday, he had morning coffee with Fiesta Bowl representatives, then breakfast with the Orange Bowl. The romancing had begun.

From now on, bowl committees would send folks to every game. Lots of handshaking and warm smiles of fervent friendship. Everybody wanted a winner. But Goin and Bowden remembered last year, when the Seminoles ended up fourth in the nation, but were snubbed for a January 1 bowl. This was business.

"My goals are simple for this football team," said Goin. "If they do their thing, I want to position them to win the national championship in a bowl game. That's the No. 1 thing. If we stay where we are, ranked at the top, we're gonna get the chance to pick our bowl, and I'm gonna pick it to give our kids the best chance to win it all."

What that meant was, he had no intention of giving a powerful team with one or two losses the chance to redeem itself as a contender for the national championship at Florida State's expense. Not while a lesser opponent with a better record waited in the wings.

If the Wolfpack of North Carolina State continued to win, they would be an ideal choice, thought Goin. Because NC State played a softer schedule than most of the other national contenders, it probably couldn't finish any higher than third or fourth, even if it was unbeaten. But if both FSU and NC State finished with perfect records, the likely teams separating the two in the rankings would be either teams Florida State beat in the course of going 12–0—Miami and Michigan—or Washington, which had to go to the Rose Bowl if it won the Pac-10 Conference.

"I'll play Washington if they want to drop out of the Rose Bowl," said Goin, laughing. "I'll play 'em in the Blockbuster Bowl for the whole ball of wax. I'll tell 'em that. They ain't gonna do that, but I'll tell them anyway.

"If I can't play them, I'm gonna position our team to win. I don't want to play a 10–1 team or a 9–2 team when we're 12–0. They've got everything to win, and we've got everything to lose. I'm going for an undefeated team.

"There will be people thinking: They oughta play Notre Dame out in the Fiesta Bowl. Well, bull. Notre Dame lost to Michigan, and we beat Michigan. Why should I give them a chance to bounce back against us? We have Notre Dame scheduled in '93 and '94. We'll cross that bridge when we come to it. If our team gets to be 12–0 and No. 1, I'm sold on positioning us against an opponent where we will be 13–0. Or at least have the chance to be 13–0."

Goin knew what was going to happen if an undefeated, No. 1 Florida State turned down Notre Dame or some other national power in the Fiesta Bowl and chose to play North Carolina State in the Blockbuster or Citrus Bowl in Florida. The Fiesta Bowl people would scream bloody murder on being denied a chance at the glamour matchup. And the media would ride him for trying to back into the national championship with an easy bowl game.

Let 'em all scream, Goin argued.

"We beat BYU out in California, Michigan at Michigan, then Syracuse here. If we go on to beat LSU at LSU, Miami here and Florida in Gainesville, then I'm not going out looking for the next-best football team in the country. If we go through that schedule and are 12–0, we've earned everything. And I'm gonna offer no excuses to anyone for positioning our team to win the national championship in the bowl game."

Despite the worry built into his job, Goin was feeling pretty good about Florida State's situation. After signing up with the Atlantic Coast Conference in July, life had gotten considerably sweeter for him and his athletic programs. Although it meant splitting bowl money with a conference for the first time, it also meant sharing in revenues from other ACC football powers. And, even more important, it meant cashing in on the conference's big-time reputation—and tournament earnings—in basketball. Already, basketball recruiting had benefited from the new relationship.

Then there was the big bowl bonus. Right after Florida State joined the ACC, the conference hooked up in an alliance that guaranteed January 1 bowl bids for champions of the Big East and the ACC and for Notre Dame—"which is its own conference," as Bowden liked to say. The arrangement, planned to begin in the 1992 postseason, seemed to be an ideal way to end the backstabbing and infighting of the bowl-pick season. Every big winner would have a place to go.

The Cotton, Orange and Sugar bowls were already tied to conferences. Champions from the Southeastern Conference went to New Orleans and the Sugar Bowl; Big Eight champs went to Miami's Orange Bowl; and the Southwest Conference winners played in Dallas at the Cotton Bowl. Under the new alliance, these three bowls agreed to choose the other teams from the pool that included the ACC and Big East champs, Notre Dame and two other national powers. The Fiesta Bowl, in Tempe, Arizona, got the national championship game if the schools ranked No. 1 and No. 2 were in that pool; otherwise, the Fiesta chose its teams from those left after the other three bowls picked.

Things were a little shaky with the alliance deal at present. Schools were worried about being shut out of big bowls if they were runners-up in their conferences. And the Blockbuster Bowl, which was not part of the alliance, was making noises about breaking up the deal with a cash offer some of the conferences couldn't refuse. But too many people wanted the alliance to work. And there would be earnest efforts to patch things together.

If it held up, the coalition amounted to a coup for Florida State, as far as Goin was concerned. The path to a major bowl now went directly through the conferences. And except for Clemson, the ACC schools had lately been playing football a notch below Bobby Bowden teams.

21

In the first half of the homecoming game against the overmatched Blue Raiders, the Florida State Seminoles scored two touchdowns and two field goals. They put up 255 yards of total offense. Casey Weldon attempted 24 passes and connected on 14 for 210 yards and a touchdown.

But the indelible impression from thirty minutes of football in Doak Campbell Stadium was that of an engine sputtering along on half its cylinders. The score was 20–10, Florida State. But it felt as if the Seminoles were down by 20 when they slinked off the field at halftime.

Two things stuck in Bowden's mind: the sight of No. 21, Middle Tennessee State's 175-pound tailback, Joe Campbell, zipping around right end for 29 yards and a touchdown; and the recurring image of his own offensive linemen struggling to control a Division I-AA opponent—and by and large failing.

In the coaches' locker room, Mickey Andrews was beside himself. "We're fooling ourselves if we think we're coaches. I don't think there's been a lick thrown the whole half."

Bowden's assistants didn't bother with drawing up halftime adjustments or tinkering with blocking assignments and defensive formations. It was clear what the trouble was.

Andrews had stormed at his defense as they came off the field. But the look he gave Bowden now reflected more embarrassment than anger. "They need to make up their minds whether they want to play football."

Brad Scott collared his linemen, then the whole offense, in the players' locker room. Fans in the end-zone seats should have been able to hear him through the metal door:

"We can't throw, and we can't catch. We let them get their hands up blocking the dad-gum passes. We got a quarterback who can't throw the ball, receivers falling down on routes, tight ends dropping touchdown passes, holding penalties on the best runs. And everybody is just feeling their way around here thinking that this team is just gonna lay down because we're so good and we're so skilled.

"Well, I tell you one thing, men, you're setting yourself up for the biggest disappointment of your life, whether it happens today or whether it happens next week."

Oh Lord, maybe this was it. They had lost control. They had let up so much in practices for fear of injury that the players had forgotten how to block and tackle. When was the last time they had put the whole team in full pads? Since before the Michigan game. Was this the price they had to pay, humiliation at homecoming against a Division I-AA team?

"You're playing like a bunch of dad-gum mullets," Scott bellowed. "Well, that's our fault. You better get your butts in gear out there and do what the heck you're supposed to do. You're fixing to live in five days of hell around here next week."

The players watched Bowden enter from the coaches' dressing room, saw him stare intently at his notes before calling them all together. He looked tired.

"C'mon in here, men."

The coaches had left their booth in the press box before official stats were available, so they never had accurate numbers in front of them. But some facts were easy to remember: an interception; five penalties; having to settle for field goals twice inside their opponent's 5-yard line; and, worst of all, nearly a four-minute deficit in time of possession.

"Now, men, that's strictly a first half of getting outhustled and outfought. That's awful. I didn't think you were capable of doing that bad."

It was the worst kind of anger, the kind that seemed built up behind some barrier and funneled to the outside through a tiny hole, like a laser.

There was no yelling. Bowden's voice was low and even, tinged with sarcasm.

"Did you see them hustle off the field at the half? They know dang well they're outplaying you. They're outhitting you.

"Defense, they had the ball the whole half. They have dominated the whole half. I could tell by the way you walked out on the field you weren't ready to play.

"What are you going to do the next half? We can get beat if we play like this. We can get beat by a One–Double-A team.

"Offensive line, forgive me for asking you to dominate. We've been on the goal line three times and had to kick field goals. What are they doing, just beatin' the hell out of you? You've been readin' those dang clippings about how good you are.

"Nobody has made a great catch. There should have been two touchdowns in the end zone. 'Oh, Coach, you don't think I'm gonna go up and try to get it with both hands, do you? Nah, I'm gonna reach up with one and get it.'

"Because it doesn't mean enough to you.

"Our goal-line offense is getting whipped. I can't wait to see the film. I tell you what, men, this second half, I'm gonna grade that film, and you better dominate your man. You better kill your guy or I'm gonna be very upset.

"Oh, excuse me for saying dominate. Just don't let him dominate you, all right?"

Bowden's intention to let Scott and Richt call the plays had lasted until the second quarter, when he put on a headset and offered a few "suggestions." That was driving all three of them crazy. So at the half, Scott told him, "Why don't you just take it, Coach."

The experimenting with the offensive line was over too. Moving Stevenson to center and inserting John Flath in the tackle spot apparently weakened the line at two positions. Robbie Baker, it was decided, had been punished enough. He would be back at center, Stevenson would move back to tackle, and the same front five that started against Michigan would now line up against Middle Tennessee State.

But not immediately. First, the Blue Raiders would get their turn with the ball. Bowden paced nervously for the first six minutes of the third quarter while Middle Tennessee State received the second-half kickoff, then drove from its own 10-yard line to inside the Florida State 40. The Blue Raiders ran 13 plays and picked up three first downs. Freshman quarterback Kelly Holcomb continued the record string of complete passes he began in the first half. But when the Blue Raiders were finally forced to punt, they had been pushed back to a fourth-and-12 situation on the 41.

The kick rolled out of bounds at the Florida State 8, where the Seminole offense got its first chance of the new half. Bowden wanted to pound it. He called four consecutive running plays, and Lee and Bennett advanced the ball to within four yards of midfield. There, Weldon tried his first pass, and he was nearly sacked in the effort. It was ruled incomplete.

On second down, Shannon Baker caught a quick out, but was stopped after only a yard. Pressured again on third down, Weldon scrambled right, directing the receivers to move downfield. He hit Kevin Knox for a 38-yard gain down to the Blue Raider 15. A holding penalty and a screen pass for negative yardage backed the Seminoles up to the 29. Weldon overthrew Knox on second down, but he hooked up with Baker for the touchdown on the next play.

Gerry Thomas, who was handling all the extra points, kicked his third point-after of the day. And the score was 27-10.

From that point on, the Seminoles controlled every aspect of the game. Holcomb established a school record of 13 consecutive complete passes, never missing in the second half. But the exhausted Blue Raiders wouldn't score again, wouldn't, in fact, get any closer than the FSU 39-yard line.

The Seminoles finished with 543 yards of total offense in a 39–10 victory. They were 7–0. Undefeated. No. 1 in the country. And depressed.

Little changed in Bowden's demeanor from the half. The frustration had drained him. He was still simmering. "Last week was nearly lousy. Today was really lousy," he told the players after the game. "It was strictly attitude. You weren't ready to play.

"Men, if we don't play any better than that, we will lose next week, I can promise you. LSU is not having a good year. But when they play against No. 1, they'll be like everybody else and be comin' after us."

Bowden had trained himself to bury the intensity of a game, especially the frustration and anger, within moments after he left the field. The players got the last glimpse of his feelings. Then, as he headed up the back stairs of the athletic center to where the press awaited in the large team meeting room, he again became the self-deprecating master of ceremonies of Southern football. Even after a loss, he would field the questions and serve up the quotable quip.

Today, however, it took him a little longer to lose the hard edge in his voice. It was the media, ironically, who tried to supply him with silver linings where the coach saw mostly dark clouds.

"I thought they really outplayed us. But again we just had more talent. We executed some plays out there today like we were in the first grade. If we don't get better, we'll lose next week.

"We'll put pads back on next week."

But how about the fact that Gerry Thomas made all four extra points and Mowrey hit on three field goals?

"I wish Dan could have hit that last one, then I would have had nothing bad to say about the kicking."

How about Sean Jackson, Tiger McMillon and Marquette Smith—the backup tailbacks who gained so many yards in the second half?

"Oh, I was happy with the way our backs ran. I just wasn't happy with our blocking. I wasn't happy with our throwing."

What about the defense, with eight sacks, a safety and two fumble recoveries? Wasn't he pleased with the way it controlled the second half?

"Well, the second half I was. But not the first half. I don't know how long they had the ball the first half. Was it something like four minutes more than we had it? With us being One-A and them being One–Double-A, people shouldn't be controlling the ball on us like that."

22

RANDY Oravetz's Monday-morning injury report was a long one. Robbie Baker was still suffering from flu symptoms. And now Marvin Jones had it. Howard Dinkins and Sterling Palmer reported to the training room Sunday with swollen knees. Matt Frier and Kevin Knox had severe hip bruises. Troy Sanders, who had his best day as a Seminole against Middle Tennessee State, could barely walk because of a severely sprained toe. And there was a growing list of bruised thighs, jammed fingers, partially dislocated shoulders and sore ribs.

Bowden grimaced impatiently. That was the last thing he wanted to hear. He had to send a message of physical intensity and mental preparedness for LSU week. The Monday workout, as usual, would be in sweats. Time to correct mistakes and stretch out those sore muscles. Tuesday would be back to full pads and 11-on-11 drills. "Not for punishment, but for teaching," said the head coach. "I want goal-line tackling. They've forgotten what those arms are for."

Wednesday, they would practice in shells, without their lower-body pads. That reduced open-field tackling, but it took nothing off the collisions on the line of scrimmage—especially in short-yardage scrimmages. And that's what Bowden wanted.

"What were y'all's opinions after the game?" Bowden asked his coaches.

"If Miami had been playing these guys, they would have beat them 70–0," said Mickey Andrews.

But if they were honest with themselves, some of the assistants argued, hadn't they all allowed their attentions to wander last week? The players sensed it in the coaches and used it as an excuse for their own lack of intensity. Even Bowden had been looking ahead, sneaking peeks at LSU video while Brad Scott and Mark Richt prepared the game plan.

"That's something I never do," admitted the head coach. When he had caught himself thinking too much about the following week's challenge, he had locked himself in with tapes of Middle Tennessee State Friday afternoon to cram for the game. "I kept thinking: 'What will I do if all of a sudden they're beatin' us and I don't know what they're doing?' It didn't help none on Saturday. But it made me feel a little better."

Perhaps Miami would have destroyed a team like the Blue Raiders, but Bowden knew "it was human nature for our kids not to prepare themselves the same way they did against Michigan. I didn't want them thinkin': You gotta win this one for your momma, die for the cause. This wasn't Alabama they were playin', and they knew that as well as we did. But I was hoping that pride would carry them through.

"Now I need to talk to the offense."

As he often did when he was troubled about game-plan execution, Bowden wanted the offensive coaches to walk him through every play in the previous week's game and explain the breakdowns. If there was a problem in personnel, he wanted to know about it. If they had to change the way they protected the passer or ran a pass route or pulled a guard to block on a running play, he wanted to get on it.

Richt wanted to make a point too. Since the beginning of the season, Weldon and the wideouts had been having trouble connecting on the 80 game, the quick outs. And the quarterback had taken his shots for failing to hit apparently wide-open receivers. What the coaches noticed when they reviewed game video on Sunday seemed to explain part of the problem.

They dimmed the lights and showed the head coach a couple of plays from Saturday's game featuring Matt Frier at the X position. Instead of cutting sharply inside as the patterns required, Frier consistently rounded his turns and drifted downfield, ending up three to five yards beyond the point where Weldon was supposed to hit him. Since those were timing patterns, designed to get the ball to a spot quickly, the quarterback's throws came low. Which was why Frier ended up diving for so many balls and why so many fell incomplete.

In the second half, the sophomore receiver had made a spectacular third-down catch in heavy traffic, taking a brutal hit and still hanging on to the ball to sustain a scoring drive. But he had slipped trying to make a cut in the first half, allowing a defender to intercept a pass intended for him. And there were those awkward second-half moves on the 84 plays.

"I'm pissed off at Casey for missing these, and it turns out he's throwing to a spot on rhythm," said Richt. "And that's all we can ask.

"Nobody works harder than Matt Frier. But what I see happening, Coach, is that these other guys are getting better, and he's not. He maybe started out ahead of them because of his work habits, but now they're learning how to work, and they're passing him up."

They all knew that Frier understood where he was supposed to end up. The problem was that he was having a terrible time making his body do it.

"He's just so stiff," said Richt.

Bowden nodded. "But I don't want to give up on him."

John Eason was torn. This was his guy. He wanted him to succeed more than anybody. But if the shoe were on the other foot, he would make the same argument as Richt. Frier had stayed after practice to work on the 84 route, to make the sharp cuts without rounding the turns. But he couldn't seem to do it at full speed.

"He doesn't have his body under control," the head coach acknowledged. "But I know how to help that: Get him to slow down. I don't want to give up on him. He's got great courage. He made a big play in that game that helped us."

No problem, Richt shrugged. He just didn't want his guy blamed for missing those throws. Besides, everyone in the room knew that competition would take care of Matt Frier's problem. He would fix it, or he would lose so much ground to Kez McCorvey and Knox, he wouldn't play. It was adapt or die.

Part VI

"WELCOME TO DEATH VALLEY"

1

"Not Just Another Joe," was the way *Sports Illustrated* headlined the feature on Casey Weldon in its October 28 issue. The lead photo spread juxtaposed two action shots, one of Weldon poised to pass and one of San Francisco 49ers quarterback Joe Montana in a similar pose. The similarity was striking. "No, you are not seeing double," read the caption.

"Weldon, a senior, presides over the country's most elegant offense," wrote Sally Jenkins, "and he is on the short list of Heisman Trophy candidates."

Well, that cinched it. The previous week, Florida papers had offered the same kind of tribute, handicapping Weldon's chances against the other likely Heisman front-runner—Michigan's Desmond Howard. And now the race was on. The final vote wouldn't be announced until December 14. But at this time of the year, Heisman speculation ranked second only to arguments about team standings in the polls.

Weldon couldn't have avoided the topic if he had wanted to. And he had no intention of trying. "Somebody's going to win it. Why not me?"

But he didn't kid himself about what it would take. Unlike the 1990 winner, Ty Detmer, and the other quarterback most often mentioned as a Heisman candidate, Houston's David Klingler, Weldon was the quarterback in a balanced run-pass offense. He wouldn't get the chance to throw 50 or 60 times a game, and Bowden would yank him whenever the Seminoles went three touchdowns ahead.

For him to win, the team would have to win. His best case was the national championship and media exposure. He would be on national television at least four more times—against LSU, Miami, Florida and a bowl opponent. All he had to do was contribute to wins in those games, and he was home free.

Of course, it would also help if he could walk and lift his arms without pain.

Weldon had not been able to practice comfortably since before the Michigan game. And each succeeding Saturday had added to his miseries.

The hip pain had been bad enough, but the right-calf bruise had kept him from pushing off with his back leg when he passed. The Syracuse defense banged up his ribs. Which brought on the standard ripple effect of athletic injuries:

His body wanted to compensate for the support he lost in his back leg and chest by transferring more force to the arm when he threw. That created a hitch in his motion and invited tendinitis. It also didn't help to be dumped on his throwing shoulder in the Virginia Tech game. Was nothing ever going to feel right again?

A couple of weeks' rest would cure most of the ailments. But that stuff was for civilians. This was war. And the stakes were getting higher every week. Weldon's personal undefeated streak was the same as the team's, 13 games. Best in Division I-A. A loss to LSU meant the end of everything—the championship, the Heisman and perhaps the chance to add some zeros on the end of his rookie NFL salary.

If you had the right kind of sense of humor—and Weldon did—you couldn't help noticing the grim irony. There apparently was an inverse relationship between Heisman credentials and working body parts. Weldon could read his clips in the whirlpool or on the training table, as he lay back, wired to some machine that would speed muscle recovery, so that he could go back out to be knocked down again.

But his prospects were improving all the time. It said so right there in *Sports Illustrated.*

2

SITTING Robbie Baker out for the first half of the Middle Tennessee State game had put the offensive line back into the spotlight. And not in an entirely positive way. Sunday, the Tallahassee *Democrat* led its inside coverage of the game with the Baker story and player quotes.

"Robbie Baker was the complete difference in the game," said Casey Weldon, who was one of the center's best friends. "When he came in, we got our continuity back."

Mike Morris, the starting guard, said losing the center "was like changing your family around." And Robert Stevenson, who was moved from his usual tackle spot to take Baker's place, told the newspaper: "This is the same line that has been together for two years, that beat

Penn State, that got things done. We showed how we could play together in the second half."

Baker himself had been around long enough to know what to say to reporters: "This past week made me thankful for my starting position. I've been very frustrated all week. I hope this teaches me a lesson."

That helped Scott declare the punishment served and the offensive line back intact. But it didn't stop the questions. Among them: Who learned the biggest lesson? And what was it?

"I think we probably played better in the second half for a couple of reasons," the line coach reflected. "Weldon and all of the rest of them want Baker to have his job back. And that's understandable. But it might not have mattered who we had in there the first half. We played better in the second half because we had a better attitude, because we ran a little harder and, I know, because we blocked a little harder.

"It's obvious that, after the experience of that half, I don't think we can give Stevenson up at split tackle to play center. That don't mean Baker came in there and played great. He didn't. But he played better than he has in the last couple of weeks.

"Now, you get into a game against LSU and you gotta put your best five on the line, the best combination. Our best combination is with Stevenson at split tackle and Baker at center.

"But it was beneficial. If Baker was to get hurt, then Stevenson will have had some snaps at center. John Flath will have had some snaps at tackle. Jeff Deremer got in there for a bit at center on Saturday. He probably should have been in there earlier, but I wasn't happy with his week in practice. He's a good kid and he works hard, but I ain't sure he's the answer."

Scott knew that the tinkering provided a hot topic for reporters, but he insisted, "I ain't interested in playing the games for the media. They all got their own opinion. But if Baker hadn't played poorly in the last two outings, I might have still gotten Stevenson some snaps. Not as starter, though. I wouldn't have put the kid through it and put the whole team through it.

"I think Baker has just lost a little focus. He got lullabied over the last few weeks. Now, a wide receiver can do that, and nobody might notice. But you take a guy in the middle of the line who's calling blocking schemes and pulling guards and watching linebackers, and when you're not sharp and focused, the whole team is in trouble.

"Maybe the shake-up will do him some good."

If there was a positive element in all this, Scott figured it was a wake-up call, an inoculation against complacency.

"I'm a man of faith, you know. And I just feel the good Lord has intervened to make sure we don't screw this up. Remember how we had that sorry scrimmage before BYU? That got our attention and sent us into the game against Brigham Young like a bunch of racehorses. Maybe if we had just breezed through these last few games we might not have been as keyed in for detail as we will be this week.

"Things are kinda happening like you would draw 'em up and almost hope they would. You still don't like it when they ain't ready to play. You can't accept it. But Florida had the same kind of game we did last week. They were more worried about the homecoming dance than playing the game."

Similar talk was coming out of Gainesville. After the Gators' 41–10 homecoming victory over Northern Illinois, Steve Spurrier had said he was embarrassed by his team's performance. He told reporters that "I screamed to our coaches in the press box that we looked like one of the worst-coached teams in the nation."

Miami, also playing at home, had beaten Long Beach State 55–0, playing mostly reserves in the second half.

The Seminoles were headed into the stretch now. Three more games until those two in-state matchups, most likely with everything on the line. And here they were, undefeated and as fit as they could hope to be at this stage.

"Maybe the Lord looks after me," said Scott. "I had no injuries in the line for twelve ball games last year. And it's been the same so far this year. No major knockouts. And you know that can be the difference in a championship season. You lose one or two of these guys and you're in real trouble."

3

IN the past few years, Louisiana State had not been the most feared competitor in Southern football. Auburn, Tennessee and, since Spurrier arrived in Gainesville, the Florida Gators had usurped the Fighting Tigers' power in the Southeastern Conference. Yet they still profited from the residual effect of their long history, from their apparently endless supply of great Louisiana athletes and from that loud, inhospitable stadium known as Death Valley.

After a half century of additions and renovations, Tiger Stadium's 1991 capacity was 80,140, including the nosebleed seats in the cantilevered section that hovered over the west stands. Since the NCAA began keeping attendance records in 1957, LSU had averaged nearly 68,000 fans for home games and had won more than 70 percent of them.

As late as 1987, when the College Football Association polled head coaches, LSU's Tiger Stadium still ranked as the most feared playing site for visiting teams. Lord have mercy on you if you got behind and let those fans into the game.

"That place makes Notre Dame seem like Romper Room," a Southern Cal player said after his top-ranked team survived a 17–12 Death Valley victory in 1979. That was the last time the Tigers hosted the No. 1 team in the nation.

Florida State and Bobby Bowden had done well in Baton Rouge. Overall, the Seminoles had won five of six games played there. A Bowden squad lost in 1982. But it was the 1979 game, when he brought an undefeated Seminole team to Tiger Stadium, that stood out most in his memory. "That was the game that really made me decide to stay at FSU."

Paul Dietzel, who coached LSU to its only national championship in 1958, was then the school's athletic director. And he was looking for someone to replace McClendon the next year. The job was Bowden's if he wanted it.

Bowden was four years into his rebuilding program at Florida State and cruising into the danger zone. In 1979, he had his best team so far, a team that would go undefeated in the regular season and lose in the Orange Bowl to Oklahoma. What if it didn't get any better than this for the Seminoles? Could he afford to hang around and keep plugging away while jobs like the one at LSU went begging? The phone would stop ringing if he stopped winning. It was one of the rules of the game.

But the 24–19 win in Baton Rouge in '79 teased Bowden in the other direction. His Seminoles, who only five years before were something of a joke in the region, beat the mighty LSU Tigers on one of those wild Saturday nights that made you think demons were coming out of the steaming Louisiana bayous to scream, "Hold That Tiger." If they could win there in that place, against all that tradition, maybe this wasn't a peak at all. Maybe it signaled Florida State's arrival at some new level, a level to build on. With the state's population booming and only three big-time universities to accommodate all those athletes, perhaps the future was in Tallahassee. So Bowden turned down Paul Dietzel.

"If we had lost that game, I probably would have gone."

A decade later, the tide had turned. It was Bowden's team that had the big-time reputation. In 1990, the Tigers had made their first visit to Doak Campbell, catching the Seminoles in a cranky mood after their 20–17 loss to Auburn the previous week. Florida State beat them 42–3. It was Bowden's 200th career victory and Casey Weldon's first. The Seminoles had been undefeated since.

The end of that game was marred by a fight that embroiled nearly all the players on both teams. Bowden, being interviewed at midfield on the occasion of his milestone victory, had to leave the reporters and help his assistants pull players out of the free-for-all.

It was a frustration fight, begun in the closing seconds when LSU players thought Kirk Carruthers had hit one of their guys out of bounds. Video of the brawl made the postgame TV shows, and there were clearly some hard feelings—especially on the part of the Baton Rouge contingent. Bowden was going to do everything he could to make sure no one from his side did anything in '91 to open old wounds.

"I seldom ever tell you what to tell the press," Bowden said to his players. "But if any of them ask you about that fight . . . well, I know what I'm gonna say when they ask me. I'm gonna say, 'No comment.' Don't let them start talking about that fight last year. They'll want to keep bringin' it up and bringin' it up."

Things were going to be tough enough without supplying LSU with extra incentive. Everybody in the country was already saying the Tigers couldn't do it. So here would come the Seminoles, wearing that No. 1 target and going into Death Valley as 27-point favorites to face an LSU squad with nothing to lose.

"Back at the beginning of the season," said Bowden, "I thought this would be one of the peaks we would have to be ready for. They had a new coach, but were returning all those guys from last year. I picked 'em as one of the dark horses in the nation."

The new coach was Curley Hallman, who had come to Baton Rouge from Southern Mississippi, a team with powerful negative connotations in the minds of FSU fans. It was Hallman's Southern Miss squad that upset the Seminoles in the opening game of the 1989 season. Florida State lost to Clemson the following week, then won all the rest of its games—including the one against the eventual national champions, the Miami Hurricanes. But since Miami and Notre Dame had lost only once that year, Florida State ended up ranked third.

It was FSU's first victory over Miami in five years. And Miami still snatched the national championship—largely because of what Southern Miss did to the Seminoles in that opening game. Without that defeat,

Florida State could have survived the early Clemson loss and made a strong argument—with the wins first over Miami, then over Nebraska in the Fiesta Bowl—that it was the best once-defeated team in the nation. If it hadn't been for Hallman . . .

"This is the same coach, different team," the Florida State coaches warned their players.

So far, however, Hallman had been having a hard time getting his message across to his new team. The gossip out of Baton Rouge was that the veteran LSU players were resisting his tough tactics. Morale had dipped in opening losses to Georgia and Texas A&M. But they had fought the Gators hard, losing 16–0 when they were 22-point underdogs. Then they had won twice in a row to even up their season at 3–3. The Seminoles could be sure the Tigers relished the thought of turning their whole season around with an upset of No. 1.

If the players needed a reminder, Brad Scott supplied it Monday afternoon in the scouting-report meeting:

"They've been talking about Florida State all year. You're setting yourself up for a big showdown in Baton Rouge before half the dad-gum state of Louisiana. It would be a big mistake to fool yourself the way you've been doin' in practice and go into one of the toughest stadiums in the South against a hungry team.

"You've become deaf to the coaches. 'It's old hat,' you think. 'They have to say those things.' You don't hear us anymore.

"Well, it's too late in the season to overcome a loss and still win the national championship. Seniors, you may look back and say this was the week we turned it all around—or the week that we lost it all."

4

"Is Troy a hundred percent out?"

Chuck Amato wanted to press Randy Oravetz on the status of his Clydesdale. Could a toe problem really stop a power-lifting, jungle-fighting defensive lineman?

Troy Sanders was playing the best he had ever played. Alternating him with Carl Simpson at the tackle spot had worked perfectly. Simpson was quick and strong; Sanders was a relentless bull. Both were getting better each week.

Against Middle Tennessee State, Sanders had been having his best game, sacking the quarterback and catching runners in the backfield for losses. So instead of yanking him with the rest of the veterans when the subs came in late in the game, Amato moved him to nose guard, playing directly over the center. Sanders was a junior. Chaney, the starting nose guard, was in his last year. Wouldn't it be great if Sanders could be of help at both tackle and nose guard next year?

It was an obvious maneuver. Sanders' first position, when he was redshirted as a freshman, had been nose guard. He moved to tackle before his sophomore year. But he still knew the basic responsibilities of the position, and his experience on the line gave him an advantage in technique over most of the younger guys.

The idea of playing both spots suited Sanders fine. Anything to increase his playing time. If it were up to him, he'd go both ways, playing offensive guard and defensive line. If he had any shot at the pros it would be as an offensive lineman. His height, 6-2, was about three inches short of average for NFL pass rushers. There had been a suggestion in the spring of '91, in fact, to bring at least two of Amato's Clydesdales— Sanders and Joe Ostaszewski—over to Brad Scott's side of the ball to solidify the offensive line. But depth on defense was still a question mark in spring and August. And the Clydesdales had stayed put.

Saturday, Sanders had one snap at nose. When he turned to pursue a runner laterally down the line of scrimmage, he stepped in a way that put all his 260 pounds on the side of his foot and big toe. Something gave. When he hobbled off the field to the bench, the trainers looked at the swelling foot and told him he was through for the day.

The injury was the kind of severe toe strain often suffered by running backs, who, during quick cuts, might shift too much of their body weight onto too small a surface of a foot. On natural grass, their feet might slide out from under them, saving them from injury. On artificial turf, however, with its near-perfect traction, there was no sliding, and jams and sprains were common. "Turf toe," they called it, whether the injury came on grass or artificial surfaces. And Troy Sanders had a very painful case.

It kept him awake most of Saturday night. He soaked the foot Sunday in the training room and took whatever treatment the trainers offered. But he couldn't bear to have a shoe on the foot; nor could he put any weight on it. "I have never felt anything like this," said Sanders, who was used to playing with bad knees and shoulders. "A damn toe."

Oravetz told him it was no use worrying about it; he was out. The only thing that could make his foot better was to stay off it and keep up the soaking. No practice. Probably no playing time on Saturday.

By Wednesday, Sanders had resigned himself to make the most of the situation. The coaches hadn't announced the travel squad for the LSU game, but it was safe to assume he wouldn't be on it. The rule was: no practice, no play. And he hadn't even been able to put any weight on his foot for the Tuesday and Wednesday workouts.

If he couldn't play, he didn't want to go to Baton Rouge anyway. "I got enough of that standing-on-the-sideline stuff my freshman year. I hate just standing there."

So Sanders and his girlfriend made plans to head up to his parents' house in Albany, Georgia, and watch the game on ESPN from there. He would get a little rest, eat some home cooking and be on the receiving end of a little pampering. Just what he needed.

That was before the Thursday-morning staff meeting, however.

Oravetz had gone through his injury report, and Amato asked the question: "Is Troy a hundred percent out?"

Yes, answered the trainer. And Bowden looked up. "Because of a toe? I hate for a guy to miss a game for something like that.

"What if he wants to play? Can we do something, give him something? Here's a guy who wants to play, and you tell him he can't because of a sprained toe.

"This is a pretty big game, men. If we lose this one, it's lost."

Oravetz nodded, the red creeping into his face. Amato had pushed Bowden's button, and pretty soon the whole room would be taking the trainer on.

"Yes, he should be out," said the trainer. "He can't push off on that foot. If he tries to play on it, he could be out for the rest of the season."

He could tell that his explanation found no takers. The coaches were too deeply into the high-pressure zone to deal with sprained toes. Troy Sanders was the kind of stud they liked in the lineup. A fighter. Indestructible. A sprained toe, c'mon!

"We used to play with something like that," said Bowden. "Now you want to X-ray and X-ray it until you find something."

The trainer shrugged. The assistant coaches were enjoying this, he knew. But there was no sense in aggravating the situation by challenging them. And there was certainly nothing to be gained by confronting the head coach. They were all wound tight. This was a big game. And they could lose it all.

Oravetz let them move on to another subject and excused himself. He walked downstairs to his training-room office, slammed the door and kicked the trash can across the room.

5

"Matt Frier, do you have willpower?"

Eason had chosen the topic for his Thursday segment meeting with the idea of involving all his receivers in the discussion. 'OMar Ellison seemed to be coming around in practice. He wanted to keep him motivated. He needed to stay on E.T. and to continue encouraging Baker. But the coach knew he especially had to focus on Frier.

In one sense, the Live Oak sophomore was the most even-tempered of the young men in Eason's charge. He was the most coachable, trained from childhood to respect authority. But he was far more sensitive than the swaggering country boy he affected. And he could slip quietly into depression after poor performances and sharp criticism.

Frier had gone over the game tapes with Eason, and he knew the problem. He worked so hard. He wanted to feel again the way he felt on those high school fields, outrunning and outfaking everybody. But everything was different here.

Eason pulled him into a dialogue. "Matt, in whose hands is the future?"

"I guess in the Lord's."

"And?"

"And mine. The Lord will provide the opportunity he wants."

"Does the Lord want you to wait and see what he intends or to go out and try to help?"

"I guess he wants me to go out and help."

"Matt, if things happen and you don't understand, can your willpower help you harness your effort and make progress?"

"Yes, I guess you've got to block everything out and just work hard. When people don't believe, that's when it gets hard."

"How do you handle things that you don't understand? Do you carry problems overnight?"

"Yes, probably. Because the problems I carry overnight mean a lot to me."

"How can that change your personality?"

"It can cause you to be an unhappy person."

Eason paused and turned to Shannon Baker. "Shannon, you dropped a touchdown pass against Florida last year. When did you get your vindication?"

"Maybe the fifth or sixth game of this year. Against Syracuse."

"Almost a whole year," said Eason. "You can be happy, but sometimes an obstacle stays in your mind for a long time. What would have happened if you never got the chance? Why were you ready when it did?"

"I guess because I kept at it," Baker told him. It was just the answer Eason was fishing for.

"Every one of you has faced adversity. The question is always how long are you going to let adversity tie you down? How long will it keep you down before you get the willpower to pull out?

"What would have happened if Shannon hadn't brought E.T. back after he quit last spring? 'OMar, yesterday the light came on for you in practice. Now, how long is it gonna stay on?

"Matt Frier, you're gonna get another chance. The question is, will you let your mind stop you?"

The coach pulled out a news clipping from the Pensacola *News-Journal.* Bill Vilona had written a column suggesting that maybe the Florida State receiver corps was finally coming into its own and out from under the shadow of the old Fab Four. Kevin Knox had caught 10 passes in two weeks, and Baker was leading the team with 19 receptions. The five regulars—Baker, Knox, Kez McCorvey, Eric Turral and Frier—seemed to deserve their own nickname. Vilona's suggestion: "How about the Fantastic Five?"

Eason looked up after he read from the clip. "Maybe, 'OMar, we can make it the Fantastic Five plus two, with you and Aaron Dely."

"The Superior Seven," Dely piped up.

It was almost time to end the meeting and send the receivers out to the walk-through practice in the stadium. But Eason wanted to make a personal point.

"You know, y'all think coaches are machines, that we don't feel things the way you do. But it's agonizing for me to see you work so hard and to know that you deserve to play, yet I can't put you in.

"Y'all are like my children. When I go to those staff meetings, and they say Frier can't run those 84s, I want to fight. These are my babies they're talkin' about."

6

Rain had soaked southeastern Louisiana for days and was predicted to continue, on and off, throughout the weekend. Just before dusk on Saturday, the sky above Tiger Stadium threatened to clear for one of those miracle evenings in Death Valley. But the weather report cautioned against optimism.

Over 71,000 people were expected. And while the wet weather had doused some of the usual daylong partying, there was still the smell of spicy sausage and barbecue in the air outside the stadium. Football in Baton Rouge was a Saturday-night party.

An hour before the game, the ground crew plodded through the mud on the track that bordered the playing field and checked out the end-zone grass. The sod squished beneath their feet. It would not be a night for Mike, the LSU mascot Bengal tiger.

Before games in Tiger Stadium, the live tiger was usually paraded around the field in his cage, with the LSU cheerleaders riding it like a float and the crowd screaming for blood. But the wheels would surely bog down in this mess.

Another game-day tradition was apparently rained out as well. When the Seminoles arrived at the stadium, the coaches were braced for the usual welcome—a crowd of LSU fanatics yelling "Tiger bait" at the buses and at each player they saw making his way to the visitors' locker room. The weather, and perhaps LSU's disappointing season, had cut back on the harassment.

The veterans of other wars in this place couldn't help feeling a little deprived. Who ever heard of a trip to Death Valley without abuse and rancor?

It would come soon enough, Bowden had assured his players Friday night. "Don't play tomorrow unless you're willing to fight for sixty minutes. You'll be a lot better off not even getting in there."

A half hour before kickoff, night had darkened the skies, making it harder to track the storms. But the unmistakable smell of rain was in the air.

Troy Sanders grumbled as he limped back into the locker room. He had suited up, had even tried to make his way through warm-ups. But it was no use. He couldn't play. The coaches saw it immediately. Now he would have to stand there, probably in the rain, and watch.

Bowden considered the weather report. If they were going to throw the ball, better make it early, before things got too slippery. It could be a night for defense—either theirs or ours, he thought.

"LSU is going to be fired up, full of emotion," he told the players in the pregame locker room. "They're going to come at you and attack you. But that's only going to last so long. We've simply got to knock it out of 'em.

"Backs, protect the ball. It's a little wet out there.

"Defense, knock the ball out of there. Stop the run first, make 'em throw."

But the Tigers' commitment to the run lasted for just one play on their opening series. When Florida State won the toss, Bowden, as usual, had deferred possession to the second half. Quarterback Chad Loup started the LSU offense on the 35-yard line by giving the ball to tailback Vincent Fuller, who picked up two yards. Then, on second and eight, LSU split two receivers left in a formation not unlike the one that Michigan had used in the attempt to spring Desmond Howard for the quick out. Terrell Buckley, who intercepted that Michigan pass, lined up on LSU's split end, Todd Kinchen.

At the snap, Kinchen made the inside move, as if the quick pass was headed his way. Buck stepped into the space between Kinchen and the quarterback to be in position for the interception. But the ball didn't come. After the inside fake, Kinchen had broken outside and downfield. Loup hit him going away for the 63-yard touchdown.

The stadium exploded. It was impossible to hear anything except the roar of the crowd and, just beneath it, the horn section wailing "Hold That Tiger." The whole place rocked.

"Welcome to Death Valley," said the enormous sign spread across the upper deck opposite the Seminole bench.

Tiger McMillon nearly broke the kickoff for the touchdown. He was brought down three yards short of midfield. Still, terrific field position for the Florida State opening drive. Casey Weldon and the offense trotted confidently onto the field.

The night before, when they settled in for their skull session, Bowden, Mark Richt and Brad Scott had agreed that LSU seemed vulnerable to the run. Especially the north-and-south game, right up the middle. But Scott warned the head coach about inviting a charged-up LSU defense to gain early confidence at their expense.

Against Florida, LSU had stuffed the Gator running game on the first couple of downs. "And you could see all 105 of them on the LSU sideline jumping up and down," said Scott. "Then they took off their helmets and waved them around. It was like some Fourth of July fireworks going off, with that crowd screaming and all."

He was all for pounding the run, said the line coach. Florida State could eventually dominate the game that way. But that's also what the LSU defense would be expecting. Amp Lee had scored three touchdowns against them last year. So why not fake it on the first play, complete a pass and drain some of that enthusiasm from their defense and their home crowd.

Bowden had agreed and announced the first play to the whole team in the locker room before the game. It was 45 Naked, a fake to Lee up the middle and a rollout that gave the quarterback the option of passing or running himself. Sure enough, on the opening play LSU was coming strong, hoping to disrupt the run. Two defenders, in fact, blocked Weldon's path as he rolled left. So he sidearmed the ball to Lonnie Johnson, two yards on the other side of the line of scrimmage. And the tight end took off for first-down territory.

But when Johnson was tackled 10 yards downfield, the ball squirted out of his grasp, and LSU recovered. Suddenly, Loup was back on the field passing, this time to the fullback, Leo Abel, for a gain of 30 yards. That gave the Tigers a first down on the Seminole 25. They made seven more yards before having to settle for a 35-yard field goal.

The game was less than three minutes old, and Florida State was trailing 10–0.

The noise was deafening. And Bowden wanted to settle things down, take control of the game. Amp Lee got the first-down call on the next series and made a yard.

All week long in practice, Bowden had tinkered with modifications of the Seminoles' screen passes. Against a pursuing rush like LSU's, he figured, the screens should work for decent gains. Second and long here was an obvious passing down, perfect for the first screen pass of the evening. And Bowden called for one. Amp Lee caught the ball for a loss of seven yards. Another roar shook the stadium.

On third and 16 from the FSU 14, Bowden came right back with the Irish Screen, targeting a wide receiver across the middle. Shannon Baker was in the open, but he couldn't hold on to Weldon's pass. Scott Player punted the ball 40 yards, but after Kinchen's 12-yard return, LSU was back in Florida State territory.

With their fans yelling and stomping their feet, the Tigers played as if they were the top-ranked team on the field. They even took a page or two from the Seminoles' playbook, picking up six yards on a reverse, then a first down with a one-handed catch by tailback Sammy Seamster.

Another tailback, Odell Beckham, gained a first down on the FSU 15, where the Seminole defense held the Tigers for three consecutive downs. But, again, they got the chip-shot field goal.

The score: Louisiana State 13, Florida State 0. It was the furthest Bowden's team had been behind all season.

Throughout the week, Brad Scott had been coaxing his offensive linemen to prepare for a night of mash football. On Friday night, he had tried to motivate them even more by telling them what the TV commentators had been saying about the strength of his group. The ESPN TV cameras might even isolate the interior line play tonight to verify what everybody had been saying. "Wouldn't it be pretty if they call all your names, then you go out and get your butts kicked?"

It was time to rise to the occasion, Scott told his linemen while LSU drove to the field goal. And when the offense went back on the field, it was all Amp Lee and Edgar Bennett: Lee for nine yards, Lee again for five and a first down, then Edgar Bennett for four and Lee again for another first down.

The FSU band took up the "War Chant," which brought loud boos from the LSU fans. This was their theater.

After Weldon had to throw the ball away on first down, Lee advanced it to the LSU 24 on three runs and a pass play. On third and four, Bowden called a fullback delay pass that began as a fake to Lee. Bennett steamed into the open over the middle, but Weldon's pass was behind him. Fourth down. No field goal. Bowden decided on another play-action pass. But Shawn King, LSU's outside linebacker, forced Weldon out of the pocket and tackled him before he could run the four yards for the first down.

While the defense had been on the field, Weldon walked down the offensive bench, encouraging his teammates and taking responsibility for the first-quarter sack. "C'mon now, that was my fault that time. But they can't stop us." And when the offense returned to the field, the momentum seemed to shift. Weldon found Knox and Baker for key passes, and Jackson, Bennett and Lee sustained the drive on the ground to get the Seminoles' first touchdown.

It looked as if Weldon and company would get another easy score when the Tigers botched a punt attempt on the next series and the Seminole defense recovered the ball at the LSU 8-yard line. But the offense stalled and had to hand the ball over on downs. Again, the FSU defense got a turnover on an interception. But Weldon, trying to drill the ball through coverage to Shannon Baker, threw it back to LSU three plays later.

Despite getting a first down on the FSU 19, the Tigers had to settle for a 41-yard field goal to close the half. But the damage had been done. By almost any measure, it was the worst half of offensive football for the Seminoles so far this year. Louisiana State had outperformed them in every offensive category except for rushing yards. Weldon had completed six of 12 passes for 44 yards and one interception. The team had 142 yards of total offense, 56 percent of its halftime average in the previous seven games and 20 yards less than LSU's first-half total.

In time of possession, the Tigers had a four-and-a-half-minute advantage. They had over twice as many first downs and half as many turnovers. Both of FSU's turnovers—an interception and a fumble—had led to LSU scores. The most important stat of all: Florida State was losing, 16–7.

7

THE exaggerated calm that suppresses panic took over the coaches' locker room. "Let's don't go back in there and think we got to make big plays," said Scott. "We've got thirty minutes."

Bowden wanted ideas. "We're ending up with three stinkin' yards on first down every time. When we get the ball, we need to drive right down the field. What do we call?"

"We can drop back and throw on these guys," said Mark Richt. "There's no pass rush."

"Throw it outside," said John Eason.

Was it beginning? LSU definitely did not respect the wideouts. And it could turn into a trend. They were at a stage in the season when defensive coaches had a library of game tapes and an earful of gossip from coaching buddies about who was hot and who was not. And the verdict evidently was that the Florida State receivers were not.

No defense could afford to spread itself so thin that every conceivable possibility was covered. So if you're playing the Seminoles, whom do you target and whom do you risk hurting you with the big play? Well, it looked like the backs were the attack this year. If you could stop them from catching passes over the middle, watch for the screens and the bootlegs, you might corral Florida State's passing game.

That theory would hold up, Eason knew, if either of two things happened: if his receivers failed to make the plays, or if the coaches and Weldon lost faith in them and stopped throwing the ball their way. If they were going to go back out there and pass in the second half, the wideouts were going to be open. Call their numbers, the receivers coach urged.

But the weather was wet and getting wetter. And the only thing that had worked consistently the first half was the running game up the middle. It would likely keep on working, said Scott. "I definitely think we can run it north and south."

Back in the players' locker room, they were having their own meeting. The two most emotional young players on the team were giving their version of a pep talk. Sean Jackson, a Louisiana native with family and friends in the stadium, couldn't imagine anything worse than losing in front of this crowd. He was pleading with his teammates to take control of the game.

William Floyd was on an obscene tirade, sounding as if he were personally threatening every player. "We're not going to lose this game!"

Bowden and the other coaches moved out into the players' area and quieted them down. "Sit down, men. Get where you can listen," said the head coach.

He walked over to where Weldon and Brad Johnson sat. "Do you see anything you like?" he asked the quarterbacks.

"Slants," said Weldon.

"Yeah," Johnson said, nodding, "slants and verticals."

Against Tulane, Virginia Tech and Middle Tennessee State, Bowden had been angry at the half. Then he had been measuring his team's performance against a standard he held in his mind. But here, the team in the other jerseys wasn't a lower-division squad or a group of tough overachievers who threatened to embarrass the No. 1 team. This was one of the Southeastern Conference's best group of athletes, who had decided, for the first time this season, to play with everything they had. And that would be enough to win if the Seminoles couldn't take control.

So the intensity in Bowden's voice now was devoid of anger. The only standard was victory. And everybody in the room had a pretty good idea what they had to do to win.

"Men, you've got the most important half of your life coming up. If we execute, we can get this thing right back in perspective. They've got to kick off to us. Everybody block your man. Let's run the kickoff right back for the touchdown.

"If we don't, offense, when we get the ball back, it's going to be hammer, hammer, hammer. Execute.

"Defense, you must cut out the penalties and you must lay off the officials. Let me worry about the officials."

The second-quarter penalties against the FSU defense had provoked them all. Bowden himself was hot over the calls, but he knew harassment of the refs just invited more flags.

"Men, it's down to guts. All we've got to do is go out there and play as good as we can play. We will be back here in thirty minutes. What do you think? Can we do it?"

Their "Yes!" was a kind of guttural rumble. It mixed with the noise of clattering pads and fists being pounded into gloves. They wanted to get back out on the field.

When they ran through the mud to their places on the sideline, the stadium was already up to full roar, and the rain was beginning again. Where on earth would all this water go?

McMillon couldn't get past the 22 on the kick return. And that's where Weldon and the offense began. Bennett carried for five yards up the middle; Lee for two four-yard gains and the first down; Bennett straight ahead two more times for a total of 14 yards and another first down. Hammer, hammer, hammer.

But then play stopped while officials and Seminole players bent over Robbie Baker, who was in obvious pain. Doctors and trainers peered at his knee, which had been gashed open by someone's cleat in a pileup at the line of scrimmage. Blood was everywhere. They called for the litter to carry him to the locker room. And Jeff Deremer came in at center.

The first-down play from near midfield was a pass, a 16-yard completion to Kez McCorvey on a slant pattern. Lee and Bennett then combined for 13 yards on three runs, and the Seminoles had another first down on the LSU 22. Bennett was stopped at the line of scrimmage; then Weldon was leveled on an incomplete pass toward Kez McCorvey, and he was slow getting up. But on the next play, the quarterback threw a perfect pass to Lee on the tailback vertical in the end zone. Thomas' kick pulled Florida State within two points.

The Tigers, however, appeared ready to lengthen the lead again. They picked up 15 yards on a run, then another 15 on a pass to Kinchen. But on second down from midfield, Loup pressed his luck with a long throw in front of the Seminole bench. All the players were on their feet. "Ball! Ball!" they yelled. And Leon Fowler, in deep coverage, turned to grab the interception at the Florida State 21.

It was as if air had been let out of the stadium. The coaches could hear themselves talk for the first time since the opening series.

On the sideline, Weldon was flexing the leg he hurt in the last drive.

He could add knee pain to his list of complaints now. Brad Johnson started warming up in case he was needed. But Weldon convinced the trainers he could play, and he ran out onto the field with the offense after the interception. He lasted only one play, for a handoff to Sean Jackson. And Johnson went in.

The sideline was beginning to look like an outpatient ward. Baker was in the locker room getting his gash stitched. Kevin Knox was out after the first half with a separated shoulder, and Bennett ran off the field holding his shoulder after the last series.

Defensive back Richard Coes had left the game with a fractured elbow; linebacker Kevin Adams had a bruised thigh. Both were lost for the remainder of the game. And while the doctors and trainers tended the wounded on the bench, the whistle signaling an officials' time-out was blown on the field.

This time, the players gathered around Kevin Mancini, who was holding his left knee. This was very bad, terrible, thought Brad Scott as he watched them carry his star tackle to the bench. Mancini's evening was over. Scott sent in John Flath.

On the next play, Johnson connected with Bennett for 23 yards on a play-action pass. But there was another whistle. A personal-foul call against the other tackle, Robert Stevenson. And he was thrown out of the game for fighting.

Unbelievable. Brad Scott jerked off his headset and yelled for Eric Gibbs. "You've waited all your life for this opportunity, son. Now it's up to you."

Three of the five starters on the OL were now gone. William Floyd, the redshirt freshman, was in for Bennett. Weldon paced back and forth behind the bench with one of the doctors at his arm, as his best friend tried to patch together a drive to capture the lead.

Lee lost a yard up the middle on first down. Frier broke into the open on a post pattern, but the wet ball slipped out of Johnson's hand and fell short. It was third and 11. Bowden called for the gadget play he'd been saving for weeks, Smoke Y Hide.

The tight end would throw himself at the feet of a defender at the line of scrimmage, faking the block and hiding near the pile of linemen. Then he would crawl into the open, away from the direction of the play, and, with a little luck, be all alone for a big gain.

Lonnie Johnson crawled out of the jam at the line of scrimmage and caught Johnson's throw back toward the left sideline. But his momentum carried him out of bounds three yards short of the first down. And Player had to kick.

The Seminoles got the ball back four downs later when the Tigers, penned at their own 16, were unable to get anything generated against the FSU defense. Weldon had convinced the doctors he could play and was back in the game.

He threw to Lee for nine yards. Then Floyd picked up four for the first down. Bowden and his offensive coaches worried over the calls. They had a gimpy quarterback, a decimated offensive line and a freshman fullback. This was no time for finesse, Scott argued. His young guys could be trusted to remember their assignments on the basic rushing package, but he couldn't vouch for what they'd do if Bowden got too fancy. So it was back to the north-and-south game.

Gibbs and Flath bulldozed their guys, and Lee, Floyd and Jackson ran the ball 19 yards closer. But then they stalled on third down on the 16-yard line. Bowden called a pass to get the most reliable player on the field, Amp Lee, open on the right side. But when Weldon looked that way, the tailback was covered and the rush was coming. He looked left and saw Floyd open just beyond the line of scrimmage and made a last-ditch toss toward him. Floyd pulled in the ball, ducked out of one tackle and headed toward Errol McCorvey's brother, Derriel, who was waiting for him inside the 10.

On an earlier play, Derriel had teased Floyd. The freshman had better come harder than that, said the LSU defensive back, because he was playing against a potential All-American. This time, the 230-pound fullback put his head down and rammed the 194-pound safety head-on. McCorvey flew backward two yards and was motionless on the turf when three of his teammates finally bulled Floyd to the ground one yard short of the touchdown.

Floyd got the 34 Wham call, the fullback's short-yardage play, on first down. But he was stopped for no gain as the third quarter ended. On second down, Weldon tried the quarterback sneak and got nowhere. Bowden called for the 34 Wham again, and this time the backup linemen moved their men. Floyd got the touchdown.

For the first time all night, the Seminoles took the lead. It was 21–16, with 14 minutes left to play.

Now the defense turned up the pressure. A 32-yard kickoff return put the Tigers in action at their own 41-yard line. But two penalties backed them up to the 19, where Todd McIntosh forced a fumble that Kirk Carruthers recovered. The Seminoles took over at the 20.

With the rain and the injuries, the FSU offensive attack was narrowed to two plays—the toss sweep to Lee and the fullback plunge. Paul Moore was in at fullback now. And he alternated with Lee to set up the third-

and-goal sweep from the 1-yard line. Lee scored his third touchdown. But on the point-after attempt, the wet ball slipped from Brad Johnson's grasp, and when he realized he couldn't get it down fast enough for Thomas' kick, he stood up, looking for a receiver. Warren Hart turned around near the end zone. But when Johnson let fly with the ball, Ivory Hilliard, an LSU safety, stepped in front. And he was off on a 100-yard dash to the opposite end zone with a rare point-after interception.

The replays would show Hilliard on his way to the goal line, apparently out in front of all pursuers, when No. 44 came barreling into the picture. William Floyd ran from his blocking position on the left side of the extra-point line and caught Hilliard from behind after 90 yards.

The fullback collapsed on the sideline. He had saved the Seminoles two points on the scoreboard. But more importantly, his gutsy play—taken together with his performance on the earlier scoring drive—elevated him out of the category of nameless faces who backed up the FSU stars.

Minute by minute, the field conditions worsened. Showers became downpours. But LSU, stymied on the ground in previous drives, had to pass. Loup, helped by a personal-foul penalty against FSU and a couple of big catches, put together a four-minute drive that ran out of gas on the Florida State 5-yard line. The Seminoles held the Tigers for four consecutive plays from inside the 5, then took over on downs after Dan Footman swatted down Loup's fourth-down pass attempt.

Six minutes later, the final score was 27–16. Florida State remained unbeaten in 14 games. And was still No. 1.

Bowden was beside himself. "That was one of the greatest wins Florida State ever had. We had everything in the world work against us, everything in the world. But you guys just played brilliantly. I'm proud of every one of you."

The coach led them all in cheers—one from the offensive players in tribute to the defense; another from the defensive players in honor of their offensive teammates.

They were on top of one another in the cramped space, laughing at one another's bruises and telling war stories of the game they'd just survived.

It felt like a bowl game, like a season-ending victory. What was it the coaches said? "Leave it all on the field"? Well, they had done that. They had paid for the win with everything they had. They had answered the hard questions. What could there possibly be left to prove?

The locker room was ankle deep in discarded jerseys, pants, towels and mud. The steam from the showers drifted into where the players were trying to dry themselves and change. It condensed on their shoulders and made their shirts stick to their backs as soon as they put them on. It didn't matter. They would be out in the wet again in minutes, mounting the buses and heading to the airport. And it would be good riddance, Death Valley.

Casey Weldon grimaced as he pulled his pants over his throbbing knee. His career and Florida State's unbeaten string had been launched almost exactly a year ago in Tallahassee by this same LSU team. He managed his best country-boy grin: "I could see the headline: 'It stopped where it all began.' "

The linemen were the last to finish dressing. Baker's leg, wrapped in a pile of bandages, had the look of a war wound. Reggie Dixon had partially dislocated his shoulder in the second half, and his arm hung limp, useless. Mike Morris helped Mancini, who was on crutches, make his way toward the showers. Bowden, still hyped from the game, was giving the last interview to a reporter with a tape recorder.

"I wouldn't say the defense won it for us. They kept us from losing. But everybody won this one. This was a team victory."

At the entrance to the showers, Mancini edged himself toward the rising steam. Morris' long arm extended shoulder to shoulder on his teammate's back, steadying him. And the two walked that way, inching along at the crutches' pace, until the cloud enveloped them.

8

SEVENTEEN players made Randy Oravetz's Monday-morning injury report because of LSU-game hurts. Forget about Mancini for a while, the trainer told the coaches. The doctors expected two torn ligaments, the kind of injury that might require extensive surgery. Weldon had strained knee ligaments and would likely be out a week to ten days.

Since Bowden and most of his coaches were of the "where there's a will there's a way" school of orthopedic medicine, they had been reluctant to pronounce Weldon out for the upcoming Louisville game. But the quarterback had done it himself, telling reporters he would likely be back for South Carolina the following week.

Brad Scott wasn't going to argue with Oravetz, but he suspected the usual training-room conspiracy. "The trainers always try to play our games for us. They figure that we can beat Louisville without Weldon, and that it would be safer for him not to play."

It didn't matter. Weldon was out.

Baker's severe laceration had required ten stitches. The trainers were still talking about the mess the patch-up created in the LSU locker room. It took ten towels to soak up the blood after the doctor cleaned the wound and pulled the skin close enough to stitch. The center had taken a little novocaine and a dip of borrowed snuff to take his mind off the pain.

Another day at the office for Robbie Baker, who was already held together with baling wire and chewing tobacco. He'd already had four operations. The latest scar would be stiff this week. But there was a chance the center could play. And because Baker was such a practiced masochist, everyone figured he would.

Leon Fowler, Edgar Bennett, Kevin Knox and Reggie Dixon all had separated shoulders of varying degrees. Dixon had played most of the half against LSU with only one good arm.

"Boy, that's leadership," said Bowden. But Bennett was in for some criticism for saying that he couldn't play with a similar injury.

Jeff Deremer, the backup center, had twisted his ankle. And No. 3 guard Patrick McNeil had reported to the training room with a sore right knee on Sunday. Scott smiled at Oravetz when he heard that. "Doesn't Patrick know that we can't afford to have him hurt? Can't we just let these guys pretend they're healthy?"

The offense was going to be practicing all week without the first-team quarterback, fullback, tight tackle and split end. The defense had six first- or second-teamers on the injury report. And the Seminoles were likely to face another desperate team in Louisville, a down-and-out squad determined to prove something about themselves at the expense of the No. 1 team in the nation.

But their players' achievement in Baton Rouge had given the coaches confidence. "How many top-five teams could have withstood the injuries we had and won in LSU with them hot as a dad-gum firecracker?" asked Scott.

"That was one of those games you talk about all the time, about how you're going to respond when everything's on the line late in the game. Will you work yourself through it? It's one thing to say you'll come back. It's another to do it.

"We've been No. 2 and No. 3 around here a few times and couldn't respond to that kind of situation. It would have been easy, with all that adversity around us, to fold our tents, to say, 'We ain't supposed to win this. It ain't in the cards.'

"Well, I don't think it was in the cards for us to win it, but our boys wouldn't let us get beat."

On Monday morning, that pride overpowered any dread about the injury situation. If they had to start Brad Johnson, they would be going with a fifth-year veteran who had been the starting quarterback in his junior year and who had probably made himself a better player in the interim. William Floyd had proved he was no slouch as a sub for Edgar Bennett. And that ragtag crew of backup offensive linemen may have come of age in Baton Rouge. It was their chance, now, to prove something.

"That game has got to go a long way in the careers and the confidence level of Floyd and the linemen that were in there," said Scott. "We might need some of these kids to beat Miami, to beat Florida. So maybe the focus out there this week will be the drawing together of this team.

"In a week that we're beat-up and bruised, there will be more spirit than ever among those younger guys. I mean, now it's time to circle the dad-gum wagons."

9

THE Louisville game looked more interesting at the beginning of the season than it looked now. Howard Schnellenberger, the coach who launched Miami on its mission of football dominance in the early '80s, had promised Louisville fans that he could do the same there. "On a collision course with the national championship" was his phrase. And in 1990, he appeared to take a giant step in that direction when his Cardinals upset Alabama in the Fiesta Bowl and finished No. 14 in the nation.

Schnellenberger's '91 team was considered young—with 12 starters gone from the previous year—but talented. Not talented enough, however, to withstand the devastating injuries that began early in the season. One of the first to go was the quarterback, Jeff Brohm, who broke a leg in the second game, against Tennessee. Fifteen other first- and second-teamers had gone down as well. And now Louisville was 2–6 and desperate for any chance to prove it was a better team than its record suggested.

This was becoming a familiar scenario to the Seminoles.

Bowden had tremendous respect for Schnellenberger, and Mark Richt had played under him at Miami. Both considered him one of college football's great motivators, even when he didn't have the hopeless-underdog theme to work with. Like LSU, Louisville would be insulted by the 31-point spread in their home stadium. And the Cardinals would have the added incentive of playing on a night when the town was full of big-time sports fans. On Saturday afternoon at Churchill Downs was the running of the Breeders' Cup, horse racing's richest purse.

When the game was scheduled, Schnellenberger may have hoped for a showcase for his program. "It was to be another opportunity to attract some national attention," Russ Brown, of the *Courier-Journal*, wrote, "a possible battle between two ranked teams. Why, maybe even national television would aim its cameras at Cardinal Stadium.

"Oops."

Bowden, though, was trying to discourage the mismatch talk. He didn't need any more LSUs this season. He complimented Schnellenberger's program, sympathized with his injury woes and predicted the Cardinals were on the verge of pulling it all together. "I just hope they wait until after this week to do that."

The game tapes the coaches were watching, however, only reinforced the perception that Louisville was going nowhere fast. The Cardinals had lost four in a row by an average of 26.5 points a game—which was very close to the average spread in Florida State's eight victories.

"What can you tell me about Louisville?" Bowden asked his coaches.

"Gigantic holes down the middle," said Richt.

And Scott pointed to the problems the Cardinals were having with the run. With Bennett out and the bigger, tougher Floyd in at fullback, the run blocking might improve. "Ol' Amp could get 300 yards," said Bowden.

10

THE noise from Mickey Andrews' practice field sounded familiar. Defensive back Chris Keene, a track decathlete who had been given a football scholarship, was on the hot spot for not tackling aggressively enough.

"Keene, go get yourself a pole and be a pole vaulter. We give you a scholarship and you won't hit anybody."

The Sky Patrol was bunched on the sideline, waiting turns in the drill, and they all cracked up. "Get a pole!" They high-fived. The coach was definitely running true to form.

But down on the offensive field, Brad Scott's usual bellows were nowhere to be heard. Instead, it was "Good, good. That's exactly how I want you to do it."

Scott was coaxing Eric Gibbs, who had been on the receiving end of a mountain of abuse in practices past. But Gibbs had shown them all something in the LSU game, earning "intimidation" awards for the way he had handled crucial blocks. "He played lower, harder, better than he ever has in practice," said Scott. And now, with Mancini down, Gibbs would start.

"Well, the Lord works in funny ways," Scott said. Maybe this was one of those classic sports stories: The beleaguered backup gets his chance, proves his worth, and they all live happily ever after. Why not?

So far, Gibbs had not turned his LSU performance to his advantage. Monday night, when the team went through its usual light workout for conditioning and assignment corrections, Gibbs had not made his gassers, and Scott had made him run extras. He was struggling, as usual, in the line drills and blocking segments. But Scott was determined to do everything he could to help Gibbs take the next step.

This was the week it had to happen. Baker, it now appeared, was going to sit out the Louisville game to protect those new stitches; Dixon's shoulder was going to bother him the rest of the season; Deremer would be playing on a bad ankle. "If we had to go out there and play tomorrow," said Scott early in the week, "we'd be in trouble."

What Scott hoped for was a steady improvement each day from Gibbs. "I'd handle him differently under other circumstances," said Scott. "But right now, I've got to make him feel like he's there, that he can do it."

With so many injuries, the practices were minimum contact all week. So it was almost impossible to tell where they stood. Fortunately, with rushing so prominent in the game plan, the assignments wouldn't require anything all that different from last week. "Don't change much," Bowden had cautioned. "I don't want to fight this team for sixty minutes. It takes too much out of us physically."

The rushing game seemed safe enough. The backup linemen had proved they could open holes for Lee and Bennett. And the Louisville defense looked even more inviting, especially if they could tie up the down linemen and get their ace backs one on one with the Cardinal linebackers and defensive backs. "No vision," Bowden had written in his notes after watching Louisville's defense on tape misjudge fakes and miss open-field tackles. "They don't seem to have any smell for the ball."

If Gibbs could just have a repeat performance of that fourth-quarter LSU drive—when he slammed defensive linemen backward through the end zone, when he locked out his arms in pass protection and kept on his man. What team was there anywhere who could reach into a grab bag of backups and pull out a 300-pound intimidator? And who could beat a team like that?

11

SATURDAY afternoon had been a brisk day at the races. Cool, but sunny at Churchill Downs. There, the Breeders' Cup athletes only had to perform for two minutes at a time; then it was back to the paddock. The Seminoles, on the other hand, had the whole evening to endure. And by kickoff time, the temperature was in the upper 20s, with a breeze stiff enough to drop the chill factor to 10. Which was at least 50 degrees below the Floridians' comfort zone.

"At West Virginia we caught weather like this about every other week," Bowden had told the players. "Just try to adapt to it. If you can't handle this, you can't handle pro football either, 'cause it's a lot colder in Buffalo. It's a lot colder in Green Bay."

Bowden hated cold weather himself. But his own little furnace of game-day energy seemed to make him oblivious. Not so with the players, who thought of little else but the cold from the moment they got off the bus.

The managers had rounded up cotton long underwear for the team, which was useless against the wind and only a minor obstacle for the freezing temperature. The heat blowers along the bench area were too small to accommodate more than three or four players at once. And besides, the coaches hated to see them all huddling like puppies under a porch when there was a game to play. One of the Cardinal coaches burst onto the field for warm-ups wearing short sleeves.

It's all in the mind, men.

But the Florida State players weren't buying that. Casey Weldon bounced gingerly on his good leg on the sideline, his hands stuffed in fleece jacket pockets. At first, he turned down the offer of the geeky-looking wool hat to cover his ears, but he had pulled it on after the warm-ups. This was no fashion show.

Out on the field, it hurt to move and it really hurt to be hit. But playing was better than standing. Late in the game, the nimble Charlie Ward would get his chance at quarterback and would trip over his own frozen feet. Cardinal Stadium was a minor league baseball facility with artificial turf. And the plastic surface made it feel even colder. It was like playing football on a refrigerator shelf.

The baseball stadium seated some 36,000, with most of the playing surface stretched away from the stands toward straightaway center field. Nothing like the cozy confines of Death Valley or Florida Field. This week, the fans were irrelevant.

Bowden wanted to pick up where they left off in the second half of the LSU game. "Men, we haven't dominated a game in so long we've forgotten how," he told the players in the locker room before the game. "People are going to wonder whether we're really the best team in the country. They're beginning to ask that now.

"Now, the main thing is to win. But ask yourself: What would Miami do tonight? They would go out there and jump on these guys so fast they wouldn't know what happened to 'em.

"Now, I want to run the ball, because it's cold."

So Brad Johnson was supposed to spend most of his evening handing and tossing the ball to Amp Lee, who would zip through the enormous holes opened by the patchwork OL and give Cardinal linebackers the most frustrating night of their lives.

It didn't work out that way. Lee carried the ball 13 times in the first half for a total of 21 yards—1.6 yards a play for an All-American candidate who came into the game averaging almost six yards a carry. William Floyd and Paul Moore added nine more yards between them. And Brad Johnson, running for his life a couple of times, was the second-leading Seminole ground gainer with 11 yards.

The halftime score was 27–9, thanks primarily to the defense's three interceptions, some drive-sustaining passes and Gerry Thomas' two field goals. The running game was not a factor. The blocking was a disaster.

When his linemen settled themselves in the halftime locker room, Brad Scott was in their faces: "We lose two players, and we're just gonna shut it down? We're outta synch, so we throw in the towel? Mike, is that what we're gonna do? Reggie? Pat? Is that what we're going to do, Rob?"

Eric Gibbs was not even addressed.

The line coach pointed his finger at the others: "You go to tight guard, you to split guard." Reggie Dixon would play in Gibbs's tackle spot, and

Mike Morris would flip to the opposite side to take Dixon's guard position. Patrick McNeil, who had started in Morris' place until the Michigan game, moved into the vacated guard spot. The new alignment moved to a blackboard to go through assignments and to update what they knew about the Louisville defensive line maneuvers. Gibbs remained where he sat.

"He hasn't blocked his guy all night," said Scott to Bowden.

The head coach looked as if he'd aged ten years. The cold and the anger distorted his face. "Offensive line, I bet we ain't gained 10 dang yards. I had planned to come out here today and run that ball at them, run it straight at 'em. We've been getting 250 yards a game rushing, and I bet we ain't got 10 yards.

"I thought you would knock 'em on their darn butts. If we couldn't throw the ball tonight, they'd be ahead of us. Well, I guess we'll just go out and throw it the rest of the night. We'll just have to wait till we get ol' Mancini back, till we get ol' so-and-so back. 'Cause these guys here don't like to play without them."

When the Seminoles ran back into the cold after halftime, half the stadium had emptied. The lights from bumper-to-bumper traffic out of the parking lots could be seen over the left-field fence. And the players headed straight for the heaters.

Behind the new blocking lineup, Amp Lee gained five yards on his first carry of the third quarter. But an interception two plays later killed the Seminole drive and gave the Cardinals the ball on the Florida State 38. They scored on a 28-yard draw play, then missed the attempt at a two-point conversion. It was the last time Louisville got into the end zone for the rest of the evening.

Florida State's defense pulled in a total of six interceptions and sacked the Cardinal quarterback six times. Gerry Thomas kicked two more field goals, which made four for the night. And Lee ended up with 73 yards on 22 carries—doubling his first-half average.

The final score was 40–15, but Bowden's voice suggested no hint of victory when he gave his briefest postgame speech of the season. "The defense did a great job tonight. The offense struggled, but played good enough to win. Men, you gotta get better. Let's get the film and look at it and see if we can get better."

Then, as if startled by his own downbeat words, the coach tried for a moment to reassure his players—and himself. "I'm proud of you, men. You did the important thing. You did what you had to do to win."

It was true. But it was not enough.

"The only thing I know is that we must get better, or we ain't gonna make it."

The coach reached out, put his hand on the nearest player and bowed his head. "Dear Father, thank you for letting us survive this cold night . . ."

12

ON Sunday, Bowden buried himself in game tapes from the night before. It was penance. He had let himself imagine a team, after the second-half comeback in Baton Rouge, so deep in talent and determination that it could overcome everything—weather, dubious officiating, devastating injuries, an antagonistic crowd. Then he had stood on the sideline on that frigid night while Louisville drained him of those illusions. Now his imagination pulled him the other way.

"What if we had been playing Miami?" That was the question that ate at him, even though he knew in his coach's heart that it couldn't be answered.

Fans were already asking it in a hundred different ways, grumbling about the mistakes and the failures to cover projected point spreads. Sports columnists and TV commentators were arguing that any team that struggled with LSU and Louisville didn't deserve to be ranked ahead of Miami and Washington. And Bowden was hearing the question more often, even from his North Florida loyalists: Do you think you really deserve to be No. 1?

The public coach argued for common sense. Given the injury situation and the hostile environment in Louisville, "the boys did remarkably well to win like they did," he told local boosters at their Monday luncheon. "Now, their play wasn't that good. When we graded the film, we weren't that impressed with the way we played. But as I told the coaches this morning, it's normal. We're catching other teams ready to rip our heads off. South Carolina will be that way too."

As for the critics: "When you're No. 1, it doesn't make any difference how bad you beat somebody. You're not going to impress 'em. We weren't going to impress anybody beating Louisville 70–0. They expect you to do that. The only way to impress them is to lose. You wanna impress somebody? Just get beat."

The private Bowden, however, was unconsoled by common sense. He was scared. More than ever now. Why on earth was that? Here he was, precisely where he had hoped to be, 9–0 and heavily favored to be 10–0 going into the Miami game. The anxiety was all out of proportion to the sense of accomplishment, as if all they had done by winning was to raise the stakes they could lose.

When was the last genuine celebration of a victory—Michigan, Syracuse? Yet hadn't they won each week since? Everyone—the fans, the media, the coaches and the players—saw the five-game stretch between the Syracuse and Miami games as a five-week audition for the role of defender of the national championship against the most successful football program in America. The coaches had cautioned one-game-at-a-time. They had warned of the dangerous potential of desperate underdogs. But all along their real message had been: Avoid the upset. The Hurricanes are coming.

That robbed the interim games of meaning. So what the coaches had hoped for was proof of a kind of professionalism, of dedication to doing a job, to honing an edge—even if the end product, victory, could be accomplished with something less than committed effort. That hadn't happened. In his head, Bowden was not surprised that his team of postadolescent amateurs had not behaved professionally. In his heart, though, was the terror of uncertainty. With all the injuries, the sloppy tackling and blocking, with the failures to throw and catch when it counted, where in the world did they stand?

He wasn't going to find answers to that in the Louisville video. But he used it to mount evidence to make the case for what had to happen next. He would now argue, with the conviction of a prosecutor: "Men, you won't win the national championship playing like this against Miami."

He began in the Monday-morning meeting with a notebook full of questions and criticisms from his weekend tape review. For two and a half hours, he quizzed his assistants about every Saturday-night breakdown. Who messed up? Why? How can we get better?

"We need to wake up as coaches," he told them. And he felt better almost immediately. He had started the process.

The coaches, however, couldn't feel any sense of relief until they had taken the message to the players. And in the three hours between their sessions with Bowden and their afternoon meeting with the athletes, the challenge they wanted to deliver grew in relation to their impatience, so that by the time the offensive team sat down to listen to the weekly scouting report, the theme had expanded to include the wider moral universe. Brad Scott stood before his group of potential All-Americans, the holders of the nation's longest winning streak, and read them the riot act:

"You just remember to yourself how you felt when this ball game was over Saturday night. How did you feel about your performance? How did you feel that a younger Louisville team was much more hungry and much more aggressive and kicked your tails all over the football field? . . . All those guys leaving the field said, 'I don't know how those guys beat us, 'cause they ain't very good.'

"We're in a crucial point in our season, 'cause now we play three football teams that if you play like that are going to beat you. We don't have a leader on the team. I haven't seen this group organized and together since the Michigan game. I'm waiting and the coaches are waiting, but it's gotta come from within you.

"We're at a low point now, in my opinion. And anybody in this room who doesn't think we are, you ain't been lookin' at the same film the last four weeks that we've been lookin' at. There's no enthusiasm, no emotion; no caring, sharing, loving. We got a bunch of individuals out there. 'I'm cold. I'm hurt. I don't feel like playing tonight.' Is that fair to everybody else?

"It's time for a family reunion on this offense. Do we have a bunch of selfish players only concerned about what they do? You're saying, 'We're waitin' on Miami.' Well, you're gonna play Miami soon enough, in about two weeks. But you're gonna play a good football team this week who would like nothing better than to beat your butt. I tell you, these sons of guns here will play football.

"And you don't think South Carolina is going to be encouraged by what they saw against Louisville? Or let 'em watch the LSU game. Or let 'em watch Middle Tennessee State. Or Virginia Tech. When was the last time we had a performance out of this offense?

"It goes all the way back to Syracuse, doesn't it? That's been so long ago I can't even remember what year it was. That's the last time this offense played together. Is that what we're all about? Is that why we worked our butts off here, some of you, for five years, through the off-season, through the summer football camp, to get to this point in our schedule and then throw it away because we got a bunch of guys who ain't ready to do it, ain't willin' to pay the price, ain't willin' to make a commitment to work their tails off in practice and do the things we have to do to win?

"What kind of message are you sending to yourself? Quit worrying about other people now. What kind of message are you sending to yourself? You got any pride in you at all?

"If there are a few of you who feel that way, then pull it up by the dad-gum bootstraps and let's rally the camp, and let's get these other guys out of the lineup. Let's play with eleven people who want to play football."

After Scott harangued them, John Eason took his shot, comparing some of the Seminoles' self-absorbed players with the "new breed" of the '60s. When his old coach at Florida A&M, Jake Gaither, complained about that "new breed," said Eason, he "was talking about the people on marijuana and other drugs. Today I see a different 'new breed' coming along. I see it when I look in this room. That's the selfish breed. I've never seen players like this. So selfish.

"Gaither used to talk about the hungry boy, playing for pride. Most of you are concerned about your stats, about how much playing time you get and about the pros. I see people on the bench, when we're winning, getting mad because they're not the ones catching passes, they're not the ones running the ball. I've never seen it before.

"You need to reassess yourself personally. Where are you going and what are you going to do? You fought to get scholarships, then once you get here you don't want to practice and don't want to play hard in the games."

Throughout all this, the players sat quietly. It was impossible to know how they were taking it. Every time they assembled like this it was to be lectured, so most of them had grown immune to preaching. But this session was a break in routine, consuming most of the time set aside for the scouting report. Which signaled the importance the coaches put on the message.

"The good news," said Scott, retaking the floor for a closing challenge, "is that you're still in charge of your own destiny this year. We've played badly enough on this offense to be defeated, but the defense helped us. Now what are you going to do from this moment on?

"It's a new season, as far as we're concerned as coaches. It's a new season startin' today, until this dad-gum bowl situation is over. You've won enough games to play in a bowl. Will it be the bowl for the national championship?"

13

THE early November afternoons in Tallahassee could be glorious. A sky so high and blue it looked as if the ceiling had been peeled off the hemisphere. And a sun that lit the practice fields in green relief. It was a welcome 65 degrees.

All week Bowden watched the offense from his usual position, deep in the scout-team defensive secondary. Maybe it was the weather, maybe his own wishful thinking, but the players seemed more attentive, the ball handling a little more crisp. So the coach let himself be persuaded that, if nothing else, the imminent approach of Miami had brought back enthusiasm for football.

"Exciting, isn't it?" He had grinned nervously when he said that to his coaches Tuesday morning. Behind him on the grease board, he had written a big "9–0." He pointed to it.

"That looked pretty danged big back at the Michigan game, didn't it? I didn't know for sure we could do it. But now, if we win four more, we'd be the first team to go all the way and never lose that No. 1 ranking."

"We're that close."

First South Carolina, then Miami. One more game to get ready.

Already, they were among the last people in college football, and certainly the last in Tallahassee, to be talking seriously about a Seminole opponent other than Miami. Elsewhere in the athletic center, assistant athletic director Andy Urbanic was worrying over the toughest security arrangements in stadium history, and Wayne Hogan, the sports information director, was preparing for the arrival of some 500 media people.

Sue Hall, Bowden's secretary, was threatening to answer the phone: "We're sorry, but there are no Miami tickets." The game had been sold out for months. But every day, Ms. Sue added to her stack of personal requests for the head coach's help. If she would just pass the message along, they said, Bobby would take care of them.

Bowden brought most of that on himself. When he came to Florida State, he was Seminole football's best salesman, steadily building attendance by his teams' successes and his personal appeals to the fans of North Florida. He was never the unapproachable Legend. He was always just Bobby. "Perfectly adaptable to us Southern Crackers and rednecks of northern Florida," the old dean had said. Even when the program became more sophisticated, it shaped itself around his image, encouraging the inference that it was Bobby who licked every stamp and dusted off every seat in the stadium. "Glad to have ya, buddy."

Big Foot. Dan Footman, the 6-5, 270-pound defensive lineman, was the comeback player of the year.

Bowden and his players in
the locker room just before
the Middle Tennessee State
game.

"Let's have a word,
men . . ."

Assistant trainer Jack Marucci and head trainer Randy Oravetz examine X-rays.

Kevin Mancini is carried off in the rain at LSU by teammate Mike Morris and Dr. Kris Stowers.

Charlie Ward shivers in Louisville with the head coach.

A battered Matt
Frier soaks his
weary body in the
whirlpool.

Backup offensive lineman Eric Gibbs succumbs to the practice-field heat.

It was that kind of day. Quarterback Casey Weldon is nailed by Miami's Darren Krein in the Game of the Century.

Kevin Mancini, in street clothes, consoles a beaten and exhausted Casey Weldon at the end of the Florida game.

"It scares me to death." The coach.

Another practice to endure for center Robbie Baker, who, by the end of the season, was held together by Ace bandages and baling wire.

Fullback Edgar Bennett honors his expelled roommate, Amp Lee, by wearing
Lee's number on his shoe at the Cotton Bowl.

The problem was that in an era in which the promotion and staging of big-time football had become a multimillion-dollar operation, there was not enough of Bobby to go around. Not enough to run a football team, to plan for games, to talk to the media and boosters—and to make good on the promises his image inspired with the thousands of fans in the region who took his warm handshake at a golf tournament as the symbol of a lifelong commitment.

"Now, y'all just call me when you need anything," he would say. And lots of them did.

Sue Hall was the filter. The bigger the game, the more the coach felt pulled into his private world of worry and preparation. But the bigger the game, the more the outside world encroached. So Ms. Sue played gatekeeper. She arranged the distribution of his private game tickets—including the ones to his family. She blocked out the appointments, protected his afternoon nap times, fed him his low-cal lunches and, most important, said the "no" word the coach resisted uttering to anyone but his players and his assistants.

Bowden was going to be 62 on Friday, November 8, the day before the South Carolina game. Since everybody knew his weakness for chocolate, there would be cakes and pies galore. Ms. Sue would hide some of them. But she'd give him a day off from his luncheon diet to splurge a little. Of course, the diet was a joke anyway, because he would sneak so much junk at home that the only official diet meal was lunch. Still, even the coach was starting to feel guilty about the way his game sweater was tightening up over his belly.

"Nerves."

Was it any different this year? Bowden was inclined to say no. His routines had been the same for years. The weight gain as the team moved toward the bowl season reflected an annual nervous binge. Right now, he was bothered by the unpredictability of the offense, by the defense's bad habit of giving up at least one big play for a touchdown every week. But if he didn't have those problems to fret over, he would think of something else. He fretted by nature.

In fact, he had a new worry that flew in and out of his thoughts: Was he turning conservative in his approach to the game?

The boosters had flirted with the issue at the Monday luncheon. All those handoffs and pitches and screen passes. Wasn't the offense playing it pretty close to the vest these days? "That was all me all the way," he told them. "The idea was to win the game and not get upset."

He knew the quarterbacks were griping about it. Weldon would like to throw for 500 yards and five TDs a game, and Johnson had felt reined in when he finally got his chance against Louisville and they had run the ball so much.

"No, I wouldn't be any different last week if I had it to do over again," he said to himself. "If I had had Casey, though, I wouldn't have been as conservative. If the weather had been better, I wouldn't have been as conservative. The weather, that was the big thing.

"When you go up there, you wonder: How are your kids going to respond to that weather? How are you gonna execute with five starters out? There were too many ifs up there to be nonchalant, throwing the ball all over the place."

Well, if he were to be absolutely honest, there was also another issue. And it applied to this whole series of pre-Miami games: "The fact that we were in the driver's seat.

"Let's say we were 11th in the nation, trying to get in the top five. I'd have to be ripping those teams, or we wouldn't make it. Now we don't have to do that. We just gotta win. And what I'm trying to do, once we get a game secure, is to make sure we won't lose it."

Was that Bobby Bowden saying that, Mr. Riverboat Gambler himself? Yes, indeed, he thought. There was a time for taking risks and a time to play the percentages. That was only common sense. Especially when you had the big guns on your side of the battlefield. Don't do anything to jeopardize your chance to win—that was the No. 1 axiom of the great coaches. It was the way champions played the game.

But Bowden's built-in second-guess mechanism never let him rest with a decision. Playing not to lose was the safe approach. And the safe approach was the predictable approach. "Louisville got into my head pretty good. They knew what I liked and decided to do something about it," said Bowden to his coaches.

"Are we too vanilla? Are we making it too easy on defenses?"

The questioning was really self-directed. But the coaches took it as criticism of their preparation. And they got defensive, immediately reminding him that they had learned to avoid tinkering too much with the usual schemes, because, in the heat of the game, he would be reluctant to call the new stuff anyway.

Bowden laughed knowingly. It was the truth. But how do you break that cycle?

"You get yourself up a game plan for South Carolina, and I might let you call it," he said.

Oh no, Brad Scott argued. "That doesn't work. You can't stand to just be there on the sidelines watching."

But you guys have to do it sometime to break my tendencies and just live with the way I act."

The group launched into a discussion of plans for South Carolina, of what they wanted to show Miami in the game films and what they wanted to hold out. Of schemes and plays. Of people and potential game plans. John Eason listened, but his concentration was divided. He had been dealing all week with the usual barrage of academic hassles, along with his coaching duties. And he had been thinking about the way things were working out.

"Y'all oughta be thinking about a Sean Jackson game plan," he interjected. "Because Amp may not be around for the bowl game. He's just not getting the work done academically. The same with E.T."

It wasn't exactly a shock that went through the room. Amp Lee had been a borderline student his whole career. He and Turral had both been dismissed and readmitted before. And because both were below 2.00 overall, they had to make even higher grades this semester to pull up their averages.

At this point, what was there to do? Threaten more penalties? Have more conferences? There was an academic support staff to help the players. And the kids, ultimately, had to do it themselves. There was time between now and the bowl game, time for tutoring and counseling and appeals to deans. But there was also less than two weeks left until Miami.

14

CASEY Weldon asked to speak to the team before Wednesday's practice.

"Now it's down to a three-game season," the quarterback told his teammates. "I'm as guilty as anybody when it comes to the point in a game when we know we're going to win and we worry more about our stats than playing together. But like the song says, 'We're indestructible.' When we are together, we are indestructible."

The coaches liked to hear that. They were all romantics, believing that spectacular feats could be accomplished with commitment and willpower. They had all been in locker rooms when a feeling took hold of a team, when something clicked perfectly and a group of individuals became one.

And they were always trying to find a way to conjure that power on demand.

Most of them were drawn to true stories of heroism and inspiration. Especially the head coach. On the last two Friday nights, Bowden had told the team stories of athletes who suffered deaths in their families almost on the eve of big games, then returned to their teams to lead them to victory. Like Scott's plea for a family reunion, though, the coach's stories went out to an audience trained to endure adult lectures with polite indifference. They were in the room. But were they listening?

In the week before the South Carolina game, however, there were two real-life stories that grabbed everyone. One was the announcement by Los Angeles Laker superstar Magic Johnson that he had tested positive for the AIDS virus. The other was the appearance of a 13-year-old cancer victim, Houston Howell, at the team's practices.

The Magic Johnson story struck a chord in the whole nation, with front-page stories in the newspapers and almost daily follow-ups for months. But it had special power with young athletes, who believed desperately in their own immortality and in that of their heroes, like Johnson. That he, in the prime of his life, could contract a disease that would likely kill him was terrible enough. But that he was stricken through sexual contact, in pursuing what most of these young men considered an important perquisite of athletic stardom—that jarred them all.

Like many people their age, the football players tended to see AIDS as something that couldn't affect them. It applied to intravenous drug users and homosexuals, not to athletes. Not to strong young men. If it could happen to Magic Johnson, it could happen to them. And that got their attention.

The imminence of death was a brand-new topic for them. Old people died. Criminals died. Unlucky fools died. But great athletes?

Young Houston's presence affected them in a similar way. He had maybe a month to live, the doctors said. But he was a Seminole fan and was excited at the prospect of meeting some of the players. On Thursday, when the team was doing its usual run-through in Doak Campbell, Houston was in a wheelchair on the edge of the field. And some of the players came over to talk and tease him during the loose practice.

The boy, weak and rail thin from his battle with cancer, thrived on the attention. They were such obvious opposites, a dying boy and athletes so full of life. But the players instinctively made no big deal about his infirmity. They shook his hand and talked sports. Weldon took a special interest in Houston, and he would stay close to him and his family throughout the boy's final days. But even the players who didn't come over to see him would look up from their huddles or glance his way as they waited in lines for their turns in drills. If he caught their eye, they would smile.

Bowden watched them, and in his Friday-night talk to the team, the coach made mortality and gratitude his themes.

"Magic Johnson. He's made millions. He's been a great athlete, one of the greatest ever. He's known and loved all over the world. But would you swap with him right now? Not now, not now.

"You oughta be thankful for what you've got. God has given you a strong, healthy body.

"Houston. He came out to see us in a wheelchair. Just 13 years old. So close to death. He's always followed the Seminoles, and this might be the last game he'll be able to see. Look how lucky you and I are compared to him. It seems so trivial, that game tomorrow, doesn't it?

"He's going to be watchin' y'all. Y'all go out there and really lay it on the line. If we win it, let's dedicate it to him.

"That's the reason I like to give y'all devotions and talk to you about the things in life that are really important. Because all of us are going to be faced with that one of these days. I'm gonna die one of these days. Sooner than y'all because of my age. But you got to be ready to go, 'cause you don't know when you'll go.

"God has given me a mind; God has given me health; God has given me desire to become a great coach. I'm gonna try to do that and somehow give it back to him. That's your calling too. You've been given this great ability. Now use it."

15

SOUTH Carolina was probably "the best-looking, weirdest-playing team we'll see all year," said Doug Hanlon, the graduate assistant who scouted the Gamecocks. Pound for pound, they seemed to measure up well against just about anybody. "Why they can't play, I just don't know."

So far in '91, South Carolina was 3-3-2. It had beaten Virginia Tech, East Tennessee State and Georgia Tech, lost to West Virginia, East Carolina and North Carolina State and tied Duke and Louisiana Tech. The Gamecocks had speedy receivers, some beefy guys on defense and a strong quarterback in Bobby Fuller. But the game tapes revealed a schizophrenic team.

"Men, this team that we're playing here, I don't know how they're going to play," said Bowden before the game on Saturday. "They got behind West Virginia 21–0 in a quarter and a half and nearly came back and won it. For some reason, they didn't play with confidence at first. Then they saw they could play with West Virginia and nearly came back and beat 'em. We must go out and play as hard as we can play."

If the Seminoles didn't immediately take charge of the Gamecocks, they were at least opportunistic. And early in the second quarter, they were out in front 7–0. Gerry Thomas kicked a 29-yard field goal after a 64-yard drive stalled on the Gamecock 12. Both touchdowns followed South Carolina mistakes, including an errant throw that gave Terrell Buckley his school-record ninth interception. But also in the second quarter, the defense allowed its near-weekly long touchdown. This one went 79 yards when Fuller connected with Eddie Miller for the touchdown pass.

Then, almost at the end of the half, the Gamecocks were aided by a fourth-down penalty against the Seminoles that gave them new life deep in Florida State territory. And as the half ended, they kicked a 22-yard field goal to make the score 17–10.

In Doak Campbell, the home crowd of over 60,000 lost interest in the game by the start of the second quarter. They amused themselves with the wave and the "War Chant." Some had brought "We want Miami" signs into the stadium with them and were just waiting until the fourth quarter to wave them for the TV cameras.

Bowden, on the other hand, was exasperated. He hated that 79-yard touchdown given up by the defense. But what really got to him were the offensive breakdowns—especially the failure to convert third downs deep in Gamecock territory. "I can't believe they stuffed us like that," he told the coaches at halftime.

"We've got to get 'em cranked. But I forgot how. See what you can do for them."

Brad Scott had rearranged his line again, looking for some combination that might make up for the loss of Mancini. This week, he moved Morris to the tackle slot and McNeil into Morris' guard position. The head coach wanted to try the straight-ahead stuff, and he had Bennett leading off two series out of a one-back set.

Before the game, he had told the players he wanted to send a message to the South Carolina defensive front: " 'We're coming right at ya, we're gonna knock your britches off.' I want to see what we're made out of that first play. If we like it, we're gonna do it some more."

The first play had gotten three yards, the only gain of the opening series. When he led another series with the same play after Buckley's pickoff, they lost two yards. Then there were those three downs from inside the 20 when they ended up settling for the field goal.

Scott's halftime pitch to his OL was simple enough: "There's no adjustment to make. You're the best we got. We've just got to execute. You want to be in the position to play Miami for it all? Well, you've got thirty more minutes."

When Bowden addressed the whole group, he began in a weary tone: "Men, we're really stinkin' up the place again. Offense, you're doing absolutely nothing. We got on the goal line and ran three downs and didn't make it. I cannot believe we're not any tougher than that.

"We had them 17 to nothin', and everybody just stopped." Now the anger was in his voice. "Even our defense is gonna let 'em have the easy one. Just when everybody seems to be working their guts out stopping them, somebody gives them an 80-yarder. I could be the worst player in the world and I could back up.

"Men, we need to go out and play like No. 1. If we don't quit fooling around, heck, we'll get beat today. We don't have to wait till next week.

"Defense, if they don't score again, we win. I know you get tired of hearing that. But the way our offense is playing I don't know what to expect. They won't hit nobody. The dang offensive line is gettin' creamed. The quarterback is rushing his throws. The backs are running easy. Nobody will go up and get the ball and make a great catch. Hey, men, we've got thirty minutes to get that straightened out.

"If I'm ticking you off, I hope I am. I hope you get mad and go do something. That score was 17 to nothin'. We could have killed 'em, but no, we kinda slacked up. Kirk, how about that defense? Are we ready to go out and kick some butt? Quarterback? Receivers?"

The third quarter relieved some of his concern. The offense held the ball for 11 of the 15 minutes, and Weldon completed seven of nine passes for 180 yards. Lee and Jackson finished off drives of 79 and 62 yards with one-yard runs for the two touchdowns.

Weldon made his third touchdown pass of the day early in the fourth quarter. Then the other three quarterbacks got their chances. But the scoring was over by then.

South Carolina didn't get any closer than the Florida State 38-yard line in the second half. The defense recorded two sacks and Buckley's interception. Favored by 24 points, the Seminoles won 38–10. It was the first time in five weeks that they covered a point spread.

Thirty seconds after the team entered the postgame locker room, South Carolina was ancient history. There was only one topic on everybody's mind. "Men, I don't care about bowls or nothin' else, you'll never play in a bigger game than the one next week. No. 1 goes against No. 2. This is full-dedication week.

"When we start back in here Monday, think of everything you can do to get better. 'Cause if we put it all together then, if you think you're happy now, you just wait until next week. The whole world will be watching.

"Okay, men, let's grab a word . . . And hey, we'll give that football to Houston."

Part VII

THE GAME OF THE CENTURY

1

ABOUT the same time Bobby Bowden began redeeming Florida State as a real university in the minds of Southerners, the University of Miami embarked on the same mission. And arrived at a similar place, by way of a slightly different route.

In the ten years before Lou Saban became head coach in 1977, Miami had only two winning seasons under four coaches. Home attendance averaged around 30,000 in the 75,000-seat Orange Bowl. And there was serious talk about discontinuing the program. Saban got the Hurricanes to 6–5 in his second year. More important, he started Miami's recruiting tradition. That first Saban recruiting class included six Florida all-staters. And eleven of the thirty he brought in that year went on to become pros.

A notoriously restless soul, Saban left after '78 for West Point. And the university hired Howard Schnellenberger, who was then the Miami Dolphins' offensive coordinator. He had just one losing season, his first, in 1979. Four years later, in 1983, the team he built won the national championship. And Miami hadn't had a losing record since.

When Schnellenberger resigned to join the newly formed U.S. Football League, Jimmy Johnson took over in '84. Under him, Miami was No. 1 in the polls for 15 consecutive weeks in 1986, then lost the championship to Penn State in the Fiesta Bowl. The next year, Johnson and the Hurricanes went undefeated and captured the championship.

Johnson then headed to the pros, becoming coach of the revamped Dallas Cowboys after the '88 season. Dennis Erickson was named head coach in Miami. And in his first year, 1989, he won the national championship with an 11–1 team.

"The Team of the '80s," sportswriters dubbed the Hurricanes. And it was true. But there was a provocative dark side to all of this.

Outside of South Florida, most college football fans hated the Miami Hurricanes. Football was supposed to be played by the sons of steelworkers and farmers in gritty little towns in the industrial North, the Midwest and the Deep South. A set of traditions had grown from those roots.

And wasn't it self-evident that Miami, way down there in tropical Margaritaville, didn't share them?

To great motivators, that was a made-to-order environment for a "They say you can't do it" approach. And Howard Schnellenberger was a master motivator. He had used the attractions of the resort city to lure a few top recruits out of the urban North, and the metropolitan area around Miami provided a seemingly endless supply of poor, hungry athletes. Schnellenberger drew boundaries around all of South Florida and proclaimed it the State of Miami. From that huge population base, you could supply two or three good college football teams. Why not one great one?

Schnellenberger also made wise use of his Dolphin connections. The locals loved their NFL team. And the new Miami head coach let it be known they could expect something similar from the Hurricanes. Miami would be an NFL-style team, with pro offensive formations and defensive alignments. In South Bend and Tuscaloosa, they might sell the tradition of the past, but Schnellenberger pitched the future to his top recruits: You play here under this system and you'll be ready for the NFL.

When Johnson replaced Schnellenberger, he built on that foundation. The underdog mentality evolved into the Hurricane Attitude—a finger-pointing, trash-talking, fatigue-wearing, fight-provoking arrogance that infuriated just about everybody else in college football. And which, in turn, only reinforced the paranoia that motivated them: The world, indeed, was against them. Everybody wanted them to lose. So they won even more.

It was a perpetual-motion motivation machine.

There was, however, an interested minority who were intrigued by what they saw: other players. If you can walk the talk, why not talk it? What the bad boys did looked like fun. It provided a sense of spontaneity to the most rigidly controlled sport in America. But when their own players dabbled in the Miami style, dancing in end zones and teasing opponents, fans were aghast. This was a disease, this Miami thing. So soon NCAA officials called meetings to invent taunting rules and to warn against unnecessary celebrations after sacks and touchdowns. And Erickson, when he replaced Johnson, made a concerted effort to tone down the Attitude.

Back home in Miami, however, the disdain of official college football worked the opposite way. Not that the president of the university and the faculty were all that thrilled with the Hurricanes' image, of course. But it clearly struck a chord with local fans, who fancied themselves outlaws too. Who cared about the rednecks and the do-gooders anyway?

Hadn't they all been looking down their noses at Miami for years? Well, let 'em come on down to the Orange Bowl and play a little football.

Bobby Bowden had come on October 6, 1990, when 80,396 watched Miami beat Florida State 31–22. That was Bowden's seventh loss to Miami in ten years, his tenth in 15 seasons at Florida State. No other team had beaten him that many times. Three times since 1980, the Seminoles had lost by just one point. And four times in that same period, it was Miami that blocked them from their own claims on national championships.

But Miami had been no picnic for the rest of the country either. Notre Dame had lost five of the last seven against the Hurricanes. After 1990, the Irish didn't want to play them anymore. Florida dropped out of the annual series in 1987 after losing three of the last four matchups. Why on earth, asked some of the Florida State boosters, are they always on the Seminole schedule?

Because if you want to win it all, you should play the best, Bowden told them. "We will always play them. And we will always play Florida."

In truth, there was a tremendous advantage in having both Miami and Florida on the schedule, especially now that everyone in the state would be playing conference opponents for most of the season. Poll voters could argue the relative merits of conference wins until they were blue in the face, but victories over the Hurricanes and Gators would foreclose the debate. Who could play a tougher schedule than that?

With fans, Bowden played the Miami curse for laughs. He told them after the '88 opening loss, "I promise you Miami will never do that to us again." Pause. "We moved the game to later in the season." But by the coach's way of thinking, the Hurricanes and Seminoles had been more or less on equal footing since 1987. They should have split their four games since then, with each winning on its home field. What upset the balance was that '87 game in Tallahassee, when the wind played havoc with the kicking and Bowden relied on a two-point conversion to win in the final 40 seconds. The Seminoles lost by one point.

In 1988, the Seminoles were embarrassed in the Orange Bowl 31–0. They won in Tallahassee in '89. Then that huge crowd in Miami in 1990 got to Bowden's young team in the first half, and they lost by nine points. Now it was the Seminoles' turn again in Doak Campbell, and Bowden had pretty much the same team he had last year. Except Casey Weldon was now the starting quarterback and everybody else was a year older. All that should count for something.

Bowden himself never got into a dither about the Miami taunting business. Intimidation tricks had been a part of college football forever.

A lot of it was showmanship, which didn't go unappreciated by a man who helped invent the flaming-spear-on-horseback routine. And a lot of it was also an invitation to bump the game to another level of physicality. Which was also a classic football tradition. Miami's edge over most teams was derived from its superior talent and disciplined preparation. That's what supplied the confidence at the core of the famous Attitude. Another team with the style and not the substance to back it up would be a collection of obnoxious losers.

There were plenty of Florida State players eager to challenge opponents—including Miami—on that same level and in that same style. But Bowden knew he and his team could never get away with it.

"If it was okay to fight, if we wouldn't get such a bad image, I would go on out there and start a fight," said the coach, whose competitive juices told him he owed the Hurricanes one from the year before.

Down in the Orange Bowl in 1990, some of the Miami players had run through the Seminoles as they were doing warm-ups, bumping and shoving the visiting team. At first, Bowden thought it was an accident, but then he read a clip from a Miami-area paper that had one of the Hurricanes bragging about the tactic. It was "the Miami way of football," the kid had said. And the Florida State coach was steamed.

"I called Coach Erickson about it and asked him, 'Please don't let that happen again.' I don't think he knew anything about it. And I'm sure he called the kid in and chewed him out. But if this was wrestlin' or hockey, and we played them here, I'd get even for that one."

He grinned at the thought, then took it all back. St. Bobby could never get away with it. "That would start the awfullest fight in the world."

2

Monday night, before his receivers headed out to practice, John Eason showed them tape from the 1990 Miami game. The image he wanted burned into their minds was that of Lawrence Dawsey, leaping for impossible catches and fighting through tackles for extra yardage.

Dawsey caught 13 passes for 160 yards and a touchdown that day in the Orange Bowl, as the dazed Seminoles tried to fight back from a 24–6 deficit. It had been a losing effort, but the senior receiver had made it a contest instead of a rout. Twelve of Dawsey's catches were in the second half. And Eason showed one of them over and over: a one-handed grab and then a determined run through a half dozen would-be tacklers.

"He made All-American in that one game," Eason told his young players. Like the one coming up, that was a big game too, watched by the 80,000 in the Orange Bowl and millions on CBS. Everybody knew who Lawrence Dawsey was after that one. Including the NFL coaches.

"Somebody right here may be setting themselves up for the future this Saturday."

Eason talked as he rewound, then played the Dawsey catches again. "He was hungry. Y'all are hungry too. But you want to be spoon-fed like babies. The bottom line is: Put it in the end zone. You may not get another chance."

That would be all the preaching he would do this week. If a football player wasn't excited about this kind of an opportunity, he was useless anyway. He would just remind them about a few things—about their assignments, about their concentration. The most important message was one he didn't know how to put in words they would believe: There is more to life than what you're feeling this week.

No matter how many times they went through this big-game trauma, the coaches were always a little surprised at the way the whole world seemed to stop for football. It was ironic. They were the ones who spent most of their time trying to get young men to pay attention to the details of the game, to block out all the competing attractions of life and focus on football. But there was also comfort in the knowledge that other people were looking out for all the things that surely were more important than football. In a strange way, that's what relieved the guilt of the coaches' obsession. Somebody else was keeping things in perspective; they were free to bury themselves in the game.

Then along would come one of these mega-contests. Everybody—the media, school officials, parents, boosters, fans and players—could think of nothing else but the Game. And all distinctions between life and football were obliterated. Didn't anybody notice how weird and dangerous that was?

Eason had been questioning himself for weeks about the effects of all this single-mindedness. Maybe it was because he also had the job of overseeing the academic side and evidence was growing that the players were having a hard time keeping their minds on schoolwork. They were skipping classes and study halls. Midterm grades looked bad. Just keeping track of all the penalties, the extra running and the 6 A.M. study halls was becoming a bureaucratic tangle.

But there was also this nagging feeling that, in his personal life, things were slipping out of balance. Coaches were always making deals with their families. Just let us get past this game, this season, this recruiting period, and we'll have time together. Most of them tried to clear a few hours a week for family time no matter what, but the march toward the championship had overpowered everything else.

And they were the adults in this organization, the guys who supposedly had their priorities in order. What about the kids?

In the Monday scouting-report meeting, Brad Scott had taken the opposite tack from the previous week. "You gotta feel good about yourselves, your teammates and your second-team players—everybody who played a part in this. You're 10–0. Congratulations for getting there. But now it's a new season.

"This has got to be the priority this week." Whenever the word "priority" came out of coaches' mouths, it usually triggered a disclaimer. The game had to be a high priority, said Scott, "along with schoolwork and, of course, your family. We would never take that out of the picture. And your faith. Some of you will be praying in a way you haven't done in a long time. The Lord will probably be saying, 'Well, I've been wondering where you've been.'

"Outside of your schoolwork, your family and your faith, nothing can come between you and preparation for this ball game."

Eason believed that too. Only if it was so hard for grown men to work that out, what was it like for these 20-year-olds, waiting to play in what everybody told them was the biggest game of their lives?

3

BRAD Johnson walked through the crowded athletic-center atrium on his way to the training-table cafeteria. It was a zoo. Light setups and camera tripods created a half dozen little interview areas for the TV guys. And the print reporters were clustered around players on the couches that lined the walls.

A year ago Johnson would have been in the middle of all this, pummeled with questions about his teammates' emotional readiness and the quality of the Miami secondary. It was the one thing he didn't miss about being the starting quarterback.

He nodded in the direction of the media tangle. "If you have to go through that to play, I'd guess you'd rather have it than not. But it gets so silly."

The sports information department expected over 500 media people for Saturday. And each day a new batch would arrive to do advance stories setting up the Game of the Century. The crush would be too much for the informal ways reporters and players did business at Florida State. So Wayne Hogan and his people organized a schedule that would make key people available without totally disrupting practices, meetings and the players' class schedules.

There was a Bobby Bowden briefing or telephone conference call every day. Each day, also, a group of four or five players was scheduled to show up in the atrium, where reporters could grab them for one-on-one interviews. Casey Weldon and Terrell Buckley were in near-constant demand.

Most of the stories gained their impact from the rich history of the FSU-Miami series. And Bowden supplied just about everything else: "Yeah, this is one of those games that has a chance to live up to the hype. I betcha whoever wins wins by two touchdowns. There's just too much explosiveness out there."

Back in another era, Bowden and Schnellenberger had posed in boxing gloves to hype the game. But now the clash-of-titans theme was self-evident. No. 1 against No. 2. Winner take all. And by the end of the week, the frenzy had escalated to a point that suggested only the winner could walk away alive.

"We understand what's at stake," Kirk Carruthers told Craig Barnes of the Fort Lauderdale *Sun-Sentinel*. "This is for the national championship. We know if we don't win, the games with Florida and in the bowl mean nothing."

This would be Brad Johnson's fifth FSU-Miami game. He had started in just one, last year's loss in the Orange Bowl. And it looked as if he would finish his college career where he began it, on the sidelines. Every day he fought off the disappointment that implied. But being No. 2 brought with it a perspective he might not have had otherwise.

"Football is not everything. It's everything we got now. But it won't be forever. This game is a special game, but it's not the end of the world, no matter what happens."

All the questions that seemed so important to the media and to the fans probably didn't have any answers. Not until the teams actually met on the field.

"You can't help doing it. I do the same thing when I'm talking to my friends," said Johnson. "You speculate and you speculate."

But here he was, the No. 2 quarterback on the nation's No. 1 team. He knew the Seminole game plan, every pass and run they might call. He had studied Miami's defense. There was a picture in his head of what a quarterback should see when he stepped to the line. For over four years he had sat in meetings and worked through practices with teammates and coaches. He was a student of the game. Yet if someone asked him what to expect on Saturday, he honestly couldn't say.

"We could win by 30; they could win by 30. We sit in the meetings and say this guy is slow and that guy can't cover. But we don't really know until we get out there. Everything depends on how we react and how they react."

Of course, you couldn't just throw up your hands and not plan anything. You had to design schemes for what you thought they were going to do. And the routines of practice helped hone the skills that would make adapting easier come game day. It was funny, though, how the need to believe in the possibility of control drove them all.

Johnson's segment coach, Mark Richt, had been watching tapes in the office until eleven-thirty each night. "He almost never does that," said Johnson. "But he's never beaten Miami. The year we won he was at East Carolina."

The team was going out a little early to practice these days, and coming in a little later. They weren't so much physical workouts as teaching and reminding sessions, with the coaches taking every chance to coax and encourage.

"Against a team like South Carolina," said Johnson, "they build up the other guys. When you play Miami, they bring them down."

Brad Scott had worked that angle Monday in the scouting-report meeting. The good news, he said, was that "this is not as good a Miami team as we've played against. I don't believe they're good enough to stop our running game."

All the little failures and breakdowns of the past few weeks were forgotten subjects. The anger had dissolved. The coaches worked to hide whatever tension they felt and to affect, instead, an air of confidence. "They want to relax so that we relax," said Johnson. But the players read a hundred other signals of competitive anxiety: the hurried tempo of the drills, the near-giddy enthusiasm for the most routine plays. "You do that Saturday, men, and we'll gut 'em," Scott would yell. "We'll gut 'em."

When you hear that kind of stuff, said Johnson, "then you know it's Miami week."

4

"IT'S beginning to sound like a done deal," said Bowden to his coaches.

Bob Goin had been keeping the head coach posted on bowl negotiations, and the annual panic by selection committees was on. In fact, the process was probably over. The bowls worried that if they waited until the official deadline of November 17 they might lose the kind of matchups that boosted ticket sales and TV ratings. So every year at about this time they began making secret pacts with schools.

Washington, which was narrowly edged out of No. 2 in this week's Associated Press by Miami, was the only other undefeated team in the nation. And as Pac-10 champion, it would automatically go to the Rose Bowl. That left Florida State and Miami as the top attractions.

Goin's dream of matching up with an undefeated North Carolina State dissolved when the Wolfpack was beaten by Clemson. Now the most attractive option was the Federal Express Orange Bowl, with its $4.2 million payoff and easy commute from Tallahassee. Miami felt the same way. So the Orange Bowl got an informal agreement from the two in-state teams to be the winner's prize.

Now, what if the unthinkable happened? There was no advantage in jumping the gun on the Sunday deadline unless Goin could get a firm commitment to an attractive bowl in the event of a loss to Miami and/or Florida. Money didn't have to be the deciding factor, since Florida State would be splitting revenues with the other Atlantic Coast Conference teams. But it was still important. Of the remaining bowls, then, which seemed to offer the best combination of revenue, prestige and geography? The Mobil Cotton Bowl in Dallas was worth $3 million and looked like the best bet. So Goin shook hands on a deal that would take the Seminoles to Dallas—regardless of the outcome of the FSU-Florida game—if they lost to Miami.

A done deal.

The difference between the two payoffs only underlined the price of defeat. Carruthers was only partly right. Losing to Miami wouldn't make the bowl game worthless. It just cut the reward by $1 million.

5

KEVIN Mancini settled back into the Cybex chair and waited for Andy Barker and Jack Marucci to readjust the leg strap to his left calf and shin. Ever since he had been carried out of the LSU game, Cheesy had put the rest of his life on hold in the effort to rehabilitate that left knee. He had to play again.

The Miami game, the national championship—those would have been incentives enough. But there was also the NFL. Mancini was a senior and down to the last three games of his college career. Miami, Florida and the bowl game. Just three more chances to attract the attention of the scouts. Three more performances on the stage of national television.

"That's No. 67, Kevin Mancini, in there, folks," the TV commentator would say. "The Seminoles were afraid they had lost him for the season, but he made a miraculous comeback to lead this offensive line to the national championship. That gritty performance will no doubt stand him in good stead with pro coaches when they start drawing up their wish lists for the 1992 NFL draft."

That's what Mancini dreamed of, plotted for. Nothing was more important right now. Even without torn ligaments, things were tough enough for a 6-3 offensive lineman with ambitions to play with guys three inches taller and 20 pounds heavier. An operation to rebuild the knee might cost him a year in rehabilitation and his best chance at making the NFL. He had to try another way.

Mancini had all but moved into the training room. He hit the weights. He ran agility drills and sprints. He rode the stationary bike. And now, on the Cybex leg machine, he was testing his progress.

The 270-pound lineman leaned back in the chair and gripped its side handles, waiting for Marucci's signal to start pumping. The machine was similar to any leg-extension apparatus in a health club, except instead of a weight rack it had electronic gear to set resistance and to measure relative power. The trainers would get readings when he exercised the leg in both directions—up in a leg extension, and down in flexion, when he pushed and pulled against resistance.

The power came from the upper leg muscles, the quadriceps and hamstrings. The knee was the hinge. And the energy transferred from the muscles to the machine was limited by the strength of the joint. Using Mancini's right-leg performance as a baseline, the trainers could compare that with the power of his left. And the results would be part of the evidence the doctors would need to evaluate the tackle's chances of returning.

When Marucci told him to go, Mancini began working, tentatively at first, edging himself toward the point where he expected the pain to begin. But then he increased the effort as his confidence built. He pushed and pulled a half dozen times, the sweat streaming from under his baseball cap and his face reddening with the exertion. The two trainers watched the Cybex dial and recorded the numbers.

For the last two weeks, it had been impossible not to be impressed by Mancini's commitment. The trainers had guided him through an intense rehab program and spent as much time counseling patience as encouraging effort. No one would have been surprised if they had carried him right off that muddy field and onto an operating table. But he had fought back. And now look at these numbers: His left leg was just 15 percent off the power level of his right.

The stress of actually playing football wasn't measurable by any machine. Everybody knew that. But these results suggested that Mancini was at least strong enough to try working himself back into the practice drills. And if he was really at 85 percent strength, he might be one of the healthier ones on the line. Dixon's shoulder wouldn't be right until the off-season. Stevenson was in constant hip pain. Morris would miss full-contact scrimmages because of ankle problems. And Baker, enduring all his usual late-season aches plus the lacerated knee, wouldn't play at full speed until Saturday. Instead of running onto the field behind Renegade, maybe they should be delivered by ambulance.

Marucci and Barker grinned at Mancini as he eased himself off the Cybex chair. The lineman let himself smile through the sweat. This was all going according to plan.

6

In the Wednesday-morning meeting, Bowden and the assistants listened to Oravetz's injury report. And the head coach was surprised to hear of Mancini's progress.

"I heard him on TV telling the guy that he still had all this pain and was not very optimistic he could come back. It disappointed me a little."

Brad Scott laughed. "Well, you know, Coach, ol' Mancini is playing Bobby Bowden. He thinks he's got his own secret game plan."

All week, the tackle had been ducking reporters. He affected an exaggerated limp in front of them. And when he was cornered, he played down his chances of coming back. Too much pain, too little progress so far, he told them. He swore his teammates to secrecy and pleaded for cover stories from the trainers. Let 'em wait until Saturday, he thought. The seniors would be introduced for their last home game, and he would come running onto the field.

"He thinks he has this big 'S' on his jersey," Mark Richt said, smiling. "And when the guys on the other side see him out there, they will say, 'Oh no, not Mancini!' "

The whole room broke up in laughter. "Hey, do me a favor," said Scott. "Don't tell him that's not true."

All week long, the meetings had been energized by a tug-of-war between the assistants and the head coach. It was the usual creative battle, only heightened by the big-game atmosphere. At first, Bowden offered his usual 100 ideas of how to capitalize on this or that defensive alignment; the assistants then gradually convinced him to throw out 95 of them. Next it was their turn to lobby for the changes they wanted, and the boss would play the conservative role.

"Are you sure we're not adding too much?" he asked on Wednesday.

"It's already in," they told him, knowing that the new plays would truly be in only after Bowden became a believer during the last two days of workouts.

Most of the new stuff was intended to give Miami a familiar look, then frustrate assumptions with some new twist—maybe a pass-route altera- tion or a new primary receiver. They were all in agreement that running straight ahead was going to be crucial, given the Hurricanes' speed to cut off sweeps and slow-developing runs. They had to have the rushing game. Look what happened to poor Houston when it tried to pass its way by the Hurricanes.

The priority on the north-and-south attack inspired the assistants to lobby hard for making better use of Paul Moore. Edgar Bennett's shoulder injury in the Louisville game had cinched the case, as far as some of the coaches were concerned. They wanted a masher in there, both on the runs and as a blocker, and Bennett was a finesse guy who seemed to be thumbing his nose at them.

Bowden had backed them when all the initial criticism of Bennett's blocking began. It was true that Bennett was not the blocker Moore and Floyd were. But he was a better open-field runner and pass receiver. He was also the guy who came back for his last year of eligibility instead of bolting to the NFL. And the coach had no intention of holding him out of the biggest game of his career.

Each day, Scott and Billy Sexton lobbied in some different way for increasing Paul Moore's role. "We gotta have No. 32 in there for this one, Coach," Scott said after he had gone over a new draw play.

Bowden let a little impatience into his voice. "Here's a guy who came back for his fifth year, and it's not fair to cast him aside. He's a captain, a fifth-year senior, and we're gonna start Paul Moore?"

Well, maybe not start, they argued. But this was Moore's senior year too. Miami was his home. And he could be counted on to turn loose all 240 beefy pounds against the Hurricanes. Why let him sit on the bench?

"If this comes down to a mash game," said Scott, "he's our best masher."

"I agree a hundred percent," answered Bowden. "But we can't forsake Edgar."

A few games ago Bowden might have been more responsive to the assistants' arguments. But there were two factors that made him back his No. 1 guy. The first was his habit of relying more and more on the veterans when the games got bigger and bigger. Depend on the dependables. The second was his natural empathy.

If Bennett had not been to see him to talk about his worries, Bowden may have found it easier to relegate him to a lesser role. But last week the two had sat in Bowden's office and talked about Bennett's plans, about his hurt shoulder and about his desire to become a better blocker. The discussion reminded Bowden of what he owed the fullback.

Against South Carolina, Bowden had tried to alternate Bennett and the other fullbacks to maximize both blocking and pass-catching potential, and the effort had cost them something in continuity. If, for this game, he had to choose the first-teamer from the whole group, it would be Bennett. They could work out a way to give Paul Moore his chance.

Just having the guys he knew best in the lineup would give him more confidence, thought Bowden. These kinds of games felt like drag races, with two high-powered machines pouring it on side by side, squeezing every ounce of energy out of their engines and drive trains. If you strapped yourself in for that kind of ride, you had to have faith in all those moving parts. And maybe a little something extra in the fuel tank.

Bowden let the assistants tinker with the running attack and the changes in pass routes. For his own peace of mind, though, he needed some brain-lock insurance. More than anything, he hated getting to a point in a game where he had nothing left up his sleeve. What if the two teams were hopelessly deadlocked and he needed that desperation first down? Two points to win the game? What would he call?

"I tell you one thing I definitely want in," Bowden told his assistants. "You can't get too many Hides against these guys."

Bowden had two versions of these gimmick plays—the Y Hide to a tight end and the Tailback Hide to the receiver out of the backfield. The principle was the same with each. The target receiver, pretending to block, threw himself on the ground near the pile at the line of scrimmage, then crawled out of hiding away from the direction of the fake play and into a position to receive the pass. He had called the Y Hide once already, in the LSU slop, but even so, it wasn't the kind of thing a team would scheme against; so it would work as long as everyone carried out their fakes convincingly and the receiver crawled out of the pile and into the open quickly enough. After that, it was simply throw and catch.

"I just feel better knowing those babies are in there," said Bowden.

So along with the new running plays and the modified pass standards, the Seminoles practiced the Hides every day. Lonnie Johnson and Amp Lee would crawl around the feet of the dueling linemen as Casey Weldon pretended to look downfield. Then the quarterback would turn and hit them as they popped up in the secondary.

It was one more headache for Jimmy Heggins, who spent most of his time trying to convince Lonnie Johnson and Warren Hart to do more than pretend to block. On Y Hide, he had to coach them to fake it, to escape the tangle at the line of scrimmage and to get into the open before Weldon was smothered by a pursuing linebacker.

Bowden teased him about the pressure: "Here we are, it's fourth and two to win the game. We call the Y Hide. And, Jimmy, there's no pressure on you at all now. 'Cause if we lose, all that happens is that we don't go to the Orange Bowl and we don't get that extra million dollars."

7

"THERE'S one second left on the clock. The crowd is roaring. This is for the national championship. You make it, we win; you miss it, it's all over."

Dan Mowrey was on one knee in the holder's position on the practice-field 20-yard line, looking back at Gerry Thomas and putting the pressure on. Nothing could simulate a real game situation, but the placekickers had their little pretend routines.

Mowrey held the ball out as if taking the long snap from center. "Hut, hut." Then he pulled the ball down into a hold, and Thomas took his steps and swung through. Boom. Through the uprights. Then they moved back a couple of yards to where they had left another ball.

"One second left," said Mowrey. "To win it all or lose it all." Boom.

Missing the extra points at Michigan and hearing the boos in Orlando had rattled Mowrey more than he let on. "I tried to laugh it off, but it really got to me." He bore down in practice, but his confidence was gone. Since LSU, he had been handling kickoffs and waiting for his chances at the long field goals. Mowrey still had the leg. Thomas seemed to have the close-in accuracy.

Mowrey didn't resent Thomas for taking the kicking job. It was more like he lost it than Gerry won it. He was still the guy on scholarship, which meant the coaches would give him every chance to win it back—if not this year, then the next. Thomas, a redshirt sophomore from the same school in Niceville that produced backup quarterback Kenny Felder and receiver Kevin Knox, was a walk-on.

The two seemed entirely different types. Mowrey was the outgoing cutup—maybe a little young even for his 19 years. A lackadaisical attitude toward school had put him on Mark Meleney's and John Eason's lists of academic problem children. Thomas was a quiet, serious junior, carrying a strong B average in a business curriculum.

But the two got along fine in practice. Kickers need one another more than other players do, since they often end up coaching themselves for long periods on a field alone, while the offense and defense bang heads elsewhere.

The two would kick somewhere between 100 and 250 balls a practice, lining them up, ten at a time, from different spots on the field. From the 23-yard line in was Thomas's territory, which meant 40-yard kicks and under. Mowrey would practice between the 20 and the 40.

"One second left," they would say. And nine times out of ten, it was boom, through the uprights.

8

THE offense trotted into the stadium at around three-thirty Thursday afternoon, earlier than usual for the last pregame run-through, because Brad Scott wanted to make sure everybody knew where they were supposed to be on the new plays. And he wanted to run the rehearsals in exactly the places on the field where the strategy would work best. Leave nothing to chance.

The sun was warm, the day nearly cloudless. It would be the same tomorrow and, most likely, on Saturday. A 70-degree fall afternoon in North Florida. No rain. No excuses.

It felt good to be in the stadium in shorts and no pads. And alone. The media and fans were locked out of these sessions, as they had been all week. Bowden wanted no cameras, no unfamiliar note takers observing his practices even from a distance. Not this week. And the isolation was reassuring.

The athletic center had taken on the feel of a media convention. Everybody needed a moment, a word, a prediction, a sound bite. With an empty Doak Campbell surrounding them and all that sun and sky above, it was possible to believe again that not everything in the world depended on football.

In the Thursday-morning meeting, Bowden had led the devotion prayer: "There's not a coach here who wouldn't have prayed for a chance to play in a game like this. Help us to realize there's much more to life than this."

He kept his head bowed for a moment before saying, "Amen." Then he looked up. "I would have prayed longer, but I couldn't think of anything more important."

Practices had been intense all week, not so much from the hitting as from the level of expectations. Mistakes seemed to annoy everyone, coaches and players alike. The tension bred strange reactions. Reggie Freeman became convinced that he had been jinxed by a voodoo curse from an old girlfriend. And he had run off the field in frustration earlier in the week. It took a Randy Oravetz incantation in the training room to convince him to return.

It was the receiving corps, though, who seemed to be feeling the most pressure. All week they had problems holding on to the ball. And their teammates had been quick with criticism.

"A little shift in the mood," said Eason. "People are angry. It's time to get down to business."

The defense, growing more confident with every week's game, could be especially merciless in the end-of-practice scrimmages. "Don't have to cover him, man. He'll never catch it."

Shannon Baker and Eric Turral were special targets, because they were the guys counted on to haul in the deep passes. Every drop brought a barrage of whistles and hoots from the sideline. And neither of the flankers was happy about the abuse.

Baker, however, could pull himself out of the funks more quickly than his teammate. Thursday afternoon, Turral remained on one knee watching while the other receivers rolled through the plays with the first-, second- and third-team offenses.

Eason said nothing. "I just want to see how long he'll wait for an invitation to practice."

Scott's mission on Thursday was to get enough reps for each of the possible combinations: Mancini in, Mancini out; Baker at center, Stevenson or Deremer at center; Morris at guard, Morris at tackle. And he took his frustration out on the scout-team defenders, who were supposed to be giving his offensive line the look of the Miami defense. It was boring work, and they didn't have their minds on what they were doing.

"Run it again," he exploded. "And this time, GET WHERE YOU'RE SUPPOSED TO BE."

The afternoon dragged on past the time the team expected to be on the field. The coaches wanted every repetition they could get, but they were fighting ever-shortening attention spans. And as it grew later, the window of isolation began to close.

Television sportscasters who had planned to use the backdrop of the stands in Doak Campbell for their live reports to stations in Miami, Tampa Bay and Tallahassee had talked their way past the guards and were setting up tripods and cameras. The mere appearance of strangers with cameras when they were going through game-plan rehearsals drove the coaches crazy. And the players egged them on by pointing into the stands: "Hey, who are those guys?"

Bowden and Scott would kick one crew out; another would move in within minutes. The sports information assistants negotiated some hurried compromises with the TV people as the team finished its workouts. But whatever illusion they had that no one was watching was gone. And as they trotted into the locker room to shower, a crowd of reporters gathered in the atrium.

9

THE clash of the No. 1 and No. 2 teams in Florida and the nation hogged the media spotlight. But the other big football power in the state was about to reach a historic milestone too. With a win over Kentucky on Saturday afternoon in Gainesville, the University of Florida Gators could win their first Southeastern Conference title and an automatic bid to the Sugar Bowl.

Since losing to Syracuse, the Gators had gone undefeated, both in SEC play and against out-of-conference teams. They were 8–1 and favored by 33 points to beat Kentucky, a 3–6 team in the SEC cellar.

It was hard to exaggerate what Saturday might mean to the long-suffering Gator fans. The school was a charter member of the 58-year-old SEC and had never officially won the conference championship. In 1990, Steve Spurrier's first year as head coach, Florida had the best record in the conference, but couldn't claim the title because it was still being penalized for NCAA violations.

Now here they were, poised to finish this glorious season as first-time champions, and they were being upstaged—again—by Bowden and the boys from the girls' school. Paranoid FSU fans could hear Gator teeth ominously grinding around the state. And they took every opportunity to let Bowden know that an ambush was surely being prepared for the Seminoles in Gainesville two weeks down the road.

One caller on Bowden's Thursday-night radio show pleaded with the coach to substitute freely on Saturday against Miami, so that the players would be fresh for the *real* game against Florida. Out-of-state media had a tough time understanding a rivalry that could eclipse a No. 1 vs. No. 2 showdown. So Bowden spent a lot of time during the week trying to explain.

"From a national standpoint, the Miami game has been much more meaningful, but the Florida State fans are paranoid about Florida. Your basic Seminole fan wants to beat Florida above all else."

The coaches and players, he said, were naturally more focused on the rivalry with Miami, because Miami was the team that stood between them and the national championship year after year. Four years in a row now they had beaten Florida teams. Which meant no player now on the squad had ever lost to the Gators. Who could blame the young guys for being less concerned about the Gator threat?

Florida State alums and fans, on the other hand, had lived their lives in the oppressive shadow of the University of Florida. *The* University of

Florida, Gator boosters liked to remind them. So every FSU-Florida game began a year of either gloating or abject misery for everybody who felt connected with the schools.

Either way you looked at it, said Bowden, it meant he was responsible for two must-win games. "They're the two biggest games that determine whether I'm St. Bobby or just S.B."

10

ON Friday afternoon, about the same time Bowden was burrowing in in Thomasville for his tape-review routine, Seminole boosters, university officials and visiting dignitaries were quietly launching the next phase of Florida State's big-time ambitions. In a tent in the shadow of the naked girders of Doak Campbell Stadium, they celebrated the ceremonial groundbreaking for the new University Center complex.

Since the Miami game was the last home contest of the season, construction would begin on Monday. An eight-story, 243,163-square-foot complex was going up on the east side of the stadium. Beginning sometime in '92, a similar structure, though half the square footage, would rise on the west side. The south end zone would be enclosed. The Moore Athletic Center would be expanded on the north end. And within five years—if everything went according to plan—an expanded 70,000-seat Doak Campbell Stadium would stand at the center of this huge $100 million Gothic nest.

"How fortunate we are," said FSU president Dale Lick, "and what a tremendous boost this is going to be for higher education in our state."

Where Doak Campbell had once been exiled to this far corner of the campus, it would now become—literally—the inner core of the school's administration. The Registrar's Office, Financial Aid, Cashier's Office, Admissions, the Advising Center and a host of others would be moving into the complex. So would the schools of Criminology, Social Work and Motion Picture, Television and Recording Arts.

In the expanded athletic center, all of FSU's sports departments would have their offices. And the football coaches would have those rooms with a view.

The massive project was the result of four years of planning, wrangling and compromising. The university—the smallest among Florida's nine four-year state schools—would free up space elsewhere on campus so that academic departments could expand into old administrative space. And the boosters, who were paying for the end zone bowl-in and the athletic-center expansion, would rid themselves forever of the Erector Set complex.

"This edifice," said Alan Mabe, president of the faculty senate, "will stand as a reminder that this university can achieve its goals and aspirations."

11

WHEN the team filed off the bus in Thomasville, the head coach was waiting for them in the small Holiday Inn banquet room. And after they had settled into their seats, he read them a quote from Winston Churchill:

" 'To every man there comes in his lifetime that special moment when he is tapped on the shoulder and offered that chance to do a very special thing that is unique to him and that is fitted to his talent.' "

Bowden looked up and removed his glasses. "That's what we're faced with tomorrow. You and I, our team, our coaches have been given an opportunity that we may never get again." Then he read the rest of the quote.

"Churchill said, 'What a tragedy if that moment comes and you are unprepared.'

"That's the good news, men. You are prepared. You have prepared yourselves. The coaches have prepared you, and you have responded."

There would be no inspirational stories tonight. No need. Just show them who they're playing, thought Bowden.

"Now, last year, men, you and I go down to Miami. Beautiful day. The stadium is rockin'. Everybody's watching. National television.

"We're out there flexing before the game and Miami runs right through us, pushes a couple of us. They ran right through us and pushed a couple of us. I remember looking at it and being glad none of our kids retaliated, 'cause that could have started a war.

"I thought it was just an accident, that we just happened to be in their way. Then I saw an article in the paper last summer. One of their football players made a statement. Well, it turns out that during a spring game one of the teams came out and ran through the other one. Somebody asked, 'Why did y'all do that?' And he says, 'Well, that's a Miami tradition. We did that to Florida State last year and intimidated them.'

"I called Coach Erickson. He hadn't seen it. He apologized. And I'm sure he grabbed that kid.

"Now, I would never want y'all to do something like that. And Coach Erickson doesn't want to do anything like that. But hey, men, I'm tired of being intimidated by Miami. We're playing in our domain. That's our castle out there.

"They've won forty-three in a row down there in their domain. But we ain't down there. They think that just because they're Miami they can come up here and take that ring away in our own backyard in front of our crowd.

"Miami hasn't been behind this year. You and I have played in the mud. You and I have been thirteen points behind in a rainstorm. You ain't supposed to come back and win them kind.

"We've played in freezing weather. We've played with a thirty-mile-an-hour wind coming up and down the field. We've played before 105,000 people. Men, we've been tested. Miami hasn't been through the test. They'll get their test tomorrow.

"We started off the year, y'all came up with the motto 'No Excuses.' Y'all came up with it. And I tell you, I can't think of a single excuse tomorrow. We got everybody healthy again. We're playing at our place. We got a heck of a ball club. We got the best material in the country. There's only one thing that can keep us from doin' it and that's not being together. If someone can divide us, they can beat us. But not if we're cheering for each other, we're clapping for each other. We. Us. Team.

"It will be a sixty-minute fight. There's no way we can expect for anything to happen in that game that will cause it to be over in ten minutes. It will be sixty minutes. One of their linebackers, Barrow, said, 'We're going to be so tired after the Florida State game that the cheerleaders will have to drag us off the field.' That was pretty good. I hope we feel that way. That we give every drop.

"Think about that now. Will you give every drop? There have been some times this year when you haven't. And there may have been some times when I haven't. Most of us are in the same boat on that. I just want to remind you of one play. That's the play William Floyd made against LSU, when he sprinted with every drop he had—when nearly everybody else had given up—and caught that guy. Will you do that? Will you do that tomorrow? If one of their guys breaks clear and he's running for a touchdown and he's got 70 yards to go and you're 15 or 20 yards behind him, will you give it all you got?

"Now, if you will, we'll win.

"Tomorrow is one of them call-anything days. I might call anything. You might get that Y Hide off our one-inch line. We ain't holding nothing back tomorrow.

"Play as hard as you can. That's all I want. Don't worry about losing. I don't think you are. You're far too smart. Just think of one thing: It's our home, our crowd.

"Seniors, this is the last time you'll hit that field. Seniors, you will not let us lose. If somebody else falters, you're gonna pick 'em up, see that they fight.

"Now, show class tomorrow. Dennis is controlling those guys real well. They can't hardly stand it. They're not used to that. But don't try to outshowboat those guys. We don't want that image. Your momma don't want that image. Your daddy don't want it.

"If he pushes me, I walk away. If he cusses me, I walk away. If he slugs me, I walk away. Then I see him after the ball game. I'll let you out early if you want to do that.

"Hand the ball to the official. Show good sportsmanship."

Then he paused and looked over his glasses. "The last thing I got down here is just this: We're gonna let the big dog hunt."

The players laughed and applauded. They liked it when the Man got into it like this. Let the big dog hunt, indeed.

12

Kickoff was at noon, so by nine-thirty traffic around Doak Campbell was already moving slowly. People in "Game of the Century" T-shirts were strolling in the parking lots and making their way through stopped cars on West Pensacola. Above the chatter of the souvenir vendors, the honking horns, the laughter and calls of the tailgate early birds, there was the sound of the taped Seminole drumbeat, amplified through the stadium's loudspeakers. It would be the morning soundtrack.

The last time the Hurricanes came to town, they attracted the third-biggest crowd in stadium history. This one should be a record.

Out the window of his second-story office in the athletic center, Bowden could see the regulars milling in the parking lot. Those would be the Seminole booster big-buck contributors. They got the spaces closest to the stadium.

He had come in early to be available for recruits and their parents. Some one hundred of the top prospects from Florida and around the country had been invited to be here for the game. And the assistant coaches would bring a half dozen selected stars to chat with the head coach in his office. Bowden nervously fiddled with papers and pins on his desk between visits.

Burt Reynolds had planned to fly in for the game. He probably would have been in the office too. But at the last minute his private plane developed problems, and he had canceled. Just as well, thought Bowden. This was going to be nervous and hectic enough.

Just before Mark Richt brought in Danny Kanell and his parents, Brad Scott ducked into the coach's office to remind him of a few keys they had discussed the night before in Thomasville. Scott and Richt had redesigned some of the formations to force Miami defenses into more predictable alignments, and Scott wanted to make sure Bowden didn't call one of his standards when the formation didn't allow it.

"If you do, Coach, one of my guys is likely to get so confused he'll call time out."

The new plays and formations had been a continuing soft sell on the part of Richt and Scott. They had brought tapes to the Friday-night skull session to show how the plays would unfold against typical Miami defenses. And they had kept Bowden from going through his three pages of notes until he seemed comfortable with what his assistants were saying.

Richt introduced Dr. and Mrs. Kanell and Danny to Bowden. They were prepared for just what the coach had to give, a few minutes of friendly, superficial chitchat: "How many children do you have? . . . Just the one son? Well, you look like you've got a keeper."

The symbolism was more important than the substance. The message: Bobby Bowden, on the most important day in Florida State football history, took time out to talk to you, son. That's how important we think you are to our program.

And Kanell was. "He's the kid we want," Richt had told the head coach the night before. "Either him or Walsh." Bowden could see why when he got a look at the 6-5 quarterback. "Oh, what a good-lookin' kid that is."

A few minutes later the coach waited in the hallway outside the projection room while Bob Goin introduced him to the rest of the recruits, parents and high school coaches. "If I were to turn my children, my most cherished possessions, over to someone for four or five years, I could find no greater person to turn them over to than this fine Christian man. Bobby Bowden, ladies and gentlemen."

The coach acknowledged the enthusiastic applause. He wanted to talk to them as a parent, he said. "That Magic Johnson thing scared us all, didn't it? You don't want these young men exposed to any more than they have to be exposed to. In college you can get into the fast lane pretty quick.

"I have raised my children. Now I'm in the grandchildren business. And when your boy comes here, I try to take your place. I think that's important.

"I've been here sixteen years. I'm not looking to move. Our coaches have been together, most of them, for seven years. That's stability.

"I guarantee any boy who comes to Florida State and wants to graduate, we'll give him every tool to do that.

"Now, it's true that Deion ain't got no degree, but he seems to be getting along all right. I had to borrow a couple of hundred from him not long ago."

He exited to the laughter and headed back down the hall to gather his game plan. Then he moved through the office and down the stairs, shaking the hands of parents and boosters along the way. He crossed the atrium floor to the door that led to the locker room and, through it, to the stadium. He smiled and waved to the people still mingling in the atrium. But once the door closed behind him, as far as he was concerned the game began.

The crowd outside cheered the Seminoles through the flexes and drills, while the long line of recruits watched from the sidelines. As the players made their traditional ankle walk to the end zone, the horns blared from the band section, and they lifted their helmets like gladiators. The fans roared.

Down at the other end, the Hurricanes were whacking one another on their shoulder pads and strutting between drills to the boos of the nearest Seminole sections. Only the south-end-zone seats, occupied by the fans who had made the trip from Miami, produced cheers for the invaders.

The Sea World blimp circled slowly overhead. The traffic on Stadium Drive and West Pensacola was nearly at a standstill. And fans were still making their way through the gates and into the last empty seats as the players trotted off the field to the locker rooms.

The half-hour wait until they could escape into the stadium always passed slowly for the players. Today it would seem interminable. Most of them sat in silence, staring into space or willing all their attention to the tunes on their Walkmans. "Those refs are just looking for something to call now. They are already wound up," said Casey Weldon to no one in particular.

More silence, then Kirk Carruthers: "The biggest game of your life, baby. Wire-to-wire champions. The first ever in history. I want to be part of it. You better be a part too."

"We got it, man. All we gotta do is do it."

Bowden had been reading his note card. He looked at his watch, then cleared his throat nervously.

"Don't worry about making a mistake." The coach nearly laughed at himself for saying it. Who was he kidding? "It's the biggest game in the country. I've never been in one bigger than this either.

"But you've already done all the work. And this is really about the only thing fun about football, playing in a game.

"Go out there and play just as loose and as hard as you can. And if you make a mistake, don't worry about it. If we get behind, don't worry about it. They've never been behind. How are they going to respond? I know this, we've been in terrible situations and come back and won.

"Every time you hit a guy, men, it's for the ring. Are you going to let him hit you harder because he wants it more than you? You make it count."

Someone hit a button on the video machine, and a short highlight tape from the last Miami game in Doak Campbell appeared on the TV screen. The '91 players watched the '89 Seminoles celebrating their victory, saw the joy in their faces and in the faces of the fans cheering the 24–10 win. Commit that to memory, the coaches told them.

"Remember, it's sixty minutes," said Bowden when the tape concluded. "If you get behind, it don't mean a darn thing. If they get behind, it don't mean anything. Just keep fighting."

Then the head coach reached out to put a hand on the nearest player's head, connecting him with all the others. And he prayed:

"Dear Father, why have you put this group of men together? These players, these coaches, to reach a game that is the pinnacle of college football?

"We can't ask you to win it for us. You've got both teams to be concerned about. We merely pray that you will help our players to do their best, to give them wisdom, to protect them from injury.

"Be with our coaches and give them wisdom in the decisions we must make. And maybe if we can win we can glorify you. In Thy Name we pray. Amen."

"Amen," echoed the team.

13

THE noise when they ran back onto the field shook the stadium. The Hurricanes were already lined up across from the Seminole bench, waiting. And they edged menacingly into the wide lane down the middle reserved for Chief Osceola and Renegade.

Both teams knew they should give the horse and rider room. And they would. But there was too much energy and emotion loose in the stadium now. They couldn't just stand there. So all 200 of the players on both sides leaned toward the center of the field. Assistant coaches pushed their players back, preserving the neutral ground. And Renegade, trained to endure these moments, danced warily at the south end of the lines.

"Now," said the stadium announcer, "your Seminole seniors, playing their last game in Doak Campbell Stadium." He read the names in alphabetical order, and each ran onto the field to applause and cheers: EDGAR BENNETT . . . KIRK CARRUTHERS . . . JAMES CHANEY . . . JOHNNY CLOWER . . . HOWARD DINKINS . . . REGGIE DIXON . . . BRAD JOHNSON . . . When he said KEVIN MANCINI, the 270-pound tackle sprinted onto the field as if Baton Rouge had been only a mud bath and the weeks since merely a honing of the edge of the offensive line's secret weapon. The ovation grew into a roar. And Mancini's teammates clapped and hooted.

PAUL MOORE . . . MIKE MORRIS . . . HENRY OSTASZEWSKI . . . JOE OSTASZEWSKI . . . SCOTT PLAYER . . . CASEY WELDON. Only the starting quarterback's reception overshadowed Mancini's.

Florida State won the toss and, as usual, elected to receive the ball at the start of the second half.

The officials signaled that Miami would be receiving, Florida State kicking. And Chief Osceola rode to the center of the field holding the flaming spear aloft. Most of the Hurricanes turned their backs as the standing-room-only crowd created the deafening noise that rose to a 60,000-voice scream when the rider on horseback planted the spear on the 50-yard line. The Game of the Century was officially on.

So far, Miami had been averaging 450 yards and 36 points per game. "This Miami team," read Jim Gladden's scouting report for the Seminole defense, "has great speed at the skill positions, an offensive line that will hold with the best and a confidence level that is extremely high. They are very cocky and think you are overrated."

And the first time they had the ball, the Hurricanes drove 74 yards for the initial score of the day, a Stephen McGuire run into the end zone from the 2-yard line. Carlos Huerta's kick made it 7–0, with less than two minutes off the clock.

Two personal-foul penalties against FSU had helped the Hurricanes move down the field, but the most frightening sight for the Seminole coaches was McGuire's open-field romp of 29 yards in the middle of the drive. Last year in the Orange Bowl, the same fullback had accounted for half the 334 rushing yards Miami gained against them. And Bowden was convinced the key to this rematch would be who best controlled the other guy's running game.

When the defense came off the field, Chuck Amato cornered his linemen and spoke reassuringly to them. The only thing he was worried about were the penalties. "Play aggressively, but nothing foolish now."

The Florida State offense got the ball at its own 23. In the locker room before the game, Bowden had told the players he would test them immediately by running out of the revamped formation. And Amp Lee took the first handoff for 13 yards and a first down. But then Lee was nailed behind the line of scrimmage, and a holding call made it second and 23 from the Seminole 23-yard line. Two plays later, Scott Player booted them out of trouble with a 44-yard punt.

Mancini took off his helmet as he crossed the sideline and plopped down alongside the other linemen on their end of the bench. "They suck, they suck," he said.

Brad Scott pulled at the headset line to give himself enough slack to reach the bench. He leaned over into the sweating linemen. It was all right, he told them. They knew what they had to do. That first play, with the big gain out of the flex, that should tell 'em something about the kind of afternoon they could have.

"Lock on 'em."

On the first play of Miami's second series, Gino Torretta, the Miami quarterback, hit Kevin Williams at full speed with a pass that could have put the Seminoles 14 points down. But the speedster couldn't hold on. And when Carruthers sacked the quarterback on third down, Miami was forced to punt from its own 22.

Now it was Florida State's turn to get help from a Miami penalty. On third and 14 from the FSU 37, Shannon Baker was mauled on a post pattern and awarded the pass-interference call. Weldon was sacked on his first attempt to capitalize on the penalty. But just before he was tackled on second down, he got away a 51-yard pass to Amp Lee gliding toward the Hurricane end zone. Lee was way out in front of the nearest Miami defender when the quarterback released the pass. But the ball floated a fraction of a second too long, and the tailback had to slow down to wait. He was smothered at the 2 as he pulled it in.

On first down, William Floyd was in the game to block for Lee on the toss sweep. Floyd went into motion, crossing from right to left behind the quarterback before the snap. When he took the ball from center, Weldon wheeled and pitched it back to Lee for one of the Seminoles' most familiar plays. And the 230-pound Floyd should have been in position to take care of the 190-pound safety blitzing into the backfield. But the safety was moving as soon as the ball was snapped. He shot across the line, knocking the freshman fullback backward and dropping Lee for a five-yard loss.

On second down, Weldon threw the ball away in the end zone when Kez McCorvey was double-covered. Now it was third and goal from the 7. And Bowden called for the Y Hide.

When Weldon took the snap, he rolled right, looking to the end zone in front of him. The Miami secondary shifted in the same direction, just as they were supposed to. And Lonnie Johnson crawled frantically into the open behind the pileup on the line of scrimmage. Maybe it was because Weldon had to fade so far right to avoid the outside linebacker in hot pursuit. Or maybe Johnson ended up too far to the left by the time he stood up, ran and turned. But the arc of the pass was a few feet short of where the tight end stood alone and waiting on the 5-yard line. Johnson couldn't seem to move himself any closer. And the pass bounced off his outstretched hands.

Gerry Thomas kicked the 25-yard field goal, narrowing the Hurricanes' lead to four points.

After two exchanges of possession, the defense handed them the biggest break of the first half. On second down in the next Miami series, McGuire took the handoff and appeared on his way for another respectable gain, when Joe Ostaszewski reached out as the fullback ran by and raked the ball from his hands. Joe's twin brother, Henry, jumped on it. And suddenly it was the Seminoles' ball at the Miami 24.

So far, Bowden had started each series with a run. Now he called for the play-action pass. Weldon faked the handoff, then hit Bennett over the middle for a 20-yard gain. Lee moved the ball two yards closer on first and goal from the 4. Then, as the second quarter began, in came Paul Moore and the mash gang. The big fullback carried three times on the same play, the 34 Wham, pushing it into the end zone on fourth down. Thomas' point-after kick gave the Seminoles the lead, 10–7.

Miami stifled the Seminoles' offense for the remainder of the second quarter. But the FSU defense robbed Torretta and the Hurricanes of any chance to gain advantage. Two Miami drives ended with interceptions, one each by Buckley and Marvin Jones. Then Sterling Palmer blocked a 41-yard field goal attempt near the end of the half.

The Florida State defense had won the battle of the first half. The most famous wide receivers in college football had caught exactly one pass in the first half. The offense that was averaging 18 points and 225 yards per half through eight games had seven points and 167 yards so far in this one. And more important, for the first time all year, the Miami Hurricanes were behind.

The bad news was that Florida State's offense seemed to be having as much trouble against Miami's defense. The Seminoles had converted just one third down, and that was with the help of a pass-interference call. Their only long drive had given them a first and goal on the 2-yard line, but they had to settle for a field goal. Their touchdown came after the defense handed them the ball on the Miami 24-yard line. And in a game the Seminoles proposed to win on the ground, two passes—the 51-yarder to Lee and the 20-yarder to Bennett—were their key plays of the half.

14

THE assistant coaches huddled with Bowden at the half. Everybody talked at the same time, as much to release the nervous energy as to explore new strategy. There were few surprises here. This was turning out to be pretty much what they expected, a pitched battle. Speed canceled speed. Power balanced power. And some small advantage, even for only a moment—a single play, a block, a great catch—would likely mean the difference between the greatest football triumph in school history and the utterly unthinkable.

From where they stood on the sidelines, it was impossible for the coaches to have a perspective other than the one supplied by a collection of images piled one upon another: McGuire rumbling through the defensive secondary with Seminole tacklers bouncing off him; Lee seemingly all alone with that long pass, then being nailed by Miami's Hurlie Brown, who seemed to cover the last 15 yards in microseconds; William Floyd's knock-back on the failed toss sweep; and Lonnie Johnson's frozen feet on Y Hide.

Dennis Erickson and his coaches in the other locker room were no doubt similarly haunted. But the fact that they shared the anxiety would bring no comfort to either side. All the little nightmares could be diluted and ultimately dissolved only by winning.

The Seminole offensive assistants crowded around the small blackboard in their locker room, arguing for two or three plays that might catch the Hurricanes in the wrong alignment and produce the big gain. Bowden listened and noted them. "I'm gonna throw that Hide again," he said. "He was wide open. I'm gonna get that Tailback Hide."

But they all knew the remaining half would belong less to strategy than to execution. And it was that message that the head coach took to the players.

"Okay, men, we're down to the most important half of the year. We're thirty minutes away from what we've worked for."

The young men were wedged into tight spaces in front of him, the sweat still glistening in their hair and rolling down their cheeks. Effort and contact had relieved them of their pregame nervousness. The only anxiety that remained was a mixture of impatience and frustration. And fatigue would soon kill that.

Outside, the halftime celebration honoring heroes of the 1990 Gulf War was drawing to a close. And soon the strains of the "War Chant" would be discernible, even through the metal door.

"Thirty minutes away," said the coach. "It's all guts."

Although they knew they shouldn't be thinking it, some of the defensive starters couldn't escape the thought: When was the offense going to show up? This was becoming a habit, this struggle until the defense broke the other guy's back and made the field safe for the offense. They had snatched the momentum before. But Miami was not Louisville.

"Defense, you're only doing two things wrong," said Bowden, who was still thinking about McGuire's first-quarter run. "Tackling. I told you to hit the guy and clutch him. You mean it doesn't mean enough to you to use your arms for the ring?

"Then the darn penalties. The score would be 10–0 now without the penalties. But, defense, if you can keep 'em off the board, we're okay. We'll be undefeated in another thirty minutes.

"Offense, we need to get the ball and drive for a touchdown, and we can take control of this game.

"We've got to have some great plays, men. Somebody has to make some great plays."

The knock at the door meant the captains were wanted out on the field, and there was just another minute left with the team.

"Men, we've got thirty more minutes. We need a hero, don't we? We need somebody who'll suck it up and go get that passer. Somebody who'll make that great catch, that great run.

"We need a hero, men. We need a hero."

On the first play of the second half, a play-action pass, Weldon was caught in the backfield before he had a chance to throw. And when he didn't get up, the trainers ran onto the field to where he lay, flat on his back. The visitors in the south end zone began the mock "War Chant" and drew the boos of the home crowd.

The blood had drained from Weldon's face as he was helped to the sideline, but it appeared nothing was broken or strained or separated. Brad Johnson took over on second and 16 on the FSU 22, and Bowden called for the Tailback Hide.

It was Amp Lee who crawled around the pile this time, as the backup quarterback rolled to the right, then swung the pass to the wide-open tailback on the left side of the field. Lee picked up 19 yards and the first down. On the next play, Johnson scrambled away from the rush and picked up nine yards. Then Lee got the first down on a toss sweep.

Weldon came back into the game. But, again, he was sacked for six yards. He got all six back on a second-down scramble and converted the third down with a 14-yard pass to Kevin Knox. That put the Seminoles at the Miami 32-yard line. And with two consecutive Kez McCorvey grabs, it was suddenly first and goal at the 8.

Lee slipped on the first-down carry and lost two yards. Then a holding penalty on second down pushed the ball back to the 22. Bennett got back eight of the lost yards. And Bowden called a third-down play to get Bennett over the middle or Baker in the end zone.

Weldon threw the ball high for Baker, who came back toward it with a defender in tow. At first Baker was sure the ball was behind him and high, but he jumped anyway and was surprised to get his hands on it. But it passed through. Was the defensive back close enough to draw the interference call? Baker looked around, but there was no flag. And he jogged off the field to where Eason stood.

Thomas again was called in to kick the field goal. And he made the score Florida State 13, Miami 7.

The Hurricanes moved from their own 28 to the FSU 34 on the next series, but were forced to punt. And Weldon and company took over at their own 7.

McCorvey got the Seminoles out of the hole on first down with an 11-yard catch on an out pattern. Then Bowden turned to the running game. First Bennett and then Lee picked up long gains on bread-and-butter

Seminole rushing plays. Then, from the Miami 38, Lee, Weldon and Sean Jackson pushed it to the 22, where Bennett caught another clutch pass for first and goal on the 10.

The Seminoles were able to move it four yards closer, but no more. Thomas' third field goal of the day made the score 16–7.

Torretta began Miami's first series of the fourth quarter on the Hurricanes' 29-yard line. And he turned again to his fullback for help. McGuire caught a first-down pass for seven yards, then picked up five more on a run. After a four-yard completion to Kevin Williams, McGuire got the call again on second and six and ran 27 yards down to the FSU 28.

Thomas caught a pass for eight. And McGuire picked up the first down with an eight-yard carry. Now the ball was on the Seminole 13. But the Hurricanes were having their problems close to the goal line as well. A penalty, an incomplete pass and two sacks by Carruthers and Simpson left Miami with a fourth-down situation on the 27, 24 yards short of a first down. Huerta came in to try the 44-yard field goal, and he hit it.

Florida State 16, Miami 10.

After Huerta's kickoff went into the end zone, the Seminoles began on their own 20 and picked up a first down on back-to-back Lee carries. Bennett picked up two more. Then, on second down, Bowden called for the modified version of the Irish Screen that used the wideout as a decoy and left the fullback open. Bennett had only one man to beat for a huge gain or even the touchdown, but the ball never got there. Defensive tackle Mark Caesar deflected it, and it bounced toward Bennett as an incomplete pass.

The third-down call put Baker 15 yards down the field on a curl pattern, and Weldon hit him. But the flanker dropped it, and the drive was over. So was Baker's day, Eason decided.

Player kicked his shortest punt of the day, 28 yards, to Kevin Williams, but Williams returned it only two yards. The Hurricanes took over on their own 42.

Carruthers sacked Torretta on first down for a loss of four yards. But the Miami quarterback hit his tight end for 21 on the second play. And McGuire picked up 25 yards on two runs. It was first down on the Seminole 16. After an incomplete pass, a McGuire carry up the middle made it third and six on the 12.

Williams and Horace Copeland, two of Miami's three receivers on the field, lined up on the right side. On the Seminoles' side of the line, strong safety Mack Knight and Buckley were covering. On the snap, Copeland, the outside receiver, ran straight for the end zone. Torretta looked, but there was Buckley, waiting.

Williams had run downfield about five steps, then cut abruptly to the outside, parallel to the line of scrimmage. Knight was on his tail. Torretta tried to lead his receiver, but the ball was slightly overthrown, and Williams stumbled and fell reaching for it.

Fourth and six.

A field goal would have left the Hurricanes three points behind with some four minutes left to play. And the way the Florida State defense was playing, this might be their last possession of the game and their only chance to win. So the Hurricanes had to go for the first down or the score.

When Miami broke its huddle, Copeland and Williams again split to the right, and Knight and Buckley got into position to cover them. Mickey Andrews, on the Florida State sideline, had thought about putting his two corners in bump-and-run coverage closer to the line of scrimmage. But why risk one of these receivers getting behind them and scoring?

Buckley was backed up about seven yards from the line of scrimmage. His sight line to the Miami quarterback was blocked by Knight, so at the snap Buck backpedaled a step or two to keep Torretta in view.

This time, Williams ran to the post, drawing Knight to the center of the field. Copeland ran at Buck, who was already on the goal line. Then, just as he got inside the 5, Copeland stopped and wheeled. Torretta later said that he was afraid Buckley would jump all over the pass. But he threw it perfectly, high so that the 6-3 Copeland could leap out of range of the 5-10 cornerback. Even that might not have been necessary, since Buck had too much ground to cover to beat the ball to the receiver.

He hit Copeland while he was still in the air, wrapping his arms around the tall wideout's legs and heaving him backward toward the line of scrimmage and away from the first-down marker. But the official spot was at the 3, three yards more than Miami needed.

The fullbacks, McGuire and Jones, pushed it into the end zone in three downs. And Huerta came on the field to kick the go-ahead point.

Carlos Huerta was one of the premier kickers in college football, a fifth-year senior at Miami who would soon find a home in the pros. But nothing was going to be automatic in this game, not even extra points. The Seminoles had already blocked one Huerta kick at the end of the first half, and game film would show that Miami had only ten men on the field when he kicked the 44-yarder. Now, for this extra point, Rusty Medearis, the defensive end, was making the long snap instead of the injured Tom Patterson. And Medearis, who had been a backup long-snapper for punts, had never centered the ball for a placekick.

The ball came back a little slower than usual, and the Seminoles' Howard Dinkins may have gotten a piece of it as Huerta kicked. But the ball made the inside of the right goalpost with six inches to spare.

Miami 17, Florida State 16.

On the bench, the defensive players who had not been on the field sat with their heads down. And on their end, Weldon and his offensive teammates remained frozen in thought as Huerta put the Miami kickoff into the Seminole end zone. The stadium was the quietest it had been all day. Three minutes and one second remained in the game when the offense ran out to the 20-yard line.

Weldon's nine-yard pass completion to McCorvey immediately got things stirring again. Fans rose from their seats. And on the sidelines, every player was off the bench watching the offense. Lee picked up the first down. Then Weldon found Eric Turral on the sideline for another 11 yards. E.T. got the call after Baker's last drop. If there was ever a time to become a player, thought Eason, this was it. And Turral's first catch of the day gave the Seminoles a first down on their own 44.

Weldon was sacked on first down, and the Seminoles called a time-out to stop the clock. Bennett picked up six yards on the next play, making it third and seven on the 47. Weldon went to Bennett again, this time with a pass. And when the fullback made the catch, he fought for the sideline and the first-down marker, as a Hurricane defender tried to drag him back onto the field. The officials ran over to mark the spot near the Florida State coaches and players.

The bench area was a circus now, with the coaches trying to keep track of what was happening on the field and monitor substitutions. The 90 players not in the game were crowding as close to the action as they could. And the coaches and officials had to repeatedly caution them to move back.

Was it a first down? Did Bennett get out of bounds? The crowd obscured Bowden's view of the officials, and it took some twenty seconds for him and the other coaches to realize the clock was still running and it was fourth down. They had to use Florida State's last time-out, so there was no question the Seminoles had to go for it with a minute and fifteen seconds left in the game.

With no time-outs, they had to stop the clock with first downs, incomplete passes or plays that took the ball out of bounds. It would be a one-minute drill, 11 on 11, for all the marbles.

Bennett got the fourth-down call, the 34 Wham up the middle, and he picked up the first down and six more yards. Weldon went to him again for a seven-yard pass that Bennett took out of bounds on the Miami 33.

Second and three with a minute and four seconds left.

Everyone in the stadium was standing, but the noise they generated had an anxious edge to it. They had been deliriously hopeful, then totally depressed, then encouraged yet again. This was too much.

But the two people who had the most to do with directing the Seminole attack felt a surge of confidence. This was meant to be, thought Bowden. Just look at the way it's working out.

On the field, Weldon felt in control of a series that could become THE DRIVE. Everything was clicking—the blocks, the pass patterns. He could see it all unfolding so clearly. It was just throw and catch now. Something they did every day in practice. They could not be stopped.

On second down, Bowden called for a play that had the same look as the previous one that sent Bennett to the sideline. Only this time, the tight end would be the primary receiver over the middle. Lonnie Johnson, however, was shadowed closely by a defender, and Weldon had to keep the ball out in front of him. Too far. Incomplete.

Third and six on the 33. One minute left.

The coaches figured the cutoff point for a Gerry Thomas field goal was the 20-yard line. That would make it a 37-yard kick from the spot where Brad Johnson held the ball to the goalposts 10 yards deep in the end zone. Closer was better. But the Seminoles were at least 13 yards away.

Bowden called for 68, a bomb that could go to the Z deep. Turral was the Z. When he pulled away from center, Weldon saw that E.T. had gotten man-to-man coverage from the cornerback, Ryan McNeil, and slipped him. There he was, wide open 20 yards down the field. The only trouble was that E.T. had run his own version of the pattern, going inside when the route called for an outside move. Now, Weldon was unsure whether the receiver planned to drift inside toward the goalposts or outside to the corner. So he hesitated a fraction of a second before lofting the ball toward the end zone, splitting the difference between the corner and the post.

As it turned out, Turral was headed outside. If the pass had been thrown to the corner, he could have kept his body between McNeil and the ball. But Weldon's throw was slightly inside. And when E.T. leaped to grab it, he had the Miami cornerback in his lap.

Still, this was the kind of catch that had made E.T. a Tallahassee schoolboy hero. And it was one reason why Eason had left his problem child in at Z for the crucial drive of the afternoon. When it was all on the line, the superstars had a way of rising to the occasion.

On the sideline, the players leaning to see the figures in the end zone blocked Bowden's view. But when he heard the crowd roar and saw his players jump up, he assumed E.T. had come down with the ball. We've won the dang thing, he thought. And he rushed down the sidelines to keep his players from running out onto the field and drawing a penalty on the kickoff.

Then someone told him. "No, no, Coach. It was pass interference." And suddenly he had to be thinking of plays again.

The penalty gave the Seminoles a first down at the Miami 18. Good. They were inside Thomas' range now, with 53 seconds left on the clock and no time-outs. Bowden weighed his options: Pass? The game could be won with a kick from right here. Why risk an interception? Even an incomplete pass left them in exactly the same position with one less down and four or five seconds less time to work with.

Run? Yes, but it had to be a safe one. No fumbles. And if it wasn't a first down, the players had to hustle to get back to the line of scrimmage for the next play.

Where the ball now sat, slightly inside the left hash, a kick would have been at a less than ideal angle. The run should be toward the center of the field to set up a field goal that would be nearly straightaway.

This game is won, thought Bowden. Don't do anything to lose it.

The call was for Amp Lee, who took the handoff and headed toward the right side of the line. But there was no room, and, instinctively, he cut back left looking for a hole. He gained one yard before being hauled down. But he also moved the spot even farther to the left. All the way to the left hash.

Weldon lost his shoe on the play and was kneeling to replace it while the clock was running. Oh Lord, thought the coach, what else can go flying off out there? And he decided to play it safe: Kill the clock, send out the kicker and win this game right now.

The head coach told Brad Scott to signal in the clock play, in which Weldon would take the snap and spike the ball to the ground. The quarterback got the signal and tried to pantomime an argument. There were 40 seconds left. Forty whole seconds.

Weldon wanted 46, the toss sweep to Lee. He would remind the tailback to keep it in the center of the field and pick up a few more for Gerry. Who knows, maybe ol' Amp could run it in, and they would be kicking an extra point instead of a field goal. How about 46? Weldon signaled.

The clock play, do it, Scott signed back.

Giving only the most fleeting of thoughts to defying the coach and calling the run himself, Weldon stepped into the huddle and repeated what he'd been ordered. When he spiked the ball, there were 29 seconds left on the clock.

Gerry Thomas, the leading scorer on either team that afternoon, ran onto the field with his holder, Brad Johnson. Johnson set up the hold on the 24-yard-line hash mark. And Thomas walked off his steps. The snap was good. The hold was the best of the afternoon. And boom, the kick was solid. Plenty of distance.

Johnson leaped to his feet and thrust his hands in the air. The crowd sighed, making a noise that was easy to mistake for a cheer. But only Gerry Thomas, the officials beneath the goalposts and the fans in the south end zone had a good view of where the ball flew.

Bowden again heard only the crowd. And again he worried about restraining his celebrating Seminoles while there was still time on the clock. He was sure the kick was good. But someone grabbed his arm. It was wide right. The only cheering left was that coming from the wild group in the south stands.

15

For ten minutes after the clock ran out, the FSU fans stayed in their seats, as if waiting for the credits to roll on some sad, gut-wrenching movie. In the near silence, eerie for a stadium filled with almost 64,000 people, the only sounds that had anything to do with what happened over the last three hours was the excited chanting of the Miamians in the south end zone: "We're No. 1, we're No. 1."

Hurricane players remained on the field, dancing in victory and saluting their fans. Some carved up slices of the Doak Campbell turf to take back to their practice field. Maybe they would start their own Sod Cemetery, they told reporters.

The Seminole players saw nothing of what went on in the stadium after Torretta killed the last twenty-five seconds. They couldn't get into the locker room quickly enough. Once inside, some banged their helmets into lockers. Some kicked stools and ripped the gear from their bodies in frustration. "Do we have to score for them too!" Todd McIntosh exclaimed through his tears. Other defensive players around him nodded, but said nothing.

Most were too numb to do or say anything. They had stumbled into the locker room like zombies. Only their eyes, glistening with held-back tears, betrayed emotion. So many months, so many games, so close. "No excuses," they had promised. Where did that leave them now?

Bowden had been pacing alone before the wide entrance to the showers. Part of him was already on automatic pilot, readying an official self to face the media, the recruits, the boosters, the friends waiting for him upstairs.

"Okay, men, let's come up front now. Come over where you can see."

He began almost as if he were talking to himself. "In 1987, we did the same thing, led 'em the whole game, then went out there and lost to 'em just like this."

He paused. And pulled himself back from somewhere his thoughts were dragging him.

"We'll find out what we're made of right now. We either come back and win the last two ball games, win more ball games than any team in Florida State history . . ." Or what? He knew all the things he had to say, wanted to say, about getting over this terrible feeling as soon as possible and moving on. But there was still too much going on in his head. His thoughts were going in a hundred different directions.

"You never know, men. Some crazy things could happen. Miami could stumble. Washington could stumble." But they won't, said something inside.

"We'll probably drop down about five or six. Maybe lower. But the main thing is, don't give up. Now, Florida is probably about as good as these guys." And when he said that, the just-completed game rushed back into the coach's consciousness.

"There was only one difference today. You probably fought as hard as they fought. They made one more big play than we did. One more big play. That was the only difference in that one point out there.

"But I liked the way y'all fought, the way you came back. I liked the way we nearly won it."

Bowden wanted them to appreciate what they had earned, despite the loss. They were going to the Cotton Bowl, one of the prestigious January 1 bowls. They still had a chance to win 12 games. Still had a chance to finish among the top three or four teams in the nation, just as they had in the four previous years. It had come to that, hadn't it? Fifteen minutes before, they were fighting to do what no team in college football had ever done, go wire to wire as No. 1. From now on, their challenge would be to avoid slipping below the mark they themselves had established over the last four seasons.

"Men, you can't let this loss cost you the next game. You can't go out and lose two games because of this one.

"It will be tough. It will hurt me. I won't even sleep tonight. And I know you won't. Coaches won't. We ain't been beat in 16 ball games.

"We gotta come back with our heads up. Come back next week. Tuesday, Wednesday, Thursday and Friday. We really need to get together on that next ball game.

"This is not the end of the world. Again, you can't tell. It still might happen. Now, somebody has got to help us."

It was time for the prayer. Let them get out of these uniforms and into the showers. Let 'em begin to feel this awful pain, then begin to survive it. But Bowden couldn't help speaking his thoughts. So much was shooting through his mind.

"I feel sorry for y'all, men. I get another chance next year." He was thinking of the seniors. All this effort for the ring. To come so close, and now they would never have another chance at the national championship.

Then he rested his hand on a player's shoulder and closed his eyes. "Dear Father, help us to be able to handle this loss. It's gonna hurt. It's gonna hurt. We can't help that. This is not life and death. We are all better off than little Houston. I'd rather be us than Houston. I'd rather be us than Magic. We've got our health.

"Help our families. Take them home safely. Help them to be able to handle this loss."

16

WHILE Bowden headed upstairs to the main projection room to talk to the largest contingent of reporters, the locker-room doors opened to the rest of the media.

Casey Weldon braced himself for the onslaught by pulling his stool into his locker cage so that the metal on either side of him made him accessible only to those who could fit themselves directly in front of him.

It was all over now. The national championship, the Heisman, everything. In one game.

He answered reporters' questions as best he could. No, he wasn't worried when Miami took the lead. Yes, he was sure they could drive the length of the field to win. "I thought we were going to have the perfect storybook ending."

Would he have liked to have another play there at the end instead of killing the clock on second down? Maybe, but that was the coaches' decision. And it was a reasonable one. They were out of time-outs, and everybody was confident Gerry could kick it from that distance. So there was no point in doing anything to jeopardize their opportunity to win.

When the reporters ran out of questions, they stayed in front of the quarterback's locker, waiting. Maybe there was something he could tell them they hadn't asked. But Weldon just looked past them, then down at his shoes. "Unbelievable," he said, over and over. "Just unbelievable."

Gerry Thomas did his best to confront the questions. But he found it impossible to speak. Rob Wilson, a sports information assistant, took him into the coaches' locker room for a few minutes to let him collect himself. Then the kicker came back to his locker to face the reporters.

"I didn't do my job," he told them. That was it, the bottom line, as far as Gerry Thomas was concerned. There was no question it was within his range. All week, he and Mowrey had boomed them through. "One second to win the game," they had told one another. One kick. One chance. "I just didn't do my job," Thomas repeated.

"I hit it good. It just kept fading."

In the headlines and newspaper leads the next day, "wide right" would be a kind of catchphrase. But no one in the locker room believed Thomas deserved the blame for the loss. It was a shared agony. They all had their own memories of opportunities squandered, of moments where the game could have been snatched from Miami's grasp.

Eric Turral sat for a long time beside his locker. It was on his fingertips. The game. Maybe the championship. It would have been a tough catch, a heroic catch. But it was there.

Shannon Baker, Weldon and lots of others on offense would have loved to have a couple of plays back. And the defensive players, despite holding Miami to less than half its weekly average, would be replaying key downs in their minds too. "We all had our chance to mess up," said Buckley.

But spreading the responsibility for the loss didn't diminish the feeling of devastation for the players. It only underlined it. Maybe the South Florida cynics were right. Maybe the Seminoles had some fatal flaw that crippled them every time they ran onto the field against Miami.

"We knew we were the better team," a depressed Kirk Carruthers told reporters. "And they knew they were going to win."

Up in the head coach's office, Bowden had his own postgame interrogations to endure. But unlike the young men in the showers a floor below, he had decades of practice at dividing his public and private grief.

He returned to his office after the postgame radio show to shake the hands of a few old Alabama friends waiting for him there. They would be at his house later, along with his huge extended family. Those who knew him well wouldn't bother with condolences. Bowden hated anything that smacked of pity—"pity pats," he called the pats on the back he got at times like these. And his close friends and family wouldn't expect much in the way of attention. Bobby, they knew, was going to go away for a while.

He might be sitting there, calmly nodding and smiling, but he was gone way inside somewhere—where he would stay until he finished torturing himself with the mental replays and was finally prepared to let the routines of everyday life and of preparation for the next football game pull him free again.

"It's like there's this big screen right there in front of me. Voices are trying to comfort me. But they can't say nothing to make me feel better."

The friends departed, leaving the coach in his office with a handful of reporters working on Bowden sidebars to their game stories. It was a familiar, if ghoulish, ritual. They wanted the heart-tugging profile of a coach in defeat, of a man who may have just lost the national championship by little more than the length of a football. And the coach would accommodate them by sending random quotes up from that place deep in himself to which he had already begun retreating.

"That's the most amazing series with Miami," he said, shaking his head. Then he sighed. "We were flirting with disaster all year."

How did he feel?

"There's a big sense of letting people down, a guilt feeling. I think all coaches feel that way."

But he seemed to be handling it remarkably well.

Against these guys—he smiled wryly—"I've had lots of practice. I'll handle it good until I go to bed tonight. It's kinda like you wake up at night with this scary feeling that you're going to die or something."

Silence. "It's a big letdown for these kids."

17

AT 10 A.M. on Sunday, after his usual early-morning session with the newspaper writers, Bowden honored a commitment he had made to Clint Purvis, the team chaplain. He was the guest speaker for Jeans Sunday, a special college service at Tallahassee's First Baptist Church. It had been scheduled for weeks, with the coach's name on the program as a principal attraction for students from schools in the region.

"Those of you who are Miami fans," joked Purvis, "we have a special place for you in our baptistery"—the chest-deep pool of water used for baptism services.

The gentle humor would have been in perfect keeping with the usual Bowden style, a charming mixture of old-time religion and self-deprecating humanism. But this was the day after the Game of the Century. And the coach had suffered through a terrible night, waking a half dozen times to the tape loop in his mind. All of the things that he could have called, could have done, could have said, played over and over until he drifted off to sleep again, then awoke to repeat it all. What time was it? Had he overslept? Didn't he have to be someplace? Oh Lord, it was three-thirty in the morning, hours before he could lose himself in the postgame routines.

Facing the reporters early in the morning was almost a relief. There was no question they could ask that he hadn't already tortured himself with a hundred times in the past twelve hours. So Bowden cruised through the press conference, issuing his tributes to Miami and joking about his reluctance to admit defeat:

"That one lousy point, and I gotta say they're better than us . . . I love our relationship with Miami. I'd love to play 'em in a game next week to atone for this one . . . It was our time to win. I don't know how we lost."

Maybe there was something to the curse business, one reporter suggested. And Bowden played along. "They're going to chisel on my tombstone: 'But he played Miami.' "

As usual, the visiting reporters were amazed at the performance. The day after his team had lost perhaps the biggest football game in school history, St. Bobby was still feeding them the quips. But talking to reporters was easy. To live the next few days, the next two weeks even, with this game so vividly replaying itself—that would be the hard part.

When Bowden strode to the First Baptist pulpit an hour later, the dark cloud had resettled in his mind. And the world seemed uncharming and unfunny. Here was a man who believed with all his heart in the New Testament message of redemption but today was consumed by the Old Testament warnings of condemnation and retribution.

"If I was to recommend something to you young students," he told the students crowded into the sanctuary, "it would be that you read the Bible, and that you pray to ask God to help you understand. And he will. Then commit your life to him.

"As you read this book, there's a theme, boys and girls, that rings from the first chapter all the way through. If you want to be happy and successful in life, you've got to be sure you follow this basic rule . . . People who obey God are blessed. People who disobey God are cursed."

Bowden talked about the responsibilities of obedience, of avoiding sin. He worried over the message that Magic Johnson might be sending. Johnson had said he was going to use his prominence to reach young people and encourage them to practice safe sex.

"Safe sex? Doesn't he realize that's a sin with anybody but a husband and wife?"

God's rules hadn't changed, Bowden argued. Not for athletes or ministers, pastors or students. Or for coaches. "The worst thing you can do is live this life away from God. I might not ever win a national championship. I might not win every game I play. But I ain't gonna live away from God. I'm not gonna go to that grave with a life unused."

Some of the students coughed and shifted restlessly during Bowden's talk. It may not have been exactly what they expected. But it was definitely the man they came to hear. And they gave him a standing ovation.

Part VIII

"GATOR BAIT"

1

I<small>N</small> the week before the Miami game, all of Tallahassee had been building up to a party that became a wake. Something had died on Saturday. And the classic stages of grief, including anger and denial, had to play themselves out.

The letters, the faxes, the phone messages poured into Bowden's office. Many—maybe most—were sympathetic, ranging from the dreaded "pity pats" to simple notes of support. Others took the form of indictments, some scrawled in illegible fury and some neatly typed. They demanded an accounting for the errors of a 20-year-old player or for the decisions of a coach in the heat of battle or for a hundred little things that had no explanation. They felt betrayed.

One alum from California sent his Florida State cap back to Bowden: "I've finally given up on you and Florida State ever winning a national championship. If it ever happens it will be because FSU didn't schedule Miami, because it appears that we'll never beat them when it counts."

At the Tallahassee *Democrat* sports department, reporters and editors were chasing a dozen phoned-in rumors: Bowden was about to call a press conference to resign; there were attempted suicides in the football dorm; a well-known player was in jail for drunken driving; players had packed up and left school. All false. But the phone kept ringing.

The players were not suicidal, just dazed. If the days after the Miami game were going to be something like a prolonged funeral, they were the bereaved and entitled to a little grief. And they intended to indulge themselves. The Sunday crowd in the training room for the coach's TV show had watched the replays and had listened to Gene Deckerhoff try to end the show with an upbeat note, looking forward to the traditional rivalry with Florida. This was a tough loss, said Deckerhoff, but there were two weeks now between the Miami game and "that big showdown in Gainesville" on November 30.

Some of the players snorted. "That big showdown don't mean nothin' now," said Reggie Freeman.

There were no coaches in the room to hear that. But they didn't have to. There was a voice of furious cynicism inside them too. Only the wildest of flukes would put them back in the running for the championship.

What separated the players from the coaches was a generation or two of experience with loss. The players couldn't conceive of feeling worse. The coaches knew they could. All they had to do was blow the remaining two games and live out the off-season with that taste in their mouths.

"It's time to redefine our goals, men," Bowden told his assistants in the Monday-morning meeting. "It ain't far from the penthouse to the outhouse. If we lose to Florida, we're in the outhouse."

With two weeks to prepare for Florida, the players had Monday off. Tuesday, Bowden called a team meeting "to get kind of regrouped," he told the players. "Our target was to win all our ball games and win the national championship. Well, we lost a ball game. That does not mean those other goals are not within reach. But I thought we'd better come in here and redefine what we're going to do.

"My feeling was that we gave it everything we had. I thought we left everything we had out on the field. We could have executed better and won the game, as you and I know. We didn't do that. But as far as effort is concerned, we did that.

"We've got a better ball club. There's no doubt in my mind about that. There's no doubt in my mind we've got the better players. For just some reason, it was not meant to be.

"What we can't do now is lose two because of that one. That's the easy thing to do now. You let that loss hurt so much and you care so much about it, you lose just a little bit of confidence. And first thing you know, you've lost another one.

"The good thing, now, is that the Florida game gives us a chance to atone for that. What if we didn't have any more big games? What if we didn't have any more television games? That's the game everyone will remember, No. 1 vs. No. 2, and Florida State got beat. But we got Florida coming up this week, who might be as good as anybody else in the country. Florida at Florida is gonna be about as tough as it gets. But that game gives us the chance to get back, doesn't it? Beating Florida, at No. 5, gives us the chance to go right back up that ladder."

Bowden didn't want to let go of the thread of hope for the national championship. If somehow Miami lost and Michigan beat Washington in the Rose Bowl, then the Seminoles would be right back in the thick of it, he argued. Stranger things had happened. But he probably had a better case when he simply pitched pride.

"This team could declare itself the best team Florida State ever had.

We've never had a team win 12 ball games. We've never had a team beat Florida five times in a row. We win the Florida game, and you'll forget about that other. I will too."

2

SURVIVE the loss to Miami? Of course they could. Forget it? Not likely, thought Bowden, who was fighting his own demons as he tried to push and pull his coaches and his team back on track.

What would he have changed about the way he called the game? The boosters, so self-consciously deferential with the coach in public, had asked him that at the Monday luncheon. And he knew that behind the question was the renewed suspicion that he had turned conservative on them, that he was now playing not to lose instead of playing all out to win.

"I would change very little," Bowden told them. "If you were drawing that game up, and you said it was gonna come down to a kick on the 17-yard line for the score, you'd take it. You would take your odds most games kicking a field goal from the 17-yard line."

It was going to be this way for a while, Bowden's years of experience taught him. When you win, bad decisions are made irrelevant; when you lose, every choice is called into question. A catch here, a big defensive play there, a kick ten inches more to the left, and they all would have been heroes. But knowing that still wouldn't stop the second-guess process, not from the fans and not from within himself.

As usual, Bowden's first response was the defensive one: "There's a difference between common sense and being conservative." All the while, his own self-analysis was spitting out the question that had been nagging him since Louisville: "Am I getting too conservative in close games?"

In his mind, he replayed the final period again and again. There were maybe two calls, he figured, that would invite the "conservative" tag. One was the third-down play on the Seminoles' last scoring drive, just as the third quarter changed into the fourth. Florida State was leading 13–7 and had moved from a first-and-goal on the Miami 10-yard line to a third-and-goal from the 4. At Michigan, Bowden had ordered up pass plays in those situations, going for the touchdown even on fourth down.

But that was when Dan Mowrey was blowing all those extra points, and Bowden just assumed he had no kicking game. His only route to the scoreboard was through the end zone.

Against Miami, though, Gerry Thomas appeared to have the short kicking game locked in. He was, after all, the leading scorer on both teams. And Bowden was determined to do nothing to take those three points off the board. "We could have passed in that situation, and Casey might have gotten something in there, as good as he is. But we might have gotten intercepted or sacked and gotten the ball pushed back even further." So Bowden's third-and-goal call was an Edgar Bennett run, which got only one yard, yet preserved Thomas' opportunity to kick his third field goal of the day. That made it 16–7, which would require Miami to score twice to win the game. Not very likely, the way the Seminole defense was playing, thought Bowden. When the Hurricanes got 10 points in the fourth quarter to win, "I guess to an outsider, that third-and-four call looked conservative."

Even more controversial, he knew, was the decision to try for the 34-yard field goal on third down in that final drive. "Why not try another down? All I could think about was all the bad things that could happen. Whatever I had to do had to go for the first down or the touchdown. Otherwise, what would you have accomplished? If you kick on third down, they're expecting something else, so they can't rush as hard.

"The only pass I would have been willing to call would have been a corner route, something at the sideline. But we had been down there before. And what was to make us believe we were going to do anything different other than risk an interception?

"What if you took a sack? Now you're out of field-goal range. What if you complete the pass or run the ball but it's not a first down? You've got no time-outs. So now you're dependent on the officials spotting the ball and your team lining up fast enough to kill the clock so that you can get the kicking team on before time runs out.

"I'm thinking this kid is nearly automatic from this range. He's that good. I hated to throw him to the wolves. But what's the smart thing to do in this situation? I know what Bear Bryant would have done. I know what Bobby Dodd would have done. I know what General Neyland would have done."

And Bobby Bowden and his team had reached the territory once ruled by those legendary coaches. They had the talent, the preparation, the motivation. All that remained was to seize the opportunity, grab the ring when it appeared before them. Bowden believed all that as fervently as he believed anything. But in the backwash of a loss, he was as haunted as any fan by the what-if issues: What if his fear of losing had edged him too far away from the bold alternatives? What if he was losing his nerve? How could he know? And who would tell him?

He tried to open up the subject for discussion in the morning meetings. "Am I gettin' too conservative in these big games? I think I did it the way I should have, but I wish y'all would talk about this among yourselves and maybe send one person in to talk to me. I wouldn't want y'all to say something just to make me feel better."

But he knew he was asking a lot from his coaches. The loss hurt them too, and they were all reluctant to wade too deeply into self-analysis. The younger players were doing enough finger pointing and sulking without the grown-ups jumping into it. The sooner they could move on, the better.

3

"This bull has gotta end about whose fault it was. It wasn't the coach's fault, it wasn't the offense's fault, it wasn't the defense's fault. It was all our faults."

Kirk Carruthers was addressing his teammates in a players-only meeting at the November 20 practice. Before segment meetings that afternoon, Bowden had called the seniors into his office to encourage them to lead the others out of their listlessness. "It's normal that y'all feel down," the coach had said. "But I expect you to gradually put this thing behind you.

"Wouldn't it be awful if we took it easy and got beat 'cause we weren't prepared? Don't you let that happen. Your leadership means everything."

Carruthers, one of the captains Bowden chose early in the year, was taking the message to the players on the practice field. He knelt in the center as they crowded into a giant huddle to hear him.

"We all gotta start gettin' back on track for Florida," he told them. "I hate to hear all that stuff too, about if so-and-so wins, and then they win, where we'll be. But we're not out of it yet. Miami is destined to lose. And we would really kick ourselves in our butts if we went down to Florida and lost and Miami and Washington lost and we could've had the ring."

The blame game is "like a disease," said the linebacker. "One guy starts it, then another picks it up, and the disease keeps on growing. Those of you who want to keep talking that way should go over to that field and play two-hand touch while the rest of us try to get something done out here."

It was the proper sentiment. It was just that no matter how reasonable the idea sounded, no one—not the coaches, not the players, no one— seemed ready to resume football at the level they left it. There were days during that week of practice after the Miami game that one group or another rose to the occasion. There were moments of crisp hits, perfect passes and catches, aggressive blocks. But they were only moments. For the offense especially, the practices seemed sleepwalks.

The assistant coaches, determined to fake what they did not yet feel, tried to put enthusiasm into their voices. For even routine drills, they yelled encouragement: "That's the way, that's the way!" But the players ambled through the periods, distracted and morose.

"This is normal. It takes time," Bowden told himself. But the fear rose in him. He had never had a team so devastated by a loss. Had he himself ever felt this way? Everyone was asking him that. One thing he knew for sure: The highs don't exactly balance out the lows. No matter how great you felt after winning big, that feeling was overwhelmed by the grief of a big loss. But was this the worst? they wanted to know. As if he could measure the pain with some kind of emotional dipstick.

Maybe it was. That one in '87 had hurt. And now, to lose again by one lousy point. How on earth . . . ? But every time he felt himself slipping into that pit, the coach fought his way back. He could look in the eyes of his players and assistant coaches and see the threat looming: Either pull out of this soon or risk losing everything.

"We can't waste these practice days," Bowden pleaded.

"We're trying," said Brad Scott. "But there are all these outside forces. We can't stop them from talking to reporters. And all they want to talk about is Miami."

By the end of the week, Bowden's patience had run low. "There ain't no sense fooling ourselves. They ain't into it. We ain't into it as coaches. I'm not saying we've lost our team, but when we come back in here on Sunday, we've got to jack these kids up.

"I'm not gonna go down there to Gainesville and get embarrassed by Florida because some people don't want to pay the price."

like coming down the road on a donkey and people were waving those palm fronds.

"At that time, Florida State had only won twice and had lost 10 in a row. And I didn't realize the importance of it for all those fans and alumni. We beat them the next three years too. And when we were winning, there was nothing to it. Then I lost six in a row, and I found out in a hurry how important a game that was."

The streaky nature of the series continued after the Gators' six-game run from '81 to '86. The Seminoles won in '87 and went on to take the next three, including the 45–30 pounding in Tallahassee in 1990. It was one of only two games Spurrier lost in his debut year as Florida's head coach, and it dampened—at least for a few months—the "Time of the Gator" talk coming out of Gainesville.

It was natural that Florida's new era of high expectations coincided with Spurrier's arrival as head coach. He was the Gators' golden boy, a come-from-behind legend as the Florida quarterback in the mid-'60s and the school's only Heisman Trophy winner. Everyone remembered the wins he engineered—like the one in 1966 over Auburn, when he passed for 349 yards and three touchdowns, punted seven times for a 46.9-yard average and booted the tie-breaking 40-yard field goal in the closing two minutes of the game. He was a first-round draft choice and played nine years with the San Francisco 49ers before moving to the Tampa Bay Buccaneers for the final year of his NFL career.

As a head coach—first with the Tampa Bay Bandits of the old USFL, then at Duke—Spurrier became famous for wild, crowd-pleasing offenses that amassed record-breaking passing stats and made superstars of unknown quarterbacks. Two of the three years he was at Duke before coming to Florida, he was named ACC coach of the year. He immediately won the same honor in his debut in the SEC at his alma mater and was a lock to repeat in '91.

But no Gator player in '91 had ever played in a game in which Florida bested its ancient rival. And as they put together the best season in the school's football history, the Florida coaches, players and fans had to read and hear, almost daily, how they—partisans of *the* University of Florida, champions of the toughest conference in America—were the state's also-rans in big-time college football. On the day they captured their first SEC championship with that 35–26 win over Kentucky, the Gators' claim on history was overwhelmed by Game of the Century hype in Tallahassee. They had won it all. Florida State had lost it all. And they still got less attention than St. Bobby and company. But now all eyes would be on Gainesville.

Bowden had suspected that would be the case from the beginning. In his preseason handicapping, in fact, the coach rated the Florida game the tougher of the two in-state showdowns. The ambush atmosphere of raucous Florida Field—that alone could cancel any Seminole advantage. Bowden always thought the Miami game would take care of itself. Playing in Tallahassee against the Hurricanes, Florida State would be primed to win it all in front of the home crowd. But if his players survived that, Bowden suspected they would be tempted to underestimate the challenge of a Gator team they had beaten four years running. Then they would go into that snake pit of a stadium and have the battle of their lives.

That would have been the logical scenario if they had won against Miami. Now it was worse. Instead of complacency, the coach had to worry about despair. And once again, he had history to haunt him. In '81, the Seminoles had beaten Ohio State and Notre Dame back to back, lost only to Nebraska and Pitt and were 6–2 and No. 14 in the country when they welcomed Miami to Tallahassee in Game 9. They lost to the Hurricanes 27–19, then were crushed at home against Southern Mississippi 58–14. And they finished the season with a 35–3 loss in Gainesville. "They liked to kill us," Bowden remembered. That launched the six-game losing streak.

Even more auspicious was the 1983 season, when the Miami and Florida games came back to back at the end of the season, just as they would in '91. Florida State was 8–2 and on its way to the Peach Bowl when it lost to Miami at home by the eerily familiar 17–16 score. Then, in the next and final game of the season, the Gators embarrassed the Seminoles 53–14 in Gainesville.

During that six-year string of losses to Florida, Bowden's teams went 46–16–3 in all the other games they played and were undefeated in five bowls. But losing to the Gators was agonizing.

"I'm telling you, if I can't find a way to beat them," Bowden said at one point during the ordeal, "I think enough of Florida State to say maybe they ought to find someone better."

Then he added, "Right now, though, I can't think of anybody."

When the Seminoles began their own win streak in '87, it was Season One of the latest chapter in the Bowden saga, the quest for No. 1. Out of all the teams in the country, only Miami had played better football over those four years. And the Gators were left a rung back on the ladder. Now, however, Spurrier was apparently pushing and pulling them higher. This would be the highest the two teams had ever been ranked, No. 3 and No. 5, before their annual game. Which, for the coaches, would add to the stomach-churning pressure that always accompanied this game.

"It's one of those games that you can't enjoy as a coach as much as you can other games," said Bowden. "The reason you can't is that you must win. You've got to win it, and they've got to win it. And that takes a lot of the fun out of it."

5

On Monday afternoon, John Eason stood quietly and watched his receivers work their way through the usual practice drills. Almost from the minute the players took the field, it became clear this was going to be a different kind of week. The post-Miami depression was still there, but in place of the near paralysis that afflicted them the week before, there was the hint of something new, a kind of free-floating anger.

Maybe that was good, Eason thought. His old coach at Florida A&M, Jake Gaither, had preached "Somebody's got to pay" after hurtful losses. Get mad, take it out on the next opponent. But seething anger wasn't always manageable. Sometimes, it could turn inward, imploding a team and individual players. It made for a dangerous additive in an already emotional game. So Eason had hoped his receivers sensed the new mood and were prepared to adapt to it. But the evidence argued otherwise.

The final practice week before the Florida game had begun with a light Sunday workout, a running session. And as usual, some of the players were late coming back from their weekend off. Among them was Eric Turral, who was a half hour late and tried to argue that the start time had not been clearly announced. When he was assigned to run stadiums along with the others who had been tardy, Turral resisted and appealed to Eason. Now, on Monday, here he was with Baker, high-fiving after routine catches and inspiring a slow burn in Casey Weldon, who definitely had a case of post-Miami mad.

Weldon wouldn't let himself off the hook for bad throws. At least two in the Miami game were sure touchdowns, he figured: the one that fell short to Lonnie Johnson on the Y Hide in the first half, and the long throw a foot or two inside to Turral in the end zone on the last drive. If he had made the big plays, they would have won. But wasn't it also true for some other players who had had the game in their hands?

"They will rise to the occasion, they will do it when it counts," he had said about the receivers all season when reporters invited him to criticize the receivers' play. But when it counted, they hadn't. Up until now, he had been reluctant to get in the wideouts' faces. With all the Heisman hype, they might have figured he was thinking only of his own stats. But all that was over now.

So when Baker and Turral began their celebration routine in the Monday practice, Weldon strode toward them menacingly: "That stuff is expected. You should make those catches every time."

The receivers bristled. Eason said nothing. This was something they had to learn. And it wasn't going to get any easier, because the most obvious by-product of the new mood would be impatience. In the 11-on-11 scrimmages, the defense was going to terrorize the receivers— especially Baker—for every tentative move, for every drop. And a dozen times during the week the receivers were going to be reminded, "Dawsey would have caught that."

Run your stadiums, Eason told Turral. This is no time to test the patience of the coaches and your teammates. The era of good feelings is over.

6

"THE key, gentlemen, is going to be our ability to motivate. We're going to win this game or get slaughtered."

At some point in the previous week, Bowden had changed his pacifier from gum to an unlit cigar. And in the Tuesday-morning meeting, he chewed on the cigar and leaned forward over the conference table.

"I want to meet with the seniors and a few handpicked leaders among the juniors today. And I don't want losers in that room. I don't want guys who don't give a darn."

The time of mourning had to end, Bowden had decided. The Monday practice had clinched it for him. There was a sense of anarchy, of things about to fly out of control. And football could not be played that way.

Once the 30 or so handpicked players gathered in the main meeting room that afternoon, all the coaches left except Bowden. He stood at the front of the room, looking more focused, more intense than he had since he left the sideline after the Miami game. "This is just me and y'all," he told them. "It's time to put up or shut up.

"We started off the year ranked No. 1 in the nation. You seniors talked about how you were going to be there. You talked about how we were going to be better than everybody else, 'cause you were going to lead us. 'We're different from those other seniors they've had here in the past. We came in here early this summer. We are goin' to do it.'

"For 13 weeks, we did it. We got one more week. We got two more games and one more big week."

In the room were the team's dozen seniors and a group of key underclassmen, including Dan Footman and Marvin Jones. They sat quietly and watched the head coach.

"I can tell you how people are going to respond. They're going to say, 'This '91 group was the best football team Florida State ever had.' Or they're going to say, 'What a disappointment! Best material in the United States.'

"We didn't think we could be beat. Have you still got that confidence? Or did that confidence go away with a one-point loss in a game that you should have won?

"Y'all ain't got nothing to be ashamed of in that game that we lost. But we lost it by one measly point, and we know we were better. Just because we didn't win it, are you just going to throw it down?

"What have you done since that Miami game to make sure it don't happen again? People who practice average play average. Men, it's time to quit talking. It is time to quit talking about what's going to happen Saturday. It's time to do it. And you need to do it in practice. It scares me when I get out there and watch you guys in practice this week. Last week I could understand, the anguish of that last loss killed me, it killed you, it killed your families. That was last week, men. Life has to go on. There's a bigger game this week. Do you realize that whoever wins the Florida State–Florida game might go on to win the national championship?

"All we've got to do is have a slip out of Miami, a slip out of Washington. The winner of this ball game is the national champion.

"That is going to be the wildest arena we've ever been in—84,000 people and all for them except for a few of our people in there. It's us against the danged world that day. You've got to inspire our game, seniors. We've got to get out there and work. Lift your buddy up. It's your ball club. That's why I called this meeting.

"That's where we are. You can inspire this football team. You made our statement: No excuses. That was a great motto. But some of you carried it a little too far. Some of you said, 'If we don't win it, we will be a complete failure.'

"I didn't want to put that kind of pressure on you. Colorado won the national championship last year having lost one game and tied one. The team that won the year before lost one. Don't give up. You're still the same people. You're still the same ball club. Best team in Florida State history right here. Or the most disappointing. I'm sorry. That's the way history works. I can't control that. You can control it.

"Florida, they think they've got you. They think you're down. They don't think you're very good. They've won seven games in a row. They're playing at their place. We beat 'em last year, and they're going to pay us back.

"But they ain't been in the arena as many times as we have, men. They haven't played for that title the way we have the last four or five years. We got to do them exactly like Miami did us. Go down there with the utmost confidence. We have to have a great practice today, and a great practice the next day. Don't let any complaining take place from guys not willing to pay the price, who don't come to practice, who want to get out of something.

"We've got the material. It's up to you."

He wanted to name new senior captains just for this game, he told them. They would all vote later on official captains for the year, but he wanted this group in a leadership role for the Florida game: Weldon and Mike Morris from the offense, Henry and Joe Ostaszewski for defense and Reggie Freeman, a junior, on specialty teams. Those five, Bowden figured, could lead by both word and deed. And they needed every motivational advantage they could get this week.

As he walked out to the Tuesday practice, the head coach ruminated about meetings and inspiration. "Well, they were attentive enough in there. But you don't really know if they would have done just as well without the talk. You just never know."

7

THE word was already out among the receivers even before the two-fifteen segment meeting on Wednesday. And before the release went out to the beat reporters later that afternoon: "Junior wide receiver Eric Turral has been suspended indefinitely from the Florida State football team . . . Turral's suspension came after he missed Tuesday's team practice without an excuse. Bowden said Turral's absence came on the heels of other team rules violations."

It had been a terrible week for John Eason. His wife was in the hospital being treated for diabetic complications. He had just gotten a new load of dismal academic reports. The papers were dumping on his receivers. And then there was E.T., who, after resisting discipline for his late arrival Sunday, had skipped Tuesday's practice entirely.

"Cut him loose," said Bowden on Wednesday morning. "Let him spend the rest of the year working on his academics." And Eason had agreed. It had come to that.

"E.T. is gone," the receivers coach told his players.

Eason hadn't slept much the last couple of nights. He would go by the hospital to see his wife, then stay up until the early morning worrying. The reports from the study-hall monitors and class checkers suggested a larger group than usual appeared to be blowing off their studies. All year, up until two weeks ago, Amp Lee had missed just one class. Now he seemed to be missing regularly and was avoiding his required study halls altogether. "What's going on?" Eason asked himself.

As the time neared when Lee would have to make the decision to turn pro or return for his senior year of eligibility, he appeared to be foreclosing his options. Eason had asked him to come by and talk. "Just to talk, but he always has excuses. The excuses sound good to him, but the bottom line is, he's not doing what he's supposed to do. I don't know if an agent is getting to him or what. He's got to make a 2.4 to avoid dismissal. E.T. has to make a 2.56."

It was miraculous that Turral had hung on this long. He deserved credit for that. But all his efforts to stay alive academically could go for naught if he didn't pull it out this term. And despite all the progress in the classroom, E.T. was still unpredictable on the practice field. No one talked about it, but the missed catch in the Miami game loomed even larger in the context of Turral's annoying unpredictability. "That catch could have changed everything," Eason acknowledged. He imagined himself talking to Turral: "If you do what we've been asking you to do all year, then you make the catch. You have a chance to go out and make yourself a bunch of money. But the way you're acting now means you might end up on the street somewhere. It's just a matter of being undisciplined."

But there had already been enough of those talks over the past three years. Maybe, thought Eason, he and the young receiver had been a bad fit all along. "I even question my own philosophy with him. I don't like to yell and holler at them. I like to talk to them one on one. 'I'm gonna tell you, and I want you to respond,' I tell them. 'I'm gonna treat you like a man. I'm gonna let you have your manhood.' But then sometimes I wonder if that philosophy was not good for E.T. Maybe he needed someone to holler at him, to curse him. Yet then I see how it's worked for everybody else." And maybe now it was time to turn his attention to the rest of them.

Particularly to Shannon Baker, who was E.T.'s best buddy on the team. As long as things were going well, some of Baker's dedication and unselfishness seemed to rub off on Turral. But when things went sour, Turral's capacity for self-destruction could dominate the relationship between the two. It could be, thought Eason, that I have to lose E.T. to save Shannon. Because this was definitely a sour period for the wideouts.

They were already chafing from the abuse of their teammates and haunted by their sense of falling short of expectations. To make matters worse, Wednesday morning's *Democrat* carried a feature on Eason's group, using stats the coaches compiled in their film-grading sessions. *Democrat* reporter Steve Ellis had copied the grades from the board in the wideouts' meeting room. So far, according to the chart, the receivers had dropped 21 passes, a higher total than any other group in recent Florida State history had racked up. Baker alone accounted for 10, including two drops in each of the past three games. And Turral had five drops and nine missed assignments.

Ellis quoted Weldon, who let some of his frustration show: "Consistency is the key at receiver, and we're still working on that." And Eason himself told the reporter that the inconsistency was forcing him to try his fifth combination of starters against Florida. Kez McCorvey would be at split end and Matt Frier would move to flanker.

When he read the story, Eason winced at the tone. It was like he was dumping on his own players. He hadn't meant to do that. And he certainly hadn't meant to help Ellis use the internal grading report. But there were the numbers, in print for all to see.

"I'm not going to put the chart up anymore. That's for us to use as a positive teaching tool," said the coach. "I didn't particularly care for the article. It was too negative." He knew there was nothing in the story that wasn't already being talked about among the other players, but that was family stuff. Not meant for outsiders to hear.

"You know," he told the receivers, "I haven't been sleeping well. I keep thinking about y'all."

How could he explain how he was torn? On the one hand, the coach felt paternal and protective. His instinct was to defend his players against every attack, even those that came from their teammates and the other coaches. Certainly from the outside world. But at the same time, they could never grow into what they had to be as players and individuals if they failed to adapt to the pressure of the world in which they had chosen to compete.

The group before the coach was a depressed lot. Most of them couldn't even look up while he talked. But Eason needed them to hear what he had to say.

"I'd like to save every one of you. You know how you come in and want to be impact players? Well, I want to be an impact coach in your lives. I want to help you reach your potential as football players, to help you do the things you're supposed to do academically and to help you understand the difference between right and wrong. I think I tried to do that with E.T."

Eason paused. It was very quiet in the room.

"You tolerate so many things, put up with so many things along the way. Then along comes something that by itself wouldn't be all that significant, but you've just had enough. That was basically how I felt this week. Most of my notes from Coach Bowden were about one person. You overlook those things because you want to try to bring somebody along. This is about the third time he's walked off, and y'all always brought him back. Now it's Sunday and all you guys had to come back at four o'clock and do what you were supposed to do. Those who didn't come back and those who missed meetings had to run ten stadiums whether they liked it or not. And they did it. But you got one player who thinks it's unfair, because he thinks the meeting is a half hour later.

"Then I looked at the practices. All of you were trying, and this one guy was making you look like fools. It is my responsibility as a coach to get you guys to do what you're supposed to do, to get the effort in practice. If y'all do not do what you're supposed to do in practice, that's not your fault. It's my fault. Because I am your coach, and I must get y'all to do that. What Coach Bowden says a lot is: 'You get what you demand.'

"I didn't sleep Monday night. I didn't like what I saw in practice. I didn't like E.T. missing. And I talked to Coach Bowden about it.

"I feel like I should try to save every one of you. You all came here to be football players. I've got to make you men. That's my responsibility, to help you become good husbands and fathers and good citizens. At the same time, I've got to make you the best football player you can be.

"With E.T., I just feel like I failed. E.T. didn't fail. I failed. But you guys are still here. You've got to get your degrees. And you've got to do what you're supposed to do out on the football field. Now, Florida is going to be a very physical game, and we need people who are going to fight."

What Eason and the other coaches feared from the beginning had become a fact. Defensive coordinators were beefing up coverage of the backs in pass patterns and daring Florida State to beat them with the wideouts one on one. And Bowden and the offensive coaches knew they would have to take the dare to win. Against Florida, they would open up the game, give Weldon more opportunities to make something happen and get the ball to the X and Z.

McCorvey was the X. He had earned the spot with steady, dependable play. And of the remaining wideouts, Frier was the one who inspired the most confidence. "I'm not sure the Miami game was Matt's kind of game," Eason had told the head coach. "But Florida is." This would not be about speed and finesse; it would be about grit and tenacity, both of which Frier had in abundance. So he would move over to the flanker spot, bumping Baker down on the depth chart. Kevin Knox would be in reserve.

Bowden had nodded when Eason indicated his preferences. It was time to depend on the dependables. All that was left was to convince this small group of sensitive souls that they qualified.

"You know," said Eason, "the only time you get a chance to see your bodies is when you look in the mirror or watch film. I get to see your bodies in motion firsthand, all the time. You can assume that you've hustled. You can assume you've done certain things. But you don't really know. It's just the way you feel. You can't see yourself the way I see you. Now, if you didn't have the talent to do what I asked, I wouldn't bother with you. But I recruited every one of you. I know who you are as people and who you can be as football players. What you've got to do, what all of you have to do, is learn to trust your coaches. Sometimes you have to trust people. You have to trust me to tell you the right thing."

8

THE Seminoles stayed Friday night in Ocala, about thirty miles south of Gainesville on I-75, to avoid the inevitable lunacy of Friday night in Gator territory. Even then, a few Florida fans would make the drive to harass the team and be discovered trying to spray-paint the Seminole bus in the hotel parking lot. Some Florida State boosters who would never miss a game at Doak Campbell and wouldn't hesitate to drive to Auburn or Baton Rouge ruled out the easy expressway trek to the Evil Empire in Gainesville. Why expose yourself to all that ugliness? they asked.

Bowden and his coaches hoped the ugliness would provide just the wake-up call their players needed. "When you run on that field, and they start booing, it should make your blood curdle," the head coach told his players Friday night. But what would really happen when they took to Florida Field was anybody's guess.

Although this week's practices had been better than the previous week's, it was still impossible to know how ready the team was for football. And Bowden had long since given up predicting performance on the basis of player mood. Which was a good thing, in this case, since the depression was still apparent. Thursday had been Thanksgiving Day, and President Lick had dropped by the players' communal meal to wish them well. He went away struck by the sadness in their eyes. "They were still in mourning."

Just one more game, thought Bowden, and then they could escape football for a couple of weeks and come back fresh for the bowl. The boosters and alumni may have been poised for the annual renewal of the rivalry. But for the players and coaches this wasn't going to be about the glory of the tradition. It was about survival. Let there be enough pride and muscle and sinew left to sustain them through one last game.

The physical condition of the team was out of everyone's hands. Every team in football, at this stage in the season, was a walking emergency room. Bowden could only concentrate on what he thought he could control—game preparation and attitude. The preparation part was over.

"We know we've got better players," Bowden told his players after their Friday-night dinner. "But are they hungrier? Are they hungrier?"

Get ready for war one more time, he told them. After this game they would have two weeks off before bowl practice. "What are you saving yourselves for?" Then he walked them through the traditional challenges: "Courage is going to be a big factor tomorrow. How are we going to handle adversity? What do we do if they get seven points on us, 10 points, 17? If we do get down, don't you dare get your head down.

"This game is on national television. You make the big play and you'll become an instant hero . . . It's a time for reckless abandon and utter disregard for personal safety . . . You seniors, you're not going to let us lose, are you? You want to go out as never having lost to Florida. You want to be the first Florida State team in history to win 11 games . . . Don't let your buddy down, men . . . Seniors, you won't let us lose, will you? . . . We can do it as long as we're together."

When Brad Scott gathered the offense in a separate meeting room, he wanted to turn the screws a little tighter. "Maybe I'm from the old school," he said. Which meant he expected a level of seriousness and dedication he hadn't yet seen as they prepared for Florida. And they might as well get down to it right now. "We're not here to play around. I don't want any talking, no horseplay."

The offensive coordinator made the starters sit down close, so he could quiz them on their assignments and challenge them directly. "If I wrote our game plan on the board up here, I would circle these words: 'Attack, attack, attack!' It's exactly the kind of offense you guys like to play. We're going for the jugular the whole game. It will be sixty minutes of full-court press. And you will make them surrender in their own backyard.

"They've been living in a dream world, playin' teams that are having their worst years. All these people are gonna be there in their new stadium, waiting for the big revival of the Gators. Well, we can throw water on it one more time.

"Men, you'll remember this one the rest of your life. What a great opportunity to be the first Florida State team to win five in a row against Florida. Wherever you go in this state for the rest of your lives, this will be one they'll dig up. This will be the one they'll talk about."

This was a little like the sermon he gave before the South Carolina game, Scott knew. The words were true. But much of the message was sure to go in one ear and out the other. These, after all, were 19- and 20-year-old boys with a hundred other miseries and pleasures on their minds. And they had heard it all before. But it still had to be said. The coaches called the players "men" in direct address, but they were always "our kids" when they were described to others. And kids occasionally needed to be reminded of the game's stakes and of others' expectations. The pursuit of those goals bound them together. And when so much seemed to threaten the cohesion of a team, the familiar phrases, even the clichés, could reassure them of all they had in common.

Like Bowden, Scott wouldn't let himself dwell on the physical evidence of the trial they were about to undergo. He couldn't heal the sick or make the lame walk. But unlike the head coach, the offensive coordinator, who was also the line coach, each day saw his players close up. He saw them limp and grimace and recoil in pain when a direct hit reminded them of where it hurt the worst. And when he let himself worry, he could conjure a nightmare.

Kevin Mancini was out. The Miami miracle had been short-lived; he had reinjured the knee in the game. And while he still resisted major reconstructive surgery that would take him out of NFL draft contention, he had submitted to immediate arthroscopic surgery to clean out residue in the knee. If they were lucky, Cheesy would be back for the bowl game.

Reggie Dixon and Robbie Baker both had nagging shoulder problems that reduced their effectiveness. Mike Morris still favored his bad ankle, and Rob Stevenson's late-season hip pain got worse with each game. Without a reliable backup for Mancini, Scott felt the only reasonable alternative was to move Morris over to the tight tackle spot and sub Patrick McNeil for Morris at guard. Although that risked weakening two positions, Mancini's and Morris', it at least put the best five players on the line.

They would probably be better off if this was going to be one of those run-at-'em games, where the linemen would be blocking the guys right in front of them. But they were calling out the air force against Florida. Which meant pass-protection responsibilities for two guys with little experience at their positions and two others with shoulder injuries that reduced their upper-body power. As offensive coordinator, Scott loved the game plan; as offensive line coach, it unnerved him.

Wasn't there something weird and ironic about all of this? Here they were at a juncture in the season where they would be judged as the best or the most disappointing team in Florida State history, and they were betting everything on the two most vulnerable segments of the team, the offensive line and the receivers. If they could survive that wager, didn't they deserve something more than the runner-up trophy in the state championship?

9

IF it was up to Gator fans, the script for the story of Florida State's season would have an ironic subtitle: "From No. 1 in the nation to No. 3 in the state." That's what one sign in the Florida Field student section proclaimed. There were others, not so carefully worded and not so neutral in tone, but more direct. The players began seeing them in the windows of cars almost as soon as they left Ocala on the team bus, which was forced to take to the right-hand emergency lane on I-75 to skirt the traffic that was building up twenty miles south of Gainesville. In fact, the Seminoles' welcome to the Evil Empire was altogether as advertised, beginning with that long ride in, down roads lined with Gator backers waving signs and gesturing menacingly, then into the new version of Florida Field.

Technically, it was Ben Hill Griffin Stadium at Florida Field, renamed in honor of the recently deceased multimillionaire who had been so generous in his support of University of Florida football. And it was a fitting monument to the region's obsession with the game. Nothing outside of the South could hope to match the combination of size and attitude.

Playing at Michigan had been a command performance in the Carnegie Hall of football. Louisiana State's Death Valley was a raucous museum of glory past. But this place had the feel of the Ultimate Arena. Newly bowled in to accommodate 83,000, Florida Field began in 1930 as a belowground stadium and was steadily expanded until the upper decks towered above the buried playing surface. On the field, it still had the feel—and the acoustics—of a concrete hole. And with tens of thousands yelling down from the canyon walls, the place shook with the noise.

The lower tiers of seats were within a few feet of the field, with the Florida student section looming directly behind the visitors' bench. An hour before the noon kickoff, the lower student seats were already crowded with those who had come early to boo the Seminoles through their warm-ups. Because of the students' traditional abuse of opponents, the Southeastern Conference was considering ordering the Gators to switch bench locations. But in 1991, visiting teams knew to keep their helmets on as extra insurance against flying objects and to turn deaf ears to the game-long chants and obscenities.

"Everything is goin' pretty much the way we expected, isn't it?" asked Bowden when he gathered his players for the pregame talk. "The crowd, the booing. And don't that excite you? They don't realize it gets our blood flowing about as good as it does theirs. They'll be excited. Just like we were two weeks ago when we played Miami. But it's a sixty-minute ball game. Can you stay excited for sixty minutes? That's the question."

The unpredictable Florida fall weather had turned warm and muggy, nearly 80 degrees, with the humidity officially at 75 percent. At the bottom of the bowl, though, it would be in the 90s with humidity to match.

"Men, it's hot out there today. But that's an advantage. On their defense, they don't play but eleven guys. And we'll run those passes, those nakeds, and we'll pound them. Let's just take it to them, and we'll own them in the fourth quarter."

Bowden's decision to go with an intensive passing game was reinforced by scouting reports that the Gators apparently were thin when it came to subbing for the starters. Nothing wears down a defensive front more quickly than chasing a mobile quarterback down after down. So the coaches wanted Weldon rolling out and throwing early and often.

It was time to let it loose, thought Bowden. Maybe some of the critics of his conservative play calling had been right. Maybe he had reined it in when he thought they had the cushion to win. But this wouldn't be one of those games. No margin was safe. Not with Steve Spurrier running the offense on the other side.

The network had asked the two teams to switch their kickoff from one-thirty to noon to accommodate a national two-game schedule. And they had complied. But Mark Richt had joked Friday night that "they won't be kicking off the next game any time soon." With the clock stopped for each incomplete pass and first down, "this could be one of those four-hour games. It will be a chucking contest."

That suited Richt and Weldon just fine. Both had been lobbying for a freer hand to put the ball up and to make decisions at the line of scrimmage. Built into the game plan this week was more than the usual number of quarterback checks so Weldon could change a play to react to coverage he suspected as he bent over center.

In the two weeks since the Miami game, Weldon had pulled himself back from depression and rethought his personal goals. "The Heisman is gone. I never really let myself think about it while it was going on. But now it's gone. One catch, one drive. To be so close, it does hurt. But there's nothing I can do about it.

"My secret goal now is to go out against Florida and throw for about 350 yards and four touchdowns and just tell the press that's what I could have done every week if I'd had the chance."

The first play, Bowden told the team in the locker room, would be 344

Z Bench, probably the most successful play-action pass in Florida State's '91 repertoire. "From then on," said the coach, "hang on to your hats, 'cause we're gonna let it all hang out."

When the team ran back onto the field, the stands were filled, and the Florida State band and Seminole fans were drowned out by the home crowd in full voice. Gator fans were still delirious over winning their first SEC title. And now this, a chance to humiliate St. Bobby and the boys from the girls' school on national television. A victory here and Florida could log its first-ever 10-win season.

Late in the practice week, the Seminoles had worked out in Doak Campbell with recorded crowd noise. But there was no way to simulate this level of bedlam. They could hear nothing but the roar. Across the field, the Florida players could barely contain themselves. They were jumping in place on the sideline and pounding one another's shoulder pads. The Florida State players eyed them curiously, as if the excited young men on the other side were part of a performance that didn't involve them. And the coaches told themselves that it would quiet down soon enough. Just get in a few licks, catch a few passes, move the chains.

Bowden got his preference—the chance to receive the ball in the second half. Florida would go on offense first. And Mickey Andrews' defense went out to face Florida quarterback Shane Matthews and Steve Spurrier's offense. Fans in the stadium and at home watching on ABC settled in for the fireworks. But the entire first quarter was going to be ruled by the two defenses. It amounted to a fruitless 15 minutes by two of the best-crafted offenses in the nation. Although they gave up ground to running back Errict Rhett and allowed a 41-yard pass to Aubrey Hill, the Florida State defense made the big plays when it counted. They shut down the SEC's most explosive offense.

By the same token, Florida's defensive front was destroying Brad Scott's patchwork offensive line and making life miserable for Casey Weldon, who was running for his life on every play. Reggie Dixon's shoulder had made him nearly useless, and he had come out of the game after the third series. Kevin Mancini was in street clothes on the bench trying to rally his teammates, and Robbie Baker was gritting his teeth through the tears of pain and frustration. But it seemed to be of no use.

From the moment the game began, the emotional edge belonged to the Gators. They were playing as if their whole season—their lives, in fact—depended on the game. They were wild men, snorting and flailing their way through blocks. And the Seminoles seemed taxed to their limits fighting them off.

Earlier in the season, Florida State had survived this kind of emotion from inferior teams desperate to prove something against the nation's No. 1 squad. Time and talent had always worn the challengers down. But this time it wasn't Middle Tennessee State or Tulane across the line. This was a powerful rival in possession of the singular advantage of being a desperate underdog on its own turf. And the only question remaining was whether the exhausting intensity of the Florida effort could be maintained for 45 more minutes of play.

They can't continue at this level, thought the Seminole coaches. Nobody can.

10

THE first Florida State series of the second quarter was a 16-play, six-minute battle down the field, beginning on the Seminole 31 and ending with four attempts to put the ball into the Gator end zone from the 1-yard line. Three times, Weldon and Frier failed to connect on 80-game passes, the three-step timing patterns that had aggravated the coaches all season. But with the Florida defensive linemen in Weldon's face on every play, it was hard to tell what was going wrong. Timing was the least of their problems.

All season, Eason had rolled his receivers, rotating four or five through the two positions. But for the Florida game, the coach decided to give McCorvey and Frier a chance to prove themselves. He had told Bowden that, because of the expected hand-to-hand combat, it was a Matt Frier kind of game. But, ironically, it was beginning to also look like an E.T. kind of game. This was everybody out for a pass and run for your life. And if there was anybody who could invent a way to get open and then fight off a defender to make a circus catch, it might have been Turral, the absent prodigal son.

Shannon Baker, who stood on the sideline with Knox, waiting for his turn to substitute, was sure that was true. He had written No. 7 on his socks and wristbands in protest of E.T.'s suspension, which didn't exactly inspire confidence from his coaches. So it was ironic that Baker accounted for the biggest gain of the drive, a second-down play that picked up 21 yards when Weldon threw up a desperation pass just as he was whacked in the face by the Gator rush. Baker pulled it in for a first down on the Florida 29.

Four plays later, with a fourth down and eight to go from the 27, Frier caught the same pass Knox had missed in the first quarter and picked up 12 yards and another first down. Then came one of the three-step timing patterns in the end zone, and Weldon overthrew Frier. But Bennett ran for five, and a pass to McCorvey advanced the ball to the 1 for first and goal.

Twice Bennett tried to get it in with the fullback Wham play. But he was stopped for no gain on first down, and somebody moved on the line of scrimmage, drawing an illegal-procedure penalty, on second. Lee got three of the penalty yards back, leaving the Seminoles with third and goal from the 2. And Bowden called for Red 88, another three-step timing throw, this time to McCorvey, who was to run under the pass in the left corner of the end zone. But McCorvey was boxed out of his route by the Florida defensive back, and the Seminoles had to settle for making the first score in the game a 19-yard Gerry Thomas field goal.

So much effort for three points. Yet that was beginning to look like enough to win, given the play so far of the Florida State defense. Dan Footman sacked Matthews for seven yards on Florida's first down. Then the quarterback tried and failed to connect with wideout Tre Everett twice.

On the punt return, an unsportsmanlike-conduct penalty put Weldon and the Seminoles in the hole, first and 25 from their own 18. And an attempt to find Bennett out of the backfield, then two screen passes, didn't fool the Gators. So Player was punting right back after three downs.

The Gators now began their best series of the first half. Making use of Rhett as a receiver and a runner, they drove from their own 24 to the Florida State end zone, making five first downs along the way. And Rhett finished the touchdown drive by running the ball in on consecutive carries from the 6. After the extra point, it was 7–3, Florida.

Buckley, whom Bowden had tapped for kickoff-return duties as well as punt returns, brought the kickoff back to the FSU 31, where Weldon threw a perfect pass to Knox on the left sideline for 24 yards. Sean Jackson, in for Lee, got six on his first carry. Then a holding penalty stalled the momentum. Even though the Seminoles completed two more passes, Weldon was sacked twice and hounded mercilessly. Florida took over on downs on their own 31 with a little over a minute to play in the half.

The Gators' Rhett lost three on a first-down carry, then got nine back on two pass receptions before Matthews tried to air it out on an end-of-half pass. Buckley, playing the ball like an outfielder, intercepted deep in

FSU territory and returned it 48 yards before running out of bounds with no time left.

In the runback, a few Florida players were riled at Kirk Carruthers' downfield blocking for Buckley, and a pushing and shoving contest threatened to escalate into a brawl. The Seminole assistants waded into the crowd to pull their players away. And they came face to face with their Florida counterparts. For a few dangerous seconds, when coaches from both teams were close enough to exchange glares and taunts, it looked as if there was no reason in the world why they all, coaches and players alike, couldn't settle this whole thing right now with their fists. But they turned from that temptation to separate their players and steer them toward the halftime locker rooms.

Brad Scott was in his linemen's faces almost immediately: "I tell you what's happening. It's very simple. For about two seconds, it's about even out there. Then the last three seconds of every play they want it about five hundred times harder than you want it. That's all it is. They're playing their butts off out there, and you're trying to survive. Have you lost some spirit, is that what it is? We're gonna let the whole football team down because five guys up here are getting their butts kicked around?"

His voice boomed over all the others in the crowded space: "You're going to hate yourselves. Is that what we've worked for since February of last year, the off-season drills, the spring, the two-a-days? Is that what we went through all this season for, to walk out of here as the laughingstock of this state? That's what's happening to you. There ain't nothing that has to be changed except the desire in your heart."

All the assistants were with their players, alternately cajoling them and reassuring them. Mark Richt masked his own edgy tension with teeth-clenched humor: "Hey, dudes, what's going on in here? Having fun yet? Are you ready to play a little ball?"

Weldon, a Band-Aid hanging from his bleeding chin, managed a tense smile. He was a mess. Grass stains were ground into his all-white uniform. And he looked exhausted. If all this running was supposed to wear down the defensive line, how come he was the one sweating and bleeding?

The quarterback leaned forward so he could see the linemen across from him. "Let's stay together now," he told them in a hoarse voice. "Everybody quit cussing everybody else. And I'm the first to apologize for that. The emotion is over now. They can't keep that up. It's over, I tell you. The second half's ours."

Bowden was waiting in the center of the long, rectangular locker room, looking at notes on a card. The jersey of No. 33, Errict Rhett, kept flashing in his memory. As usual, Bowden had been too involved with the offense to pay much attention to what was happening when Florida was on the attack, but he saw all he wanted of No. 33. Rhett had gained 93 yards on 14 carries and caught four passes for 31 more yards.

If it weren't for that 41-yarder, Spurrier's passing attack would have been held to 65 yards. The Seminole defense had recorded two sacks, and Buckley had grabbed two interceptions. That would put Buck into the NCAA career record books. The bad news was that the Gators had done the same thing to Bowden's offense. Weldon had managed to complete just nine of 22 passes for 101 yards. And he had been sacked twice as well.

Bowden looked at his watch, then at the sweating players in the room. "This is like the LSU ball game, men, when we showed all heart the second half.

"Defense, don't be outfought. That No. 33, he wants it so bad. If everybody in here played with that kind of heart, we'd have no problem out there.

"Offense, you won't protect our passer. I can't believe it. All they do is come and stand there, and when you relax they run by you.

"Now, this is a replay of the LSU ball game. They've got to kick off to us. We've got to run it right back down and score. Hey, men, thirty minutes of guts. We owe it to our seniors. You owe it to yourself.

"Receivers, you can't fall down when we call your number. We've got to get the running game going. Backs, you've got to slash. Their No. 33 is. He's running over everybody. He's a wild man. We have got to take our ability and do it.

"Offensive line, if you don't block, there ain't none of it no good. It's down to heart and down to poise. Courage, men. They're playing as good as they can play. But they're playing with more heart than some of our guys.

"Casey, you've got to lead 'em. Thirty more minutes. This makes our season. Every man, you must fight your heart out. Is there anybody here who doesn't want to do it?"

The players were on their feet, encouraging one another, pushing whatever sounds their tired bodies could muster up and out of their throats. They pounded fists into palms and slapped pads.

"It's time . . . It's time . . . Thirty more minutes, baby."

As all the other players filed out into the tunnel, Reggie Dixon remained in his locker stall, tears streaming down his face. Kevin Mancini sat next to his teammate, his arm around him.

"C'mon," said Mancini softly. "Let's go."

Dixon couldn't lift the arm below his dislocated shoulder. He was in terrible pain, and the frustration of hurting so badly with nothing to show for it was overwhelming. But he rose from the bench, his face contorted with pain, and walked with Mancini out the door and back onto the field.

11

THE Seminoles and Gators picked up pretty much where they left off in the first half, exchanging possessions in the first two series. When Florida took over with just a little under eight minutes to go in the third quarter, the biggest plays had been by the two punters, FSU's Scott Player and Florida's Shayne Edge, who forced opponents to begin each drive deep in their own territory. On first down from the Gator 28, Matthews tried to find Hill again for a long pass. Buckley was closer to the ball, however, and was pulling in his third interception of the day when Hill tackled him, separating the defensive back from the ball.

Matthews and Buckley had played together at the same Mississippi high school and had been the subject of double profiles all week in the Florida papers. No one missed the irony of Buck trying to add to his career interception record at the expense of his old teammate. But Matthews had his chance to tweak the All-American cornerback as well. On second down, the Florida quarterback took the snap on the left hash mark and was forced to roll right looking for a receiver or running room, with the Seminoles' Dan Footman in hot pursuit.

Buckley was 25 yards deep, helping out with double coverage of receivers and watching Matthews run out of time. He thought the quarterback's only option was to run, and he sprinted forward to cut him off as he crossed the line of scrimmage. One of the receivers Buckley was supposed to be helping cover was wideout Harrison Houston, who slipped behind linebacker Reggie Freeman as Buck ran toward Matthews. Matthews saw Houston in time to pull up and throw. And as he did, Freeman slipped and fell trying to turn and leap for the ball. There was no one left between Houston and a 72-yard touchdown.

The 24-second drive put Florida ahead 14–3. Yet the Florida State offense seemed inspired when it took over on the 20 after the kickoff. Weldon completed passes to Frier and Sean Jackson on the first three plays for a total of 46 yards. And three plays later, the Seminoles had a first down on the Gator 24-yard line. Knox was sandwiched between defenders on a jump ball on the 3, and the first-down pass fell incomplete. Frier moved the ball to the 16 with an eight-yard reception. And on third down, Weldon dumped a pass to Jackson at the 17, who slipped one defender at the 12, dodged another at the 5 and leaped into the end zone. But the touchdown was called back, because time had run out before Weldon could get the play off. Delay of game.

The home crowd loved that. Whatever chances the Seminoles had of hearing Weldon's signals through the noise were definitely over now. But on third down, Weldon miraculously escaped the rush in time to flip the ball toward McCorvey before being sacked. The freshman receiver had been almost in the end zone, then had run back toward the quarterback when he saw Weldon in trouble and made the leaping first-down catch at the 11. Weldon and Frier looked as if they would connect on a sure touchdown on the next play, when Frier was tackled from behind to prevent the catch. Pass interference. In the confusion down at the goal line, the officials spotted the ball at the 2, instead of half the distance to the goal. So the Seminoles had four downs to push the ball in from two yards away.

On first down, Jackson lost two yards. Amp Lee came into the game, and the second-down call was a pass that should have put the starting tailback into the flat, where a linebacker would be the overmatched defender. But Lee heard the call wrong and went inside, forcing Weldon to look to Baker, who was covered in the left corner of the end zone. The quarterback intentionally overthrew the pass.

On third down, Lee was to be the primary target over the middle, but Weldon was overtaken from behind and fumbled. The ball bounced around and ended up all the way back at the 27 before Reggie Dixon, dislocated shoulder and all, recovered it. That forced Thomas to try a 44-yard field goal, and he missed.

Florida Field erupted in a roar fueled by nearly two hours of nervous energy. But the Gators got no advantage against the Seminole defense. Matthews and the offense were three downs and out. And after the punt return, the offense got off one play, a six-yard pass to Frier, before the fourth quarter began.

Jackson and William Floyd picked up the first down near midfield. But two passes fell incomplete, including Bowden's only "rooskie" of the game—a handoff to the tailback, who tossed the ball back to Weldon for the throw downfield to Baker. The Florida defensive linemen were all over the play from the beginning, however, and the hurried pass was out of Baker's reach. On third and 10, Weldon tried once more for Baker, who was triple-covered. And the tipped ball fell into the hands of cornerback Lawrence Hatch, who returned the interception 41 yards to the Seminole 49. There were 14 minutes left in the final quarter of the season. The Gators were ahead 14–3, and Bobby Bowden's famed offense hadn't scored a touchdown in five quarters of football.

It would have been understandable if the game was ripped from the Seminoles' hands at that moment. The loud, hostile environment; the fired-up Gator defense; the heat; the mental and physical exhaustion— all of that amounted to an oppressive combination. And the Florida offense seemed determined to take advantage of it.

Matthews, using a running and passing mix, directed a drive that began near midfield and made it to the Florida State 7-yard line before a delay-of-game penalty pushed the Gators back to the 11. A loss of one by Rhett made it third and 12 from the 13, and Matthews dropped back to pass, looking for a receiver in the end zone. Wide receiver Willie Jackson was the target, but Seminole safety Lavon Brown came down with the ball. The interception quieted the stadium and sent a confident Weldon back onto the field.

The defense will not let us, thought the quarterback. If he was given this many chances, it would just be a matter of time before they overtook the Gators. And there was all the time in the world, seven and a half minutes.

On first down, the quarterback immediately found McCorvey for 20 yards. Then, chased by half the Florida team, he got the ball to Lonnie Johnson for another five. Weldon had to rush and throw out of Matt Frier's reach on second down from the Florida State 45. But on third and five, he squirted out of the Gators' grasp to connect again with the tight end, this time for eight yards.

The first-down play from the Florida 47 was a repeat of the first call of the series, and McCorvey again gained 20-plus yards. On first down from the 25, Weldon dropped back, looking for his wideouts downfield. But both were covered. The pursuit pushed him left, where he faked the throw downfield, freezing the coverage. Lee, seeing Weldon scrambling, slanted back inside. He was wide open when the quarterback dumped the ball off and only had to fake one inside move to run the rest of the way into the end zone untouched.

Weldon never saw the reception. He had been knocked off his feet and into the Florida bench area as soon as he released the ball. He lay on the ground a minute and was still dazed when he saw Brad Johnson come into the game to attempt the two-point conversion. Two points here would make the score 14–11, in range of a tying field goal. Which was the last thing on Weldon's fuzzy mind as he tried to make it to the Seminole bench and yell at the coaches at the same time. "Kick it! Kick it!"

It was an irrelevant issue, since a touchdown could win the game whether or not they made the conversion. Getting the two points would just give them one more option. "I was out of my mind," Weldon later admitted. "I don't know what I was thinking about." But Johnson's pass attempt for the conversion was deflected anyway, and the score remained 14–9.

There was a little more than five minutes remaining in the game, and confidence surged along the Seminole bench. The momentum had shifted with Brown's end-zone interception. And, for the first time all day, enthusiasm entirely overpowered the sullen depression that had haunted the offense for two weeks. Even with all the mistakes, even with the mismatch of emotions, this game could be snatched from the Gators in the final minutes. Every Seminole player sensed it.

The defense crowded excitedly along the sideline, waiting to run onto the field after the kickoff. Stop them one more time, they told one another. One more time. The Florida return put the ball on the 35, where Matthews completed only one pass for eight yards. On fourth down, Spurrier was faced with the prospect of whom to trust more to preserve the win—his offense, which had to make two yards to get the first down and continue the drive, or his defense, which had held the Seminoles to nine points so far. And the Florida head coach wanted Bowden to keep guessing.

First the Florida punter ran onto the field and prepared to kick. Then Spurrier called a time-out and sent his offense back out. Bowden called time to get the Florida State defense back. And the Gators took an intentional delay-of-game penalty with a long snap count, hoping to get the Seminoles to jump offside. But the trickery ended in a net loss for the Gators when the line of scrimmage was backed up five yards and Buckley returned the 39-yard punt to midfield. When Weldon ran into the huddle with four minutes and nine seconds left to play, he felt as if the game was all but won.

In the huddle, the players tried to rally one another. They were exhausted, but they could see the fatigue in the eyes of the Florida defense too. The offensive linemen had come into the game hurt and dispirited. And the only thing that changed up until the last series was more hurt. Because of Dixon's shoulder and tentative play by the backups, Brad Scott had moved Mike Morris all over the line in a desperate attempt to stop the bleeding. And for most of the game, Weldon had returned battered to the huddle, pleading for better pass protection. But in the last series, a little of the old confidence had returned. And now, the potential of victory, despite all that had come before, was enough to energize them.

The first-down pass to Lee was incomplete, but Weldon and the tailback connected on second down for 19 yards. Then McCorvey caught the first-down pass at the Florida 22 and ran to the 15 for another first down.

Lee jumped a little too soon on his first-down carry and was called for illegal procedure. But Weldon and Lonnie Johnson immediately regained the five yards with a pass on the repeat first down. Now it was second and 10 on the 14. The call was 344 Fanny, a play-action pass that made Edgar Bennett the No. 1 target over the middle. The tight end was the outlet in the flat. And the wideout, Kevin Knox, would run a takeoff to the end zone, pulling coverage his way and out of the territory where Weldon intended to pass.

The defensive pursuit forced Weldon to roll out right as he was looking for Bennett. But since the Florida coverage had folded inside, the middle of the field was clogged with players. The cornerback on the right side had let Knox run by him, evidently assuming the Gator safety would pick him up deep. But when the wide receiver crossed the 5 and headed into the end zone, he was alone. Weldon was on the run when he spotted the wide-open Knox. It was a sure touchdown. But the ball was wet from sweat, and Weldon couldn't get a grip. He flipped it over, rolling it in his hands, feeling for the laces and running for his life. Knox was doing jumping jacks in the end zone.

By the time the quarterback could get a grip, cock and loft the ball toward Knox, the Gator defensive backs had realized their mistake and were able to move between the waiting wideout and Weldon's pass. "All the time, I kept thinking: I'm going to win the game. I'm going to win the game," said Knox. But the defenders batted the ball away. Now it was third down with a little more than two minutes left in the game.

Brad Scott signaled the call—Red 68 Cobra. Normally, McCorvey would watch the cornerback covering him on the play and either stop just beyond the line of scrimmage or continue slanting across the middle, depending on the coverage. Weldon, however, wanted no confusion on the play, and he told McCorvey to continue to run on the slant no matter what. Before they got to the line of scrimmage, however, Bowden wanted a time-out to talk.

On the sideline, the coaches discussed alternative calls, but settled on the same play, the Cobra. But by the time he ran back to the huddle, Weldon had forgotten his instructions to McCorvey. And when the cornerback set up in a coverage that normally would have called for the wideout to stop and take the quick pass, Weldon automatically assumed that's where his receiver would be.

Everyone in the stadium was on his feet. At the snap, McCorvey, obeying Weldon, continued inside on the slant toward the goalposts. And he was wide open. But Weldon's pass was to the spot McCorvey would have occupied on the normal sight-read. And the ball fell incomplete behind McCorvey.

"If there was one play I'd love to have back," Weldon said later, "that would be it. Kez did exactly what I told him to do, and he could have walked into the end zone."

Now it was fourth down. And Bowden took another time-out, knowing this was likely to be the Seminoles' last shot.

They could get a first down if they made it to the 4. That was ten yards away. But getting into the end zone on fourth down would be no harder. The call was Smoke, which would put Frier into first-down territory on a 10-yard curl pattern to the right with McCorvey dragging across the middle from the left. Frier would normally be the primary receiver on the play. But in the huddle Weldon told McCorvey to look for the ball.

When the quarterback came away from center, the chase was on again. He scrambled right, looking downfield. Frier curled inside the defensive back but was still covered, so he continued maneuvering for position as McCorvey crossed toward the right side of the end zone. McCorvey was briefly in the clear in the end zone, and Weldon wanted to get the ball there. But again, on the run and under pressure, he couldn't set and throw. And with receivers and defenders maneuvering frantically in the space between the line of scrimmage and the end zone, 15 yards away, the play dissolved into a kind of sandlot chaos.

As Weldon ran toward the line of scrimmage on the right side, he saw open ground in front of him. If he chose to cross the line and run for the first down, could he make it? No way, he thought. He had nothing left in his legs. And besides, there stood a defender nine yards deep who would move up and nail him before he could make the first down. So Weldon passed.

McCorvey, near the end-zone sideline, was the target. But by the time the ball got there, Frier had moved into the same territory, bringing his defender with him. And there was a crowd of Florida jerseys jumping with McCorvey for the ball. The tip came toward Frier, who, for a moment, saw the game within his grasp. But as he moved to make the diving catch, a defender cut his legs out from under him, and the ball fell incomplete. It was over.

Shane Matthews ran out with the Gator offense to kill the final two minutes. And the party began. After the final gun, Gator players leaped onto the field and rolled on the ground in the end zone. Fans spilled over the stadium barriers and onto the playing surface, heading for the goalposts, but police turned them away and even hogtied a couple of the rowdier ones in the end zone.

The fans cheered and chanted and sang. It was the fitting end to the most spectacular season in University of Florida history. The Gators were undefeated champions in the SEC, undefeated at home on their new field, and victors, for the first time in five years, over their archrival. Now the guy in the end zone could hold his sign high. Indeed, the Seminoles, formerly No. 1 in the nation, were suddenly No. 3 in the state.

12

THE shock of losing was absent from the Florida State locker room this time. Those who were honest with themselves knew that, from the beginning, this one had the feel of inevitability about it. If the Syracuse game had been the fifth quarter of the Michigan game, this was the fifth period of the Miami agony. Still, there was anger, especially from those on the defensive side of the room who couldn't understand how so few points could be enough to win against Florida State. The Seminoles hadn't been beaten by a team that scored 14 points or fewer in 10 seasons.

The haunted look that Bowden had worn after the Miami loss was nowhere in evidence now. There was only frustration and fatigue. What was left to say? The season was over. A bowl game awaited them, but that was nearly a month away.

"I'm sorry about the loss, men. Defense, I thought you played great. But it doesn't help when you lose, does it? Offense, you kept fighting. You did everything today except one thing—goal-line offense. You got down there three times and didn't get it in. That's the only thing we failed at.

"Don't take it too hard. Don't be too down. Get you some time off."

He sighed and paused. "Men, we can't do it with guys who decide they don't want to practice. You're either in it or out of it."

But he didn't want to leave them with a negative thought. It was just like Miami. They were so close there at the end. "I did like the way you fought back," he told them.

Someone from the Cotton Bowl was at the door. "We know you've had a rough week here. Anything I can say is not going to make you happy. But you've had a great season, a great year. We want to reward you for that. And we're inviting you to come to Dallas for a reward. If you don't have a good time, it's your own fault."

The players looked at the bowl representative as if he'd alighted from another planet. Dallas was the last thing on their minds. They had been to bowls before. A good time? Unthinkable at this point.

They would have at least a week off to become students again before their next practice. It was time for final exams. "Next week is the fourth quarter of your academics," Chuck Amato reminded them.

Sean Jackson had been holding back the tears since he left the field. He wanted to speak. And when Bowden gave him the floor, the words came out in barely controlled sobs.

"These past two games, I don't think I've ever had two games that I ever wanted to win so bad. Even though we lost, I'm not about to give up on you guys. I think it's important that we stay together as a team. Even if the Cotton Bowl has no determination on the championship, we've still got to win the game.

"I just want the seniors to know I'm not about to give up on you guys."

There was an awkward silence. Few in the room had any emotion left to bare. They had been drained. And Jackson's sincerity, in the face of the indifference they longed to affect, unnerved them. At this point, caring only meant hurting more. They had invested 12 weeks in caring with all their hearts for something that was no longer possible. Now they wanted to be left alone.

Bowden watched his team's reaction to Jackson. "Hey, seniors," he said, before leading them in the final prayer, "you've got to hold this team together now."

The coach stood in the middle of the room, reached out to touch the nearest shoulder pad and bowed his head. "Dear Father, thank you for this opportunity. We pray that you'll heal any of our injured and take us all home safely. We're sorry that we were unable to win these last two ball games. And both of them we could have won as easily as we lost 'em, but we lost them. We pray that you help us to learn from it and grow from it and become better men and a better ball club because of it.

"Take us all home safely. These things we pray in Thy Name. Amen."

The players groaned when Wayne Hogan told them the doors were about to be opened to the reporters waiting outside. "Ah, man, can't you give us a minute or two?" But most of the pressure from the media was going to be directed toward Bowden and Weldon. Hogan took the coach to a separate interview area and announced that the quarterback would be available in a few minutes. Weldon was in the training room getting seven stitches in his chin.

When he appeared, still in full uniform and a new bandage on his chin, Weldon looked as if he were sleepwalking. Someone got him a stool, and invited the quarterback to sit on a raised platform where the TV and print reporters could all see him. They crowded four deep, pressing in close so that a half dozen mikes were inches from his teeth. He stared at them through the stupor of exhaustion, struggling to focus on their questions and to mumble responses that made sense.

Fifty-one times he had tried to pass, and it felt like 45 times he'd ended up on his back with some monster on top of him. Was it the worst he had felt after a game?

"Yeah, probably."

Could he have run for the first down on that last play?

"I don't think I could have made it."

How about the offensive line?

"We were hurting. The chemistry wasn't there, and that's a big thing with the offensive line. We were missing Kevin Mancini to begin the game and then Reggie Dixon, who came back to fight like the warrior he is."

What happened in these last two games?

"I think the big thing is that, being No. 1, we were the target all year and we might have just run out of some juice."

Has a great season now become just a good season?

"I wouldn't even say it's a good season."

Part IX

"THIS WILL BE THE
LAST TIME . . ."

1

O<small>N</small> Sunday, December 1, Bowden's assistants escaped the agony of the immediate past by giving themselves over to the demands of the distant future. December and January would be the months of full-time hustling for next year's freshman class. And while they would soon tire of the frustrations of romancing 18-year-old superstars, they were ready to welcome any distraction from the nightmares of the past three weeks and from the unsolicited advice from boosters and fans that would tie up their phones and stuff their mailboxes between now and the bowl game.

Instead of a film review of Saturday's game, the coaches' Sunday session was devoted to recruiting. Over the season, Ronnie Cottrell's list of prospects had been narrowed to a core of about one hundred, fifty of whom would be prime targets. What effect the two losses at the end of the season would have on recruiting, no one could tell. It would be considerably less than paranoid boosters imagined, though. As long as a program remained in contention for maximum TV exposure, for "graduating" its stars into the NFL and for having an annual shot at the national championship, a big loss here or there seemed irrelevant. For every prospect discouraged by a defeat in a key game, another saw it as an opportunity.

Many high school stars were used to thinking of themselves as franchise players, as athletes who could turn a program around or supply the missing ingredient for the long-sought championship. And, naturally, recruiters did nothing to discourage that inflated sense of self-importance—at least not until a recruit showed up for his first practice. Many of the current Seminoles had signed on convinced they would be part of history, and just as many others, still in high school, shared the same excited hope.

There was even a downside to success, especially when it came to recruiting for specific positions. There was a widespread perception, for instance, that Bowden's team was so deep at some positions that top prospects would be better off going elsewhere. Tailback, for instance, was a four-deep position, with junior Amp Lee leading three other

345

underclassmen. All of them high school stars with big-time college prospects. What chance was there to break into that lineup?

None of the receivers were seniors. They would all be back, crowding the competition for newcomers. But John Eason could be comforted by the thought that the ego factor would prevail in the kind of athletes he sought. They would have seen the kind of season the receiver corps endured. And they would dream the missing-link dream, imagining themselves as the clinching factor in the next run for the championship. He knew Tamarick Vanover, the Tallahassee all-everything receiver-back, was thinking precisely that. And in his case it might be true. Vanover could be the championship Z. If he could get that kid and maybe one other reliable X, thought the receivers coach, it would be a great recruiting year.

The big battle, ironically, might be with offensive linemen. Despite the troubles all season, there was going to be an enthusiastic pitch from those recruiting against FSU that Brad Scott had too many studs in waiting to give a serious look at a freshman.

That argument was already starting to drive Scott crazy. Last year's freshman crop, all redshirted in '91, was indeed one of the best line classes in recent memory. But all of them were unproved and some would be hurried into competing for starting jobs in '92 because of the lack of reliable backups among the juniors and sophomores. A talented freshman—such as Reggie Green, an athletic 300-pounder from the Tampa Bay area—might walk onto the field in the fall as a true freshman and immediately find himself second or third on the depth chart. Scott was trying to get that message across, especially to Green, but other recruiters would be urging the hot line prospects to count the bodies in front of them. So Scott's season-long ordeal was merely shifting from the Seminole practice fields to the high school athletic offices and to the homes of the young giants he coveted.

Most of the fan attention, however, was going to be directed toward the hunt for a future quarterback. Kenny Felder and Charlie Ward would be redshirt juniors in '92. Jeff McCrone, last year's only QB signee, would be a redshirt freshman. Richt couldn't be happier with the prospects of Felder and Ward, both great athletes and gifted offensive leaders. Weldon naturally overshadowed everyone at the position this year. Yet there was no one on the Seminole staff who doubted they could win big with an offense directed by either of the juniors. Still, it was a little scary to have everything invested in them for the next two years.

Both were also stars in other sports, baseball for Felder and basketball for Ward. If either chose to concentrate exclusively on the rival sport or were lost to injury, Richt would have only McCrone to fall back on. McCrone had been trying to recover from tendinitis all season and might never develop, even as a reliable third-teamer. Which meant that the quarterback they picked this year might be No. 2 as a redshirt freshman and the starter in his sophomore season. So he had better be a great one.

All year, Richt had been juggling his list. And he had narrowed the top tier to three: Dan Kanell, the baseball-football star from Fort Lauderdale; Chris Walsh, brother of former Miami and current NFL quarterback Steve Walsh, from St. Paul, Minnesota; and Danny Wuerffel, from nearby Fort Walton Beach. Richt didn't have Scott's problem. The QB prospects could see they were needed immediately. But they were likely to be more concerned than other players about who else was being recruited at their position. And they all talked to one another.

The quarterback coach would have loved to have two of the three, but assumed that was unlikely. Kanell and Walsh were on everyone's priority list, and Wuerffel would be a hot prospect with FSU's regional rivals. In fact, to make sure he landed one of his choices, Richt had to be prepared to cut a deal, promising he would take no other quarterbacks if that's what it took to get his top choice. But so far, no one had asked.

The coaches sat around the meeting table Sunday afternoon adding and subtracting names on their recruiting lists. They worried aloud about what the competition was saying and about the studs they most wanted making their grades and scores. The only topic was the future.

From now through the bowl game and into the last days of January, the assistants would be on the road, visiting players and parents and clearing the way for Bowden, who would fly in to meet with the top prospects. After the bowl would come the players' official visits at university expense. Then, the first week of February, the players would sign letters of intent.

Between now and then, the competition for top high school players would mirror the competition in games. The regional powers—Georgia, Alabama, Auburn and Clemson—would all be rivals. But it would be the state championship that would concern them and the fans most. Bowden and his assistants were convinced that there were enough great athletes in Florida to fuel each of the state's three big-time programs, keeping them at the very top of college football for years to come. Yet that conviction didn't spare any of them from the anxiety of the process. There was still the paranoia that everybody else was bending rules to get the upper hand and still the recurring nightmare that, come February, every young star who had pledged his love for Florida State would show up on local TV wearing a Gator or a Hurricane jersey.

The more experienced they became in the annual ritual, the more the coaches tried to resist the temptation to let 18-year-olds drive them crazy. But this year, they welcomed the diversion. It was going to feel good to hit the road, to sit in high school coaches' offices and talk football and to feel firsthand again the respect Bobby Bowden's program inspired in people who knew the game. The world didn't stop in Doak Campbell on November 16 or on Florida Field two weeks later. There was a past to take pride in and a future to look forward to. There was a life full of urgency and meaning divorced from those games and, more important, from the game itself. It was just that sometimes you had to get out of town to remember.

2

WHEN Charlie Barnes introduced Bowden at the weekly booster luncheon on Monday, he offered a tribute wrapped in a reluctant recognition of the bottom-line realities of big-time football.

"It's not true that winning and losing college football games don't matter. A couple of weeks ago we broke ground on a complex made possible in no small part because Bobby Bowden has won games like these last two. It shouldn't really matter, but it does."

Bowden accepted the warm applause and stepped to the mike. "I'm reminded," said the coach, "of this older lady who was talking to her son, who had just quit the team. She said, 'Son, you need to go back to the team.' He said, 'No, why should I go back? They talk about me, they criticize me, they fuss at me, they won't let me have my way. I'm not going back. Name me one reason why I should go back.'

"And she said, 'Well, the first reason is that you're 40 years old. And the second is that you're the head coach.'"

The Civic Center luncheon erupted with laughter. "And I guess that's what brings me here today."

The coach was more relaxed than he had been in several weeks. Losing gnawed at him. He hated the fact that the Seminoles had lost on Saturday. But he had been so leveled by the Miami defeat, maybe without knowing it, that the reservoir of sorrow had been depleted. The grief had left him empty and strangely relieved. It was true that the opportunity for a historic achievement was gone, at least for this year. But gone too was the pressure that had built steadily since two-a-days, pressure the coach handled from a lifetime of experience without realizing its cumulative, suffocating effect. Now he could breathe again.

"It's amazing how a season goes," he told the Monday audience. "The last two games we lost came down to the last play. If you're successful, you win. If you're not, you lose. We were that close to maintaining the dream that we had before the season began. That baby's gone now."

Although they surely had grown older by what they'd been through the last few weeks, Bowden's players were too young to have developed a memory of survival. They hadn't realized until the final minutes of the Florida game that they could play winning football again. They hadn't realized, in fact, that it even mattered to them. Then it was too late. Bowden knew how they felt, because he felt it too. Defeat destroyed him. But even though the Miami loss was the worst in his career, he had survived other losses. The only antidote for the poison was to play and win again. It was the singular advantage of sport over the rest of life.

Until they could play again, the Seminoles were going to have to live with the taunting of critics and the despair of their fans. Those were the unwritten rules of the game off the field. It had been a tradition for years that the winners of the Florida–Florida State game would torment the losers with the score until the rematch. That morning, Barnes reported, Gator backers called the Seminole boosters office at exactly 9:14 to ask if they knew what time it was. "And I suspect we'll be hearing from them regularly until November 28 of next year."

The fans at the luncheon were polite. But their questions to the head coach, many preceded by long sighs, barely masked their frustration. Like fans everywhere, they believed their team was supposed to win and lost only because of miscalculation and lack of motivation. Why didn't we try this, Bobby? Why didn't we do that?

Bowden reminded them that the Gators had something to do with the Seminoles' problems. "We have to give a lot of credit to the University of Florida. Especially to their defensive line. They played as if possessed. They played like a team that had been beaten the last four years by you, and they were going to get you. And they did."

But he knew, said the coach, that "just about everything I say sounds like an excuse." And wasn't this supposed to be the year of no excuses?

Though this was the part of losing that players and young coaches hated most, Bowden had learned to steel himself against fan reaction. He would make all the speeches, submit to countless interviews and shake every extended hand. But he had a filter thickened by a quarter century of winning and losing in plain sight. "When you win, you get too much credit. When you lose, you get too much blame." And, at this point, his shield was fully erected.

"I scan the papers to see what's being said. But I will not clutter my mind up with things I don't need to hear. I tell Sue not to put any negative letters on my desk.

"I've been through this all my life. You learn how to get around it. This is where you separate the coaches who are new at it and those who've been around a long time."

Bowden had avoided the trauma until he graduated to Division I-A. "I was head coach at South Georgia and Howard. "When we used to lose, who cared? I didn't see my name emblazoned the next day: 'Bobby Bowden lost.' "

His initial year at West Virginia, 1970, was when Bowden got the big reality lesson. "That was my first year as a head coach in the big leagues. And we were having a pretty good year. I think we got upset in the homecoming game, and I caught a little criticism for that. We might have been 5–1 when it happened. We go up to play our biggest rival, Pitt, at Pitt. We're leading 35–8 at the half. So what happens? Most of the Pitt people go home, and the West Virginia people march around to the other side of the stadium and get on them Pitt people. Then in the second half, we don't score, and they come back and beat us 36–35. And them West Virginia people can't handle that.

"I remember going back inside the locker room and talking to the kids. They were dejected. They took it almost as hard as our guys after the Miami game. It was the big game, and we had it won.

"So everyone gets dressed, and I'm the last one getting out, as usual. And I hear people outside screaming. A mob. Kinda like they're going to kill me. 'Bring him out. Bring him out.'

"What you had was four or five drunks, but I had to go out there and face that. I didn't know if they were gonna kill me, shoot me or what. I'd never been through anything like that. I had to have a police escort to get back on the bus to Morgantown. Ann's crying. She's heard all kinds of abuse.

"You see that happen, you catch all that criticism, and it gets to you. People would call. I even had death threats. Some guy would call me: 'We're going to kill you.' I was so mad I was wishing they'd come by. That was the toughest day of my life."

In 1973 and 1974, Bowden's West Virginia teams struggled with 6–5 and 4–7 seasons. And the signs started coming out, including the ones attached to coach dummies hanged in effigy. In 1975, he was back on a winning track with a 9–3 team and a trip to the Peach Bowl. But Bowden had already made up his mind that whatever he owed the school and its fans had been satisfied by his teams' performances. And whatever claim they had on his loyalty was undercut by the conditions they put on their affection. The name of the game was win or else.

During that period, Bowden started doing two things. He began keeping a notebook of Bible scriptures and motivational sayings that helped him keep disappointments in perspective. And he protected himself and his family from hurt by keeping fans, boosters and university officials at a discreet distance.

For the next twenty years, whenever he felt the devastation of a loss, Bowden would take from his desk the notebook with its handwritten aphorisms. The collection was classic Bobby Bowden—a celebration of authority, individuality, pride and self-deprecation all at once. "O Lord, help my words to be gracious and tender today, for tomorrow I may have to eat them," was one reminder. But No. 1 on the list was this: "Get mentally tough, or get out of coaching."

The effort to shield himself from betrayal produced its own set of contradictions. He became widely beloved as one of the friendliest men in the South. But in the twenty-one years Bowden had been a head coach at two universities, his circle of really close friends remained restricted almost exclusively to those who knew him in high school and college in Alabama.

If he intends to stay in the game, said Bowden, every coach must come to terms with the reality of the business: "There are two kinds of coaches—ones that have been fired and ones that have not been fired yet. I might yet survive that. But it's part of the dad-gum territory. A guy who can't handle that or a guy whose wife can't handle that, they die by the wayside."

3

THE players had no football responsibilities until December 11, when they would be finished with final exams and begin workouts for the bowl game. They would take a break for Christmas, then return to Tallahassee for the trip to Dallas. All that seemed a long way off. So since returning from Gainesville, the players had all but vanished from the athletic center. Mark Meleney wanted to round up the 22 who were in danger of flunking out for a talk, but he had a tough time. Only eight of them showed for a Thursday-afternoon meeting.

What the academic adviser wanted was to remind the players of how important their final grades were. This was no time to slack off.

"The university is changing. They're not going to give you more than one dismissal. The days when you could be kicked out and readmitted a couple of times are long gone. If you've already been dismissed once, your days are numbered.

"Where we are right now in this process is crucial. This needs to be a very serious weekend for you guys."

The coaches had already begun preparing themselves for the possibility that Amp Lee, Eric Turral and a couple of other well-known players wouldn't make the grades to continue in school. Technically, NCAA rules would permit them to play in the bowl game, because the next term hadn't yet begun, but the university interpreted its own rules to block their participation.

The announcement that the starting tailback had flunked out would be shocking enough. But things could get worse. Meleney almost certainly would have to act as go-between with college deans who would have to approve the readmission of at least a dozen other guys who would be officially dismissed but hadn't used up their chances to be placed on probation instead. That list could include Lee's next two backups, Sean Jackson and Tiger McMillon. And Edgar Bennett, who had been slow to get a professor to change a grade, was also on the official danger line.

The public reaction was going to embarrass the athletic department. And that would increase the pressure on John Eason—as the department's academic liaison—and on Meleney and his boss, Dr. Beverly Yerg, who directed the advising program.

Eason wasn't looking forward to the battle over academics. About the only encouraging thing was that the only player in his group at risk was the perennial problem child, Eric Turral. Eason hoped Eric Turral had used his suspension time to work on his academics, because any talk of bringing him back to the team would be irrelevant if he didn't make his grades. Kevin Knox and some of the other receivers had been lobbying hard for another chance for E.T., and Turral and his mother had come in to talk to Eason. Bowden was open to whatever Eason suggested. Officially, the receivers coach hadn't decided what he thought. But as the pressure of the football wars dissipated, both Bowden and Eason had softened.

To cut Turral entirely loose would trouble him, Eason knew. "What else is he going to do? I don't want him to end up on the streets. My first thought was to keep him out of the Cotton Bowl, no matter what. But I'm keeping an open mind.

"I may talk to some of the other players. You don't want to be unfair to Eric, but you want to be fair as far as the rest of the team is concerned too."

4

Eric Turral's suspension from the team was lifted in time for the resumption of practice on December 11. But six days later, final grades came in, making him ineligible for readmission and for the Cotton Bowl. Amp Lee was gone too. As were at least two others.

When Mark Meleney prepared his report for Dr. Yerg, he totaled the dismissals—18. Only four of the threatened 22 had been able to make high enough grades to pull their cumulative averages over the 2.00 cutoff. "I was expecting about 13," said Meleney, shaking his head as he stared at the computer screen.

It was true that many of the recruited football players, because of their academic backgrounds, were at a disadvantage when it came to competing in the classroom with the rest of the FSU student body. But given the support system that surrounded them, almost all should be able to make reasonable progress toward degrees. And in a normal year, almost all would, thought Meleney. Yet it was impossible not to see all the things that pulled at the players during a season like this. The media- and fan-generated attention, the exhausting demands of practice and of playing in games, the focus on winning it all—then the crush of defeat. How many 19- and 20-year-olds, even those with impressive academic credentials, could put all that on a back burner and hit the books?

Meleney and other academic specialists sympathized. A certain amount of unfairness was built into the system, especially now. The squeeze was definitely on, both from the university, anxious to enhance its academic reputation, and from the football program, which was determined to push players and coaches to the ultimate level, year after year. The pressure made the risk of failure so gigantic that players inevitably were robbed of the very experience most likely to contribute to their long-term success—the experience of independence, of taking responsibility for their own actions.

Scholarship athletes in big-time programs such as Florida State's lived arranged lives. They had little or no say in scheduling their meals, their travel, their practice times, their study halls, their dorm arrangements and their outside employment. They were told how to dress on trips and when to schedule classes. It seemed nearly the opposite of the way they had gone through high school, where rules that governed other students didn't apply to them as long as they excelled in sports. But the effect was the same. They seldom had to take personal responsibility for anything.

Over the next five years, the NCAA planned to phase out jock dorms and cafeteria training tables, with the announced purpose of better integrating student and athlete populations. Bobby Bowden was all for the idea. But he and other coaches also argued that the effort would be meaningless if universities, legislators and fans continued to hold athletic departments responsible for off-the-field behavior of players. Faculty members weren't held accountable for students in their classes who didn't graduate. And deans weren't taken to task for not being able to control students who got into trouble off campus. Why were coaches?

The argument was appropriate and convincing. And irrelevant. One certain effect of the sweeping reforms in college sports would be more pressure on athletic departments to guide the social and intellectual lives of student-athletes, with no lessening of the pressure to win. For coaches, it meant another set of things to get fired for. And when it came to academics, folks like Meleney and Yerg were going to take the pass-along heat from the fans, the university administration and the athletic department.

To their credit, Turral and Lee faced reporters and took responsibility for their academic failures. Turral told the Tallahassee *Democrat* that he had no quarrel with the rules. "Lately, I've been doing well. I had a pretty good semester. It's just that I dug a hole when I first got here. I didn't take school seriously. I'm a smart kid, and I know what I have to do."

The route back would require an Associate of Arts degree from Tallahassee Community College. With five courses in the spring and summer, Turral could get the degree and be readmitted to FSU in time for two-a-days in August of '92. Would Bowden let him resume his scholarship? The head coach promised nothing, but he left the door open.

Amp Lee said he would head to TCC too. At least for now. But there was also the pull of the Next League. Draft speculators were already suggesting Lee could be a second- or third-round choice. "I want to come back and play my last year. But I just don't know what I'm going to do. I'll go home and talk to my mother, and then I'll make some decision."

5

AFTER exams, the Seminoles had about a week and a half of practices before they got to join other students on the Christmas holiday break. The time off had healed more than aching muscles and strained joints. Scar tissue had begun to grow over some of the emotional hurts as well. And while habit required a certain seriousness in the drills and scrimmages, there was a level of looseness they hadn't allowed themselves in months.

The defense, now, was a swaggering, taunting force. Buckley talked constantly during the scrimmages, daring the receivers and quarterbacks: "Get those kindergarten plays outta here! Y'all ain't gonna do nothing with those." And even the defensive linemen waiting their turns in the 11-on-11 substitutions yelled from the sideline at the missed blocks and failed pass protection of the offensive front five.

In their own drills, of course, the defensive secondary couldn't escape Mickey Andrews' steady barking: "Do you call that hitting? I said DRIVE through that tackle." But the noise of it was too familiar now to irritate them. It had accompanied the defense through every week of practice. And every week they seemed to improve. Even in those awful back-to-back losses, the defense had held two of the nation's top offenses to their lowest point totals of the season.

Bowden, still bothered by the conservative-play-calling insinuations, had tweaked the boosters on the subject in the Monday luncheon after the Florida game. "People keep talking about conservative football, conservative football. I wish somebody would define that term for me. I do not know what it means. But I think I do, though. I think it means somebody else's defense is pretty good.

"Didn't Miami play conservative against us? And didn't ol' Spurrier play conservative down in Gainesville?"

Well, the Seminoles were going to face another one of those opportunities for conservatism in the Cotton Bowl. Texas A&M had the country's

top-rated defense. But unlike the opponents Florida State had faced in
the last two games, the Aggies didn't seem to have an offense capable of
squeezing out the points their defense could protect. So Andrews'
players were feeling frisky and looking forward to the comparisons
commentators would be forced to make between them and the guys who
were supposed to be No. 1.

The looseness on the offensive side of the ball, however, seemed to
have less to do with confidence than with resignation: Let's play this
game and get out of this season.

Casey Weldon had left just about everything he had on the field in
Gainesville. On December 14, he had made the trip up to New York to
sit among the Heisman Trophy finalists, knowing he didn't have a chance
to beat out Desmond Howard. And when he was announced as runner-
up in the balloting, he had done his best country-boy act of appreciation.
And he had meant it too. It was an honor.

But what he almost had, what they almost had as a team in the closing
moments of those two heartbreaking games—that's what he remembered most. In every way that counted to him, this season was over. He
had graduated officially the same day he was in New York at the Heisman
ceremonies. College was the past. The NFL was the future. He had
probably lost hundreds of thousands of dollars in NFL bonus and salary
money in those last two games. But no doubt hundreds of thousands
more were waiting. And the pressure was off. Weldon figured a bad bowl
game wouldn't hurt him much, a good game might help—but not signifi-
cantly. He had nothing to prove. As long as they won, he would be
happy. And the way the defense was playing, one score could win it.

Except for Turral and Lee, the offense should be pretty much intact
by the bowl game. Mancini, who had submitted to less intrusive arthroscopic surgery after the Florida game, was planning to be in the lineup
again. And Dixon, Morris and Baker were postponing their shoulder
surgeries until after the bowl. Which suggested that the original starting
five on the offensive line, playing at about 75 percent strength, would be
available.

Among the receivers, Matt Frier and Kez McCorvey were both feeling
good about their strong performances against Florida. If they could stay
on a roll, they would go into spring as projected starters in '92. But the
player with the most to gain from the bowl was Sean Jackson. "This is
the way stars are born," Bowden had told Texas reporters in a phone
interview during the week.

Jackson had gotten his academic reprieve to continue in school. And
now, as the sophomore heir apparent to Amp Lee, he would be starting

on national television in a January 1 bowl game. "I ain't seen nothing so far that scares me about playing Sean Jackson," Bowden said.

The fact was, the emotional Jackson, who played as if he were ready to give his life for the team, might be just what they needed at this point. Florida State would have athletes ready to go in Dallas, but the coaches had reason to worry whether they had a team. Especially on offense. And a player like Sean Jackson could be just the glue they needed to hold them together for one more game.

6

BOBBY Bowden, the winningest bowl coach in college football history, had never been to the Cotton Bowl. That provided one kind of personal motivation for the coach. And the fact that the '92 Cotton Bowl was the 50th anniversary of a game that Bowden remembered vividly from his youth was another.

In 1942, Alabama, the beloved team of 12-year-old Bowden, met an earlier version of the Texas Aggies. And Bowden remembered listening to the game in his bedroom in Birmingham. Hold Rast, one of his favorite players, intercepted a fourth-quarter pass and ran it in for an Alabama touchdown in that game. Bowden remembered cheering at home as his Crimson Tide won the wartime bowl 29–21.

He had been thinking of the coincidence ever since they struck a deal to go to Dallas after the Miami loss. It meant even more that A&M was where Bear Bryant coached just before he got the Alabama job. And Gene Stallings, the current Tide coach and an assistant under Bryant when Bowden was at Howard, was A&M's head coach between 1965 and 1971. All those Alabama connections. "Ain't that somethin'?" The coach even called Rast back in Alabama to reminisce a little over the Cotton Bowl connection. And he was looking forward to walking onto that field on January 1.

What he was not looking forward to, however, was presenting his battered Seminoles as a target for one last hungry challenger.

Since Jackie Sherrill left the Aggies three seasons before under a cloud of recruiting controversy, R. C. Slocum had been rebuilding the Southwest Conference powerhouse into a national contender. Under Sherrill, A&M had been ranked as high as 6th in 1985, but cheating allegations had muddied the school's record during that era. Now, in his first three seasons as head coach, Slocum had a clean reputation and a steadily improving record. In fact, in the nearly 100 years the Aggies had been playing football, he was the only coach to have led teams to three bowl games and 27 wins in his first three seasons. In '91, his Aggies had swept the Southwest Conference competition and lost only one game, by one point, to Tulsa, in a game in which their all-star quarterback was sidelined with an injury.

Had it not been for that 35–34 upset in Game 2, Texas A&M "could just as easily be playing for the national championship on January 1," Bowden told reporters. And there was every reason to believe that Slocum and his ambitious young Aggies were planning to use Florida State to prove to the nation that they were undervalued at No. 9 in the AP poll.

Except for the three Texas high school products on the Florida State team, the Seminole players couldn't be less interested in the intrigues of the Southwest Conference. They didn't know who these guys were and didn't care. As far as most of them were concerned, if they weren't playing for the national championship, this was just another meaningless bowl game. And to make matters worse, their buddies from Miami had told them to be sure to pack long underwear, because Dallas was nasty in January.

Bowden and his coaches were going to have to convince their players one more time that they were facing a lower-ranked team with both the talent and the motivation to embarrass them. Only this time they weren't battling to stay No. 1 or to preserve a long-shot chance at the top. The only thing really at stake here was pride. And after the last month and a half, there was no way to know how far even that could take them in another pitched battle.

The big challenge would be A&M's well-stocked defense. Slocum had been defensive coordinator before he took the head coaching job in 1989, and the team was still dominated by the "wrecking crew" persona. The stud was linebacker Quentin Coryatt, who was a Marvin Jones-type unguided missile, except 20 pounds beefier and two inches taller. He was projected to be among the top three players taken in the '92 NFL draft.

Kevin Smith, a Buckley-like corner, was another defensive All-American. And he was eager to showcase his talent alongside Buckley's, after losing out to Buckley in the competition for the Thorpe Award for the nation's top defensive back.

On offense, Bucky Richardson was one of those tough, throwback quarterbacks who excited coaches and fans. Mark Richt, who rarely looked at offensive film of opponents, had been talking about Richardson's toughness for two weeks in staff meetings. A 6-2, 220-pound player with great athletic ability, Richardson was the conference's all-time leading quarterback in rushing—2,095 career yards. And he might end up as someone's running back in the NFL.

The other dangerous player on A&M's offense was Greg Hill, a freshman running back who had run for 1,216 yards in '91—better than the freshman conference record held by Earl Campbell.

The Aggies were not the Miami Hurricanes on offense. But at this stage of the Seminoles' degeneration, they might not have to be. At a press conference in Dallas, Slocum did everything he could to sabotage story lines that might suggest A&M was in perfect position to take advantage of Florida State's miseries. "This is not a team that has had its confidence shaken. Florida State is as big a team as there is. We fully expect to go out there and play one of the best teams in the country."

As for the Aggies, Richardson said, "We're just happy to be here. Happy to be playing a team we've seen on television."

Bowden had heard all that before. Had said it. And it scared him to death.

7

"This is our last chance to go out as winners," said the head coach, standing before the entire squad on New Year's Eve. They were in Loews Anatole Hotel, a sprawling luxury complex that was part of a sprawling business strip along an expressway headed into downtown Dallas. The lobby alone, with its cathedral-high ceilings, could have swallowed most buildings in North Florida. And the sense of Texas hugeness, of money made and squandered and made again, overwhelmed the routines of the Seminole Cotton Bowl contingent.

That didn't seem to bother anybody, least of all the players and coaches, who were weary of being the stars on a media-shrunken stage. Here, as in Anaheim in August, the event and its sponsors were bigger than the game and its participants. The difference, of course, was the 55-year history of this annual party by Dallas bigwigs and Texas football fans. Every event had the feel of practiced hospitality. No expense spared.

After the season, the Tallahassee *Democrat* would print the names of Seminole boosters and university guests who had helped Florida State spend a major chunk of its $1 million expense money from the Cotton Bowl. In a time of education budget cuts, the tab struck many as imprudent, even though rewarding friends of the university with a bowl trip was a long tradition in college sports and even though none of the money came directly from taxpayers.

As usual, the money issue was irrelevant to the people who had the most to do with Florida State's invitation to Dallas. Under NCAA rules, the players were allowed some expense and meal money, but not enough to sustain more than a couple of nights on the town in an expensive city with no transportation. By Monday, two days before the game, their entertainment, between practices and meetings, had been reduced to hanging around the lobby waiting for something to happen.

The practices, held in the Dallas Cowboys' Texas Stadium in Irving each day since December 26, had been spirited. "You looked like your old selves today," Bowden had told them, hoping to make it true by saying it. But everyone knew better than to draw conclusions from what they saw in practice.

The weather, so far, had been cool, yet within the adjusted comfort range of those who remembered Louisville. If the rain and wind held off, the only things left to worry about were the state of their own preparations and commitment and the untested resolve of Texas A&M.

"Now, we had some boys in that last ball game who were not willing to have some pain," Bowden continued. "I don't know how you play football without pain. That's what separates you from other people. You're a football player, and you're expected to play with pain.

"We're going to play a team tomorrow where there's no finesse way to beat them. It's strictly line up and knock their tails off. We can play that game as good as anybody in the country. We've got as fast a football team, we've got as tough a group of football players here—if they've got their minds on it—as anybody in the country.

"I tell you what, if you get in that ball game tomorrow and you don't push yourself to the limit, you're unfair to your teammates. If you get out there tomorrow and you don't play the best you can, you're not going to hurt Bobby Bowden. You won't even hurt yourself. But you'll hurt your darn teammates.

"You make up your mind. We have less than twenty-four hours before that kickoff. You be sure that everything is geared right now to do what you've got to do tomorrow to win that ball game.

"Now, the ball game tomorrow. National television. We will not be the favorite with the crowd. It will be all Texas. They're out there to root on those Aggies, but that's what makes it challenging.

"Seniors, I cannot impress on you enough. This is your last showcase. If you have pro ambitions, this is your last chance to showcase it. And I'm gonna tell you, for some of you, your stock has gone down. Somebody has been telling you guys you're gonna go this round, that round. And I hope you do. But them agents will tell you anything. You had better be able to put out some film and show them coaches.

"This is your last chance. Men, give it all you got. You got the rest of your life to loaf. Turn it loose. I won't get a penny out of it. I hope you do.

"No foolish penalties. A perfect snap. Don't push, don't shove, don't taunt. Don't let them trick you into hitting back.

"Defense. Texas A&M has the No. 1 defense in the nation. Is that the stat I'm reading? I don't know if we don't have the best defense in the nation. Let's hammer that quarterback. He's the guy that they rally round. He's their leader.

"Offense. We started off with the best offense in the nation. We scored nine points last week. That's embarrassing. I can't believe that. We've got so much talent on our offense, I just don't understand it. Nine points.

"Offensive line is the key. Our offensive line has not been the same since the LSU ball game because of injuries. Now we've got everybody back. Offensive line, I promise, you are the key. We made 37 yards rushing in the last ball game.

"Goal-line offense, that's where we fell. First down and two, and we don't even score. We can change all that tomorrow. I'm just telling you what we have to do to win the game. Goal-line offense. Knock the ball in.

"Receivers, we've got to have the great catches. We quit making the great catches after Michigan. 'You got to hit me in the chest if you want me to catch it. You throw it in the middle, and I will not go in and get it.'

"Well, this is a courage game, men. If you don't feel like you fit in that category, just tell me, 'I don't think I should go in there this game, Coach.'

"Men, we need for all this to come together tomorrow. We have got the best football team in the country, I am confident of that, right here. And that's the way we ought to go out tomorrow. This time tomorrow night, we want to be Cotton Bowl champions. Then all you seniors can look back and say, 'Gee, except for two plays, except for two plays . . .' "

He was only repeating what had been on all their minds for weeks now, Bowden knew. No matter how they added it up, the difference between the season's dream and the disappointment of the last two games boiled down to two plays. Two of a half dozen plays that could have won both games. Two stinking plays. But the coach didn't want their last meeting to drift into self-recrimination.

Whatever happened on New Year's Day, this had been a season of soaring accomplishment, though none of them could yet accept that notion. This team had won more awards than any in Florida State history. They had played one of the toughest schedules in college football and held on to No. 1 for 12 brutal weeks. And in the next few months, when ligaments and bones were on the mend, when teammates had gone on to the Next League and when they all began thinking of next year—then, surely, they would reclaim their pride. Let it begin tomorrow, thought Bowden.

"Men, win or lose it, I'm really proud of you guys. I've gotten on you a little bit tonight. But y'all have practiced as good as any football team I have ever had. Whatever we said you had to do, you've done it. I'm proud whether you win or lose. I just hope you win."

8

For one last time, the team broke down into meeting segments. First, as offense and defense, then in groups by position. With Brad Scott, the offense was going to go over key blocks, fakes and pass-protection calls. But first Scott needed—as much for his own sense of closure as for the players' benefit—to issue the last game challenge.

"Everything that's happened to you, men, has happened to the coaches. The good times have been good, and the bad times have been horrible. Anybody that feels different in this room is not a team player.

"You're a part of history. This is going to go down as one of the great Cotton Bowls. There have been some great ball players here in the past. Now, wouldn't it be a shame if we went out there and didn't play with the kind of emotion, the kind of intensity, the kind of oneness that we've got on this football team?

"It's time to go out there against the favorite sons of this state and prove to them that they can't stay on the field with our Florida talent, with Florida State University. We've got some tradition that they want, and they want it badly."

No one had begun talking about it yet. But this was the new truth of Florida State football: "They want our tradition." When Bobby Bowden had come to Florida State, that tradition was all but nonexistent. He built it with raids on the turf of others. "They say we can't do it," he had told his players, who seized the underdog advantage and used it against the old powers who wrapped themselves in their tradition as if it were armor. Now it was Florida State's turn to defend the castle.

The old magic may have inspired them against Michigan, who obligingly lent the Seminoles the underdog tag for one last time. But now there was no one left in college football to say they couldn't do it. Every team was going to make them defend their territory. Miami had demanded it. And though the Florida–Florida State drama was set in Gainesville, it was the Gators who played with the desperate intensity of invaders.

Now here they were about to appear before a stadium full of Texans against a school that had begun playing football before the turn of the century. And it was Florida State's tradition that inspired the opponent's fervor.

"You know everything they're going to do, but just to know it is not enough," said Scott. "You've got to stand up and accept the challenge. When they come into those gaps, you got to hit them dead in the mouth. Then you stay on 'em, you step on their toes and you lift 'em up out of their shoes. Don't let 'em penetrate that line of scrimmage. It's a brick wall, like it was at Michigan."

Then Scott turned to the oldest of traditions on nights like this, reminding the seniors that this was their last game together. "Morris, you don't have another game . . . Mancini . . . Reggie . . . I know this game means something to each one of you. 'Cause you love that guy, and you love that guy. All that comes together in games like this.

"They're a good team, but they ain't been where you've been this year. And they don't deserve to take the glory and thunder away from Florida State. And they will not if you don't let 'em.

"The whole world is watching. There ain't no other game on TV when we're playing. This is a great bowl of tradition. It will mean something to you. But you know what will mean the most? You will never be together again. Being boys like you are, you say, 'Good.' But the truth of the matter is, you'll miss each other. You will kill for the opportunity. All of those guys who went on to the pros wish they had that opportunity you'll have tomorrow.

"It's the last time you eleven will hit that field together, the last time, Mike, you and Mancini will play side by side. I hope them shoulders hold up. I hope you'll play through that pain, that you'll forget that you have torn rotator cuffs and more screws than you got muscles, that you'll fight your heart out.

"Togetherness. Oneness. Laying it on the line. 'Cause we'll never be together again."

9

"How do you feel, Bake?"

"I feel great, Coach," said Shannon Baker to John Eason.

"Kez?"

"I've got a few butterflies."

"Matt, how do you feel?"

"I can't wait, Coach."

"Knox?"

"The chemistry is definitely there, Coach."

Eason spent almost no time on plays. Whatever was missing from the receivers' understanding of tomorrow's game plan or of their roles in it wasn't going to be changed by a New Year's Eve cram session.

Instead, he asked for New Year's resolutions, both in football and in the rest of their lives. "I'm going to try to work on my quickness," said Matt Frier. "And I'm gonna try to get closer to the Lord."

Kevin Knox told the group his spiritual life needed work too. "And I want to cut down on cursing." In football, "I know I can do so much more. I can be awesome. That's where I want to get to."

His teammates laughed. And the rest of them went through their resolutions one by one. "How about you, Coach?"

Eason thought for only a moment. "For the first time since I can remember, my resolution isn't about my weight or my diet. It's about inner peace. I want to work on inner peace. I think I've prayed more this year than at any time in previous years."

Since he had arrived in Dallas, Eason had let the built-in distractions of bowl week dilute his anxiety about Eric Turral, about the academic

problems, about his players' readiness to perform. He knew there was
no reason to expect a revival of the offense that had beaten Michigan and
Syracuse. Too much had happened since then. But the talent was still
there, if they could just tap it.

"You know, I was thinking as I was listening to our resolutions," said
the coach. "All of them are within the realm of our control. Nobody
asked for houses or for money. We can all do something about what we
want."

The receivers nodded. And they chatted for a few moments about
what could and could not be controlled and about John Eason's inner
peace. Everyone in the room but Jeff Beckles, the senior walk-on, was
an underclassman and would be back in Eason segment meetings in '92.
Yet they were still a little reluctant to break up the last meeting of the
year.

When they did, Eason asked Matt Frier to lead them in a prayer.
Everyone gathered in the center of the room, placing their hands on one
another's shoulders and bowing their heads. Frier's words were brief:

"Thank you, Father, for this New Year. Thank you for Jesus for saving
us. And bless our families and ourselves."

10

WHEN the Seminoles ran out of the tunnel and onto the artificial turf of
the Cotton Bowl, the temperature was 46 degrees, cold enough to annoy
the Floridians without hampering their game plan. The steady rain,
however, was something else entirely.

The Aggies won the toss and deferred possession to the second half,
giving Casey Weldon and the Florida State offense first crack at the ball.
Shannon Baker picked up 14 yards on a second-down reverse. But the
Seminoles got nowhere in the next three downs and ended up kicking
from their own 33.

Bucky Richardson of the Aggies immediately picked up five yards on a
keeper, then directed a drive, using Greg Hill as his primary receiver
and rusher, to push the ball to the Florida State 40. On second down
from there, Richardson pitched the ball back to Hill, who ran 38 yards
down the right sideline before Errol McCorvey overtook him from
behind. Hill fumbled as he was going down, and the ball bounced through

the end zone and out of bounds. It was a spectacular break for the Seminoles, who, according to the rules, took possession of the ball at the point of the fumble.

That meant Weldon was backed up into his own end zone as he rolled right on first down looking for a receiver. Quentin Coryatt, the all-everything A&M linebacker, seemed to appear out of nowhere to pound Weldon to the turf. And the Aggies were on the scoreboard with the two-point safety.

After the required free kick back to A&M, the Seminole defense held the Aggies to just two yards. So the Florida State offense got its third chance with the ball with nine minutes still remaining in the first quarter. Bennett picked up two yards. Then, on second down from the FSU 22, A&M's Patrick Bates picked off Weldon's pass to Kez McCorvey. It was Richardson's turn again.

The Aggie quarterback found Tony Harrison in the end zone, but the end dropped the pass. And a 47-yard field goal in the rain was nullified by a delay-of-game penalty.

The tone was set. The backs and receivers on both teams were having a terrible time holding on to the wet ball. And with aggressive defenses blanketing offenses, a turnover-fest seemed likely. Before things got out of hand, however, Weldon was able to put together one solid drive.

Starting at the A&M 46, the quarterback completed passes to Frier, McCorvey, Sean Jackson and Lonnie Johnson to move the ball to the 7-yard line. Jackson picked up three yards on the first-down carry. Then, out of the same formation, Weldon faked a handoff to the tailback and ran the ball in on a naked bootleg. It was 7–2, with 2:21 left in the quarter.

For the rest of the half, the two defenses tormented the offenses, and loose balls splatted all over the rain-soaked field. Texas A&M turned the ball over four times, three by fumble and one by interception. Florida State reversed the stat, losing one fumble and giving up three interceptions.

Weldon was having a terrible day. In addition to the three interceptions—already the most he had ever thrown in a game—he had been sacked three times and had completed just seven of 16 passes for 51 yards. The rain was a crucial factor. But he would admit to himself later that it was more than that: "In the practices, I had tried to get into it, but it just wasn't there."

If there was some good news, besides the 7–2 halftime score, it was the performance of Sean Jackson in his first start. Already he had run for 67 yards and caught two passes for 13 more.

There was no panic in the halftime locker room. When the assistant coaches gathered with Bowden, they seemed confident their scheme, with only minor adjustments, could win. The weather, the ferocious A&M defense, the excited crowd—those would not be enough to beat them if they could just take a little more control. It didn't matter how they won this, how weird or sloppy it appeared to fans and TV viewers. The point was to survive and win.

"We've got thirty minutes to reestablish ourselves as champions," said Scott to his linemen. "They're arguing and fighting among themselves right now. We get one more score, and it's over."

Bowden had decided to accent the run. He read off the plays: "44, 46, 45, 34." He challenged the defense one more time: "Show 'em you're the best in the country." Then, as he sent his players out to the second half, he reminded them, "This group of men will never get together again as a ball club."

Texas A&M fumbled the second-half kickoff, and Reggie Freeman recovered to set up a Seminole scoring opportunity from the Aggie 30. Weldon and company moved it to the 15 on a Shannon Baker reception, but then fell short on three chances because of an out-of-bounds catch in the end zone, a holding penalty and a tipped pass. On fourth down, Dan Mowrey kicked the 42-yard field-goal attempt wide left.

For the remainder of the third quarter, the offenses exchanged possessions without scoring. The Aggies added two fumbles and another interception to their turnover totals during the period. But FSU managed to confine its surrenders of the ball to punts.

Then, a little less than two minutes into the fourth quarter, with the score still 7–2, Weldon threw his fourth interception, giving Richardson and the A&M offense a shot at the Florida State 16. But the Aggies lost two yards on first down, then fumbled the ball back to Florida State in a double-reverse attempt. That was the 13th turnover of the game, tying a Cotton Bowl record.

With Jackson and Bennett running and Baker pulling in a 14-yard catch, the Seminoles took the ball the length of the field, but Gerry Thomas missed a field goal from 37 yards out. They got another chance for a drive less than two minutes later. And this time, Bennett and Jackson ran the ball close enough for Thomas' 27-yard field goal, making the score 10–2.

Texas A&M had one more chance with two and a half minutes left to play in the game, but was forced to surrender the ball on downs in its own territory. The Seminoles had a first down on the A&M 19 when time expired.

After the game both coaches celebrated the play of the two defenses.

And the fans and media complained about the ugliness of a contest that ranked as one of the lowest-scoring Cotton Bowls and tied a bowl record for turnovers.

"We won this game about the way we lost the last two," said Bowden. And it was true. In the Dallas papers the next day, columnists would be analyzing the two or three plays that made all the difference in the Aggies' loss.

There was no one in the Florida State locker room, especially the players posing with the Cotton Bowl trophy, who gave a moment's thought to the sloppiness of the game. There were postgame smiles and laughter for the first time in forty-five days. Sean Jackson, with 27 carries for 135 yards, was the Offensive Most Valuable Player. And the entire FSU defense was third in media voting for Defensive Player of the Game.

Casey Weldon laughed when he was asked about his career-record four interceptions. "I don't care, I don't care. All I care about is the win." It wasn't until later that someone told him that his performance tied the mark for second-highest number of interceptions established by Joe Montana when he quarterbacked Notre Dame against Houston in the 1979 Cotton Bowl. Weldon had no problems with anything that tied him with Joe Montana.

Bowden gave his postgame interviews and rejoined his family back at the Anatole to watch the later bowl games. When Florida lost to Notre Dame in the Sugar Bowl, after Gator fans had spent the last month moaning about being stuck with such a low-ranked team, there was little sympathy in the Bowden suite.

The Gator loss would drop them to seventh in the AP poll. Miami and Washington, with assertive victories over Nebraska and Michigan later that afternoon and evening, would end up tied for the national champion-ship. Florida State would finish fourth.

It was the fifth year in a row that Bowden's team had finished ranked fourth or better and also the fifth consecutive 10-win season for the coach. Only Bear Bryant and Bud Wilkinson had accomplished that before Bowden.

None of that struck Bowden as particularly meaningful on the evening of the first day of the New Year. Winning—or, more to the point, not losing—was all that registered at the moment. The win was crucial, more crucial than he could have gotten his players to understand. Now he and they wouldn't have to spend the off-season worrying and explain-ing about what happened to Florida State.

They were that close to falling off the mountain, to having the worst team in the last five years after having, potentially, one of the best in college football history. How strange this new territory was. You could go from best to worst in two plays.

Before the Florida game, when Bowden was having his Friday-night skull session with Mark Richt and Brad Scott, they had wondered at the line of thinking that held that Florida State couldn't win the big game. All those games that placed them among the top-ranked teams in the nation, weren't some of them big games?

"This is the way it's going to be," said Richt. "If you beat Miami and lose to Florida, you can't win the big one. If you beat both of them and lose the bowl game, you can't win the big one."

"Boy, ain't that the truth," said Bowden, shaking his head in amusement. But there was nothing about the logic that surprised him anymore. So the question he put to Richt was purely rhetorical.

"So what do you do?"

"Well, I guess," said the quarterbacks coach, "you can't ever lose again."

EPILOGUE

On February 5, 1991, twenty-three high school and junior college prospects signed letters of intent to attend Florida State. Among them was Danny Kanell, the highly sought Fort Lauderdale quarterback, and Tamarick Vanover, the Tallahassee receiver. Reggie Green, the big offensive lineman Brad Scott dreamed of adding to his group of future stars, decided to go to the University of Florida. And when Kanell made his choice public, the other top quarterbacks headed elsewhere. Chris Walsh picked Miami, and Danny Wuerffel signed with Florida.

With the addition of Green, Wuerffel and *USA Today* defensive player of the year Dexter Daniels, a linebacker from Valdosta, Georgia, the University of Florida had its best recruiting year in recent memory. Miami, as usual, signed a group of highly skilled speedsters. So who won the state recruiting war?

"A toss-up," *USA Today* reported. "Florida, Florida State and Miami all rank among the top five classes, according to most experts."

Two weeks after the Cotton Bowl, Amp Lee ended the suspense and announced he would enter the April NFL draft.

Eric Turral, keeping his vow to make up his grades, enrolled at Tallahassee Community College and passed all his courses in the spring term. "After I graduate from TCC in the summer, I plan to return to FSU and see what happens," he said.

Terrell Buckley's choice to forgo his senior year was validated by his selection in the first round of the NFL draft by the Green Bay Packers. He was the fifth player chosen.

Amp Lee may have made the right choice too. He was picked in the second round by the San Francisco 49ers.

Howard Dinkins, the outside linebacker troubled for most of the season with back pain and other hurts, impressed NFL scouts enough to be chosen in the third round by the Atlanta Falcons.

The three most disappointed Seminoles in the draft were probably Casey Weldon, Edgar Bennett and Kevin Mancini. Weldon lasted until the fourth round, when the Philadelphia Eagles picked him as the 102nd overall choice. "It's ridiculous," Weldon told reporters on draft day. "I thought the third round would be the latest for sure. I'm looking forward to proving a lot of people wrong."

Bennett, touted by many to be a first- or second-rounder, was picked right after Weldon by Green Bay. Mancini was not drafted at all, but he was invited to the New York Giants camp as a free agent. Similar try-out deals were made by Henry and Joe Ostaszewski, Kirk Carruthers and Paul Moore.

Brad Johnson, hoping to prove he could play quarterback in the NFL, may have gotten his chance when he was taken in the ninth round by the Minnesota Vikings. He was the 227th overall pick, three places ahead of 1990 Heisman Trophy winner Ty Detmer.

After leading the Seminole basketball team through its debut season in the Atlantic Coast Conference, Charlie Ward changed from starring point guard into college quarterback for spring practice. And he edged out his good friend Kenny Felder for the No. 1 spot in the depth chart. Bobby Bowden could barely contain his enthusiasm for Ward.

"He gives you a dimension you can't coach," Bowden told the Tallahassee *Democrat*. "You better contain him; he'll kill you outside the pocket, and we haven't had that in years."

No matter who ended up taking the snaps in the fall, it would be the beginning of a new era at Florida State. Either Ward, who earned a 3.23 grade point average in the fall and was elected vice president of the student body in the spring, or Felder, a marketing major with a 2.64 grade point and a career waiting in major league baseball, would be the Seminoles' first black starting quarterback.

But the field of competition at quarterback narrowed in June, when Kenny Felder was chosen No. 12 in the Major League Baseball draft. The Milwaukee Brewers offered Felder over a half-million dollars to forgo football and begin his baseball career immediately. Felder signed.

"I would have done the same thing," said Bowden.

Spring practice left no doubt about the potential of Andrews' defense. Almost all the starters would return, and the coaches were tinkering with new pass rush alignments that would turn Dan Footman, Carl Simpson and Sterling Palmer loose on opposing quarterbacks. Against those imposing defensive veterans, Brad Scott's young offensive line began the spring looking tentative and overmatched. By the end of the workouts, however, some of the youngsters had improved enough to encourage Scott and the other coaches.

Among John Eason's wideouts, the mood was decidedly upbeat. "They've been calling us the 'young receivers' for a couple of years now," said Kevin Knox. "Now, we're the veterans. And instead of being seen as the weak link on the offense, we should be the leaders that hold it together. You just wait and see."

By the end of spring practice, Matt Frier had won his starting role back on the split end side and Shannon Baker overtook the competition at flanker. In the fall, Vanover was likely to join the mix.

The best news of all for Bowden was that his underclassmen seemed ready to make up for lost time in the classroom. In the spring term, most pulled up their grades and none flunked out. That meant that all his returning players would be eligible for play in the 1992 season.

After the bowl game, the names of both Mickey Andrews and Mark Richt were on the lists of schools seeking new coaches. And both interviewed for openings. But they remained at FSU, leaving Bowden's staff intact for another run at the national championship.

Handicappers began guessing at preseason rankings in February. The 1991 coholders of the national title, Miami and Washington, were again expected to be favorites for the top spot in 1992. Florida State would begin the season ranked as high as No. 2, reporters told Bowden.

"None of that means much right now," he said in April. "But I tell you one thing, I won't mind a bit if somebody else gets to carry that No. 1 load for a while."

ACKNOWLEDGMENTS

Few prominent figures in American culture would allow a writer unlimited access to his life and work at the very moment he faced one of the greatest challenges of his career. Yet Bobby Bowden did exactly that. On the basis of a five-minute conversation in May of 1991, the coach agreed to an unusual deal:

He would grant me the exclusive access I needed to write the inside story of his and Florida State's pursuit of a national championship; he would share in whatever earnings such a book generated; but I would retain complete editorial control. And true to his word, from August 1, 1991, through March 1992, in even the most traumatic of circumstances, he made a place for me at the heart of his football program.

I owe special thanks to many in Tallahassee. Bowden's assistant football coaches—especially John Eason—welcomed me into their private meetings and spent long hours answering stupid questions. And the players, who make the biggest sacrifices in college sport and get the least in return, shared their lives when there was nothing in it for them.

Sue Hall, the head coach's secretary, cleared a corner of her office and provided motherly protection throughout the season. And I wouldn't have gotten far without the help of Dr. Beverly Yerg and Mark Meleney of the academic support staff; football secretaries Sheila Singletary, Mary Jo O'Donnell and Carol Moore; and the team's unofficial den mother, Pam Eaves.

This book owes much to Doubleday editors David Gernert and Joel E. Fishman and to Richard Woods, who balanced the demands of agent and friend.

I owe the most however, to my wife, Christine Gardinier, who fed me, nursed me, counseled me and helped chase away the demons.

If "No Excuses" was the motto for Florida State's football team in 1991, it applied doubly to me. With the access and freedom I enjoyed, I have no excuses for failing to measure up to the experience Bobby Bowden, his coaches and his players provided me.

I will be forever grateful.

ABOUT THE AUTHOR

BEN Brown, a Florida native, has been a reporter, feature writer, columnist and editor since the mid-1970s. He has worked on the staff of *USA Today* since its inception in 1982 and has since written about media, outdoor recreation and sports. Brown lives in Washington, D.C.